FOUNDATIONS OF
Educational Administration

FOUNDATIONS OF

Educational Administration

A BEHAVIORAL ANALYSIS

WILLARD R. LANE

Professor of Educational Administration
University of Iowa

RONALD G. CORWIN

Associate Professor of Sociology
The Ohio State University

WILLIAM G. MONAHAN

Associate Professor of Educational Administration
University of Iowa

THE MACMILLAN COMPANY · New York
COLLIER-MACMILLAN LIMITED · London

PREFACE

THE EVENTS of recent years clearly support the observation that school leaders function in an environment in which they must continually confront particular kinds of human behavior. Actions, attitudes, sentiments, and values constitute a significant aspect of the social system of American schools; and whether the behaviors with which the educational executive must deal arise from within or are external to the educational organization, it is through the context of that organization that they must be interpreted. This book represents an attempt to analyze some of the important parameters of educational administration in terms of the behavioral environment.

The volume is the product of nearly seven years of profitable collaboration between a sociologist and two professors of educational administration. It was our belief that the discipline of sociology can contribute as much to the analysis of educational organizations as it has contributed in the past to a better understanding of industrial organizations. Sociological concepts have provided a point of departure and a framework for interpreting typical concerns of educational administrators, and the direct experience of two of the authors with the day-to-day problems of administration and their own competence in the social sciences has added substance to the analysis and helped to guide the questions and interpretations underlying the book.

The book is organized in three broad sections which we have labeled "foundations," each of which focuses upon a particular context. We have designated these three contexts as *process, organization,* and *function.* Each of these, in turn, contains five chapters.

The resources, skills, and training requisite to the management of organizations can be viewed in terms of many contexts; we do not lay any claim to the effect that the three contexts into which this book is organized constitute the ultimate boundaries of administrative behavior and the total territory encompassed. They merely represent what we conceive to be a logical framework for attempting a relatively systematic analysis. We rather guardedly use the term "systematic" because the extent to which systemization should be attempted, the breadth of generalizations that should be tendered, is still somewhat elusive and the path to systematic analysis is at best awkwardly undertaken. Some persons suggest rather broad and perhaps meandering paths of generalization and speculation; others suggest a more pedestrian route to systematic analysis through the rigorous study of routine detail. In this book, we are more concerned with a kind of middle ground between these two views and have attempted to establish as our frame of reference the *relationships* between administrative events. As a consequence of that frame of reference, the reader will find few specific prescriptions for completing administrative tasks; there are no formulas to follow guaranteeing success, and the administrator's job is nowhere in this book presented as a "push-pull, click-click" procedure. When one deals with the kind of complexity that is compounded in modern organizations, it is vain to hope that success will come from "cutting along the dotted line."

When a student enters a field of study in which he hopes to prepare himself for organizational administration, our view is that he must first discover the nature of the parameters with which he will be involved. If one wants to label the study of administration as a choice between "micro" analysis and "macro" analysis, this book is clearly in the latter category. But the book is written with a strong conviction that administrative effectiveness is best realized when the administrator is clearly aware that an organization is a special kind of behavioral environment. Educational organizations are different from other kinds of complex organizations, certainly; but the differences are due primarily to the purposes that organizations serve and the system of values that they are designed to sustain. The processes which govern the pursuit of purposes do not differ from one organization to another—information must be collected, activities coordinated, and resources marshalled and applied. In our view, therefore, administration is a process; moreover, administration *assumes* some manner of organization, whether large or small, formal or informal, public or private, permanent or temporary. And though organizations may be administered in different ways, there are particular functions that they perform by virtue of the goals they seek. We hold that administrative significance rests on the leadership function rather than on routine mechanics. In this book, we have merely tried to point the directions that have been taken and might be taken in a social approach to school administration. The book is primarily directed to graduate students or upper level undergraduates preparing for more technical and specialized courses in general school administration.

During the preparation of a book such as this, many people contribute. The authors' colleagues and students—past and present—have provided valuable comment and constructive criticism at various stages of the work. Particular acknowledgment is due to Professor Franklin Stone, University of Iowa, for his wise and patient counsel and to Mrs. Geraldine Sheridan for a variety of significant contributions including typing, proofreading, and general assistance in the preparation of the manuscript. The authors wish to express their appreciation to the editors of the *Educational Administration Quarterly* for granting permission to reprint the article entitled *Professional Persons in Public Organizations*. We are also grateful to Appleton-Century-Crofts for permission to adapt materials from *A Sociology of Education* for portions of chapters 4, 13, and 14.

W. R. L.
R. G. C.
W. G. M.

CONTENTS

Part One

Part Two

Part Three
THE THIRD FOUNDATION
The Functional Context of Educational Administration

PART

ONE

THE FIRST FOUNDATION

*The Process Context of
Educational Administration*

I

Introduction

In the real world, the isolated individual does not
exist; he begins always as a member of something
. . . and his personality can develop only in society, and in some way or other he always embodies
some social institution.

John Neville Figgis
(Lecture II)

I N T H E last fifty years or so, a great deal of scholarly and professional interest has been devoted to the "science of administration." But
unless one is willing to accept some particular administrative view, the
term *science* is still premature; there is still a considerable body of expert
opinion which maintains that much of the activity which characterizes
administration is as much art as it is science.

Unfortunately, those who tend to view administration as mostly artful
behavior have been generally content to leave it at that. On the contrary,
those who have viewed it as a science have tried to make it into what they
believe it to be. Therefore, one can find a variety of influences left by the
science-seekers. Most of them have enjoyed some success and a few have
been almost revolutionary.

Some Historical Considerations

Administration as *art* is much older than administration as *science*. The
artful administrator was successful in antiquity while the artless one was
not. In general, the significant leaders seemed to possess a talent for management; they were perceptive about human motivation and skillful in
their use of position and reward. Thinkers and wise men took note of this
art and tried to articulate aspects of it in such a way that others less

endowed with charisma who may be faced with some form of directorial responsibility could profit therefrom. For example, Confucius advises that persons charged with administrative duty should seek honest, capable, and unselfish public officials.[1] Even Socrates has suggested that ". . . over whatever a man may preside, he will, if he knows what he needs, and is able to provide it, be a good president . . ." [2] The art of successful administration was thus usually characterized as a charismatic phenomenon—emotional, powerful, and genetic.

Following the Industrial Revolution when the need for management skills became a crucial aspect of the competition for markets, resources, and organizational techniques, entrepreneurs became increasingly concerned with the training and development of managers. Although the two terms, *management* and *administration*, are frequently used synonymously today, whatever distinction there has been between them is primarily political. *Administration* was usually preferred when describing appropriate organizational know-how with reference to public or quasi-governmental enterprises, and *management* was preferred in describing capitalistic enterprises. Consequently, management came of age after the Industrial Revolution, but long before that administrative skills were required by the military, the church, and the empire-builders.

MILITARY ADMINISTRATION

The earliest forms of administration undoubtedly accompanied man's first attempts at organized cooperation; but historical evidence permits us to infer that the rudiments of modern organizational management were evolved from very early military structures. In his study of the development of the military staff, Hittle credits Philip of Macedonia with a most advanced staff organization. In addition to possessing an inventive genius for new weapons, Philip also organized commissaries, transportation, hospitals, and even a post akin to the modern provost marshal for the regulation and supervision of encampments. Hittle asserts that "It is evident that present day staff organization is in some ways similar to the system established by Philip more than 2,000 years ago." [3]

With the coming of the Middle Ages when feudal man was expected to bear arms as a part of his general obligations in fealty, there was not a notable advance in military staff organization. It is interesting to note that with the coming of the mercenary armies military staff organization began its modern development. This is interesting because it suggests the importance of the influence of personal profit on organizational efficiency. Mercenary soldiers such as those maintained by the merchant cities of Italy in the fourteenth century were, in a sense, history's first recognized professional managers; their services were available in the open market to whomever could afford them, and in order to sustain their marketability, these men studied warfare carefully and seriously. They were professional soldiers who were well-acquainted with the risks—both in employment opportunities and in physical survival—of not learning all that they could about their craft.

The professional military organization was brought to a high degree of technical competence by the Swiss in the fifteenth century; it was not long after that similar armies were being developed in France and in Germany. The military staff organization came of age with these professional armies through the introduction of such military "offices" as *sergeant-major,* who was the principal staff officer, and *quartermaster,* whose early responsibility of riding ahead to seek and arrange for quartering of the troops led to his being used for reconnaissance purposes as well.

As armies continued to increase in size and with the advancing sophistication in weaponry, the need for competent and well-trained staff functionaries demanded more attention from military leaders. This need, in turn, was compounded by a growing difficulty of commanders to secure enough information. The importance of information and its subsequent influence on the development of staff theory is reflected in the work of Paul Thiebault. Thiebault had been promoted through the ranks to lieutenant general on Napoleon's staff. Once he was questioned by the Emperor regarding such things as the strength and location of his detachments, the nature of his armament, the supply situation, and the condition of the enemy. Thiebault's lack of information about such things greatly embarrassed him. As a result, he studied and collected as much data on staffing as he could and then developed and published the first manual of basic staff theory and technique.[4]

Officer training followed these developments. Traditionally, the source for officers were the families of the well-to-do, but growing specialization and complexity necessitated particular training programs. In 1832, the Nicholas Academy was established in Russia for the purpose of training officers for the Army. A Swiss, Baron Henri Jomini, was instrumental in the establishment of the Academy; having risen to the rank of general in Napoleon's army, he left because of animosity between himself and a high-ranking officer on Napoleon's headquarters staff. Another training school for officers was established soon afterward in France, but perhaps the finest of such schools during this era was the Prussian Academy of War.[5]

By the middle of the nineteenth century the relationship between military success and administrative efficiency was well established. Every beginning student in the study of administration, regardless of his institutional specialty, knows that his basic model has been derived from the military. Ironically, changes in that model in modern military organizations have not been readily adapted by many organizations built on the older one.

THE LINE AND STAFF LEGACY

When the Industrial Revolution introduced the factory system, its revolutionaries looked for someone with experience in dealing with large numbers of people engaged in highly uniform activities. It was natural for them to look toward the military. These experts from the military merely applied their basic knowledge of staff theory to the problems they faced in the mass production of goods. Even today, management theory is still replete with "principles" directly derived from military staff theory. Among such legacies perhaps none is better known than the concept of *line-and-staff*.

The line-and-staff concept persists in the terminology of management far beyond its usefulness. It is merely one conceptualization of an operational definition of authority in organizations, but as such it tends to obscure that more important concept as well as discourage rigorous analysis of it. The idea of line-and-staff encompasses a doctrine of command, control, direction, and communication through prescribed channels; it is philosophically derived from a time in the world when human lives were conceived only as a means to an end and the doctrine of absolutism prevailed. The military and the church were authoritarian institutions and administration traced its ancestry directly to them. From this, the so-called *rational model* of organizations was directly derived.

THE DEVELOPMENT OF THE RATIONAL MODEL

The rational model has much to recommend it; it has considerable appeal to the administrator who faces the real world every day and who therefore tends to view other perspectives as idle schemes or academic conversation. Rational organization theory has a long and productive history: beginning with the military and the Roman Catholic church, it was refined through the Industrial Revolution, given theoretical expression by Max Weber, extended by Frederick Winslow Taylor, and adapted to large modern-day structures by, among many others, James D. Mooney and Alan C. Reiley. It is important to this discussion to examine—however briefly—these developments.

The rational model maintains that administration in any organization is composed of a number of rational functions—for example, planning, organizing, coordinating, evaluating, delegating, controlling, and so on. These functions are usually considered synonymous with leadership, and thus administrative leadership is conceived as something to be superimposed upon the organization in such a way that organizational goals are more effectively pursued. In using this model for analyzing organizational behavior, Gouldner states that one must assume ". . . that decisions are made on the basis of a rational survey of the situation, utilizing certified knowledge, with a deliberate orientation to an expressly codified apparatus." [6]

As the rational model implies, organizations are rather mechanistic to the extent that particular elements can be manipulated within the confines of a master plan. If errors occur it is comforting to dismiss them as distortions under the convenient label of "unintended consequences." It was such unintended consequences, however, which led various people through the years to continually work toward more sophisticated versions of the rational model. In all cases, they accepted the assumptions upon which rational organizational theory is built and busied themselves tinkering with its operational characteristics.

Weber's Bureaucratic Model. Although he is often regarded as an historian since most of his work was historical in nature, Max Weber is familiar to social scientists for a significant view of formal organizations. His bureaucratic theories were the result of his interest in uncovering the "laws of social behavior." Working in Germany at about the turn of the century, Weber became intensely curious about the nature and exercise of power in social and political relationships. This led him first to an analysis of bureaucracy and secondly to the development of an "ideal type" of bureaucratic structure. Bureaucracy and the organizational myths that it fostered are discussed in some detail in Chapter 5 of this book. It is mentioned only briefly at this point as an important aspect in the development of administrative thought.

Weber held strongly to two related views: that rationality in human behavior was most desirable, and that bureaucracy offered the best means for achieving such rationality in organized endeavors. He suggested that the growth of bureaucracy was primarily due to ". . . its purely technical superiority over any other form of organization. The fully developed bureaucratic mechanism compares with other organizations exactly as does the machine with the nonmechanical modes of production." [7]

Weber's analysis and postulations regarding bureaucracy can best be understood by first examining certain conclusions that he reached regarding the primary sources of power and influence. Although power is an extremely complicated concept, Weber concluded that there are three important fundamental sources of it: (1) cultural rules and societal values; (2) charisma, the creative and personal genius of individuals (largely emotional perhaps, and mystical, but tremendously influential); and (3) those legions of administrators who generally regulate the codified social order. For many persons, Weber's inclusion of the charismatic leader—an *irrational* notion—seems incongruent with his concern and belief in rationality. Actually, Weber maintained that bureaucracies occur *as a result* of charismatic personalities; that is, the bureaucracy is established in order to sustain that which the leader inspired. On this point, Gerth and Mills point out that ". . . Weber sees the genuine charismatic situation quickly give way to incipient institutions, which emerge from the cooling off of extraordinary states of devotion and fervor." [8] By "incipient institutions," Weber would not mean bureaucracy; whether a charismatic movement would ". . . be routinized into traditionalism or into [bureaucracy] . . . does not depend primarily upon the subjective intentions of the followers or of the leader; it is dependent upon the institutional framework of the movement, and especially upon the economic order." [9] Not only was Weber able to fit the irrationality of charisma into his own deep desire for rationality, but it also offered him a solution to the problem of unpredictability in rational structures. Consider the following statement, again from the Introduction by Gerth and Mills to his *Essays:*

> In general, Weber's construction of historical dynamics in terms of charisma and routinization is an attempt to answer the paradox of unintended consequences. For the charisma of the first hour may incite the followers of a warrior hero or prophet to forsake expediency for ultimate values. But during the routinization of charisma, the material interests of an increased following are the compelling factor. [10]

There are a great many facets of Weber's bureaucratic thought that were woven into his final structure, among them the theories that the appointed official was always likely to function more "exactly" than the elected official; that prestige or "social esteem" of officials is especially low where the demands for expert administration are not high; that the development of a money economy is the predominant presupposition of bureaucracy (the reader may recall a previous statement that the development of military staff theory received important impetus with the advent of mercenary armies). Weber also pointed out that bureaucratization is intimately related to and dependent upon the development of specific administrative tasks; the increasing demand of any society for protection and security; and, of final importance, the development of means of communication and transportation.

Perhaps the most meaningful of Weber's assertions regarding bureaucracy to the majority of people who are only dimly aware of what it is, was his statement regarding its permanence:

> Once it is fully established, bureaucracy is among those social structures which are the hardest to destroy. Bureaucracy is THE means of carrying 'community action' over into rationally ordered 'social action.' Therefore as an instrument for 'societalizing' relations of power, bureaucracy has been and is a power instrument of the first order—for the one who controls the bureaucratic apparatus. [11]

The Ideal Type. For Weber, the ideal bureaucracy was one incorporating a number of elements which together constituted a *formal* structure. Weber repeatedly emphasized the "form" of the structure, and although he did not hold that a bureaucracy had to include all of the characteristics of his ideal type, the more such characteristics it included the more likely it was to function longer and more effectively. There were five basic elements which, taken together, constituted the form of Weber's ideal type:

❴ 1. *An hierarchical structure.* Each official in a higher office has control and supervision of an official in a lower office.

❴ 2. *Functional specialization.* Individual office holders are selected on the basis of their ability to perform particular tasks.

❴ 3. *Prescribed competence.* This is derived from number 2 above; it stipulates that each position in the hierarchy has particular and known rights and obligations attached to it.

❴ 4. *Files and records.* Pertinent acts, decisions, and so on should be recorded to provide basis for the establishment of policy guides. This is essential toward reducing alternatives and thereby insuring predictability.

❴ 5. *Rules of behavior.* Unless there is a codified apparatus, the problem of unpredictability is omnipresent. Codes of behavior established through policies represent an essential process in the rational structure.

Perhaps the most significant and irritating problem, both theoretically and actually, presented by such a highly structured formal organization is its tendency to feed upon itself, to grow in size without a clear and distinct relationship to its productivity. Weber was aware of this probability, but asserted that where rationality also governs this aspect of the structure, growth would be in terms of scope rather than detail. He states: "Bureaucratization is occasioned more by intensive and qualitative enlargement and internal deployment of the scope of administrative tasks than by their extensive and quantitive increase." [12] Whether such an observation was an accurate reflection of what was really happening with the bureaucracies that Weber studied, or merely wishful thinking on his part, the facts that have accumulated since 1900 support the opposite view, namely, that administrative tasks have increased in quantity more than in scope.

What Weber was not in position to take into consideration during the time that he wrote were a number of sociopsychological factors within organizations which have contributed to the proliferation of indirect, or nonproductional, tasks as opposed to the direct tasks associated with production. Each individual specialty in an organization wants attention and status; this is one of those sociopsychological factors and helps to explain the increases in the number of indirect tasks which are created. Interestingly, such jobs apparently continue to increase even though fundamental production functions may be *declining*. It was this condition that prompted C. Northcote Parkinson to formulate his now famous "law." In support of his contention that indirect jobs make more indirect jobs, Parkinson cited a situation that occurred with the British Navy; in a period of little over a decade (1914–1928) the number of ships in service was decreased by about two-thirds and naval personnel by one-third, while at the same time shipyard officials and administrative personnel at middle levels increased by forty per cent and high echelon or headquarters personnel increased by seventy-eight per cent.[13]

Although the extent and number of administrative tasks is increasing, this in itself is an oversimplified reason for being either critical or apprehensive of bureaucratic structures. One must also take into account the impact of automation and of research and development (R&D) activities within large corporate as well as public enterprises, and, perhaps even more important, the fact that national productivity continues to rise both as an absolute figure and per capita. The latter fact tends to support Weber's early contention that bureaucracy functions exactly.

The Advent of Scientific Management.   Max Weber's influence on the organization of human enterprises was immeasurably powerful. The kind of "rationalism" that he espoused was evident in large, formal organizations throughout the world. Some of them doubtless attempted directly to adapt his ideas to their purposes; in most, however, the observations he made about bureaucratic tendencies were descriptively accurate because Weber was an incisive analyst whose scientific orientation led him to accurately and coherently record what he observed and deduce events from these observations.

But Weber's work was largely empirical and somewhat idealistic, and there followed not long after him a new group of scientists whose pursuit of rationality made Weber's activities seem dull by comparison. The movement which has been labelled "scientific management" was distinctly American, and, like many American movements, quickly established itself almost as a cult. Its founder was an industrial engineer named Frederick Winslow Taylor. Taylor was liberally educated in American and European schools but found himself idle during the economic depression of 1873 and therefore applied for training as a machinist. Not long after, he secured a job in a Philadelphia steel company and in 1884 was promoted to chief engineer for the plant. Taylor's subsequent preoccupation with *efficiency* was the result of years spent observing and analyzing the actions of workers while handling materials and machines. It should be remembered that the "principles" he later developed were almost entirely concerned with the function of men and machines and his famous work, *The Principles of Scientific Management*, dealt not so much with the *management* of men but rather with the *efficiency* of men. He referred to time and motion study as the "cornerstone of scientific management." [14] Taylor and the disciples who followed him (of whom there were legions) became so engrossed in the manual and temporal aspects of the work that the job somehow became separated from the man. It was the task itself which became the focal point of scientific enquiry and measurement. The Taylor point of view has frequently been epitomized in terms of stop watches and measuring tapes because its basic purpose was to break down work—any kind of work—into whatever component parts could be determined for it. Short, stout men were to be preferred for work which demanded bending or stooping (like shoveling, for example) since it could be demonstrated that they were more efficient at this type of work.

Although Taylor himself was primarily interested in the shop level of organizations and the component parts of work, the same ideas were applied by others more interested in positions further up in the hierarchy. The establishment of "departments" in which certain functions were brought more closely under the supervision of certain individuals was a direct result of Taylor's work studies. Closely related was the "principle of span of control" which held that the number of departments under any particular individual's control should be in proportion to his ability to give them adequate supervisory attention. And adequate attention, in turn, could be measured in terms of productivity. The single value system and maximization of financial return consequently became the major criteria for good management. These criteria established the rule of increasing productivity per man hour, and financial incentive was based on measured production, time and motion study, and piece work. The system came under violent attack at times and ultimately gave way to a more humanistic view; of it Pfiffner and Sherwood state:

This was a philosophy of human motivation which viewed labor as a commodity, each individual being his own agent operating within the laws of the marketplace. Under the single system of values, owners and managers did not view themselves as their brother's keeper and regarded themselves and their enterprises as insulated from the broad problems of human welfare.[15]

Authority was implicit in the scientific management movement. The authority of results was congruent with American philosophical pragmatism as interpreted by many entrepreneurs who neither clearly understood it nor could efficiently afford the time to study it in any detail. Moreover, this implicit authority was within the organization where it "rightfully" belonged—at the top. "All wisdom resided at the top of the hierarchy and any resistance to its edicts was regarded as subversive." [16]

Between 1910 and 1925 practically no aspect of American life escaped the application of the principles of scientific management—at least no organized part of it. Even the church and the family were criticized as being inefficient, and proponents of the "principles" were ready to correct even these institutions' inadequacies. It is little wonder that schools and their administration were early targets of the new management cult.

EDUCATION AND BUSINESS—THE NEW RELATIONSHIP

As a result of the influence of business practices, not only were the management and administration of schools profoundly affected but their purposes and curricula were also acted upon. Morphett, Johns, and Reller point out the influence of business when they state:

A literature on school administration was being written. The words "efficient" and "businesslike" appeared frequently in that literature. The dynamic, bustling, aggressive administrator was confident that he could use the proven methods of business and industry to solve all of the important problems.[17]

A well-documented and detailed account of the ways schools were influenced by business interests is contained in Callahan's *Education and the Cult of Efficiency*.[18] He points out that not long after the turn of the century American business became alarmed by the threat of competition from German industrial expansion and attributed that country's economic good fortune to its emphasis on excellence in industrial education. So excited was the business community that on two occasions arguments were presented during meetings of the National Education Association (in 1905 and 1907) demanding modifications of American public education along the lines of Germany's educational system. And it should be remembered that Weber's influence was significant in Germany. With the advent of World War I, all things "German" fell somewhat out of favor and little more was heard about German education; but the time was ripe for a new force for educational improvement—scientific management.

By the beginning of World War I, the demand for the application of the principles of scientific management to public school administration had grown into a full-scale campaign. Schools were castigated in popular as well as professional periodicals for inefficient management, curricula, teaching method, and personnel. Among special publications, the *American School Board Journal* was particularly notable for its criticism. This is understandable since the majority of school board members throughout the country exercised important influence on their national association and its policies, and they were first of all businessmen who had become converts to the new "science."

By 1913, efficiency and education were effectively married and the honeymoon lasted longer than anyone might have guessed. It was in that year that the National Society for the Study of Education published a yearbook devoted to efficient education.[19] This paper, which probed the application of the Taylor principles to school administration, was the work of Franklin Bobbitt, an instructor in Educational Administration at the University of Chicago. Bobbitt went through the principles one by one, indicating, sometimes in elegant detail, the appropriate ways each might be applied to the processes of education. It was a hard-headed, rational, and at times cold-blooded statement. And, contained in it here and there were curious rationalizations regarding the development of a better society. Consider the following statement summarizing Bobbitt's comments regarding application of the principle which requires the establishment of qualitative and quantitative standards for work:

The greatest obstacle appears to be, not the complexity of the problems, not the lack of technique, but rather the inability of school people to cooperate and the lack of a desire to cooperate. Owing to the nature of the training, the nature of the weeding process along the line, and the nature of the work to be performed, the school man is necessarily an intellectualist; and the intellectualist is, by nature, whatever the field of his labor, an independent individualist, a man of wide vision and of large capacity for self-help and self-direction. By nature he is a leader of men. He dislikes nothing so much as to sink his personality into a cooperative task where he is not the leader or director. Impatient of restraint for himself, he is sympathetically impatient of restraint for his colleagues. Each educational worker desires therefore for himself and for all others in the field of education the greatest possible degree of individualistic freedom. The result is . . . the relative autonomy of a very large number of small units—in other words, a low and primitive form of organization, direction and management. All this stands in the way of accomplishing any large cooperative task. It results in a constitutional tendency to place the welfare of the worker above the welfare of the organization and the welfare of both above the welfare of the total society of which school men and school institutions are but agents.[20]

The great attractiveness of scientific management for American business—and subsequently for public school administration—was not merely provocative excitement about a novel notion (although there was much of that in it too at the time), but the real explanation for the rapid assimilation of Taylor's ideas into the general structure of American management was the enormous fact that it did indeed result in increased production and greater economy—that is, while production tended to rise, costs tended to be more carefully controlled using the new principles. Unquestionably, this *had* to appeal to those guardians of the public weal who were much more concerned with the stabilization of taxes in the public sphere than they were with industrial investment in the private sphere.

In the same year as the publication of the NSSE yearbook, 1913, the annual meeting of the American Association of School Administrators (then the Department of Superintendence of the National Education Association) being held in Cincinnati, devoted a considerable portion of its deliberations to the subject of the application of scientific management to the conduct of American public education.[21]

Education and the business community apparently discovered that they had much in common following the events of 1900–1920. Nothing *does* quite succeed like success; a few shrewd and opportunistic young school-men quickly absorbed the lessons of scientific management and began to emphasize the more thrift-oriented aspects of efficiency with regard to the maintenance and operation of public schools. Rather quickly, an important criterion of effective school management rested with the amount of an annual budget that could be turned back at the end of the fiscal year—the consequence of efficient and thrifty management, scientifically based and rationally pursued with no apparent loss of "effectiveness" demonstrated in the instructional program. Since about 1920, the relationship between public school administration and American business practices has become well established and seldom questioned. It seems fair to say, however, that with the advent of professionalized school administration, the relationship was no longer a highly relevant one after about 1940. But though it is true that the commitment to efficiency as advocated by Taylor's disciples has now generally eroded away, its legacy for schools and other public agencies has continued to be a strong faith in thrifty administration. To that extent at least, the economic implications of the scientific management movement have left an indelible mark on public education that even the affluence of recent years has been unable to erase. "Cost per square foot" is still a more important criterion in the construction of an educational facility than the problem of whether it is an appropriate environment for intellectual and vocational learning activity.

Before turning to another highly important phase of administrative evolution, it is of almost ironic interest to note that as recently as 1960, the issue of whether school administrators were educators or businessmen was still the subject of public discourse. Writing in *Look* magazine in that year, George B. Leonard espoused some concern that business orientations were dominating educational ones to the detriment of the latter.[22] In a sense, one might feel disposed to comment that in about sixty years, the circle had come full around.

Toward the Natural Systems Model

The emphasis on rationalism in the management of human enterprises with its focus on the job rather than on the worker produced an image of corporate structures that has been aptly characterized as "organization without people." It would be only a matter of time when growing resentment against such dehumanization in organization would develop into a notable revolt. The revolt was fully established during the 1920's and by the late 1930's its tenets had effectively permeated much of American management theory—so much so, in fact, that by the end of World War II there was sufficient basis for describing enterprises as "people without organization."

THE HUMAN RELATIONS ERA

The sources of the revolt against what had become traditional management theory were varied, and there certainly was not unanimous agreement among the revolting factions; still, the movement seen in retrospect tended to produce a general point of view which seemed more than anything else to emphasize as its basis the relationships between people. Pfiffner and Sherwood identify three important sources of strain which provided momentum to the movement: (1) students of management who attacked traditional "principles" as being untested proverbs; (2) public administrators who rejected the notion that administration and political process were separate—that is, that the administrators were *not* merely technicians who carried out political mandates; and (3) social scientists who were strongly oriented toward the preservation of human values.[23]

Undoubtedly, the work of Elton Mayo and his associates—the now famous "Hawthorne Experiments"—represented the most significant event in the genesis of the ideological revolt.[24] But it should be of particular interest to students of educational administration that concern over the value of human relationships as a factor in certain school functions was expressed much earlier. It is curiously ironic that in an appendix to the same yearbook in which Bobbitt meticulously explicated the application of scientific principles of management to school administration, there is contained a suggestion of the importance of a highly personalized relationship between teacher and supervisor. Under the title, "Supervision of Beginning Teachers in Cincinnati," John W. Hall, a professor of elementary education at the University of Cincinnati, concluded a report of that city's program of supervision with the following statement:

By way of summarizing the personal elements of supervision as they appeared in the work in Cincinnati, we are moved to say that—with absence of the feeling or the attitude of superiority, with full appreciation of the conditions, the difficulties, and the efforts of the teacher . . . with fairly good judgement and resourcefulness in suggestions for substitution or improvement, with fair-minded estimate of its [the lesson's] value—it is remarkable what difficult cases may be handled without interruption of friendly working relations.[25]

It remained, however, for the work of Mayo and his associates, through careful attention to scientific objectivity by experiments conducted in the real world of American industry, to establish a firm basis for re-humanizing the world of work. The fact that the effort was sponsored by the highly respected Harvard Business School and was carried on with the full cooperation of the giant American (Bell) Telephone and Telegraph Company in its Hawthorne plant of Western Electric lent an aura of credibility to the studies that in turn provided the work with an enormous respectability.

There were three important works which resulted from the Mayo studies. The first of these, Mayo's *The Human Problems of an Industrial Civilization*, lay the groundwork for the other two more technical works.[26] It was discovered in effect by the Hawthorne experiments that increased productivity on the part of a worker was an unanticipated consequence of the social relationships between workers and the situations in which they were embedded. It was an unanticipated consequence because originally it was assumed that the manipulation of certain variables in the working environment, such as lighting, heat and ventilation, opportunity for rest periods, and so forth, would be reflected in measurable production changes. A special room, which came to be known as the Bank Wiring Room from the nature of the particular work that was done there, was used for the experiments, but regardless of the amount of variation exerted on any factor, production constantly increased. Such increased productivity was concluded, rightly, to be the consequence of the social situation and interaction among the workers.

It is obvious that work in process by persons concerned with the nature and function of group dynamics received impetus from the Hawthorne studies. As Wallace Donham stated in the Foreword to Mayo's *The Social Problems of an Industrial Civilization*, ". . . the net result of the three reports, as they came to the interested reader, was emphasis on the individual, including of course, emphasis on him in his social surroundings."[27] Indeed, F. H. Allport's work on the effect of the group on individual behavior preceded the Mayo work, and since he too performed many of his experiments as a member of the psychology staff at Harvard, there can be little doubt that the building science of social psychology as it was developing at Harvard and elsewhere provided empirical bases for explaining much that was included in the findings of the Hawthorne studies.

The resulting emphasis on human relations which reflected management thought after 1930 and which somehow came to be operationalized under the broad dictum of democratic administration has overshadowed a far more significant relationship which was established by Mayo's work; we refer to the recognition by the business and industrial community of the importance of behavioral scientists as contributors to more effective management. In the early years of the new thought when entrepreneurs were busily engaged in shedding the vestiges of the scientific management epoch by seeking ways to translate the new myths into a useful language, this relationship between the behavioral scholar and the corporate enterprise was a consultancy based almost entirely on the latter's terms. But the relationship was effectively established thereby; it is not unreasonable to assume that it ultimately broadened to include the university as a full-fledged partner whereby service became as legitimate as research and teaching. The assumption is at least supported by the application of cybernetics to organizational productivity, as well as the present dominating emphasis on "R and D" (research and development) by almost any company with as many as ten employees. Both of these concepts owe a considerable portion of their origin in management to academic institutions.

Human Relations and Democratic Administration.   By the end of the 1930's, human relations had become the watchword of American organizational thought. Its proponents were even more zealous than their counterparts a generation earlier who were crusading for Taylor's principles. There are probably a dozen good reasons for the excitement that this movement generated: it flowered fully during a period of desperate economic depression; corporations had continued to grow larger in size, and the new doctrine appealed to salaried, professional managers whose limits of sympathy when faced with difficult personnel decisions were much more expansive than they might be had they owned the businesses themselves; American political thought was conducive to it, as was American philosophy and American literature.

But how does one encourage people to be "human" in their relationships, to recognize that the man is so much more important than the work, and still, somehow, get the work done? Moreover, the work must still be done well, directions must still be given, policies made and abided, personnel hired and fired. The answer, of course, was democratic administration. At least this phrase seemed to satisfy as an answer, although it certainly did not reveal much of the mechanics, nor seldom did it allow much enlightening additional discussion. We were slaughtering sacred cows on the one hand, and creating new ones on the other.

Democratic administration was particularly appealing to school administrators. Their discontent with the creed of scientific management principles was especially acute whenever they were confronted with the need to *evaluate* the efficiency of schools. Whereas the businessman could merely determine whether he made a profit or a loss, or calculate over time how much of a loss he should sustain until the ink turned black, the school administrator's search for such a simple dichotomy always ended in frustration. The plain fact is that public school's effectiveness can be truly evaluated only over long spans of time, but such a notion was obviously distasteful to those who were accustomed to more precise and immediate assessment. In addition, school administrators were still required under the regulations governing their licensure, to have had teaching experience; their pre-service training demanded much in its curriculum—and still does—that was primarily pedagogical. The child, learning, educational philosophy and educational psychology constituted important elements in the school administrator's frame of reference. It was assumed that he must know about these things in order to appropriately direct the purposes and activities around which schools were organized. Such a frame of reference was not compatible with a point of view which held that people were only so much raw material to be manipulated in terms of the product that was being dispensed. This certainly does not suggest that there were not a great many autocratic school administrators, nor that authoritarianism was not prevalent, but merely indicates that the sources of authoritarianism are many—religious as well as economic—and the great majority of school administrators, no matter what their leadership style, viewed the child as the primary and fundamental object of their responsibility. The majority of them were therefore sensitized to human values and became convinced that democratic administration would provide solutions to the role conflicts apparent in the teacher-turned-administrator situation.

The schools long had been epitomized as the "wellsprings of democracy" and no one could question their enormous role in the socializing of the young. The advent of the human relations movement merely provided schools with a new avenue for expressing, and realizing, a point of view that had been crystallizing for decades. It culminated in the so-called "life-adjustment" education view that rose to a peak in the early 1950's. An important early impetus was provided to the foundations of this point of view by Dewey and his disciples, although Dewey's ideas were badly distorted in it. And it also received impetus from a willing acceptance on the part of American school administrators of democratic administration. Unfortunately much of what passed for democratic administration was anything but that. In many cases, subordinates were allowed to decide on issues that really made little difference to anyone.

What is highly important, and apparently was not even dimly perceived by the great majority of school administrators, is the fact that "democratic administration" was a label that was used to stand for an immensely complex plethora of sociocultural concepts which themselves were equally complex. The process through which theoretical ideas from several different disciplines pass ultimately into practical applications is extremely involved and little is known about it. Outside the physical sciences (and only rarely there) such a process seldom is allowed to complete its cycle before generalizations are applied; moreover, in the conduct of human enterprises, applications of theoretically generated ideas are frequently put to use by persons who know very little of their development.

The popularity of "democratic administration" is a classic example. It was analogous to presenting a person, skillful in driving an automobile, with an airplane and saying to him, "Look, here is a vehicle that will do a lot more for you, but we do not know much about it yet." The man sees it as a vehicle that will get him from here to there quicker than what he's been used to and has been unhappy with, and since he knows about vehicles, he decides not to wait until its developers know more about it. He is free to use it, renames it a flying car, and hops in. Certainly a few people who attempted to use it found it not too difficult to cope with, but others were not so fortunate. Teaching people to swim by throwing them head first into the deep water is probably an effective method, but one does lose a disproportionate number of learners with it.

Early publications which attempted to explicate the new administrative technique were not much help either. One of the best known in educational administration divided the tasks of democratizing school administration into the following five aspects:

([1. Social responsibilities of education must be defined.

([2. Democratic concept of leadership must be developed.

([3. A democratic form of organization is needed.

([4. Participation by all is required.

([5. The role of the teacher must be defined.[28]

The Koopman, Miel, and Misner book certainly opened an important door; it was not, in fairness to its point of view, presented as the last word on democratic administration; more accurately, it could be characterized as the "first word." Its discussions of such seminal concepts as *power* and *authority* were therefore superficial, almost as if such concepts were subversive to the new approach. Group techniques rather naturally received considerable treatment in many of the early publications dealing with the democratic approach, but the underlying motivations upon which much of the basic group research was founded as well as the sociopsychological data regarding needs, ego satisfaction, status relationships, personality conflict, sentiments, wishes, fears, and other similar states were seldom treated in the "applicational" literature. Naïve psychology prevailed and some people had more talent for it than others.

THE SYSTEMS-PROCESS VIEW

The human relations era actually encompassed two significant phases of administrative inquiry and practice. The first of these, which may be characterized as the period of "democratic administration," lasted through the late forties and into the early fifties. The second phase of the era is still current and, for lack of something better to call it, might be labelled the *system-process* period. This second phase came about because of the growing recognition that to realistically apply some of the worth-while tenets of democratic administration, persons in administrative positions had to know about more than interpersonal expectations, morale or group cohesiveness. They had to learn more about the principles of social organization which *structure* human relations. For, whereas the human relations approach focused on interpersonal interaction and sentiments in organizational contexts, the context itself usually was "assumed" as a given in the system and was therefore seldom the *subject* of inquiry. In the current phase, by contrast, more attention is being given to the distribution of power, the function of roles, the degree of specialization, the centralization of decision making and the character of the prestige system—all of which can more appropriately be considered to be properties of the organization itself than of the membership. The phrase that has come to dominate the field today, though no more appropriate than those of other periods, is *administrative theory*.

A number of factors have contributed to the prominence now being given to behavioral sciences in the study of school administration. Administrative theory has become a sort of catch-phrase for reflecting that prominence, and although a great many practicing school administrators are still somewhat dubious about this newest emphasis, their number is dwindling. This is so because, first of all, the number of school administrators in the position of the superintendency is itself being startlingly reduced through district reorganization; and since fewer jobs are available (and are more and more complicated in terms of problems, size of district, salary, and staffing), the competition for such positions is quickly becoming limited to persons who hold doctorate degrees. Secondly, much of what has been done under the label of administrative theory has produced knowledge that *is* useful to the administrator, and—perhaps most important—his training and inclinations developed in graduate school have provided him with a frame of reference which accommodates theoretical constructs in meaningful ways. The administrator is then in a position to find many kinds of applications in the real world of administrative tasks for knowledge that he is increasingly prepared to understand and use.

Certainly an important factor, briefly touched upon previously, which has also contributed to application of behavioral science knowledge to school administration was inherited from the early emphasis on human relations, and, as we have pointed out, the applied behavioral sciences still constitute a logical part of that human relations emphasis, not only in educational administration but in all phases of management. In all fields of administration, students and practitioners alike learned over a period of time that the residue of shibboleths and slogans, and of cook-book type formulas for engaging in "good human relations" was simply not enough; on the contrary, it sometimes seemed to make more problems than it solved.

FROM PRACTICAL TO THEORETICAL ANALYSIS

The five years following World War II brought with them criticisms of public schools that erupted into sometimes vitriolic attacks on personnel, purposes, and methods. Alarmed by the intensity of the criticism, school administrators and professors of educational administration through their professional organization, the American Association of School Administrators, proposed a massive study of public education with its primary focus on the management and administration of schools. With financial assistance from the W. K. Kellogg Company of Battlecreek, Michigan, the now famous Cooperative Program in Educational Administration came into being. The CPEA, as it came to be known, called for the establishment of eight centers to be situated, or based, in universities geographically distributed throughout the country. The program was to run from 1951–1956 but was continued to some extent after the first five years. The Kellogg Foundation invested more than five million dollars in the program, and universities, school districts, and individual administrators contributed additional millions. It was an awesome attempt ultimately aimed at attacking some of the most basic and long-standing problems confronting administration. Among them, school-district reorganization, improved preparation programs, analysis of recruitment and selection factors in school administration, upgrading the quality and utility of graduate research in educational administration, experimental programs in in-service education (an aspect of training that administrators generally favored for teachers but avoided for their own continued education), and, of course, attention to the status and role of the school administrator as he now arrived at the mid-point in the twentieth century. In a real sense, this latter interest encouraged the school administrator to confront broad societal and cultural issues which impinged on the school and thereby generated a new interest in the goals of public education and the purpose-defining processes by which such goals were decided.

This was an exciting time to be involved in school administration. The CPEA centers initiated hundreds of conferences devoted to a wide variety of content and rather quickly the complexion of research in school administration began to change. There was a noticeable increase in graduate research of an analytical nature and a corresponding decrease in much of the purely descriptive, survey type research which had brought some justifiable criticisms from other disciplines. Interestingly, the greater part of the analytical research originated in school districts though most of it was pursued in the colleges and universities. School administrators themselves began to encourage scholarly inquiry in staff studies; community power structures were analyzed, as were communication patterns, administrator–school board relationships; and many practicing administrators became as interested and knowledgeable about the *economics* of education as they were about budgeting and financial accounting.

The CPEA influence accomplished something else that was extremely significant for future developments but which has received little comment. Those who administered the various centers worked diligently to encourage sociologists, economists, political scientists, and anthropologists to participate in CPEA conferences and action programs. It was this effort, more than any other, which profoundly influenced the present status of school administration.

From practical though sophisticated analysis, and with a considerable tolerance at times of behavioral scientists with prejudices about school administrators, there began to emerge a more theoretically oriented analysis. Instrumental in reinforcing the theoretical approach was the National Conference of Professors of Educational Administration. NCPEA was begun at a meeting of the American Association of School Administrators in Atlantic City, New Jersey, in 1947. At that time a meeting of professors was held to exchange information and get better acquainted. Under the leadership of Walter Cocking, E. T. Peterson, Paul Mort, E. B. Norton, and Worth McClure, additional plans were made to meet together for a longer period of time. A special committee composed of Norton, McClure, and the late Dr. Cocking, began planning that resulted —with the help of the International Business Machines Corporation and a grant from the General Education Board—in the first meeting of educational administration professors. It was held at IBM's "Homestead" club at Endicott, New York, in August, 1947, and has convened annually since then.

It was at the 1953 meeting of NCPEA that a new emphasis began to emerge. Discussing this particular conference, Robert S. Fisk, Dean of the University of Buffalo's school of education, stated:

> To this writer it seemed apparent that the Conference as a whole was characterized by an attempt to break through on some of the more theoretical problems which appear to be related to the quality of educational leadership. Prior to this Conference a good many of the concerns had been more specifically related to training techniques and procedures. At East Lansing it seemed that several of the groups were more concerned with the underlying theories and principles, if any, of educational administration.[29]

There were distinct differences between the concerns expressed by NCPEA at its second meeting in Madison, Wisconsin in 1948 and the meeting at Michigan State University in 1953. Fisk's comments above regarding that 1953 meeting are amplified in a comparison of topics considered by the assembled professors. Consider the lists in Table 1.

TABLE 1.

Comparisons of Topical Concerns by NCPEA 1948 and 1953 [30]

At Madison, 1948	At East Lansing, 1953
1. What is involved in the improvement of community living?	1. Implications for school administration of recent developments in the theory and practice of communications.
2. What is involved in the process of democratic, socially intelligent educational leadership?	
3. How can the desired type of leader be developed?	2. Decision-making in school administration.
4. How may the program of evaluation be continuously evaluated?	3. School administration and community development.
5. What is a desirable policy at the state level relative to certification of administrators? What are the present practices in the states?	4. New approaches to structure and organization of public education.
	5. Administrative behavior and personality: emerging concepts and hypotheses.

The Applied Behavioral Sciences. There were a number of reasons for the surge of interest among both professors of educational administration and practitioners in analysis of the process of administration. Perhaps most important was the nature of the changing American culture as we approached the mid-century; as examples, there was an awakening of the American people to the problems of minority groups as reflected in the Supreme Court's desegregation decision; growing realization that the transition from a predominantly rural culture to an urban one was substantially complete, bringing with it a complex of human problems which confronted city school administrators with immensely difficult decisions. In addition, a highly sophisticated technology was rapidly accumulating, and one of its notable consequences was an ability to change work skills and patterns faster than institutions were able to change human beings. The nation's economy, assessed in terms of the startlingly growing gross national product, was clear testimony of national affluence.

Naturally, many strains and pressures accompanied these events. The role of the federal government as a full partner in the economic fortunes of the nation was now taken for granted but required adjustments in most of our institutional structures. These various changes touched the lives of everyone—the family, the church, the schools, communities across the land were experiencing the consequences of change. C. A. Mace, in an incisive paper dealing with this very problem, discussed some of the consequences of affluence in the following fashion:

Under these conditions [of affluence] there is a reversal of means and relations characteristic of the state of nature. Man no longer eats to live, he lives to eat. Man no longer builds to live, he lives to build. He no longer kills to live, he lives to kill. What he does he does no longer because he must, but because he *enjoys* it.[31]

But of course another problem is illuminated by the affluence—the problem of poverty. In the last few years, the attention of the American people has been focused on this segment of the culture which in turn has created still a new dimension of decision-making for educational administrators.

In order to generate substantive content in preparation programs for school administrators that would provide them with the kind of training skills and knowledge necessary to their tasks in the changing twentieth century, the first requirement was rigorous inquiry and study of the phenomena which composed the emerging problems of administrative process. Traditionally, the quality of research in educational administration was far below the standards that this new requirement placed upon it. This was due, in turn, to the fact that there was little consensus among researchers regarding the most crucial parameters to be investigated, or, stated another way, there simply was no general theoretical model from which researchable hypotheses could be derived. It was this realization which led to the search for theory.

Needless to say, there still is no fundamental theory, but students of administrative process now know enough not to seriously seek an overall theory. The search for one has uncovered a variety of theoretical constructs that have been both productive and useful and, more than anything else, this search has drawn together teachers of educational administration with those in the behavioral disciplines. From their collaboration a new respect has developed between them, as well as new modes of cooperation. The watchword now has become "interdisciplinarian." In curricula, the consequences have also been fruitful. The aspiring school administrator now studies leadership, system theory, cybernetics, social psychology, sociology, and organizational behavior. Moreover, methodology has been refashioned; the use of simulation, computer-assisted instruction, case studies, and individual investigation of a variety of topics now tends to dominate programs.

Leadership has traditionally occupied an important place in the preparation programs of school administrators, but in the last two decades it has become a major focus of attention. Coordinated with the new interest in leadership has been the study of organizations and organizational behavior. The school administrator is no longer merely the caretaker-manager of a public enterprise; the pressures and problems of his job demand that increased attention be given to his role as executive and less to his role as expediter. And he has quickly learned that to be a successful leader, he must be able to predict human behavior much more accurately in varying situations. In this regard, Bass has stated:

To understand and predict a person's behavior . . . it will often be necessary to determine his cultural background, his social class and ethnic group, and the nature of the present situation, as well as his past history, motivation, and biological status.[32]

That's rather a tall order. In effect, one who aspires to a leadership status requires understanding of sociological and anthropological data, political and economic data, and, particularly, knowledge of the psychology of interpersonal relations. Moreover, he must be adept in analyzing the structure of organizations and the nature and function of group processes in the organization. In short, his grounding in the behavioral sciences must constitute a significant portion of his total training, but to be effective, it must be studied in the context of the institution in which he expects to exert leadership. Thus for the school administrator, the organizational context that he must constantly focus upon is the social system of the school.

The systematic study of educational administration, as social process, has come into full bloom in the 1960's. The work begun by NCPEA has been complemented and reinforced by the University Council for Educational Administration, an organization now composed of more than fifty doctoral-granting institutions. A landmark in the social process emphasis (the "new movement," as it has been characterized by Roald Campbell) [33] was the first of a series of career development seminars sponsored by the UCEA, devoted to theory and administration. Growing out of that conference was the publication of *Administrative Theory in Education*, edited by Andrew Halpin; [34] this book, with an earlier volume by Coladarci and Getzels,[35] provided important impetus to the application of the behavioral sciences to educational administration. Under the auspices of the UCEA, the University of Alberta initiated a conference in 1962 looking toward more specific relationships between administration and the social sciences. During that conference Paul Lazarsfeld suggested the importance of a knowledge of social science in administrative work when he observed that ". . . the administrator attempts to fulfill the goals of the organization, with the help of people, in a setting which increases the possibility for creativity, for development, and for change. This view of the tasks . . . leaves little doubt as to why the administrator must be familar with at least some aspects of the social sciences." [36]

In 1964, the National Society for the Study of Education devoted its sixty-third yearbook to the relationship of the behavioral sciences to school administration. Commenting on the status of the relationship, Griffiths and others stated in the introductory statement to the yearbook:

The present posture is toward operationalizing concepts, testing propositions, and developing theories based upon evidence . . . a change in the direction of thought in educational administration is discernible and it may well be *the* direction for the coming decades.[37]

An interdisciplinary seminar for administrators at the University of Oregon led to the publication of another recent volume which explored the relationship between educational administration and behavioral science.[38] Composed of political scientists, economists, sociologists, and social psychologists, such seminars are rapidly becoming the rule rather than the exception in the preparation of school administrators.

The New Rationalism

There has now emerged a sort of "new rationalism" in all areas of administration. Its genesis is fundamentally mathematical and its implement is the computer. But it is the necessity for precision in computer programming that has led to the "new rationalism," and its basic methodology has evolved from information theory. In a sense, this new emphasis on rationalism is therefore much more precise—in a mathematical sense —than was the rationalism of either Weber or Taylor. Weber's rationalism was fundamentally philosophical and Taylor's was basically observational, although neither of these descriptions is little more than adequate. Still, the new rationalism is founded in the assumption that problem-solving is dependent upon information and specifies a systematic method for retrieving such information.[39] In general, it can be traced to the development of operations research. It would be a mistake to assume that what has here been referred to as "new rationalism" is a departure from the relationship of management to social science; nothing could be farther from fact. On the contrary, new management procedures and methodologies are now generated almost entirely from the applied behavioral sciences.

A Concluding Comment

The present text is not another *exploration* of the relationship between the behavioral sciences and school administration. It is, rather, an attempt at the integration of certain social science concepts into the context of the administrative process.

The authors recognize, of course, that with reference to administrative competence and administrative effectiveness there is still much that is more art than science, but even here there is the assumption that the artful administrator must be knowledgeable about interpersonal relations and the nature of sociopsychological and cultural phenomena in the conduct of social institutions. Schools, after all, are particular social systems which incorporate networks of human relationships within special cultural arrangements, organized for unique ends. Wherever one finds organizations, one also finds administrative structures. It is toward a better understanding of the interaction between the organization and the administrative structure that this book is aimed.

SUMMARY

In this chapter, we have traced some of the significant developments which have directly and indirectly influenced the present practice of American educational administration. Through even so brief an historical review, the relevance of the behavioral sciences and its integration into the substantive content of preparation programs in educational administration can be more clearly understood.

As has been suggested in this chapter, one of the highly important consequences of a greater emphasis in behavioral content has been a search for a more coherent theoretical base; consistent with this point of view, the following chapter explores aspects of the nature of theory for it is at that point that careful analysis must always begin.

BIBLIOGRAPHY AND NOTES

1. L. S. Hsu, *The Political Philosophy of Confucianism.* New York: Dutton, 1932, p. 124.
2. Plato and Xenophon, *Socratic Discourses,* Book III, Chap. 4. New York: Dutton, 1910. (From Socrates' discourse with Nicomachides.)
3. J. D. Hittle, *The Military Staff.* Harrisburg, Pa.: Military Service Publishing Co., 1949, p. 20.
4. *Ibid.,* p. 91.
5. *Ibid.,* pp. 101–107.
6. A. W. Gouldner, "Organizational Analysis," in R. Merton *et al., Sociology Today.* New York: Basic Books, 1959, p. 404.
7. M. Weber, "Bureaucracy," in H. H. Gerth and C. W. Mills, *From Max Weber: Essays in Sociology.* New York: Galaxy Books, 1958, p. 214.
8. *Ibid.,* p. 54.
9. *Ibid.*
10. *Ibid.*
11. *Ibid.,* p. 218.
12. *Ibid.,* p. 212.
13. C. N. Parkinson, *Parkinson's Law.* Boston: Houghton, Mifflin, 1957, p. 39.
14. R. F. Hoxie, "Scientific Management and Labor Welfare," in *Journal of Political Economy,* Nov. 1916, p. 818.
15. J. M. Pfiffner and F. P. Sherwood, *Administrative Organization.* Englewood Cliffs, N.J.: Prentice-Hall, 1960, p. 99.
16. *Ibid.*
17. E. Morphett, T. Reller, and R. Johns, *Educational Administration: Concepts, Practices and Issues.* Englewood Cliffs, N.J.: Prentice-Hall, 1959, p. 105.
18. R. Callahan, *Education and the Cult of Efficiency.* Chicago: Univ. Chicago Press, 1962, pp. 12–13.
19. National Society for the Study of Education, *The Supervision of City Schools.* Chicago: The Society and Univ. Chicago Press, 1913, p. 119.
20. *Ibid.,* pp. 49–50.

21. Callahan, *op. cit.*, pp. 19–25.
22. G. B. Leonard, "Educator or Businessman?" in: *Look Magazine*, vol. 24, 1960.
23. Pfiffner and Sherwood, *op. cit.*, p. 100.
24. *Ibid.*, p. 101.
25. J. W. Hall, The Twelfth Yearbook of the National Society for the Study of Education, *The Supervision of City Schools*. Chicago: The Society, 1913, p. 105.
26. See: T. N. Whitehead, *The Industrial Worker* (1938), and F. J. Rothlisberger and W. J. Dickson, *Management and the Worker* (1939), both published by Harvard Univ. Press, Cambridge, Mass.
27. W. B. Donham, "Foreword," in E. Mayo, *The Social Problems of an Industrial Civilization*. Cambridge, Mass.: Harvard Univ., Graduate School of Business Administration, 1945, p. viii.
28. G. R. Koopman, A. Miel, and P. J. Misner, *Democracy in School Administration*. New York: Appleton-Century-Crofts, 1943, pp. 7–12.
29. R. Fisk, "Historical Marker, NCPEA, 1953–57," in W. R. Flesher and A. L. Knoblauch, *A Decade of Educational Leadership*. The National Conference of Professors of Educational Administration, 1957, p. 40.
30. W. E. Arnold, "Historical Marker, 1948," and R. Fisk, "Historical Marker, 1953," in Flesher and Knoblauch, *ibid.*, pp. 12 and 38–39.
31. C. A. Mace, "Human Motivation in an Affluent Society," in S. M. Farber and R. H. L. Wilson, eds., *Man and Civilization—Control of the Mind.* (New York: McGraw-Hill, 1961, p. 157.
32. B. M. Bass, *Leadership Psychology and Organizational Behavior*. New York: Harper & Row, 1960, p. 7.
33. A. Halpin, *Theory and Research in Administration*. New York: Macmillan, 1966, p. v.
34. A. Halpin, ed., *Administrative Theory and Education*. Chicago: Midwest Administration Center, Univ. Chicago, 1958. Reissued by Macmillan, 1967.
35. A. P. Colardarci and J. W. Getzels, *The Use of Theory in Educational Administration*. Stanford, Calif.: Stanford Univ. Press, 1955.
36. P. Lazarsfeld, "The Social Sciences and Administration: A Rationale," in L. W. Downey and F. Enns, *The Social Sciences and Educational Administration*. Edmonton: Univ. of Alberta, 1963, p. 4.
37. D. Griffiths, R. O. Carlson, J. Culbertson, and R. C. Lonsdale, "The Theme," in *Behavioral Science and Educational Administration*, 63rd Yearbook, National Society for the Study of Education, D. Griffiths and H. Richey, eds. Chicago: The Society, 1964, p. 3.
38. Cf. D. E. Tope *et al.*, *The Social Sciences View School Administration*. Englewood Cliffs, N.J.: Prentice-Hall, 1965.
39. For a cogent discussion of this particular approach to problem-solving, cf. C. H. Kepner and B. B. Tregoe, *The Rational Manager*. New York: McGraw-Hill, 1965.

2

The Nature of Theory

There is an increasing awareness that organization (or system) is a basic property of life—if not
life itself. If one takes this literature seriously . . .
then one arrives naturally at the assumption that
the basic properties of human or social organizations are fundamentally similar to those of organizations existing on different levels of analysis.[1]

. . . American school administrators seem to
proceed according to a collection of rules of
thumb, without any consciously worked-out guiding theory.[2]

The Need for Theory

THE NEED for a general theoretical perspective on school administration has long been recognized. As early as 1916, Mort lamented
the lack of comprehensive theory in the field, charging that it is
largely made up of rules of thumb. His own principles, however, seemed to
have been more humanitarian than theoretical. He stressed the importance
of the individual, local participation in the school system, and called for administrative simplicity.[3] A book of essays edited by Halpin constitutes
one of the important statements of the need for systematic theory in administration. In that volume Thompson describes the core of administration as a complex of "simultaneously variable factors" rather than a set of
specific techniques, and he calls for a theoretical approach which stresses
processes and relationships rather than techniques. On this point, Griffiths
states:

If any one statement could be made concerning educational administration
at this time, it would be that as a field of study it is undergoing radical change

. . . Present day textbooks are characterized by a search for the *substance* of administration and for the theory which binds the substance together.[4]

One reason that theorization has not flourished among educational administrators in the past must be related to the fact that many of them have had to be involved in the mundane, technical aspects of organization, which perhaps has smothered some of their natural theoretical curiosity. One writer observes that most literature on school administration over the past twenty-five years deals with the technical aspects of organization, the legal and physical matters of organization which include details from purchasing and maintenance to performance ratings of teachers, and this writer attributes the basis of this former era to the "efficiency cult." [5] Charging that the so-called "principles of administrative theory" are little more than sheer doctrine, Cornell calls for an analysis of educational administration from the standpoint of social structure—that is, such features as operations, coordination, interaction, customs and informal organization; he believes that these, not the more technical elements, are the essential processes of administration. Of this, Griffiths states:

An adequate theory must be concerned with the dynamics of human activity, not the mechanics of organization. While the administrator must take account of finance, building, buses, and the like, these must be considered in their proper perspective; they are of secondary importance in determining how people behave in the educational system.[6]

Currently, there has been a more widespread awareness that the administrator is not the "manager" who is aloof from his organization, but that he is rather a worker who is a part of it. This awareness alone forced widespread acceptance of the view of administration as human interaction, which in turn has increased the relevance of social science and interdisciplinary research for administrative skills. This renewed enthusiasm for a social science of administration, however, has created still other problems, as Halpin notes. Science is a "sacred cow" in our culture and, as Halpin cautions, it tends to be sanctified by scientists and administrators alike who take themselves too seriously and tend to accept speculation as truth regardless of the validity of the speculative statement.[7] This faith in science can be especially embarrassing to the social scientist whose wildest speculations may be regarded as confirmed knowledge. Yet, if theorization is wanted, someone must be willing to take a chance occasionally; however, such speculation must not be confused with scientific generalization.

From the social scientist's point of view the layman's faith in science may be equally disappointing when it becomes evident that what he wants is not confirmed knowledge but information useful in solving the practical everyday problems that administrators face. Since much social science theory does not have this objective, administrators are sometimes disillusioned with theoretical analyses. Thus, the social scientist is disappointed to learn that even those administrators who verbalize about the potential utility of sociological theory sometimes are not willing to support it in terms of necessary research, nor to accept some of its discomfiting and disconcerting conclusions.

These precautionary statements suggest that it is necessary for the social scientist, the educational theorist and the practitioner alike to formulate some common understanding about both the nature of scientific theory and the direction in which the field is expected to evolve if a full-fledged theory of scientific administration is to materialize.

There is much common sense at the basis of all theory. One of the fundamental reasons for theory development was provided more than six centuries ago by William of Ockham. Sometimes known as the "principle of parsimony" Ockham's dictum is perhaps best known as "Ockham's razor." The dictum maintains, in effect, that understanding becomes clearer as we are able to explain a variety of effects with very few principles. Or, put another way, understanding of phenomena is least complete when a different principle is required to explain every observation.

One particularly coherent statement about the general function of theory is the following by Bernard Bass:

In any science, our aim is to understand the phenomena we study. We understand a phenomenon when we are able to account for it by means of a set of principles, principles which are sufficiently general to apply in various combinations to other phenomena. We check our principles through testing the accuracy of our predictions, using the principles. Finally, we may achieve control over the phenomena by appropriately using the principles.[8]

The Elements of Theory

As an extension of common sense, theory consists of some of the same essential elements. The difference is in the degree of self-conscious precision with which each element is used. What are the essential elements of theory? Merton suggests six types of activity that are often considered to comprise social theory: methodology, general orientation, analysis of concepts, *post factum* interpretations, empirical generalizations, and quantified knowledge.[9]

Methodology. Precision of generalization usually increases with refinements of measurement. Measurement enables typologies to be transformed into variables; for example, when temperature became measurable, the single concept "heat" replaced the common sense hot-cold typology. Indeed, the primary utility of gross classifications generally resides in their promise of eventual transformation into such variables. Authoritarian and representative bureaucratic types of bureaucracy, to be discussed in later chapters, is an example of a gross dichotomy which will eventually be refined into not one, but a set of variables, including the degree of centralization and standardization, the degree of specialization, the amount of personality, and a relative stress on rules and record keeping. It should not, however, be assumed that dichotomies always represent opposite ends of the *same* continuum, for they often turn out to represent different classes of events: for example, bureaucratic and professional characteristics of organization, discussed later, are probably two different kinds of continua rather than polar opposites of the same continuum.

The advantages of methodology which make it most useful can also be its shortcomings. Merton charges that there is often more attention paid to the methods of hypothesis testing than to knowledge of the theory from which the hypotheses are derived. It is to be expected that in a technique-oriented, practical culture, "how-to-do-it" disciplines and "methodologies" will have a special place, but it may obscure the more basic aim of science, the discovery of knowledge. Correctly understood, method is not separate from theory; method is *part* of theory.[10] The methods used to arrive at a conclusion influence that conclusion; this implies that the theory being tested should *determine* the methods used. To assess personal attitudes toward power, for example, questionnaire methods are often adequate; but to understand the actual operation of power, asking individuals about their beliefs may produce conclusions with gross inaccuracies, particularly because laymen have usually not been trained to observe power systematically, and also because power is often self-incriminating.

The demand for precision is often motivated by a desire to copy the physical sciences. It is part of a general glorification of "the scientific method." That "method" seems to amount to a ready-made "prescription" revealing the way knowledge is discovered: the scientific method seems to promise the investigator that if certain rules are followed "an act of science is being done." The most popular of these rules states that hypotheses must be proposed before investigation begins. The rule implies that the connection between knowledge and the process of knowing has already been determined. It is significant that important hypotheses often emerge in the process of investigation, initiated without preconceived hypothesis.[11] Insistence by educators and fund granting agencies on prior statements of hypotheses or similar rules represents a confusion between the process of theory *construction* and retesting of established theory. It often leads to sterile, unthoughtful research because attention is directed away from significant events which may have the misfortune to be unrelated to the initial hypothesis. More refined methods become necessary at advanced stages of hypothesis testing, but at the elementary stages of theory development the more creative rather than the more exacting skills of the scientist are required.

Despite the prestige and ultimate utility of the mythological "rigor," validated and reliable instruments, and well-formulated hypotheses that are preferred by the private and government foundations sponsoring research on such problems, a premature attempt to imitate the more advanced sciences at this point would be not only pretentious but misleading. "Let's not," says Hall, "make the mistake of rushing toward a unified theory! There can be no theory of *school administration* as an operating field of endeavor until there are well-tested theories explaining all the relevant operations in all the situations which make up the administrative field." [12]

General Orientations. Because the orientation sets the context for inquiry, it is extremely crucial. Administrative theorists are still debating their orientation—whether social relationships are the core of discipline in the organization, and whether value prescriptions, lists of functions and tasks, and endless lists of other concepts are essential subjects of investigation. Social scientists are also still arguing over a general orientation and are not even agreed on types of variables that ought to be accounted for (some are still debating whether a social science is possible). One theorist, for example, proposes that a theory of administration must include such variables as value patterns, situational patterns, aptitudes, skill and knowledge, personality, physical energy, and capacity of the administrator in addition to individual and organizational performance. [13] This is indeed a comprehensive list, but admittedly too abstract to be meaningful until these types of variables are refined under more specific situations. The crucial question is *which* variables are important? One primary move in this direction is being made by Haas and others who are studying the possibility of an empirically derived typology of organization using ninety-nine variables. [14] No one project could possibly consider all relevant variables and their specific applications; there must, therefore, be a conscientious selectivity at this stage of the theory construction. Because of the elementary level of theory construction in the field, this book will have achieved its purpose if it does little more than suggest guidelines for an orientation to administrative theory by illustrating the types of variables that promise to be important.

Concepts. Language provides a perspective. Concepts sensitize the observer. Concepts point to important aspects of the situation to observe and implicitly determine what is not to be observed. Therefore, conceptual development is a crucial phase of theory construction.

It is difficult to define a concept because it is normally used to stand for the very words one must rely on to describe it. A concept is a kind of "bucket term"—and it is useful because, analogously, it is easier to carry the bucket than what is in it. Theory is, of course, a particularistic form of conceptualization; the theorist must deal first of all, therefore, with concept construction and must exercise both care and precision in their construction. It is to this task that the theorist applies operational definitions. Such definitions not only provide a measure of logical precision to the particular theorist's constructs, but they also protect him from others' meanings (which might be quite different) for the concepts he is using. Bass has characterized this quality of operational definitions as follows:

> The operational definitions and their meanings are critical for empirical verification of the adequacy of the theoretical model developed to account for the phenomena under study. But their meaningfulness to the public has nothing to do with the validity of the deductive proofs of the relations between the constructs defined by the operations.[15]

Thus, if a reader understands that morale in an organization means *esprit de corps*, then whatever principles or theorems relating to morale that a particular theory produces will be applied, in that reader's case, to *esprit de corps*.

Post Factum Interpretations.   The term *post factum* refers to interpretations of observations after they have been made, as opposed to empirical testing of predesigned hypotheses. Explanations construed in this way after the facts are in can be extremely consistent, and hence convincing; but precisely because they are convincing, they may obscure alternative explanations. Moreover, since new explanations can always be constructed to account for the exceptions, this type of explanation is not subject to disconfirmation. Yet, despite these inadequacies, *post factum* interpretations are extremely useful as plausible starting points during the creative stages of theory construction. There is no mistaking that school administration had been in this creative stage at least until about 1960. *Post factum* explanations are as vital to the following chapters as reviews of more rigorous studies.

Empirical Generalizations.   Establishing empirical generalizations constitutes one of the main theoretical tasks. These generalizations are sometimes mistaken for theory. For instance, the discovery of a correlation between the level of administrative success and amount of scientific training might be construed as a "theory." This is not precisely theory, although it is true that empirical generalizations are important elements of theory.

Before a generalization may be considered appropriate, several conditions must be fulfilled. First, there must be more evidence that confirms the statement than disconfirms it. This seems obvious enough, but untested hypotheses are easily mistaken for generalizations. Complete confirmation would require a systematic search for evidence to modify or refute the hypothesis, but sometimes all that one investigator is able to do is provide examples that *support* the hypothesis. In this sense, initial investigations take the form of a "grand jury investigation" to determine whether there is a "case," or in other words, whether there is reason to explore the hypothesis further.

Second, the *conditions* under which the generalization is valid must be specified. So long as the prediction occurs under the stated conditions, the statement is true regardless of the infrequency with which these conditions might occur. For instance, it may be found that Catholic school administrators are less geographically mobile than Protestant administrators, but the generalization is limited to the South and not in the North. Any such limitation does not destroy the statement's validity and theoretical utility. The point is that generalizations need not be "universal"—that is, applicable to all situations (even the law of gravity is limited by vacuums). At the early stages of theory formulation, exact limits often remain unknown, and the theorist must content himself with establishing whether or not certain relationships occur at all and must postpone more refined analyses of the limiting conditions for further research.

Finally, precision of generalization is increased as the exact form of the relationship is discovered. Crude hypotheses are usually only first approximations which assume a simple linear relationship. For example, it may be hypothesized that the level of ambition progressively declines with age; it could be true up to a point, but a more refined analysis might reveal that near the age of retirement it rises again. Increased precision in stating the nature of the relationship is essential at the later stages of theory construction, but cannot be demanded during the initial stages.

Codified Knowledge. Although theory consists of generalizations, one generalization does not equal a theory; nor does a body of generalizations in themselves constitute a theory. For theory to exist, the empirical generalizations must be related logically. This logical component is an essential feature of full-blown theory. The test of theory, in turn, is whether other generalizations can be derived from it. For example, codified knowledge might take this form:

(*Law 1:* Ambition to achieve economic success is greater for minority groups than for the general population.
Observation: Jews are a minority group.
Derivation: Jews have greater ambition than the general population.

To be tenable such a postulate rests partially on the confirmation of the derived statements. If true it would apply to other minority groups as well. If it does not apply to Negroes, Italians, and Puerto Ricans, the initial premise must be modified. This is, of course, a simplified illustration.

There are two common misunderstandings about theory: (1) that it is speculation, and (2) that its goal is only to predict. The tendency to distinguish between "theory" and empirical fact is a false understanding of the term. Correctly understood, an empirical theory *is* fact—that is, an organized body of empirical generalizations (and the assumptions on which they are based). The other misunderstanding is that the goal of theory is only to predict. If theory is a logical set of laws, then the goal is not to predict, but to derive other laws.[16] Once such a logical relationship is established, prediction more easily follows. While prediction is, of course, extremely important, its importance to theory construction rests merely on its utility as a *tool* of science; it is employed to *test* the validity of theory. That is, if a derivation does not accurately predict, of course, the theory is inadequate. But the ability to predict in itself is not the distinguishing feature of theory. A set of random predictive statements does not constitute theory, no matter how practical they may be.

This point is not purely academic, because a search for predictive statements often proceeds differently from a search for theory. For example, if it were learned that body build is related to administrative success, the person who visualizes prediction as his goal would be satisfied, but the theorist would be puzzled. While prediction may have great utility and while it may be a point of merging interest between practitioner and theorist, it is not a substitute for the scientific goal of theoretical explanation. So long as school administrators demand of social science only that it solve their practical problems of management, they are not, no matter how great their faith in social science, directly contributing to the development of explanatory theory. Of course practical research may bear some theoretical implications, by accident if not by design, but zeal for practical solutions may actually divert investigations which otherwise would have been more directly focused on explanatory work.

The whole question of the relevance of theory to daily problems partially involves the question of what is practical. It is not entirely clear that solving the daily problems is more practical than developing more fundamental understandings about them. It is not by accident that the most advanced of the applied sciences—notably medicine and engineering—are grounded in such theoretical disciplines as physiology and physics. In the words of Walton, "It is perhaps because of impatience with theorizing and because of eagerness to get at practical applications of our knowledge that we overlook the essential practicality of sound theory, out of which sound practice can be developed." [17] Yet, at this point even many of the sympathetic administrators who otherwise express a fondness for "theory" tend to retreat under the daily pressures of work to what seems for the moment the more practical affairs of administration.

Implications. Empirical theory, then, may be defined as a logically coherent body of confirmed generalizations that have in common certain assumptions and concepts that can be specified with a degree of precision. Theory develops, when it does, as a result of a series of modest attempts to imaginatively think through problems in conjunction with rather close and systematic observations. Despite some claims, there is no formula for achieving this success. In order to evaluate the current state of progress intelligently, it is imperative to first identify the particular stage of theory construction that the field has achieved. A realistic appraisal of the current state of administrative theory reveals that social science is still wrestling with problems of the elementary stages of orientation and conceptualization. Criticism must fall within the range of reason set by this current level of theory. The contemporary theorist cannot properly be criticized for failing to provide a full-blown theory before its basis has been established. Such criticism often reflects the disappointment of persons who are zealously interested in achieving the more advanced stages of theory without bothering with the preliminary turmoil. This book is hardly dedicated to the promulgation of that turmoil, but the authors are resigned to live with some of it for a while longer. We are aware, however—and comforted by that awareness—that theory is, above all else, heuristic—that is, theory begets theory. And perhaps at this point, we are back to common sense. There is startling scientific clarity in the adage that one must crawl before he walks.

Perhaps it is also well to remind ourselves that in the field of administration rigorous and systematic study of organizational process must candidly recognize the difficulties imposed by the bifurcation of practice and science. Halpin states this dilemma incisively:

Our problems . . . are exacerbated because administration may be approached from the point of view of a normative discipline as well as from that of descriptive science. Both approaches are important, but the researcher must keep the two realms straight and must know at all times which approach is being used. Administration as a normative discipline deals with how an administrator ought to behave and is predicated on an ideal situation in which time is theoretically infinite and choices are not coercive. In studying administration as social scientists, our concern is with how administrators actually behave in a real world where time is limited and choices must be made . . . Research in administration has been severely impeded because the language of these two realms has been confused.[18]

Underlying Assumptions of Theory

Theory construction probably best begins with an exposure of the critical underlying assumptions. The assumptions of the theoretical orientation to be developed in subsequent chapters are outlined below.

1. There are certain administrative problems which are shared by all

types of organizations. Educational administration does have much in common with other administrative fields from which insights can be drawn.

2. The nature of administrative problems and effective principles are more a function of the *organizational* structure in which the administrator works than of his line of work. That is, the nature of administration is as much determined by such conditions as the size of the organization, and whether it is privately or publicly controlled and whether it is complex or simple, than whether it is educational, business, or political. (This does not mean that the administrator can function in ignorance of his particular institution; on the contrary, in order to exert leadership in any area he must appreciate its basic values and goals. However, given a school administrator and businessman each of whom understands his respective field, the similarities and differences in the problems they face will be greatly influenced by whether or not they work in the same size of organization, and so on.)

3. The administrator works with organized *groups* rather than directly with individuals themselves. The problems of administrators are better understood from the perspective of social organization rather than from the psychology of individuals.

4. The educational leader is not a "manager" aloof from the organization, but a *part* of it. Therefore, administration is best understood as a *relationship* between persons and groups rather than techniques and rules of administration. Accordingly, the factors of subordination, cooperation, conflict, and the principles of leadership, coordination, and organization are the primary tools that administrators must understand. With regard to relationships, administration must be understood from the standpoint of the subordinates—that is, the teachers' as well as the superior's standpoint. This will mean that "school administration" is not an exclusively executive function, but that it is distributed throughout the organization in terms of these interrelationships between teachers and supervisors.

5. Modern organization is characterized by internal contradictions among the various principles on which they are organized. These contradictions, often produced by environmental pressures, are a source of internal conflicts "built" into the organization itself. The administrator and his employees "inherit" problems from the situation.

6. The important supervisory and leadership decisions concern the regulation of these internal contradictions and environmental pressures. The operating decisions often inadvertently lead to organizational "drifts" between social policy and practice.

7. The significance of these contradictions within organizations has been insufficiently stressed in the past, and much of formal theory, consequently, amounts to little more than assertions of myths about organization. A theory of organizational process as well as structure is needed.

8. Validated knowledge ought not be confused with the *process* of theory development; codified theory cannot be achieved without beginning systematic analysis at less ambitious levels. Synthesis of abstract hypotheses with illustrative material and concrete examples is a convenient point of departure.

Sometimes assumptions are most clearly exposed by the model of society which the investigator imagines. Attention is now turned to a review of some of the available models.

Models of Organization

Models are often used in the name of theory. Sometimes an advanced theory in one area may act as a model for a less advanced area, but theories and models are not equivalent. While a theory is a logically related set of confirmed generalizations, a model is constituted of propositions confirmed for one set of problems but applied to another class of problems. The major difference is that empirical theories are first empirical laws from which more abstract relationships can be derived, while scientific models first consist of abstractions which are later interpreted into empirically testable hypotheses.

In general, one subject is a model for something else when the concepts of both subjects are *isomorphic*. This means that (1) there is a one-to-one correspondence between the concepts and assumptions of the model and the observed world, and (2) the relationships take the same form.[19] Isomorphism suggests hypotheses. For example, if a school system is like the human body, then the main office of the system may function like a brain, and decision processes may be likened to a nerve center. Since a disturbance in one part of the body affects all other parts, the same may be expected of the school system. However, some of the disadvantages of models should also be apparent in the same illustration: because models are seldom perfect analogies, they can be seriously misleading. Yet, sometimes they are used to the point of seeming real; they may become so sacred that the investigator is more interested in preserving the model than in interpreting reality.[20] Because of such disadvantages, a model may actually obscure the actual relationships. This is especially true when models are chosen on the basis of their prestige or their success in other fields rather than any isomorphism or inherent similarities to the subject matter being studied. The prestige of physical science models may be a consideration that underlies their prevalence in the social sciences. For social science has relied heavily on physical, geological, and ecological models, and none of them are particularly relevant to *social* conduct. Models derived from cultural activities, such as the dramaturgical or even the musical model, have been ignored despite their possible relevance to everyday life.

RATIONAL MODELS OF ORGANIZATION

Models in which conflict is the basic process are implicit throughout this book, but, since the biological models stressing structure have been among the most popular sociological models, the conflict models will be contrasted with them. Rational-biological models of organization in particular have widespread popularity among the most eminent contemporary theorists of organization, including C. I. Barnard and Talcott Parsons.[21]

Gouldner describes the rational model as that model in which organization is conceived as a means for the realization of announced group goals. Stress is placed on rationally directed, long-range development of the organization, or a *system*, toward explicitly stated goals. The model, as Gouldner points out, has called attention to the most distinguished characteristic of modern organization, its rationality.[22] Its premises are that decisions are based on a rational survey of the situation and implemented through a codified legal apparatus, and that significant changes result mainly from planned efforts to increase efficiency. Because nearly complete rational administrative control is assumed, any recognized departures from rationality are attributed to random mistakes, ignorance, miscalculation, or other impediments to rationality. Gouldner suggests that from this "mechanical" (systemic) perspective on organization, the structure appears to be purely manipulatable, designed solely for purposes of efficiency and the idea that "things can always be made better."

There are a number of considerations which the model ignores and, in fact, obscures. First, attempts to rationalize the organization may obscure the less formal and less rational elements of organization that also contribute to its effectiveness. The rational attitude that "nothing is sacred" in organization also ignores the fact that people become emotionally involved in the established ways of doing things; problems of organization arise precisely because the organization becomes a sacred end in itself. Nor do executives, in fact, have complete control over the organization because it is dependent upon outside forces which divert the organization persistently from its long-range goals.

The rational model is grounded in a biological model of society that underlies the structural-functional view of society. The model rests on the complacent belief that "good" organizations are essentially harmonious and static, an unmistakably selective perception of the way organizations operate. It is assumed that societies exist in a state of harmonious equilibrium maintained by the consensus of their members, and that conflict, irregularity, change, and dissent are, accordingly, a "sickness" which disrupts the harmony. This view of conflict as a disease having primarily "dissociating and disfunctional consequences" is sharply criticized as utopian by Dharendorf in an essay with a provocative title, "Out of Utopia." [23] His observations merit extensive reflection by persons interested in building an administrative theory. He observes that all utopias, from Plato's Republic to Orwell's brave new world of 1984, have several elements in common. First, they are all societies from which basic change is absent, with the exception of orderly change, or a "moving equilibrium," which occurs so uniformly throughout the society that it is never upsetting to anyone. Also, utopias are uniformly consistent and based on a universal consensus in regard to prevailing values and institutional arrangements. In these perfectly agreeable societies there is a caste-like relation between the leaders and the oppressed, who would never revolt against their superiors. Recalling that Socrates finally decided that justice really means that everyone does what is incumbent upon him, Dharendorf notes, with some disgust, that modern theorists have also discovered that justice means that everybody "plays his role." Although some writers add a clever touch of realism by inventing an individual nonconformist who is considered to be a pathological case, according to Dharendorf his only role is to highlight the inherent good of conforming. Finally, it is uniformly true that utopias are isolated from all other communities. Since citizens of utopias are seldom confronted with demands from the outside world, the society maintains complete control over its environment and complete autonomy to establish and fulfill its goals. Dharendorf asks "if the immobility of utopia, its isolation in time and space, the absence of conflict and disruptive processes, is a product of poetic imagination divorced from the commonplaces of reality—how is it that so much of recent [sociological] theory has been based on exactly these assumptions, and has, in fact, consistently operated with a utopian model of society?" [24] The same question has implications for administration.

A way of looking at society is also a way of not looking at it. The conception of school "systems" and stress on the "socialization" functions of schools already suggests selective perception about their fundamental nature. Dharendorf writes: "One of the more unfortunate connotations of the word 'system' is its closure . . . there is no getting away from the fact that a system is essentially something that is . . . self-sufficient, internally consistent and closed to the outside." He concludes that ". . . it is only a step from thinking about societies in terms of equilibrated systems to asserting that every disturber of the equilibrium, every deviant, is a 'spy' . . . The system theory of society comes dangerously close to the conspiracy theory of history . . ." As a consequence ". . . it introduces many kinds of assumptions, concepts, and models for the sole purpose of describing a social system that has never existed and is not likely to ever come into being." [25] It also contributes to a series of myths about administrative organization, to be examined in Chapter 8.

THE CONFLICT MODEL

Dharendorf observes that advocates of "empirical research" and defenders of abstract theory are stubbornly similar in one respect. They have both dispensed with the prime impulse of all science, the puzzlement over concrete intellectual *problems*, the simple curiosity to solve "the riddles of experience." Problems, as opposed to topics or fields of inquiry, exist because they are puzzling to the investigator. Their solution demonstrates, above all, critical examination of facts, observations, and testing which generates new problems. Dharendorf believes that this loss of problem consciousness explains the utopian state of modern theory.

One of the curious riddles of society concerns the problem of "social glue," or in other words: what holds organizations together? Why do people join organizations and "play" roles? If the bonds of organization are personal harmony and group consensus, why do they persist despite the facts of organized resistance, internal friction, intrinsic competition, and sometimes radical cleavages that characterize organizations? It is unreasonable to dismiss so common a phenomenon as conflict as "accidental" and "exceptional" to the normal process. On the contrary, perhaps it is not the presence, but the absence of conflict that constitutes the surprising and the abnormal. At the very least, what seems to be called for is a model of organization in which power and power conflict have a central place. It is proposed that power has as vital a place in the maintenance of social order as consensus, and that conflict itself, as a natural adjunct of power relationships, provides a form of cohesiveness. Some premises of a conflict theory of organization follow:

1. *The Group Nature of Conflict.* Contrary to a popular view, conflict is not purely personal, or the subjective expression of individual psyches. Conflict is a group phenomenon and extends beyond the subjective attitudes of persons as group members. Barnard points out, for example, that just as a thousand loves between soldiers and enemy women is not equal to peace, so a dozen disputes between American tourists and French cab drivers is not equivalent to a French-American conflict; parties in conflict may even display affection toward one another, as in the cases of conflict between the sexes or age groups and the numerous wars fought by "peace-loving" people.[26] Since conflict can exist independently of personal hostility, personal attitudes reveal little about group relations. Moreover, Barnard maintains that improving interpersonal relations by "getting people together" (as in the comprehensive school) does not necessarily reduce conflicts which are based on institutional differences (for example, race), and in cases where enemies definitely have something to fight about, getting them together may simply expose their basic differences and drive them to their extremes.[27]

2. *Cultural Relativism.* Historically the "good" people have usually

fought the "good." Nations participating on each side in the religious crusades claimed religious justification. Modern nations each establish elaborate moral justifications for their inhuman acts of violence. The neighbors who dispute their property lines are likely to be "good" citizens, just as "progressive" educators and "essentialists" and "authoritarians" are equally "good" people. That is, the "good" man is generally the supporter of his own groups' values, while the "bad" man is usually on the opposing side. Thus, the problem is not which side is "good," but what the fight is all about.[28]

3. *An Organization Is a Balance of Power.* What is defined as "good" may have had a long history of struggle for acceptance, as, for example, did Christianity, which was at one time the religion of a downcast minority. In this sense, the world, a society, or an organization, as each exists, is the outcome of historical power struggles and is the remnant of resulting animosities. All organizations are subject to some incipient cleavages on the basis of their previous history. Since the defeat of an idea or of a group seldom requires complete annihilation, scars remain which provide the basis for cleavage in new conflicts. For example, the relationship between North and South in the United States cannot be understood apart from the Civil War and the events that preceded and followed it. Similarly, playground fights are not entirely due to personality problems; those fighting may represent different community groups and families in conflict—social classes, racial, religious and ethnic groups. Like schoolboys' fights, the more sophisticated battles between their parents, teachers, administrators and other school personnel, often reflect deep-seated animosities nourished by past events. Relationships between the school and its community are likewise molded by past struggles which may recur.

4. *Conflicts Create Cooperation.* Cooperation and conflict are not polar opposites, but are in fact closely related group processes; conflict between groups promotes cooperation within groups.[29] Because groups must cooperate intensively in order to wage conflict, the cohesiveness and discipline of a group may be indicative of impending disputes with another group. Also, as new conflicts occur, new forms of cooperation emerge. For example, competing groups within a school system will nevertheless work together when their mutual interest is jeopardized by outside groups. Superintendents intentionally employ this principle when they cast the blame for certain internal problems onto the school board. This alternating conflict and cooperation between groups, which can take place among the same individuals, provides an element of unpredictability and flux in the organizational structure.

5. *Groups Must Be Visible to Conflict.* Conflicts cannot occur between groups that are not identifiable; each side in a conflict must have some physical or symbolic identity. This requirement of visibility helps

to explain why certain minority groups which are in opposition to the established order, such as the Mennonites and, more recently, the Beatniks and "hoods," deliberately maintain a uniquely characteristic appearance. Members of such groups who do not maintain the symbols (such as Mennonites who wear lipstick, or Beatniks without beards) are outcast by the group, not so much because their acts are mortal sins, but to prevent further erosion of the group's identity. The members of one branch of Mennonites are not permitted to have telephones in their homes, but they may freely use public telephone booths because the public telephone is not identified with them. Identity is so important that as groups in conflict lose their symbolic character, the conflicts between them decline. Some distinctive groups, such as Negroes who cannot modify their appearance, must endure conflict longer than ethnic groups, such as the Italians who quickly become acculturated and accepted. Quite often conflicts disappear in this way without being resolved as the identity between those in conflict disappears.

6. *Conflict Is Sustained by Ideology.* Symbolic identities have their highest expression in the statements of ideologies justifying the group's position in conflict. For example, each side of the "town-and-gown" fights between colleges and their communities around the country has its rationale or its justification. Professors are viewed as potentially dangerous liberals of an impractical bent by a nation that is grossly anti-intellectual, while many professors delight in thinking of laymen as crass, unsophisticated, conservative materialists. The ideology of local democratic control over the schools bolsters resistance to consolidation or to any interference in local affairs from state departments of education, while state departments justify their interference on the basis of elaborate ideologies about raising the standards of education, benevolence, and professional expertise.

Perhaps there is no more elaborate rationale for the different positions that educators take in conflict than those provided by philosophies of education. Two dominant philosophies, as described by Conant and Nock, will be briefly compared to illustrate the function of philosophy in maintaining and justifying conflicts.[30] The two philosophers differ on the meanings of the doctrine of equality, realistic and instrumental conceptions of education, and programs of education.

a. *The doctrine of equality.* Conant's basic value premise is "equality of opportunity, not equality of rewards." Consequently, he emphasizes that there should be a minimum of social class distinction to facilitate social mobility. Yet, while he is interested in maintaining an open class structure, he does not advocate homogeneity of social groups either, and he encourages diversity.

Nock also implicitly accepts the doctrine of equality, but he is less interested in explicating what it implies than in what it does *not* imply about education. Denying that all men are "educatable," he asserts that the doctrine is applicable only to those who are able to learn. Therefore, equality of treatment must be tempered by ability. While he grants that democracy and political equality are acceptable political values, he maintains that there is no implication from this political philosophy that the economic and educational areas of life need also be egalitarian. Therefore, while Conant concentrates on initial social opportunity, Nock emphasizes the desirable and logical outcome of the resulting competition, the survival of an intellectual elite based on ability.

b. *Conceptualizations of Education.* Conant perceives education in its pragmatic, utilitarian aspects. First, it is a way to implement a fluid social structure, providing a means of social mobility. Second, education for Conant is more than a way to train an elite; it is a way to train citizens to live in a democracy. He sees education, then, as a way to make democratic society work. This is most clearly seen in his exaltation of the "comprehensive" high school, which he believes will develop mutual respect among persons of diverse backgrounds who attend. He asserts that the American nation could not have developed its current coherence without the unifying influence of the public schools.

For Nock, on the other hand, there is a fundamental distinction between education and training. Education is for him a way of finding "truth," not of achieving the practical goals, even those so noble as developing an appreciation of democracy. Nock assumes that achievement of this truth requires more than direct contact with the world; it requires a "mental" grasping, which only a sophisticated intellect can achieve. And here is the fallacy that Nock sees in science, for with it, he charges, anyone can claim knowledge merely with sense experience; however, he argues that achievement of knowledge is not a democratic process, but a specialized one.

c. *Programs of education.* Conant believes that education must train persons for a variety of disciplines. He would like to have a variety of programs, designed to benefit all types of students and all types of intellectual abilities. He believes that specialized education should be at a relatively late age so that persons are not prematurely "forced" into a career pattern before their interests and abilities are known.

Contrary to Conant, Nock favors early specialization for promising students. He believes that intellectual ability can be identified early, and this allows for greater cultivation of the intellectual elite which he feels will develop anyway. Furthermore, since the object of education is to find the truth, a "bargain counter" education is uncalled for; this is merely a way of admitting that we are not sure of what the truth is. Furthermore, since "truth is truth," it can be found in Greek and Latin literature as well or better than in science. He prescribes a nonelective curriculum weighted heavily with classical studies and mathematics.

d. *Interpretation.*[31] This brief summary of the two positions should be sufficient to suggest for the reader two basic philosophical positions under controversy today in public education. From the standpoint of conflict theory, Nock and Conant are representatives of two identifiable groups in competition over a limited social value; their philosophies are used by groups in conflict as justifications. The middle class is being justified by Conant and the upper class has been justified by Nock. From this view, one function of education is to transmit a group's values to its young; it is a training program for "new young warriors" to staff groups in conflict. Nock's distinction between education and training is illuminating. He defines training in terms of those subjects (science) which help to promote the social mobility of the middle class, and equal opportunity for all classes. Yet, it is equally obvious that "education" in Nock's terms also amounts to a training program—the training of a cultural elite. Latin, Greek, and math are symbols of identification with the upper social class, the landed leisure class that once controlled the society and still struggles for survival against the newer commercial and industrial middle class.

7. *Conflict Influences Goals.* Due to conflicts which normally exist within and between organizations, some personnel have aims which are not expressed in the official statement of purposes. This situation nourishes a diversity of organizational goals and unplanned cleavages between departments which further compromise the original goals. The operating goals, consequently, are partly forged out of the conflict process. As a note of caution, perhaps the conflict model is too preoccupied with these spontaneous and unplanned developments of goals,[32] but it is a preoccupation which at least counteracts its systematic neglect in the rational model of organization.

IMPLICATIONS

The important question at this point is not which model is more "real to life," but which raises the more significant questions. In the conflict model, "organization" is problematic. It calls for an investigation of organization as an initially "unnatural" state of affairs and forces the question to be asked: What causes organization? Answers to this question will provide answers to the question about the role of the school administrator.

The Special Nature of Educational Administration

School administration is viewed in this book from a general perspective on organizations. General principles of organization and conflict are borrowed from literature on other types of organizations. This does not imply, however, that problems of administration are unrelated to the *type* or organizational goals, the organization's complexity, and its degree of centralization and standardization. There are certain characteristics of education suggested by Campbell which make it a somewhat special case.[33] Yet, it will be clear as they are briefly discussed in the following paragraphs that far from denying the relevance of a sociological perspective and a conflict model, each special feature seems to support the critical relevance of the conflict model.

First, education is a service that deals directly and intimately with people; perhaps this hardly makes education a belligerent enterprise. However, the school does things *to* people as well as *for* them; parents will be especially suspicious of some types of changes which may occur in their children, as indicated in Chapter 8. The conflict centers partly on which services the school is to render to a community with diverse interests and high hopes, and partly on the authority of the school to make that decision and to control the means of implementing it. Parents have exercised a long and, in some sense, legitimate control over administrative decisions which, however, is also legally delegated to the school boards and which is often usurped by professional doctrines of authority. The possibility that schoolmen may oppose the interest of parents lays the groundwork for incipient conflict.

Second, the development of a critical attitude is a central part of most educational philosophies, and some objectivity is generally expected of the public school system. This analytical attitude, supported by ideologies of academic freedom, is sometimes directed toward highly valued aspects of society. Consequently, there always exists a remote possibility that schools will lead pupils to revolt against certain aspects of the established order which some members of the community uphold. Public sensitivity to this possibility increases interest in the school from outsiders who can exert sometimes overwhelming pressures. Teachers, children, parents, and administrators may differ on the utility of critical thinking in practice if not in philosophy. This and the first condition suggest the inherently unstable, triadic relationship that characterizes the school's relationship to pupils and parents. There is usually some competition between home and school for the allegiance of children.

Third, there are explosive impediments to accurate *evaluation* of the success of schools. Policy statements tend to be so abstract that they are useless in establishing criteria of success. What is "good citizenship"? Does it include critical attitudes toward the American government or not? What are the criteria of good teaching? What is a "successful" student? Often many years are required before attitude changes effected by high schools are revealed in behavior. This ambiguity in evaluating teaching success is less apparent in some phases of business, particularly in sales, where effectiveness can be measured in terms of sales volume and effectiveness of promotion campaigns. The actual criteria of success used by teachers and administrators have been left directionless by the ambiguity of goals and standards of success, and these criteria must be hammered out in practice from the different available expectations.

Fourth, education differs from other organizations in the structure of the forces that control it. School boards represent various special interests of the community and have almost complete legal control over school policies; school administrators have almost no legal status, and their job is subject to the school board's pleasure, which greatly impairs the administrator's control over his organization. He is forced to compete for the support of various special interest groups which attempt to influence school practices, and he must often act as a mediator between them. Because these groups are inexperienced and untrained in education, the administrator may wish to resist some of their demands; but because they control his job, he may be in a poor position to do so.

Fifth, the school staff is professionally trained; many teachers have as much education as the chief administrator. Professionalization requires autonomy over work, a requirement which is often at variance with actual control by the administration. Their level and type of training, together with legal tenure provisions and the support of several professional organizations, gives the teaching faculty more legal autonomy than, for example, unskilled factory laborers. At the same time, teachers do not have as much authority over their spheres of work as do those in many of the more established professions. In fact, perhaps no other professional group, except perhaps nursing, is so completely subordinate to its administration as are teachers. The traditional authority of laymen over the schools, the ensuing professionalization of teachers, and the delegated power of administrators and school boards over teachers are basic characteristics of teaching that breed conflict between laymen, the administration, and their subordinates.

Finally, the school's physical structure and organization merit special attention. Unlike many organizations, such as the hospital, the school cannot be understood as a separate unit, for it is part of a system of units physically dispersed throughout the community and state. The fact that the superintendent's office is physically remote from the principal's office may be of some consequence for the development of unauthorized autonomy in some schools, problems of communication, and the kind of criteria used to evaluate teachers.

School administration is obviously, then, not identical to other forms of administration in all respects. The differences, however, should not be permitted to obscure the similarities; and in fact they may merely serve to highlight many of the same characteristics found in other modern organizations to which conflict models have demonstrated relevance. In any case, the concepts that have proved fruitful to us in studying complex organizations are those that have common rather than specific application.

A Conceptual Perspective

The concepts which underlie models are tools of analysis. They set the perspective and point to the questions that are to be raised. Concepts have a fundamental role, therefore, in directing the investigation of organizations. Some of the major concepts that will appear in subsequent chapters will be previewed below. Their applications will be developed in more detail in the chapters which follow.

POWER AND AUTHORITY

Organization is primarily supported by two types of force, power and authority. Power is sometimes conceived as the nonlegitimate or illegitimate threat of force to achieve an end, while authority is the *right* to use force, which is granted either by the consensus of those over whom it is wielded, or by delegation from other authorities. Power, then, will refer to the potential of force, and authority will refer to the right to exercise that force. Power is calibrated from minor *influence* at one extreme, to complete *control* at the other. While both power and authority involve the threat of force, force need not be actually applied in order to exert either power or authority.[34]

Excessive display of authority may in fact dissipate power as repeated applications use up the available alternatives.[35] Unexercised power may also lose some of its threat, of course, but the more significant fact is that power is directly proportional to the number of alternatives available and is diminished when they are used. It is, for example, evident that persons who are willing to use illegal and unethical alternatives have more power than those who feel constrained by legal and ethical principles. Similarly, within the legal and ethical limits, each application of power consumes an alternative and simultaneously commits the organization to a line of action which further restricts its alternatives in the future. For example, in March, before the annual contracts have been signed, principals have a source of power over teachers that is not available in April after they have been signed. Similarly, a principal has more power over an incompetent teacher before the disposition of her case is decided than after she has been demoted.

A person may have authority without actually having the power to implement it. In fact, because power is a function of the alternatives available, authority and power may be inversely related. That is, the very legitimacy of authority constrains the kinds of alternatives that an authority may use in order to exercise its power. Authority is constrained by popular expectations, values, and traditions, which necessarily bind the use of power. The restraints on power that accompany authorization are apparent in the fact that fraud and bribery are very effective kinds of power which are precluded to persons in authority. The power of the principal to fire incompetents is similarly constrained by the existing community sentiments toward the incompetent, opinions of his colleagues, and humanitarian concern about how it will affect his personal life. The number of persons who can be demoted or negatively treated by the chief executive in any one year is limited; at some point resistance will develop. Therefore, the availability of each negative alternative is diminished every time it is used. Moreover, the way that the principal handles a particular incompetent will set a precedent that in turn restricts the alternatives which are proper for dealing with incompetents in the future.

To summarize, power is based on the ability to control rewards—an action which may be seen as a threat; to be effective, it must be used occasionally. However, just as power increases as the range of alternatives increases, it diminishes as alternatives are actually consumed, for each application sets a precedent which precludes other alternatives. Authorized power is regulated by public opinion or organizational consensus. In the long run, though, there seems to be a tendency for those who exercise sheer power to gain public respect and legitimacy over a period of time. Because the greatest power is held, at least temporarily, by persons who are not constrained within the limits of legitimization in its exercise, there is a tendency for power to become separated from authority.

REPRESENTATIVE AND AUTHORITARIAN TYPES OF ORGANIZATION

To a considerable extent, recent controversies over the appropriate models of social organization are repetitions, in another tongue, of age old controversies about the foundations of society. To the question "What makes organizations tick?" some have answered, in company with Hobbs, that it is sheer *power*—the threat of loss of job, the indirect forces of gossip and chicanery, or a compelling need of the rewards which conformity to the existing power will bring. Others prefer a more civil answer, the one Locke advocated, that it is the mutual consent of the governed which provides the *authority* to rule organizations.

The anthropologist, Bronislaw Malinowski, has implied that rules as they relate to purposes, make organizations tick. Malinowski maintains that all human behavior begins with organization and that the particular nature of any organization is understandable in terms of the relationships between its goals and its functions on the one hand, and the relationships between its rules and its activities on the other. The goals prescribe *ideal* expectations and the functions represent *reality;* in the same fashion, the rules define *ideal* behaviors and the activities represent *real* behaviors. Organizations change, therefore, to the extent that they are able to tolerate the degree to which *reality* deviates from ideality.[36] He would hold that organizations are necessarily representative.

These various viewpoints also seem to underlie the major dichotomies of modern organizational theory. Depending on the emphasis given to each viewpoint, organizations are primarily authoritarian, or primarily representative, in terms of the power of subordinates to influence decisions. In the authoritarian (or "punishment-centered") organization, power to make decisions is concentrated at the top of the formal hierarchy, while in the representative type of bureaucracy, the entire membership has opportunity to express its consent and dissent and to influence the final decisions.

OFFICIAL AND INFORMAL STRUCTURES

Uses of authority and power form several distinct structures within organizations. A *structure* includes both a set of positions which prescribe broad functions and specific duties to incumbents, and a system of norms which regulate the relationship between incumbents of different positions. Official positions in organizations will be referred to as *offices*. Each office constitutes a system of jobs, or roles, which prescribe the responsibilities (rights and obligations) of that office with respect to other offices in the system. Accordingly, the superintendent's office cannot be understood apart from the responsibilities of other offices in the system, including the roles of classroom teachers.

Although the term *structure* implies a stable pattern of relationships, it may be viewed as a variable; organizations can be more or less structured in several respects. The most structured system is the official authority system. The official obligation of superintendents is to provide facilities for teachers and to influence their direction; the principal is responsible for staffing and coordinating classrooms; the teacher is supposed to instill knowledge and values in pupils without showing favoritism, and so on. There are, however, contradictions even within the official system. Authority may have several bases. It may stem from traditional rights to make decisions, it may be delegated by political powers vested with legal and institutional authority, it may be assumed by mutual agreement among personnel, or it may be assumed by some individual because of a special competence. These forms of authority may be inconsistent, and rifts and power conflicts may develop among personnel within the organization who are committed to different authority systems.

Moreover, there are competing systems in the school, besides the official one, which create even further variability in the extent to which the overall system can be said to be "structured," or coordinated. These competing systems give rise to several different *informal* authority structures in addition to the legal and official ones. Informal leaders develop among teachers on the basis of the esteem of their colleagues. Since the authority arising from these unofficial sources is independent of the legal-official structure, it in effect constitutes a separate system of authority—the *informal authority* structure. The informal authority structure is intermediate between the official structure and the informal *power* structure. In the sense that such uses of power are not officially authorized, they technically constitute a power structure, yet, in the sense that they are authorized by group opinions, they are authority structures.

Systems of completely unauthorized power, or *power* structures, complicate the picture still further. Informal power structures exist simultaneously with, yet independently of, the informal authority structures, being unauthorized even by mutual consent of colleagues.

To summarize, there is a structural connection between authority and power and, respectively, the official and the informal organizations which they underlie. It is a crude relationship since some facets of the informal structure are authorized informally, and because competing bases of legitimization exist which are decided by power conflicts. Because authority relationships are infinitely more predictable than power relations, which by definition may exist outside the normal structure of expectancy and group control, authority is an understandably popular approach to organizational theory and planning. However, because structure is a variable and because there are a variety of structures (some based on unstable power relations), change and instability must be recognized as inherent to organizations. The notion of process must be incorporated into attempts to predict and plan organizational behavior.

The problem of predicting *events* based on unstable, semistructured power relations seems to be overwhelming at this point. The problem, however, of dealing with such dynamics as a *class* of events does not appear as forbidding. It may be necessary and useful to incorporate a set margin of error into predictions—that is, a specific measure of error to be expected from unforeseen disturbances, shifts of power, and environmental changes. In any event, attention needs to be given to the conceptualization, prediction, and explanation of power relations as distinct from authority relations.

Status and Office.[37]   It is by now a truism that the official and informal structures of an organization are drastically influenced by the society in which they exist. The statement, nevertheless, is a reminder that administration cannot be viewed apart from the general status system of the society and the manner in which the status is translated into organizational practices. The concept of status refers to a position in the general *society;* it parallels the term *office,* which designates positions within a particular *organization.* The distinctiveness of organizational and societal positions, or office and status, is illustrated by Lazarsfeld and Thielens in a study of academic freedom.[38] College social science professors believed that they were ranked low in esteem by businessmen, congressmen, and college trustees. That is, they sensed that they held a low social status in the society. But the professors who had higher official and professional ranks within the educational system felt they had lower social status than the lower ranking professors. In other words, the professors felt that their official achievement was not accorded sufficient recognition by members of the broader society.

There are sometimes contradictions between what treatment a person may expect because of his status, and what the actual duties of his office are. A superintendent, for example, assumes the status of "educator," but his official duties may be more akin to those of a businessman and, in some smaller communities, of a records clerk. Conversely, different social statuses may be bestowed on offices with the same rank in different associations. In one study, for example, it was found that school superintendents of wealthier school systems were accorded more prestige than superintendents of the same rank in less wealthy schools.[39] It is the variations in status between offices of the same official rank which, of course, motivates mobility patterns within the school system.

Contradictions between status and office are also sources of dilemmas. For example, *age* has a different meaning within the status system of the broader society and the official system of the school. For, while it may be officially proclaimed that ability is the only important consideration for promotion, within the school age *is* important. Because responsibility is supposed to be relegated to older persons, a young principal or superintendent in command of older persons can create a problem. Female high school principals who command a predominantly male staff may create a similar dilemma. Women officers occupy positions of incipient conflict because of inconsistent expectations of the subordinate place of women in our society.

Institution and Organization.[40]   Statuses and offices comprise different "social orders." Offices constitute the fundamental element of an organization, while statuses are the basis of social institutions. Together, the offices constitute the responsibilities of the school system, its jobs, or its "roles," which outline rights and duties with respect to other offices. They comprise, in other words, the *organizational* structure providing the organization's regularity and stability; conflicts between offices provide its dynamic quality as well.

Organization behavior is to be understood in terms of offices rather than exclusively in terms of members' personality characteristics. Modern man lives in a "contract" society in which people react to each other without knowledge of their personalities. Administrators do business with teachers, contractors, students, and parents, sometimes with almost no knowledge of their personal characteristics, yet with relative ease and success because people are *expected* to behave according to their status.

Little insecurity is felt by school officials when they entrust the schools' monies to bank tellers who may be virtual strangers, because even though the teller may have dishonest tendencies, he will nevertheless tend to conform to the obligations of his office rather than give in to his personal inclinations. Similarly, teachers may be personally prejudiced against Negroes, but strive to be equalitarian with Negro students in schools where discrimination is condemned, and, conversely, personally unprejudiced teachers may be forced to racially discriminate in some systems.

While the official system is not determined primarily by the personalities of those who are in it, it is primarily affected by the institutional system that underlies it. The institutional "order" consists primarily of the statuses that compose each institution. Institutions are rules that link cultural values to specific situations. They have no official name and location as organizations do, and institutions are more abstract than organizations, comprised of values and rules that transcend a location and specify the general organizational forms. Thus, while teachers are employed by the New York City Schools, for example, and presumably have some allegiance to these organizations, they also are subject to the institutional values of teachers and citizens in other parts of the country, including the political, religious, economic, professional, and educational values that dominate the society. Each of these institutions is distinct in the sense that it is comprised of a network of interrelated statuses which are less related to other institutional areas. For example, politics is comprised fundamentally of relations between politicians, governors, cabinet members, the voting citizens, and so on. Education is comprised basically of relations among school board members, the citizens of the community, the state boards of education, superintendents, teachers, and pupils.

Since there is, in each institution, an element of the ideal, these statuses and expectations can be more or less compatible within a single institution. Thus, the job of "educator" is straightforward; he is to develop in children knowledge and character. But what is distinct about the institutional order is that there may be inconsistent expectations among institutions. A "good family man," for example, is expected to spend his evenings at home with his family, but the good community citizen is expected to spend his time working on community projects, and the good businessman is expected to use his evenings to work overtime and "get ahead." The point then is this: a single institution, such as education, is implemented in a number of different organizations besides the schools, such as the church and businesses and the military, all of which have educational programs; and a single organization, such as a particular school, is comprised of a variety of often inconsistent institutional statuses. The job of a teacher at school X is hardly described simply by her status as an educator; that job is comprised of a variety of institutions, among them business, politics, religion, and so on. In addition to teaching the children, she is to keep attendance records, chaperone parties, sell war bonds, encourage patriotic and religious devotion, and provide spiritual and vocational guidance. In these activities, educational values must be *compromised* with recreational, business, patriotic, religious, and other institutions in the work place. The "official" job then, comprised of a variety of institutions, is an arena of institutional conflict where compromises among political, religious, business, educational, and other value systems are carved out of the daily work routine. In the process, educational ideals are sometimes implemented, sometimes usurped, by other institutional means. This implies that the character of the public schools cannot be understood solely in terms of educational principles and philosophies, but must be understood within the context of the broader institutional order, including politics, business, religion, and other basic value systems. It also means that the official system is inherently one of conflict, the same conflict that persists in the more abstract institutional order. But the inconsistencies and conflicts are more notable and severe as the teacher experiences them on the job because it is on the job where they must be reconciled and translated into action.

Again, lest it be misinterpreted, it should be noted that such conflict is not always debilitating; on the contrary, it can be and frequently is highly productive. The school like any other organization is a dynamic system. It is by virtue of the dynamic interaction of its various components that the organization maintains what Parsons and others have called its *equilibrium,* or "steady states." When conflicts are severe enough to create imbalance in the system, they are responsible for readjustments, which in turn may result in or intensify other tensions.

Locals and Cosmopolitans. The simultaneous existence of the institutional and organizational orders poses conflicts of loyalty for employees. Loyalty to the employer, to the school—its customs and regulations, or its administration—is often a precondition of success; but, on the other hand, teachers may be more or less attached to various institutional principles that transcend the particular school. For example, if the school's policy forbids the teaching of religion, some teachers will feel guilty about ignoring it, or will teach their own brand of religion anyway. School systems differ greatly in their attitude toward the part which different institutions play in their operation. Some teachers may stress the educational aspect (that is, the transmission of knowledge) more than others, while other teachers may stress efficiency, or the use of business techniques, or the "politics of the game" more than others.

Institutional loyalty creates a particularly acute problem in a mobile society where the local place of employment, and particular family boundaries, no longer constrain a person's career nor exclusively define his standards of achievement. In a time when one part of the country may serve as a model for another part, it is no longer apparent that compliance with the job requisites is any assurance that the major institutional values are being fulfilled. It is possible for a teacher to be "successful" without actually contributing anything toward development of the nation's educational goals.

Members whose primary commitment is to the school's *local* community will seek to win the community's support for their school program and their place in it. This makes it more likely that the community will influence the basic character of the school. However, those members whose primary loyalty is cosmopolitan in nature (that is, committed to the broader national values) will be more influenced by national and international pressures on education which, as a matter of fact, can adversely affect the interests of a particular community or region. Thus any attempt to curtail a vocational agricultural program in a predominantly rural community would probably meet resistance despite the well-known decline of agricultural opportunities, just as zealous attempts to integrate Southern schools in the national interest will be unwelcome.

Professional and Bureaucratic Orientations. The dilemmas of employed professionals constitute a peculiar form of the local-cosmopolitan dilemma. The bureaucratic employee is expected to reserve his primary loyalty for the school where he is locally employed, particularly to its administration. The professionally oriented teacher, on the other hand, will probably be more influenced by the stands taken on issues by professional societies, by professors at influential training centers, and by colleagues across the country. Conflicts in the professional and employee orientations can become particularly acute when the issue involves racial integration, school consolidation, or relative importance of seniority and merit.

Commitment. Although exercised by individuals, power and authority describe characteristics of the organization. Commitment and involvement, however, provide a parallel set of concepts which describe the power system from the standpoint of the individuals in it. While commitment and involvement tend to be correlated processes, they can be distinguished analytically. Considering the extremes, a person is completely "involved" when he does something solely because of personal desire without any formal obligation to do it. While there is an element of compulsion implicit in a commitment, it arises largely from the ethical and social pressures from precedented acts rather than from threat of direct force.

These concepts are useful in analyzing the strategies by which individuals and organizational leaders handle their problems. In complex organizations, persons often must do what they dislike in order to obtain their preferences. As a result a person may commit himself to something and be involved with an entirely different matter. In other words, people exchange obligations for rights. Their life becomes a dynamic balance of commitment and involvement. Such systems of exchange are regulated by norms of *reciprocity,* which means that when a person gives up something, he can expect something in return.

The concept of commitment is also useful for the analysis of power, which, as indicated, is a function of the number of available alternatives. Every major commitment consumes one or more alternatives by binding the organization to an irrevocable line of action. Moreover every decision creates still other commitments, ones that are often unforeseen. Informal commitments usually accompany the formal ones. For example, when a school attempts to recruit a teaching staff that is entirely middleclass, white, and Protestant, it is also committing itself to distinct practices, curriculum, and operating goals which, in turn, limit the school's alternatives for dealing, for example, with lower class Negroes.

These unforeseen and compulsory types of commitments create considerable *institutional drift* from long-range goals. Selznick cites two sources of these strains between actual and operating goals.[41] First, the daily minor decisions can lead the organization in directions it did not set out to travel. Old techniques of administration and teaching have a way of becoming sacred; thus, the goal of efficiency may actually be subverted by a seemingly minor decision to hire a tradition-directed accountant when planning to mechanize the records-keeping system. Second, drift is partly a consequence of a limited administrative prespective that naturally occurs because administrators tend to stress rationality and formal organizational goals. In stressing the rational formal goals, unintended outcomes of decisions on informal goals tend to be overlooked, or are considered to be irrelevant because they are *logically* irrelevant. The task of simultaneously "keeping an administrative eye on the ball" (as Selznick puts it), *and* systematically observing conditions seemingly irrelevant to the goals that arise independently of intentional acts, introduces a complexity into administration which is difficult to manage. However, both the relevant and nonrelevant conditions obviously do shape the character of organizations.

The concept of commitment, then, implies a *strategy of organization* as well as individuals. The act of commitment is potentially an act of change which may eventually affect the organization's structure and goals. There is a need for organizational theorists to study this class of strategies, for the notion of commitment as a strategy calls attention to the simultaneous structure and change that constitutes the science of administration. The view stresses the flexibility of organizational structure and helps to offset some of the traditional emphasis on structure and goals as "given" qualities. It suggests the feasibility of viewing organization as a development over time by analyzing its strategic acts. The decision-making process is a particularly important crux of such analyses.

The analysis of organizational process had been so neglected, and the need for new departures so urgent, that there is some justification for taking the opposite viewpoints—that process, strategy, and sheer "accident" are the "normal" states of organization, and structure is the "abnormal" state.[42] Pursuit of such a view would require special conceptual tools. A few of the most promising of these tools include *interplay, co-optation,* and *reciprocity. Interplay* stresses the strategic character of organizational decision-making. It is a tactical relationship wherein the action of one person depends on the unknown *outcome* of a previous act; an administrator's decision to fire or retain a teacher, for example, depends in part on anticipated community reaction. *Reciprocity* refers to the norm of exchanging favors. Persons may often engage in conduct that is not personally approved by them, but which promises the fulfillment of an obligation or the return of a favor. *Co-optation* refers to type of compromise in which an opponent is incorporated into the leadership structure of a group in order to control him better; some control over organizational affairs is sacrificed in exchange for greater control over the opponent. These concepts describe some of the types of commitments by which organizations are guided and *compromised.* The important function they play within organizational processes also suggests another basis of the organization's cohesiveness besides power and consensus—that is, *constraint.* These terms will be explored throughout the following chapters.

SUMMARY

This chapter has explored the elements of theory, its underlying assumptions, and the particular relevance of certain theoretical concepts to educational administration. The attempt has been to orient the reader to the general place of theory and its value on the one hand, and, on the other, to provide a perspective for the analysis of the administration of educational organizations contained in the following chapters.

Because of its fundamental importance to organizational management, the following two chapters are devoted to discussions of some important dimensions of communication.

BIBLIOGRAPHY AND NOTES

1. C. Argyris, "Understanding Human Behavior in Organization: One Viewpoint," in *Modern Organization Theory,* M. Haire, ed. New York: Wiley, 1959, p. 124.
2. E. V. Sayers and W. Madden, *Education and the Democratic Faith.* New York: Appleton-Century-Crofts, 1959, p. 419.
3. Cf. J. Walton, "The Theoretical Study of Educational Administration," in *Harvard Educational Review* 25, Summer, 1955, pp. 169–178; also, P. R. Mort and F. G. Cornell, *American Schools in Transition,* New York: Bureau of Publications, Teachers College, Columbia University, 1941. In his research Newlon had a content analysis made of eighteen textbooks on educational administration. The results showed that "over four-fifths of eight thousand pages are devoted to the purely executive, organizational, and legal aspects of administration." He found that almost the entire emphasis was on the mechanics of administration with virtually no

critical examination of the educational and social implications of the structure and procedures. (J. H. Newlon, *Educational Administration as Social Policy*, New York: Scribner, 1934, p. 93.)

4. J. D. Thompson, "Problems in Developing a Theory of Educational Administration," in *Administrative Theory in Education*, A. W. Halpin, ed., Chicago: Midwest Administration Center, 1958, p. 3; D. E. Griffiths, *Administrative Theory*, New York: Appleton-Century-Crofts, 1959, pp. 1–2. This statement may be an exaggeration. In 1960 superintendents from all over the nation were asked which fields of study were of most importance. School finance was at the top of the list and public relations, human relations, and school business management within the first five (*Professional Administrators for American Schools*, p. 47).

5. F. G. Cornell, "Administrative Organization as Social Structure," *Progressive Education*, vol. 30, 1952, pp. 29–35. For an account of the historical developments behind the efficiency movement in education, see R. E. Callahan, *Education and the Cult of Efficiency*, Chicago: Univ. Chicago Press, 1962. For an assessment of the state of administrative theory as of 1957, see H. A. Moore, Jr., *Studies in School Administration*, Washington: AASA, 1957; and R. F. Campbell and R. T. Gregg, eds., *Administrative Behavior in Education*, New York: Harper, 1957.

6. D. E. Griffiths, "Administration as Decision Making," in *Administrative Theory in Education*, A. W. Halpin, ed. Chicago: Midwest Administration Center, 1958, pp. 120–121.

7. A. W. Halpin, "The Development of Theory in Educational Administration," in *Administrative Theory in Education*, ibid.

8. B. M. Bass, *Leadership, Psychology, and Organizational Behavior*. New York: Harper & Row, 1960, p. 24.

9. The following discussion is based on Merton's discussion of theory. Cf. R. K. Merton, *Social Theory and Social Structure*, rev. ed. Glencoe, Ill.: Free Press, 1957, Ch. 2.

10. Cf. R. G. Francis, *The Rhetoric of Science: A Methodological Discussion of the Two-by-Two Table*. Minneapolis: Univ. Minnesota Press, 1961.

11. Cf. R. Francis, *op. cit.*, for a number of related insights on the method of science.

12. R. Hall, "Research Priorities in School Administration," in *Research in Educational Administration*, S. P. Hencley, ed. Columbus, Ohio: University Council for Educational Administration, Ohio State University, Jan., 1962, p. 26.

13. C. L. Shartle, "A Theoretical Framework for the Study of Behavior in Organizations," in *Administrative Theory in Education*, *op. cit.*

14. J. E. Haas, "Toward an Empirically Derived Taxonomy of Organizations," unpublished manuscript.

15. Bass, *op. cit.*, p. 27.

16. R. G. Francis, "Prediction and Science," *Midwest Sociologist*, 1956, pp. 7 ff.

17. Walton, *op. cit.*, p. 172. This disdain of "theory" in the study of administration is imbedded in a long tradition, one spokesman for which was Frank Spaulding, who believed the purpose of the course was to meet the present needs of administrators; he proposed that "It should be intensely practical, not at all academic; doing, not mere knowing, should form the goal and the atmosphere of all the work" (F. E. Spaulding, *The Aims, Scope, and Methods of a University Course in Public School Administration*, Iowa City, Univ. of Iowa, 1910, p. 11).

18. A. W. Halpin, *Theory and Research in Administration*. New York: Macmillan, 1966, p. 71.

19. M. Brodbeck, "Models, Meanings and Theories," in *Symposium on Sociological Theory*, L. Gross ed. New York: Row, Peterson, 1959.

20. See, for example, I. D. J. Bross, *Design for Decision*. New York: Macmillan, 1953, pp. 171–172.

21. For reviews of general theories of administration as they apply to education, see D. Griffiths, *Administrative Theory, op. cit.*, and S. P. Hencley, ed., *Research in Educational Administration*, UCEA, Jan. 1962, especially Section II.
22. A. W. Gouldner, "Organizational Analysis," in *Sociology Today*, R. K. Merton, L. Broom, and L. S. Cottrell, Jr., eds. New York: Basic Books, 1959, Ch. 18.
23. R. Dharendorf, "Out of Utopia: Toward a Reorientation of Sociological Analyses," in *American Journal of Sociology*, vol. 64, 1958, pp. 115–127.
24. Dharendorf, *Ibid.*
25. *Ibid.*
26. J. Barnard, "Where Is the Modern Sociology of Conflict?" in *American Journal of Sociology*, vol. 56, 1950, pp. 11–16.
27. *Ibid.*
28. George Vold's treatment of the crime problem is an example of the conflict approach to society; G. Vold, *Theoretical Criminology*, New York: Oxford, 1958, Chapters 11, 12, and 13. Also R. E. Park and E. W. Burgess, *Introduction to Science and Sociology*, Univ. Chicago Press, 1924, pp. 504–510.
29. Cf. W. Bagehot, *Physics and Politics*, 1869. New York: Knopf, 1948, pp. 44–84.
30. J. Conant, *Education and Liberty*, Cambridge: Harvard Univ. Press, 1953 168 pp.; and E. Nock, *The Theory of Education in the United States*, New York: Harcourt, Brace, 1932.
31. The question being raised here is not whether the world is "really" as the philosophies say it is; it is sufficient that the theory consistently explains the facts.
32. A. Gouldner, "Organizational Analysis," *op. cit.* See also P. Blau, *Exchange and Power in Social Life*, New York: Wiley, 1964.
33. R. Campbell, "What Peculiarities in Education Administration Make It a Special Case?" in *Administrative Theory in Education, op. cit.*
34. Cf. R. Bierstedt, "An Analysis of Social Power," in *American Sociological Review*, vol. 15, Dec., 1950, pp. 730–736; and H. Goldhammer and E. A. Shils, "Types of Power and Status," in *American Journal of Sociology*, vol. 45, 1939, pp. 171–78.
35. E. Abramson, H. A. Cutler, R. W. Kautz, and M. Mendelson, "Social Power and Commitment," in *American Sociological Review*, vol. 23, 1958, pp. 15–22.
36. B. Malinowski, *A Theory of Culture and Other Essays*. New York: Oxford Univ. Press, 1960, pp. 52–74.
37. Cf. K. Davis, *Human Society*. New York: Macmillan, 1949, pp. 88–89.
38. P. Lazarsfeld and W. Thielens, *The Academic Mind*. Glencoe, Ill.: Free Press, 1958.
39. W. S. Mason and N. Gross, "Intra-Occupational Prestige Differentiation: The School Superintendency," in *American Sociological Review*, June, 1955.
40. Cf. E. Hughes' discussion in *An Outline of the Principles of Sociology*, R. E. Park, ed. New York: Barnes & Noble, 1939, pp. 283–88.
41. P. Selznick, *TVA and the Grass Roots*. Berkeley: Univ. California Press, 1949, pp. 250–259.
42. T. Burns, "The Forms of Conduct," in *The American Journal of Sociology*, vol. 64, 1958, pp. 137–151.

CHAPTER

3

The Communication Process

Man, the talking animal, not only talks but he talks about talking.[1]

If we can map the pathways by which information is communicated between different parts of an organization and by which it is applied to the behavior of the organization in relation to the outside world, we will have gone far toward understanding that organization.[2]

The Significance of Communication for Human Action

SCOPE OF THE PROBLEM

COMMUNICATION is fundamental to human life. It is likely that without communication there would be no human beings as we know them. There would certainly be no human communities. Several recent developments have made communication of even greater importance to our society than it has ever been in the past, because maintaining communication has become an even greater problem. The most notable development is, of course, the emergence of the mass media. Fifty years ago, all but one of the four major mass media (the press) were virtually unknown. By contrast, today more than half of the average adult's leisure time is consumed by mass media; the average child spends more of his time with mass comunications than with any other activity, including school. One-sixth of the waking hours of children six to sixteen is filled with television-viewing; seventy-five percent of the average person's mass communications time is occupied by radio and television.[3]

Two other developments especially have created special communication dilemmas. One of these developments is the nationalization of society (made possible largely by the mass media) and the growing prospect of its internationalization. The other is specialization, the result of recent explosions of knowledge.

Nationalization. The United States has come of age as a national unit —politically, economically and socially; yet it could be argued that its national boundaries are solidified by little else than the mutual appreciation of Coca-Cola and a network of mass communications. Because of mass communications, every local community recently has been subjected to what C. H. Cooley called "world-wide gossip." Local events assume the proportion of nationwide significance. A local teachers' strike, students protesting the cafeteria cooking in school X, a high school basketball player guilty of accepting bribes—these stories spread across the country like spilled coffee over a tablecloth. The vehicles for these messages are both public (newspapers, television, magazines, and radio) and official (school reports distributed through state departments of education to school executives around the country). With these developments, the horizons of the north, south, midwest, east, and west fuse into a common awareness, eventually, perhaps, into a community. Yet, ironically, the maturation of a national audience is precisely the force which has extended the problems of ignorance; as the audience has increased, it has become increasingly difficult to disseminate complete and accurate information about the distant events which people have come to consider relevant. Unlike citizens of small, isolated towns who can "get together" or see the event in person, nationwide publics are forced to accept the *selective perceptions, interests, and skills of reporters who specialize in disseminating what is sometimes worldwide gossip.*

The effect on school and community relations is apparent. As will be discussed later in this chapter, the trend toward a more urbanized society has confronted school executives with increasingly greater difficulty in sending out communications capable of even *reaching* the majority of the city's residents, who (even if they hear the information) often remain indifferent and ignorant about most of the school program and its aims. Their interest in the school is probably more easily aroused by those mistakes and criticisms of the school which reach the headlines, than by its basic achievements.

Specialization. Specialization has increased the degree of unfamiliarity that people would normally have with the expanded world. The more energy one devotes to understanding an area, the less energy he can muster to understand other areas and the more superficial his knowledge of them becomes. In specializing in one subject, the person learns a perspective, attitude, and special vocabulary providing him with a knowledge which sets him off from others, all of which compounds the communications problem. In a former era, when the educational level of teachers and administrators was still relatively low and the school system was relatively simple, the community backgrounds and language of educators in the public schools were not as dissimilar to those of laymen. This permitted them to work closely with laymen who, in fact, could understand the school program well enough to appreciate it and help direct it. But many teachers now talk in terms of "field theory," "stimulus-response," "pragmatism," and "new math," and other equally esoteric notions, and the result has been that teachers have alienated themselves from laymen.

It can be said of a great many people that they are suspicious of cleverness. The development of the special professions of teaching and of administration has made laymen wary of them and has lowered teachers' respect for the judgment of those laymen who are authorized to advise them. For their part, principals and superintendents are charged with the delicate task of explaining to the school board, in the language of laymen, the latest theory or philosophy without reducing it to mere slogans. And though the level of general education is rising, school-community relations can be expected to become even more complicated as education develops an increasingly professional perspective based on special skills and a technical language.

Thus, specialization, like the developing national community, nourishes ignorance even while it extends knowledge because of the very fact that it broadens some horizons to the exclusion of others. It is no wonder that most school executives, facing specialized teaching staffs in large, partially anonymous communities, express frustration in attempts to communicate with their own personnel and with the public, and express despair at the relative indifference and ignorance which their efforts sometimes net.

The Functions of Language. Problems of communication cannot be considered for long without coming to grips with the problem of language, the fundamental form of human communication. Without language, men could not "think," for thought *is* the manipulation of word symbols. Without language man could not recall the past nor imagine the future; like lower animals, he could only communicate with gesture about the present. Since there could be no planning, there would be little need for executives. There could be no learning from past experiences without language, and thus there would be no need of teachers.

Abstraction. Above all, without language the scope of man's world would be greatly diminished, for, beyond its descriptive function of "indication," language permits abstraction. Language as abstraction opens up another world, one that is beyond personal experience. Mastery of the concepts necessary for this level of thinking makes up the bulk of classroom teaching. The most descriptive of words may actually include a whole class of events in its description, most of which the speaker has never experienced. Hayakawa puts it in a simple rural way: "One not only experiences the cow that he sees, but a whole class of cows. Cow 1 is not cow 2." He says, "There is a sense in which we all live in two worlds.

First, we live in the world of happenings about us which we know at first-hand. But this is an extremely small world . . . So far as this world of personal experience is concerned, Africa, South America . . . New York, or Los Angeles do not exist if we have never been to these places." [4] Regardless of emphasis on experience, which many educators are prone to stress, most of our knowledge is acquired second-hand—*verbally* from teachers, friends, strangers, and the news media. What is even more significant is that in the future an increasing proportion of our knowledge will be abstract, conceptual—in the way that an atom is conceptual. These developments will perhaps render the experience-oriented curriculum somewhat archaic.

Instrument for Action. Kluckholn describes language as an instrument for action; the meaning of a word is "not in the dictionary but the differences its utterance makes in the situation." [5] This principle is illustrated by Chase, who points out that because a Japanese word *mankusatsu* has two meanings, the destiny of the world may have been changed. The word means either to *ignore* or *to refrain from comment*.[6] In July, 1945, the Emperor was ready to end the war but the Cabinet wanted a little more time to discuss the terms of the ultimatum. A press release was prepared announcing a policy of *mankusatsu* with the "no comment" implication. But it was translated on the wires as *ignore*.

A Map of Reality. Each person fabricates a particular view of the world which becomes his map of reality. Needless to say, these maps, which are constructed primarily from a person's verbal experiences, are seldom truly representative of the real world. It is in this sense that man lives in a world of fictions, stereotypes, myths, and half-truths which, though false, are nevertheless real to him. Some of this fictitious world is a function of a conflict between implicit and explicit meanings of words. Sapir advises that language is so rich in meaning that it is dangerous to rely on language where clear communication is required; he notes that signal lights and hand signals are used for safety purposes on railroads.[7] Language, then, stands for reality. We define and then see, not the reverse. "Accurate communication . . . is quite as vital to the man on the street as it is to the logician or the student of semantics . . . Every human interaction hinges upon the communication of meaning . . . Inadequate communication thus leads to disappointment and frustration . . . It is no wonder, then, that the child learns to depend for the "correct" version of his world upon communication with his elders. . . . If you can communicate about something, if you can understand and are understood, then it is 'real.' " [8]

A number of classic experiments help to illustrate the process by which communication creates reality. Sherif placed subjects in a dark room and asked them to estimate the distance which a pinpoint of light moved.[9]

The movement of the light was illusionary. The light was, in fact, stationary, but in the dark room it appeared to move. In psychology, this is called the "auto-kinetic effect." But, completely without an objective frame of reference, the subjects were able to agree on a common standard which seemed to them to define the reality of the movement. Asch used a series of experiments in which objective reality was a little more apparent.[10] Subjects were asked to match the length of a given line with one of three obviously unequal lines. In one version of the experiment, one person was placed amidst a pre-informed unanimous majority who were instructed to give incorrect answers. Confronted with a conflict between objective reality and group pressure, one third of the individuals in this situation distorted their answers toward the majority. There were no errors in a control group where there was no group pressure of this kind on the subjects. Coffin reports evidence that susceptibility to influence by communication with others increases with level of difficulty of the task performed and decreases with years of training in the task.[11] Lewis reports that the prestige of the source, and expert opinion, influence the impact of shared communication on definitions of reality.[12]

The extent to which the communication that is shared with a group can determine "reality" is revealed in a report describing the efforts of a fanatic group preparing for doomsday.[13] The group, convinced that the last day of the world was at hand, believed that they were among the few to be spared in a helicopter rescue mission from Mars. Despite several discomforting failures in their prophecies, the group was able to sustain its belief with rationalizations that it sought to make increasingly public with each failure of prophecy. The role that communication played in the maintenance of the fiction is indicated by the fact that members of the group who became geographically dispersed, who did not maintain frequent communication, changed their convictions soon after the first prophecy failed.

Although most people would not be easily convinced of the world's impending demise, the way most people do perceive the world is determined by shared conceptions. In a sense, the world is constructed of labels which provide filters through which the world is interpreted. Language tends to reflect experience, and in turn it calls attention to certain aspects of experience, while obscuring others. Eskimos, preoccupied with cold weather, have a refined nomenclature to describe types of snow—blowing, falling, fallen, wet, dry, and so on. By contrast, the North American with artificial shelter is concerned with only a few words pertaining to snow ("sleet," "hail," and "snow"). Hiller says that Arabs have about six thousand names connected with the camel, again because of the importance of the camel in their economy.[14] The Arab and American accordingly "see" a different world. Similarly, the school administrator who thinks in terms of efficiency perceives a different world from his teachers who may think in terms of educational objectives, student problems, and working conditions.

Man's world is so conditioned by language that the meaning of everyday experience is changed by the words used to denote it. Kluckholn, for example, tells of a Christian Scientist who refused to take vitamin tablets on the grounds that they were medicine, although he took them after they had been defined as food.[15] We use a whole array of words to redefine certain unpleasant situations; the fact that death is cushioned by the terms "deceased" or "passed away" is more than a "polite fiction"; it is a reorganization of reality. Drunkenness is similarly disguised in a parade of innocuous terms—"stewed," "oiled," "high," "tanked up," and so on. Similarly, students don't fail; they "do poorly," or "don't measure up," or are "at the bottom of the class," or are "not using their potential." Cass is amused by a recommendation from educators that lower class children be described as "children unable to secure much beyond the necessities of today's world because of the modest finances of the family," and adds "Who's kidding whom?"—the children are just plain poor.[16] Speaking of the agencies that accredit schools, Koerner notices that "accreditors, it seems . . . never make plain visits. Like supernatural beings, they make only 'visitations.' " [17] Names, then, classify a disorderly world in a relatively orderly manner; labels constitute the structure of experience.

Definitions of reality are facilitated by what can be called "fictions." They are often factually inaccurate, oversimplified, and exaggerated. Ethnic groups, for example, are a common subject of stereotyping. One study found that Negroes are considered to be superstitious, lazy, happy-go-lucky, ignorant, naïve, and slovenly.[18] "Rochester," on the Jack Benny program, is the archetype of the subordinate, faithful, and humorous Negro. A "Turk" seems to imply such negative connotations as dirty, treacherous, revengeful; Katz and Braly found that people use elaborate defenses to sustain these false stereotypes. People project these qualities on the Turks they meet, while those who do not fit the stereotype are simply regarded as "different" rather than disconfirming the stereotype.[19]

The school executive is commonly stereotyped as a rather anti-intellectual, hard-boiled businessman, hired for his administrative efficiency and good sense rather than for his educational values and intellectual capacity. Also, according to popular stereotypes, teachers come in several common varieties. The males are underpaid, unambitious drudges; the females are "nice" young people interested in children and Sunday schools, or old, semi-kindly, frustrated matrons. Waller presents the following caricature of the teacher: "Self-sacrificing, gentle, kindly, self-effacing creature, overworked, underpaid but never out of patience and always ready to 'give freely of her time and money' for school purposes."[20] In one study it was found that students identified pictures of teachers on these bases: stern, dignified, determined, intelligent, serious, thoughtful, prim, studious, tired, and bored.[21] On the other hand, after a session with the state education associate lobby representatives during a legislative year, one state senator described a teacher as "overpaid, over vacationed, overly grasping and overrated."

Language and Group Structure. Language is also instrumental for group solidarity. The group's purposes, norms, and attitudes depend on shared communication. Language has a number of basic functions in the formation of groups. First, language *establishes* status relationships; this may be termed its "status-casting" function. The use of titles between teachers and students ("Doctor," "Sir," "Mister") clearly casts the parties involved into their official roles. Conversely, the use of first names between a principal and teacher connotates a modified official relation in which personal considerations may be taken into account; this personal element may in turn introduce certain ambiguities into the relationship.

If titles, stereotypes, and other terms help define the relationship, then changes in salutation denote changing status relationships. After his graduation, a graduate student, for example, may be embarrassed when some of his former peers now insist on calling him by his title; or when he is now encouraged by some of his former professors to address them by their first names while other professors still resent a first-name address.[22] Similarly, although some superintendents use the first names of their teachers, the teachers may feel obliged to address the superintendent by his title; the resulting ambiguity can create a disconcerting sense of ambivalence toward superiors. Schneider and Homans illustrate the significance of changes in terms used by family members in reference to one another.[23] "Father" indicates more formality than either "Dad," "Pop," or "Pa"; these terms were not interchanged by the respondents in their study. It was found that informal relationships over a period of time became more formal with parents of the opposite sex.

Second, besides its status-casting function, language permits *access* to the group. This might be called its "password function." Most groups and all occupations have a special set of terms, or "jargon," that must be mastered by members. Even though a person may be technically a member of that group, he will remain an outsider until he has mastered the jargon of the trade. Outcast is the school administrator who is ignorant of the designation "ADA," or the problems of the "intermediate unit," "democratic administration," and so on. The full-fledged educator must be able to espouse with appropriate passion such passwords as "meaningful experience," "subject matter related to life," "creating permissive atmosphere," "fostering creativity," "individual interests," "student-centered learning," "flexibility," and "team teaching." This is not to imply that there is insincerity in the use of passwords; on the contrary, they are used because they are considered to be of extreme importance.

Besides granting an individual acceptability by the group, passwords continue to function after admission—they are used to reassure, support, and embellish the basic beliefs and perspectives which they represent. Passwords become part of the social relationships of the group, binding members together by providing a vehicle for utterance, even when there is nothing new to be said. The primary function of what Hayakowa calls the "Niagara of words" is to ease social insecurities and to keep communication channels open. This is why Kluckholn can say, "Very often, what is said matters much less than that something is said." [24]

Language has still another function. It acts as a group philosophy, a sort of "institutional exchange" whereby the ideas expressed in the language of one group are restated in another, more meaningful if slightly different, form, by a different group. What one nation attributes to chance or demons or gods, another will attribute to impersonal scientific principles. In education, the old problem of the class "cut-up" has been reinterpreted in a variety of philosophies expressed by different nomenclatures. At one time the "cut-up" was simply a "naughty," bad boy full of evil to be purged by punishment and resurrected with discipline. With the advance of psychology, he became the "unadjusted" child who needed to be "reintegrated" into the group, or eventually the "sick," disturbed, and misunderstood who needed "treatment." The more recent melancholy "contribution" of sociology has been to view him as a "hood," a gang member, a rebel of the "beat" generation who is acting out the "normal aggressive impulses" of a delinquent subculture which is doomed to a legacy of discrimination in an unjust society.

Maintaining Social Cleavage. If language is instrumental in establishing group rapport and clarifying its structure, it has an equally important role in tearing it asunder. In fact, Sapir maintains that organizational warfare would be impossible without ideologies to sustain the motives and rationale behind its original impetus.[25] Purely personal hatred is insufficient to maintain an extended conflict; but words sustain the natural dissipation of merely personal hatred. Simmel suggests that the most violent fights are those whose causes have been embodied in slogans. These slogans do more than provide a common purpose; they lend a sense of deep personalized objectivity by implying that the individual is acting as a *representative* of a group, thus releasing him from personal responsibility and providing him with a noble air of self-righteousness that is impossible to gain without words.[26] So, campaigns to raise teachers' salaries profess humanitarian motives which portray overworked teachers, which affirm the intent to raise the quality of education, and which declare the worthiness of it all. Public antagonism toward teachers, in return, is similarly bolstered by unfavorable stereotypes and slogans. Clark's description of female teachers is perhaps as descriptive of the public's rationale for refusing to raise teaching salaries as it is of reality: "Teachers are women of average or slightly above average intelligence from lower-middle-class and lower-class families who probably, it can be guessed, tend to be plodding and unimaginative." [27] Whether it is true or not, the impression is widely shared, and the mere statement of it depersonalizes and justifies ensuing regimentation, discrimination, and low salaries. Similarly, charges of "socialism and leftist tendencies" and parallel slogans about "academic freedom" support both the communities' and the teaching professions' respective claims over the classroom.

The general stereotypes that teachers hold in regard to young people may help to justify their irritation with them and sustain conflict with them. Speaking of the stereotype that people commonly hold of adolescents, Friedenberg says: "Here is a people that are unusually carefree, exuberant, long of limb and fleet of foot. Noted for athletic and (it is whispered) sexual prowess, they are nonetheless essentially child-like, irresponsible, and given to outbursts of unrestrained violence. They are undisciplined. With the aid of jazz that they seem almost to have in their bones, they work themselves up to erratic frenzies in which they abandon themselves to utter license. . . . So might an embittered segregationalist speak of the Negro . . . " [28]

Words bolster an entire garment of "status fictions" that cloak the relations between persons of different status. The problems of interaction involving social scientists in the process of interviewing a Southerner about Negroes have been suggested to one of the writers by Professor Roy G. Francis.[29] Although, technically, the term "Negro" is proper and preferred among the literate population, prejudiced Southerners used the term "nigger"; what, asks Professor Francis, is the effect of asking a Southerner his attitude about "Negroes" if he is accustomed to the derogatory term? The mere use of the polite term defines the situation as one of propriety rather than one of frankness; the respondent is more likely to speak accordingly in terms of the polite fictions that the interviewer has introduced than to reveal his true feelings. The pose of middle class teachers before slum children may present a similar problem; the very process of belittling their morals, discipline, and language usage sets the teacher apart from the child and precludes his confidence in discussing more fundamental problems.

The propriety of swearing between the sexes provides still another example of the effect of words on status interaction. Schoolmen who swear before women teachers introduce a note of familiarity that (whether or not she swears with other women) calls for increased social distance on the part of the woman and/or her embarrassment. By contrast to the social distance that swearing creates between middle class male and female teachers, swearing among male teachers may have the opposite

effect; such familiarity among males may pave the way for mutual frankness.

In general, administrators tend to prefer people who talk as they do,
who see the world similarly. Thus, there tends to be more communication
among administrators than between them and teachers. Each group associates mainly with those who reinforce its established view and avoids
those whose views would threaten it. Conversely, if teachers and administrators see the world differently, it will be reflected in their language.
The very fact that they have different statuses and responsibilities within
the organization suggests that they will use a different language. Administrators may see the world more in terms of "efficiency" and the brutal
facts of "budgeting," while teachers may be more prone to think in terms
of more and more costly needs, smaller classrooms, and the individual
problems of their students. In the same way, the technical nomenclatures
of teachers, which they are certain to display before parents, administrators, and students ("good sex identification," "autistic," "guilt-ridden,"
"reaching out,") drives a fine wedge between them and their publics.
Thus, some of the very language which creates group solidarity symbolizes cleavages with other groups.

Nonverbal Communication. There is an unspoken language as well as a
spoken one. It is a rhetoric of physical symbols and signs. Symbols and
signs constitute a separate language which communicates as effectively, if
less obviously, than words. Stone has recently called attention to the way
clothing symbolizes the situation.[30] The formality denoted by a man's
white starched collar and black business suit is obvious, but its side effects
are less visible. What is the effect of a white collar in a slum classroom? It
may create more resentment than respect.

Part of the teacher's personal dilemma also centers on clothing. Students may respect the female teacher who is "in fashion," but public pressure is on the conservative side of dress insofar as teachers are concerned.
Teachers and administrators, in turn, have long struggled with a similar
problem concerning students' dress in the classroom. These problems,
however, have seldom been considered from the standpoint of educational psychology. It may be assumed that a person tends to dress as he
feels, and that he also tends to feel as he dresses. Blue jeans, white socks,
short skirts, long hair, and bermudas define the situation for students as one
that is relaxed, conducive to self-expression and freedom; informal modes
of dress defy the formality which is so prohibitive of self-expression.
Modern teen-age attire and the fashionable, revealing, or relaxed dress of
female teachers, then, express precisely the kind of informal classroom
atmosphere that many liberal educators have long sought to establish—a
relaxed classroom led by a teacher in touch with the contemporary. Conversely, a situation that calls for more respectable attire is unlikely to be
particularly conducive to "self-expression" in the classroom.

Clothing is not the only significant symbol. But the clothing dilemmas in the public schools reflect as much as any symbol the changing, ambiguous status of teachers and students in relation to each other. The problem of dressing the modern teacher and student is a derivative of a larger problem: the modern educator's uncertainty about who is his *audience*. In a complex society, people do not present themselves to the public as a whole, but only to certain segments of it. Clothing, school buildings, and other physical symbols connote a variety of meanings for these various publics. Before teachers can decide how to dress themselves and their students, they must decide not only what to communicate but also to whom they wish to communicate *primarily*—to the conservative adult world or to the teen-ager?

IMPLICATIONS

Since the very basis of social reality is embedded in communication— verbal and symbolic language—the act of communication assumes a major role in the subculture of schools. Much can be learned about group solidarity and conflict from observations about the language and communication patterns of the participants; it is important to recognize as well that both social reality and group cohesiveness can in turn be modified by language. What is real for the administrator—the outside pressures, the logic of efficiency, cost accounting, and increasing budgets—need not be equally real for the taxpayers whose world is one of rising costs, layoffs, new cars, and piano lessons. Similarly, the administrator, living in a different world of fictions than teachers, may be appalled to find that his self-styled kindly "benevolence" causes him to be regarded by teachers as an unknowledgeable old Scrooge; just as certainly, the teacher who is impressed by her own long years of loyalty and devotion may be startled to find that she is "deadwood" in the principal's office. These communication gaps are part of the broader problem of communication patterns.

Patterns of Communication

There have been a variety of attempts to visualize the mechanics of the communication process. In general, the models fall into one or more of three broad and overlapping categories: mathematical, physical, and social.

MATHEMATICAL MODELS

Mathematical models are perhaps the most advanced, and probably the least comprehensible to most laymen; they are at least the most impressive. DeFleur proposes:

$$\Delta\rho = \frac{\alpha\,\Delta\,r}{r}; \text{ and } H = -\,K\overset{n}{\underset{\iota=1}{\Sigma}}\,P_\iota \, \log \, P_\iota$$

Concerning the latter formula, he explains that H (the information source) is a "monotony increasing function of n, and K is a positive constant." [31] Beyond general recognition that such models exist and acknowledgement of their technical complexity, further consideration of them is beyond the scope of this book.

PHYSICAL MODELS

The typical communication models are usually cast in the image of electrical transmitters and receivers and diagrammed as a series of stages. These stages frequently parallel Lasswell's shorthand statement of communication processes: "Who says *what*, in which *channel*, to *whom*, with what *effect?*" [32] One visual form of the physical model interpreting this formula is shown below.[33] The effectiveness of communication at each step of process will be briefly discussed.

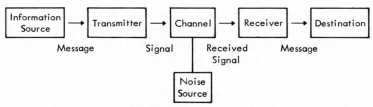

FIGURE 1. An example of a physical communication model. (From M. L. DeFleur and O. N. Larsen, *The Flow of Information*, New York: Harper, 1958. p. 8. Used with permission)

Information Source. The effectiveness of a message partially depends on how much credibility the audience attributes to the sender. For example, Kate Smith's bond-selling campaigns were successful during her World War II radio marathons because the public accepted her sincerity and purity of motives in conducting the campaign.[34]

The significance of the credibility of the information sources was further demonstrated in a study of college students who were presented with information on medicine, welfare, steel shortages, and the future of movie theaters. For some students the information was attributed to trustworthy sources (*Journal of Medicine, Fortune*) and for others it was attributed to untrustworthy sources (*Pravda* and a movie gossip columnist). There was no significant difference in the amount of factual information acquired by each group, but students receiving the high credibility source initially changed their opinions more than those who received low credibility sources.

However, the quality of the source is not entirely significant. A month later, there was a decrease in the extent of agreement with the high credibility sources and an increase in agreement with low credibility sources; the change was attributed to a decline in initial resistance to the untrustworthy source.[35] As Lewis suggests, a person will not be convinced by the U.S. Weather Bureau that it is not raining when it is. Only if the person is not present in the vicinity will he probably believe the U.S. Weather Bureau rather than the local chamber of commerce. Lewis demonstrates that the prestige of persons alleged to have asserted or endorsed a slogan usually does not affect students' judgments of it, and when it does it is because the source to which it was attributed created *new meanings*.[36] Thus, whether or not a person is receptive to suggestion is not due to the "suggestibility" of his personality, but to the *context*, or the knowledge of the source's ideological position, which influences the meaning of the message.

The credibility of information is enhanced if there are consistent reports from several sources; conversely, it is questioned if there are inconsistent reports. Thus, a monopoly over communication channels assures success. This is more than an academic proposition, for, as will be discussed below, in many cities today the mass media are virtually monopolized by a few groups; the support of certain communication cliques might virtually guarantee certain school programs and school bond issues; and these can be defeated in the same way.

Message Transmitted. There has been a great deal of attention devoted to the message content, its style, form, and other characteristics. A major issue relating to content concerns the ethics of implanting implicit messages, or *slanting*. Slanting is unavoidable, but it is sometimes intentional. The same news story will be interpreted differently by changing the heading. Note the difference between "President Takes Rest" and "President on Vacation." When the terms "Needed Rest" and "Another Vacation" are added, the implications become more obvious.

A message can be slanted by presenting only one side of the story also. In one series of military studies, it was learned that in the case of soldiers initially opposed to a point of view presented to them orally, presenting both sides of an issue was more effective than giving only the supporting argument.[37] If, however, the argument did not include *all* of the important negative arguments, the presentation boomeranged. For men already convinced of the point of view, on the other hand, presentation of both sides was less effective than presentation of only the favorable view; presentation of both sides was less effective for poorly educated than for well educated people. Also, it is probably more effective to build up one's own position than to attack the opposition without building up one's position.

A related issue is the effect of fear-arousal messages. One series of studies suggests that strong fear appeals are less effective than mild ones.[38] These studies also indicate that messages which contain conclusions are more effective than messages which request the audience to arrive at its own conclusion. Other effective devices include the "band wagon" effect ("everyone is doing it") and "glittering generalities" ("the Pepsi Generation"). Although the principle of repetition of messages is widely used by the mass media, people tend to build up a resistance to messages after a while and "hear without actually hearing." If repetition is effective, it is probably because with repetition the message reaches more people rather than because it overwhelms those who hear it repeatedly.

"Canalization" is one of the most effective persuasion principles. The term refers to the implementation of existing wants and attitudes (rather than developing new ones). Girls probably want boyfriends more than they want to be clean, so soap is sold as a means to that goal. Similarly, because most people want high income more than they want an education, educators use the income appeal to encourage students to stay in high schools or to enroll in colleges.

Most of the attention to content has dealt with its explicit, intended meanings. As a result, the implicit meaning of communication has been slighted. One exception is found in Bales' research. He distinguishes between "instrumental" (or informative) and "expressive" (or tension releasing) communication.[39] Interpersonal communication seems to consist of alternating instrumental acts which create strains between the members and expressive communication which helps to ease that strain. Conceivably, the relative balance between instrumental and communicative or emotion-based acts is a significant determinant of the effectiveness of the communication. Hartmann earlier found that emotional appeals asking voters to cast their vote for the Socialist Party were more effective than so-called "rational" appeals.[40] Merton's study of Kate Smith's war bond campaigns revealed that "sacrifice" was frequently used as a theme of the campaign; the audience was made to feel that the soldiers, Kate Smith, and other listeners were all sacrificing, which developed in them a sense of unworthiness and guilt that the purchase of the war bonds swept away.[41]

Channel. Some educators are probably as familiar as many communication experts with research on the relative effectiveness of different means of communication. The persistent crusade of teachers against "lecturing" in the classroom in favor of "discussions" is indicative. However, the evidence is by no means conclusive. Lecture and discussion methods are probably of equivalent effectiveness in transmitting information and concepts, although discussion may be more effective in transmitting attitudes and values.[42] The problem of the lecture is that the audience does not have to make decisions; this problem can be overcome if the lecture is followed up by personal contact requesting a decision afterwards; this was one of the major appeals in effective war bond sales campaigns. If, in addition, the person who makes the personal request for a decision is an acquaintance or neighbor, the decision is likely to reflect on the person's neighborhood reputation; this principle is used by most community fund appeals where neighbors collect the money. A similar procedure might very well be used by PTA's in sponsoring school bond issues.

One series of experiments on the influence of speaker versus loud-speaker revealed that the voice of a speaker who is personally present (whether visible or not) commands more attention than the radio voice. In fact, from one study it was concluded that radio had a slightly dulling effect upon the mental processes.[43] In the radio situation, the listener was less alert, less personally involved, and more passively receptive.

The channel *structure* also has come to the attention of researchers. In a series of small group experiments using simple problem-solving games, Bevalas and Leavitt found that the decentralized "circle pattern" of communication, where no one position is more strategic than the others, is relatively ineffective. Members were unorganized, without a leader much of the time, made errors, and were relatively more unsatisfied. By comparison, persons organized into a centralized "wheel" structure, consisting of four persons connected with a single person in the center, communicated more effectively. The center man linked all others, providing leadership for more organized operation; their talks were completed relatively quickly. It is significant, however, that participants of the circle were unsatisfied with their tasks.[44]

Receiver and Destination. It has long been recognized that messages often do not reach the intended audience. Audiences often "overlap" (that is, the people who use one medium use them all), which tends to give an "all or none" effect to the message. Riley and Riley conclude that often implicit in the traditional approach to audience research are "notions of a communicator concerned only with sending his message and making it as pervasive as possible and a recipient, alone in his ivory tower, coming to a decision—often purely rational—about how to act upon the message." [45] They charge that this simple view does not adequately take into account the total organizing process of social interaction which influences the reception of messages. The interactional context is best approached in terms of the so-called "two-step flow" of information to which attention is now turned.

SOCIAL MODELS:
TWO-STEP FLOW OF COMMUNICATION

The "social reality" function of communication already mentioned provides the thread of significance that connects communication with virtually every aspect of social life. Although some aspects of reality are probably shared universally, much of what is real is group determined—that is, specific to one's social circles. One's opinions are "anchored" to groups which filter and interpret information for him. Conversely, a person is unlikely to be receptive to communication which is at odds with the opinions of his group. The acceptance of contrary views may jeopardize the person's social world.

The Relay Function. Messages are relayed in the group by the group's opinion leaders. When the communication process is viewed as part of the leadership structure, the mainstream of communication is not from sender to receiver, as the mechanical model would suggest; it is from sender to an intervening opinion leader to receiver. Opinion leaders serve two functions. First, they act as "gate-keepers" for the group, filtering out some transmissions and relaying others. Katz and Lazarsfeld refer to this as the relay function of interpersonal relations.[46] People who are exposed to the information and impressed by it pass it on to those who are less exposed. Second, opinion leaders act as judges, interpreting the communication as they pass it on. This is referred to as the *reinforcement function;* if opinion leaders are favorably disposed, the communication is more likely to be effective.[47]

The basic communication process is, then, a two-step flow from the source to gate-keepers and from gate-keepers to the audience. The effectiveness of communication will, therefore, strongly depend on patterns of personal influence. From a study of personal influence in a midwestern city of 60,000 persons, Katz and Lazarsfeld report that opinion leaders are not identical with persons who are usually thought of as power leaders in the community.[48] These were distributed in all occupational groups and on every social and economic level. They conclude that although opinion leadership is often equated with high status, which would presume a vertical process downward from high prestige levels, this image of leadership must be revised to include *horizontal* opinion leadership, which is found at every socioeconomic level. In general, the leader was only slightly more exposed to the media and slightly more interested in the topic than those he influenced. The characteristics of opinion leaders, they found, varied considerably according to the type of topic involved. For example, fashion leadership was primarily related to age and gregariousness, while leadership in public affairs was primarily associated with frequency of marketing. The interest that a party showed in a subject was found to be an important factor in leadership, but interest was only part of the story. When interest was equally high, age, social status, or social context made the difference in who influenced whom.

It is significant for school administrators that social status was less important than gregariousness and age in every area except public affairs. In public affairs, influence within the family was from old to young and from men to women. By contrast, intrafamily influence regarding fashions was from young to old. With regard to the community, high status women had more influence in public affairs opinions than women in other statuses.

There is corroborating evidence from another study.[49] Leaflets were distributed by airplane over eight communities; the ratio of pamphlets per person ranged from one for every four persons (low stimulus) to thirty-two for every one person (high stimulus). Under high stimulus conditions, about half of the target population learned the message from other persons; under more limited opportunities for direct contact with the message, about two-thirds of the target population learned of the message via social channels. "The findings stressed the important role of children in collecting and passing on leaflets, not only to other children, but to adults." [50] Child-to-mother transmittals were more frequent than child-to-father transactions, but male adults received leaflets more often than women from children in the neighborhood, and more often from adults in the community.

However, while children acted as "gate-keepers," more active at some points than others, they did not judge the communication as adults attempted to; they were neutral transmitters. Accordingly, adults who received information from children were more apt to comply to it than adults who received it from other adults. These findings demonstrate that the two functions of primary group communication channels—relay and reinforcement—can vary independently. The two functions may each be fulfilled by a separate set of opinion leaders in the communication's chain: relay leadership and reinforcement leadership.

Sociologists have found that voting is also a group experience. There is an almost perfect agreement between husband and wife on political affairs, primarily because of undisputed male dominance in political situations. In politically mixed families, the persons who changed in the 1940 elections changed toward the party favored by the rest of the family. It was found that the formal media were more effective than were personal relationships as sources of influence on the opinions of "opinion leaders," but the opinion leaders engaged in political discussion much more than the rest of the community. These political conversations in which leaders engaged were more likely to reach the people who were still open to influence.[51] This suggests that flow from the radio and printed page to opinion leaders and from them to the less accessible and uncommitted sections of the community is a major pattern of influence.

The implications are clear. The mass media need not reach all of the citizens of the community in order to be influential. It need only contact the relatively few key leaders of opinion. It is equally clear that these opinions are group products. The patterns of influence within the group and between groups vary depending on the type of issues—perhaps the particular issue—but the fact is that the school administrator is dealing with groups, not with individuals, when it comes to such issues as school bond and school board elections. It seems obvious that the success of the school administrator, and the entire school program, depends on the school official's ability to identify and reach group leaders in horizontal, as well as vertical, structures.

Group-Directed Opinion Change: Reinforcement.   The reinforcement function of primary groups may either reinforce the intent of the message or provide a defense against any communication which may be incompatible with the group's norms. A person may read an editorial, and then forget about it. If, however, his friends begin to discuss it he will recall it. If his friends critically appraise it, he is likely to reinterpret it in this perspective. Thus, personal conversations act as *filters* to what people remember of what they read and hear. Because of the increased interest that discussions with others can create, the effect of exposure to the mass media may actually increase over a period of time, rather than decrease.

The problems of reinforcement and opinion change are problems of group conformity. There are at least two reasons why a person would be reluctant to accept an opinion that is not shared by his group. First, the acceptance of a deviate idea tends to jeopardize his sense of reality which is otherwise shared in terms of the perspectives of his group. Second, it will disturb the group's sense of consensus, its identity; other group members will apply pressure to bring the deviate back into line, to re-establish the group "boundaries." As two authorities put it, ". . . if he wants to 'get somewhere,' either within the group or via a group, he must identify himself with the opinion and values of those others." [52]

Interpreted in terms of group conformity, there appear to be two alternatives for effecting a significant change in a person's opinions. Either he must be persuaded to deviate, or the whole group must change. Regarding the first alternative, it might be expected that readiness to change contrary to the group's opinion is related to the individual's initial relationship to the group; such change is more likely to occur among marginal members. Kelly and Volkhart found that Boy Scouts who valued their troop highly showed more resistance to attempts to change their attitudes toward the scouting program than Scouts whose membership was less important to them.[53] Newcomb found that girls who remained conservative in a liberal college environment were marginal and able to resist peer group pressures because they were strongly dependent on their families, who provided a conservative, outside insulation against a liberal environment. Girls who changed their opinions in college were less likely to be so firmly cemented to their own families.[54]

People who perceive the same object in identical ways derive a sense of pleasure from this reinforcement; similarly, if two persons view an object differently, the person's own satisfaction is affected. Festinger hypothesizes that the amount of change in an individual's opinion as a result of persuasion by others in his group will increase as pressures toward uniformity in the group increase and as desire to remain in the group increases for the members; but it will decrease in the degree to which the opinions involved are anchored in other group memberships.[55]

These facts have enormous implications for the classroom teacher as well as for administrators. Teachers are not teaching the mythical "child" referred to in textbooks, but groups of children whose opinions are unlikely to be altered far in advance of their peers. Counseling as well as teaching must be seen in terms of group relationships.

The fact that people have a number of "reference" groups must be taken into consideration. Sometimes a person's opinions change as the salience of his reference group's opinions change. For example, a member of a conservative taxpayers group may be persuaded to increase school revenue taxes by appealing to him as a father, or a national patriot in the Cold War. Charters and Newcomb studied the possibility that a person's attitudes would change as his awareness of one or another of his membership groups was changed.[56] An "experimental" group of Catholics was intentionally made unambiguously aware of their identity by the group leader. When this group was compared with Catholics for whom the salience of religious membership was not deliberately increased, the experimental group's views more closely approached the orthodox position than the control group's views. But neither Protestants nor Jews responded in this same way to increased saliency because, it was felt, religious orthodoxy was not an important influence in the lives of Protestants; in the case of the Jews, public awareness of their identity caused them to moderate their expressed religious differences. The general point is that opinion changes can be effected by manipulating the salience of reference groups.

A series of studies suggest that the second alternative, modifying group opinion, is sometimes effective. During World War II Lewin found that group discussions were more effective than lecturing in persuading women to buy less popular cuts of meat.[57] The reason appeared to hinge primarily on the fact that lectures did not as frequently force the audience to make a definite decision, and that individuals listening to the lecture were so isolated that they could not determine whether others like them were willing to change as well. This precluded any group reinforcement. Group discussion, on the other hand, permitted the group to collectively adjust its norms in such a way that individuals were aware of the fact that any change in them did not imply deviation from the group. The isolation of group members can be an important reason for the conservative stability of group opinion under changing circumstances. In one study, for example, it was learned that each member of a particular small town church thought that all other members disapproved of card playing, though each member played cards himself.[58]

There are several specific states of group change which have been noted by Lewin and his associates. The state of "no change" is visualized as a state of stable equilibrium between positive and negative arguments ("forces"). This "equilibrium" (a group norm) can be changed either by applying pressure in the desired direction, or by diminishing opposing forces. In the first case (applying pressure) the new norm would be accompanied by a high state of tension. In the second case, "If the resistance to change depends partly on the value which the group standard has for the individual, the resistance to change should diminish if one diminishes the strength of the value of the group standard or changes the level perceived by the individual as having social value. It is usually easier to change individuals formed into a group than to change any one of them separately." [59] It also follows that the importance of the group, and its influence on determining opinion change, is a function of its cohesiveness.

THE MODELS CONTRASTED

The mechanical model performs valuable services. It points up the significant variables in the process of communication, and it provides a blueprint for depicting the logical sequence of transmission. However, the mechanical model does little more than delimit and highlight the major variables; it does not specify the full range of variables involved, particularly the variables that intervene as interference or as reinforcement of the message—the characteristic attitudes of the parties involved, and the effects of different channels and messages, in various combinations. It can, in fact, be misleading because of the focus it casts on the *logical*, intended sequence. As the Rileys point out, its major shortcoming is the implicit image that it gives of communication as a singular, one-way event between an active sender and a semi-isolated, passive recipient. [60] In emphasizing the logical sequence, the mechanical model ignores the reciprocal *interchange* of communication back from audience to sender, which occurs as part of a larger transaction between groups.

The fact that communication is a reciprocal *process* is not adequately portrayed by the mechanical image. Human communication is not mechanical, but precisely its opposite. The depersonalized model tends to obscure an element recently found to be the most significant determinant of communication effectiveness—the element of interaction. Messages are not merely electrical or impersonal impulses, but significant symbols packed with meaning. The "noise source" must be understood as something more than "interference" with the true message; human "noise" reshapes, interprets, and often intensifies and clarifies messages. These reinforcement and relay functions can be portrayed only with a model that capitalizes on communication as two-way interaction between and among groups.

Communication Barriers

The media used and the audiences to which it is directed have each received much attention by mass media researchers, but the significant variables are those which intervene between the media and the mass. These "intervening variables" have in common one underlying factor—the human element. The human factors stressed in the social model of communication reasonably enough also erect the crucial communication blocks. This does not mean that all communication failures can be traced to the human barriers, for some of the failure must be blamed on the sheer mechanics of the process already discussed—the source, type of presentation, and the channel. However, the human barriers are impressive.

SOCIAL PSYCHOLOGICAL BARRIERS

In their discussion of why information campaigns fail, Hyman and Sheatsley identify five major types of human factors which prevent effective communication.[61] They fall into two categories: (1) exposure to the media (lack of attention, awareness, and interest); and (2) effect of media exposure (prior attitude, selective interpretation and rigidity of attitudes).

Exposure. Inexposure can be traced to institutional developments—inefficiency of the media, economy of purchasing the media, level of education of the nation, and so on. It is also due to personal and social characteristics, which will be considered here.

Lack of Attention. Hyman and Sheatsley charge that there is a hard core of chronic "know-nothings." "There is something about the uninformed which makes them harder to reach, no matter what the level or nature of information." [62] In one study, fourteen per cent of the population sampled had no knowledge of five pressing national and international political problems, with a small direct relationship between size of community and awareness of issues.[63] At the height of the 1948 presidential campaign, twelve per cent of the adult population did not know who was the Republican candidate and nine per cent did not know that Truman was running for re-election. Only about one-half of the population could identify the vice presidential nominee of either party.[64]

Disinterest. A great deal of this ignorance can be attributed to the disinterest that a substantial proportion of the population has in public affairs and similar topics. There is a direct relationship between interest in a topic and the knowledge about it.[65] Disinterest, in turn, is a function of one's prior attitudes and values.

Selective Attention. From a readership study of midwestern newspapers several years ago it was reported that only one-fifth of those who read the paper recalled reading a story about revision of real estate taxes in the city, but sixty per cent recalled reading the story about a dog who awakened his master when he smelled a gas leak in the house. Here the audience's natural interest in money was outweighed by the "human" element.[66] During the war, the Treasury Department distributed messages to the public attempting to change their opinions about why the government issues war bonds. Although pamphlets were distributed to most householders in the nation, eighty-three per cent of the sample of one city did not recall receiving the pamphlet and one-third of those who recalled it reported that they descarded it without looking at it.[67]

Postman and others have demonstrated that initial attention and inattention depends to a great extent on personal values. In a study of word recognition they found, for example, that the more a word is valued, the more rapidly it is recognized. One process at work is "selective sensitization," or lower thresholds of recognition for highly valued words. "Perceptual defense" has the opposite effect of erecting mental barriers against threatening words or ideas; it sometimes takes the form of avoiding the meaning. Finally, "value resonance" provides a generalized mental set which keeps people responding to objects valuable to them when they are not present.[68]

Selective Exposure and Recall. People tend to submit themselves to messages which are congenial to their prior attitudes and values, and avoid disconfirming messages. Audiences for whom a program is intended often are the ones least likely to listen to it. People read news editorials which confirm their opinions and ignore those which do not. Those who do most of the reading are least subject to change.[69] Beyond affecting perception, prior values seem to determine what is recalled and forgotten. From cross cultural studies Bartlett reports that people recall from a new situation that with which they are familiar in their normal activity.[70] For example, a tribal people that deals with herds of animals remembered minute details about cattle when visiting this country, although they forgot many other details that an American would have considered important. Personal attitudes and values may also cause a message to be forgotten after it has been perceived. In one experiment, pro- and anti-Soviet Union audiences were given pro- and anti-Soviet reading selections. It was found that individuals not only learned more quickly that which supported their attitudes, but they forgot more quickly that which conflicted with prior attitudes.[71] Time alone does not cause forgetfulness.

For readers who like to remember their wisdom in the form of slogans, the above discussion can be summarized in a phrase of Lazarsfeld's: A message will *select* its audience before it *affects* its audience.[72]

Effects. Exposure in itself does not insure that the desired effect will occur. A message may be received, even retained, and yet not be "communicated" if the receiver misconstrues its intent, or simply does not act upon it.

Misinterpretation. Selective interpretation is as prominent a barrier to effective communication as selective exposure. A series of cartoons designed to reduce prejudice, for example, was regularly interpreted by the prejudiced in a way that reinforced their own beliefs. In one cartoon, "Mister Bigot," the central character, was specifying only "sixth generation American blood" for a transfusion that he was receiving. Prejudiced persons thought that the cartoon had ridiculed Mr. Bigot depicting him as a fraud since he was not from the old American stock that actually "deserves" sixth generation blood! [73]

Misinterpretation of certain messages is institutionally required by the fact that every individual is compelled to participate in a variety of groups which have variant value systems. Evasion of some messages and self-imposed overexposure to others is a way of achieving uniformity in everyday experience. Mechanisms of avoiding the meaning of a message were identified by Cooper and Jahoda.[74] First, the message may be simply perverted, or misunderstood. Second, the receiver may invalidate the message in one of two ways: he may either admit the general principle but dwell on the many exceptions in practice, or he may admit the particular message as convincing, but claim that it is not a correct picture; this is often the fate of dramatized messages which are interpreted by the audience as mere stories. Third, the message may actually be too difficult. Jahoda and Cooper conclude that those more subtle messages which are easily misunderstood are more appropriate for neutrals and inactive sympathizers who do not show a tendency to intentionally evade the message, and that the ". . . less a person has rationalized his prejudices, the greater will be his tendency to evade an attack on them." [75]

Rigidity of Attitudes. Assuming that a message has been received by the intended audience, that it has been interpreted correctly and retained, it may still be ineffective insofar as effecting a significant change in those who hear it. It should be evident to any schoolman that information does not necessarily change attitudes. If change does occur, it may be in the direction of the prior attitudes rather than in the intended one. Hyman and Sheatsley report a National Opinion Research Center study of attitudes of the American public toward financial loans to Great Britain. They conclude, "It was apparent that a large group opposed to the loan were rooted to the belief that the money would not be repaid, and the mere information that England had *agreed* to repay the loan was of no effect in changing their attitudes." [76]

SOCIOLOGICAL BARRIERS

The above impressive set of psychological barriers to communication is by no means uniform under all conditions. It remains to be determined *when* prior attitudes block messages, *when* a message will be interpreted favorably or unfavorably, and *under what conditions* information changes attitudes or does not. Chances are that the roots of these problems extend beyond the merely mechanical problems of speaker versus loud-speaker, or the number of people reached. They are cemented in the broad social structure of which both the communicator and audience are a part. Age, sex, political affiliation, religion, social class perspectives, occupation, and official rank are all sociocultural characteristics that have a bearing on each of the barriers so far mentioned. It is probably true, for example, that whether or not a person is "interested" in a message is more determined by his place in the flow of communication than by the rigidity of his attitudes or other personality characteristics. "Interest," for example, is an aspect of social relationships; it changes as a person's relations with others change. Thus, a citizen who is normally disinterested in education suddenly becomes intrigued with the subject when he finds himself discussing the topic over cocktails with the superintendent of schools. The older person who is adamantly against the "fads and frills" of the school program delights in remembering the first high school football team in his days. The apathetic PTA member suddenly becomes an eager enthusiast when elected to its presidency. The teacher who resists the principal's program suddenly "sees his point" after spending an evening at his home. A few of the major types of social relations which affect communication will be briefly considered below.

Local-Cosmopolitanism. Local leaders have different circles of acquaintances than cosmopolitan leaders. There is an aura of social distance and respect which the cosmopolitan leader brings with him by virtue of his wider circle of contacts; unlike the local leader, his past does not haunt him so closely. Local and cosmopolitan leaders therefore are "on different daisy chains," each likely to have access to different kinds of inside information. The cosmopolitan leader is part of a wider information clique, while the local leader specializes in local information. It is likely that information passed along to a cosmopolitan leader will take a route different from that in the local communication pattern.

Suttoff reports on a study completed at Stanford in which six forms of participation in school affairs (other than voting and organizational membership) were measured.[77] It was hypothesized that the local or cosmopolitan orientation of an individual toward the immediate community was related to the various forms of participation in school affairs. It was found that locals and cosmopolitans differed in both the form and degree of participation in school activities. Locals in Suttoff's study were more likely than cosmopolitans to demonstrate loyalty to the PTA and to be involved in its activities. But cosmopolitans were closer to their school psychologically, as exhibited by more communicated interest in school affairs; the cosmopolitan was reported to have read more and talked more than locals about school issues and problems.

Some implications of the study were suggested by Suttoff: (1) Locals would be loyal participants and contributors to financial campaigns, citizens committees, pupil census taking, and so on; (2) Cosmopolitans would be best used (*sic*) for disseminating information about the schools' future plans and long-range needs; (3) When the superintendent turns to the public he appeals to two audiences who frequently have conflicting values: locals expect the administrator to maintain the *status quo*. The success of his attempt to change from the *status quo* could depend on his being considered a "native or close neighbor by those in the community."

Blome attempted to study the community power structures in two Iowa communities (one rural and the other urban).[78] Each community had both successful and unsuccessful bond issues within the past five years. He attempted to identify people who were influential in passing and defeating bond issues in these two communities. Using a modification of methods employed by the Lynds and Warner, Hunter, and Rossi, he identified knowledgeables and community influentials and key influentials in the school bond election. One of the tests used in the interviews was composed of factual information about the school district and its plans. His study found that the key influentials in each district were extremely knowledgeable about the schools. This was true whether the person interviewed was influential in passing or in opposing the bond issue.

These two studies reveal that the public relations function of the school administrator consists of far more than merely giving out and interpreting information. The relevant information for each group and how each group perceives the real world are major considerations in any public relations campaign.

Age. The natural communication barriers erected between age groups and between the sexes have been discussed in Parsons' illuminating essay.[79] His discussion will provide the basis for the following comments. Parsons suggests that differential treatment of children of different ages is not characteristic of American families or neighborhood play groups; there appears to be no special preference shown to the first child, and it is common for children of several years apart to play together. Age grading, however, is firmly rooted in the American school system where children get their first paralyzing taste of separation by age as a basis of grouping, which eventually permeates relationships among peers and siblings in family and neighborhood as well. Yet, even by the time of adolescence age grading is not completely established, there being little more than a broad category of "teen-agers" and "young adults." Not quite children, not yet adults, adolescents attempt to carve out a clear self-identity from an essentially ambiguous status by separating themselves from both the adult and the child world. The "youth culture" which bolsters this age group is unique, faddish, and extremely romantic—a period of adolescence prolonged after biological and social maturation and characterized by strong future orientations to marry, work, and achieve recognition as adults. They are doomed to frustration during that period.

The youth culture is characterized by Parsons as contrasting with the adult culture in the following ways: the irresponsibility of youth contrasts with the responsibility of adults; prominence of physical beauty and athletic prowess in the youth culture contrasts with emphasis on task achievement in the adult world; the pattern of sexual behavior, drinking, and smoking in the youth culture is aimed at rejecting adolescent status, as contrasted with a more positive orientation to these behaviors in the adult world. Such differences produce deep lacerations between the adult and adolescent world which makes communication difficult.

The special vocabulary of the adolescent—"cool," "wheel," "cat"—is sufficient to indicate the extent to which age erects communication barriers. As each succeeding generation is required to attend school longer and enter work later, as the vocational opportunities for the young decline, as minimum wages are raised, the period of adolescence is extended. The problems of "growing up" for each generation are quite unlike those of the preceding one, the era which their parents knew. The misunderstanding and resentment between the generations that these conditions create is most pronounced between adolescents and the very old, the retired. Retirement removes the person from the active world and steals his prestige as breadwinner. With retirement, the person acquires a different viewpoint from which he recalls his own youth and sees a present and future that is less relevant to him. He is required to pay increasingly higher taxes for education, which may appear to him as a frivolous activity; and those taxes come at a time when he is deprived of his full income. So also the new school building seems pretentious to the older person, as do fads and frills, all of which increase the costs of education. The older person fails to understand the present generation, but more important, he fails to understand the problems from which it emerges and the needs which the adolescent culture is intended to fulfill. He sees the teen-agers' idolatry of singing crooners as sheer nonsense without acknowledging the paucity of adults whom teen-agers can respect. In a changing society, parents quickly become "squares," out of touch with it.

It can be expected that the most effective communication occurs between persons of similar age. The school executive's dilemma is that his program is most likely to be understood by the present generation of parents, but the community influentials are likely to come from the older, more conservative generation. Similarly, the younger generation is better understood by young teachers, but parents may be more impressed by the middle-aged teachers, and no one knows how to evaluate the extremely old teacher whose years of experience seem outmoded by younger persons with more education and better training. The notion, frequently heard, that old people vote against school bond issues because of low retirement incomes is a grossly oversimplified and naïve explanation.

Sex. Since the status of women is currently changing rapidly (only fifty years ago women could not vote), sex identification for females is probably more difficult than for the male. When during the Industrial Revolution, the woman lost her role as a partner in a common household enterprise, her role of housewife became a residual status, low in prestige if high in security.[80] The "working" wife who enters the male world seems more glamourous by comparison. With "emancipation" and financial independence, a "glamour" role based more directly on sexual prowess also became a direct path to prestige for women in the male world; this is at best a temporary role jeopardized by strong immoral undertones and by increasing age. The women's role as "good companion" to man evolved as a substitute role from the career and glamour roles. It is symbolized by bobby-socks, jeans, ponytail haircuts, a "fun-loving" attitude, and athletic interests which match those of males.

The existence of independent careers—housewife, vocation, glamour, and good companion—makes it difficult for women to communicate among themselves; and the situation makes it difficult for men to identify the type of woman with whom they are talking. The treatment which is acceptable to one type of woman may be offensive to the other; the "good companion" tolerates swearing and enjoys athletics while both swearing and athletics are alien to the middle class housewife. Familiarity from a male may imply only friendship to the housewife, but to the glamourous girl it may imply an impending illicit relationship. The persistent possibility, says Parsons, that latent glamour girl roles will influence the relationship between a man and woman prevents close communication between the sexes, despite any mutual objective interests they may have. This is undoubtedly one reason that women professionals find themselves excluded or segregated within male occupations.

Parsons points out that communication among men, moreover, is plagued by increasing specialization of their work roles, special interests, and viewpoints, which set them apart from one another. Highly specialized professionals in different fields have in common little other than the weather and sports, politics, and perhaps their crab grass. In an expansive field like education, even a single occupational group such as teachers in the same school may be so specialized that they have little in common.

When Goodenough showed the same lists of words to men and women, there were distinct differences in response between the sexes.[81] Men responded in terms of opposites and adverbs, while women responded with synonyms and adjectives which referred to domestic activities. Mead notes that for men, "mother" is a cherishing and love-inducing individual who, if loved too much, defines a male as a "sissy." Sex for men means arousal and pursuit, while for women it means caution and skill in maintaining male interest without permitting fullfillment. She conjectures that for women, marriage means a fulfilled aspiration and life of love and security, while for men it denotes loss of freedom and increased responsibility.[82]

Men are more likely than women to believe that the woman's place is in the home, although higher occupational groups have a more liberal attitude toward women than do lower occupational groups. The latter appear to fear the competition of women for jobs.[83] One of the major complaints of male public school teachers is that women do not work hard enough to improve their teaching salaries. The fact is that what is a poor salary for males is often a good one for women. At best, the vocation of a housewife is part-time in terms of years, energy, and interests available for it, and therefore women who are not usually principal breadwinners will consequently work for less salary than men.

On the basis of a study of picture appeal by MacLean and Kao, it was found that ". . . women of different age groups, with financially or morally secure backgrounds, valued pictures of art and scenery most highly, pictures with people in a 'cute' situation second . . . They avoided and disliked pictures of death, violence and destruction most." [84]

For men, this study found that those with less education and lower incomes tended to value pictures of war, violence, and social problems. For men in general, sports, sex, and action photographs were valued most highly.[85]

Social Class. Some of the problems of communication between social classes will be discussed in Chapter 4. Hartley says, "If the lines of group demarcation impede the flow of communication within as closely structured an organization as an industrial plant, where the needs of the total operation enforce at least minimal contact, we must recognize the force with which they operate in the complex society, in which the mores and norms for interaction militate against intergroup contact." [86] The lower classes see the machine technology of our society as something that creates unemployment, while the upper classes characteristically have more confidence in the modern machine. Higher occupational groups tend to define their status as due to their innate ability while persons in lower statuses see it as a matter of chance, luck, pull, or good opportunities. Upper occupational groups are more likely than lower occupational groups to believe that their child has a good opportunity to rise in the world.[87]

People of different social classes not only learn different orientations to time and money, but they have a different language and use different child-rearing methods, manners, and morals. Free communication with other people is further impeded by the enthnocentrism of one's own social class; good middle class mothers, after all, will not let their children play with the ignorant, dirty, common people.

Hierarchy. The American soldier data showed that officers believed that their men were more favorably disposed on any given issue than the men actually claimed to be. There is a noted tendency for commanding officers to project their own views upon the men under them.[88] Ninety-two per cent of the officers thought that all or most of the officers were the kind of men who are willing to go through anything that they asked them to, while less than half as many enlisted men were thus disposed toward their officers. Also, nearly half of the officers disagreed that more friendship between enlisted men and officers would improve the Army, but only fifteen per cent of the enlisted men disagreed with that statement. Eighty per cent of the commanding officers overestimated their subordinates' pride in their outfit and their desire to be good soldiers. Three-fifths of them overestimated their enlisted men's satisfaction with their jobs and the importance of the infantry to them. Fifty-four per cent of the enlisted men agreed that most men do not respect the officers, while only twenty-five per cent of the officers perceived this. The authors concluded that ". . . whether in the Army or elsewhere, completely candid interchange of attitudes on all subjects does not ordinarily occur between those who wield power and those who are subject to that power. . . . Officers could be easily misled by the rituals of deference exacted from all enlisted men. They were 'sirred' and saluted and rarely answered back. It is easy to understand how during the course of time they could come to mistake these compulsory outward symbols of deference for voluntary respect and failed to perceive underlying hostilities and resentments." [89]

The military officers also failed to appreciate the basic problems of the men under them, even when the problems were expressed. Superiors tend to view with amusement the exaggerations and the gripes of a small minority. Nearly sixty per cent of the officers, for example, thought that the enlisted men's "gripe column" in the Army newspaper would give a very untrue picture of the problems of most soldiers, but only sixteen per cent of the enlisted men viewed them as so irrelevant.[90]

Gardner reports similar communication problems between foremen and top management in industry:

They [the foremen] . . . feel that, while top management often talks of them as being part of management and expects them to identify with the interests of the company and top management, it does not make them feel that they really belong. They feel that they are expected to take whatever is handed down to them from above no matter how arbitrary it may seem to them, nor how difficult it may make their jobs. Obviously, these feelings of resentment interfere with cordial relations between superiors and subordinates and lead to a less than optimal performance . . . And they arise essentially from the lack of communication between status levels.[91]

Some of the communication problems within the educational hierarchy will be mentioned in the following chapters.

Implications

This chapter has had something to say to the practicing administrator. It appears that people become almost immune to much of the enormous volume of messages that reach them daily. People look but do not see; they hear but do not listen. These facts have enormous implications for strategies of communication, implications of special relevance to school administrators and teachers. As one group of educators have observed, "Some administrators acquire an enthusiasm for communication as an end in itself, a conviction that establishing a formal system—a newsletter, a weekly page in the newspaper, or even a multiplicity of memos—will in some not quite identifiable way take care of communication problems automatically. Repeated messages without particular substance, however, will actually develop a tendency in the recipient to pay little attention to anything . . ." [92]

Since exposure does not guarantee effective communication, "The thoughtful memo from the superior concerning the objectives of education in a troubled time may reach the teacher's desk without reaching his mind." [93] The difficulty of reaching a neutral or hostile audience makes communication with the public a serious task. Communication problems are not solved merely by increasing the flow of information, by "getting people together," by changing the wording of the message, or even by shifting the channels of communication. Barriers to communication will not be eliminated simply by determining whether lecture or discussion or print is more effective. Communication failures are more fundamental, reaching into the sociopsychological forces of group and personal values. This does not mean that the barriers between the school and community are insurmountable, but it does mean that they need serious study and reflection. It is especially important to realize that it is groups, not individuals, which are being reached. Unless the defenses of groups are taken into account, neither logic nor emotion, lecture nor discussions, will be completely effective. The communication between students, their teachers and parents, between janitors and their neighbors, may have a more important impact on the community's image of the school than a weekly news release passed out to a disinterested public.

It seems obvious that in order to be effective, school administrators must train themselves to listen as well as to talk, and to talk in a way that will be meaningful to the party intended to receive it. To the extent that administrators stick to themselves and associate only with persons on the same level and who think as they do, their circle of acquaintances acts as a barrier to accurate perceptions of the problems or of the views of subordinates or the larger community. As one publication states, "administrators have come to grief because they were convinced that they were talking to the community when they were talking only to persons who agreed with them on a particular matter." [94] To be effective, the school executive must learn the opinions of others and assume the attitudes of his audience. He is undoubtedly as guilty of selective attention recall and exposure as his intended audience, and he has all of the techniques of distorting and avoiding messages from his audience that are at their disposal. In other words, he must be seriously able to "take the role of the other" before he can communicate effectively.

SUMMARY

Undoubtedly, the nature of the communication which permeates an organization is significantly related to the organization's effectiveness in achieving its goals. This chapter has therefore presented a brief conception of the communication process including some of the psychological and sociological factors which complicate it. In the following chapter, a particularly important aspect of communication within the organization will be discussed; we refer to the avenues by which information is diffused within the school system and between it and the larger community of which it is a part.

BIBLIOGRAPHY AND NOTES

1. M. L. DeFleur and O. N. Larsen, *The Flow of Information.* New York: Harper, 1958, p. 31.
2. K. Deutsch, "On Communication Models in the Social Sciences," *Public Opinion Quarterly*, vol. 16, 1952, p. 367.
3. W. Schramm, "Mass Media and Educational Policy," *Social Forces Influencing American Education*, 16th Yearbook of the National Society of the Study of Education, Part II, N. D. Henry, ed. Chicago: Univ. Chicago Press, 1961.
4. S. I. Hayakawa, *Language in Thought and Action.* New York: Harcourt, Brace, 1949, p. 31.
5. C. Kluckholn, *Mirror for Man.* New York: Fawcett World Library, 1957, Ch. 6.
6. S. Chase, *The Power of Words.* New York: Harcourt, Brace, 1954.
7. E. Sapir, "Language," in *Encyclopedia of Social Science*, vol. 4, pp. 78–80.
8. T. Newcomb, *Social Psychology.* Dryden Press, 1950, p. 292.
9. M. Sherif, "Group Influences Upon the Formation of Norms and Attitudes," in *Readings in Social Psychology*, G. Swanson, T. Newcomb, and E. Hartley, eds. New York: Holt, 1952, pp. 249–61.
10. S. E. Asch, "Effects of Group Pressure Upon the Modification and Distortion of Judgments," in *Readings in Social Psychology, Ibid.*, pp. 2–10.
11. T. E. Coffin, "Suggestibility and Levels of Difficulty," in *Readings in Social Psychology, Ibid.*, pp. 11–17.
12. H. B. Lewis, "An Experiment on the Operation of Prestige Suggestion," in *Readings in Social Psychology, Ibid.*, pp. 18–29.

13. L. Festinger, H. W. Riecken, and S. Schachter, *When Prophecy Fails*. Minneapolis: Univ. Minnesota Press, 1956.
14. E. T. Hiller, *Principles of Sociology*. New York: Harper, 1933, p. 115.
15. Kluckholn, *op. cit.*
16. J. Cass, "Who's Kidding Whom?", *Saturday Review*, Oct. 20, 1962, p. 80.
17. J. D. Koerner, "Teacher Education: Who Makes the Rules?", *Saturday Review*, Oct. 20, 1962, p. 80.
18. D. Katz and K. W. Braly, "Verbal Stereotypes and Racial Prejudice," in Swanson, Newcomb, and Harley, eds., *Reading in Social Psychology, op. cit.*, pp. 67–73.
19. D. Katz and K. W. Braly, "Racial Stereotypes of One Hundred College Students," *Journal of Abnormal and Social Psychology*, vol. 28, 1833, pp. 280–90.
20. W. Waller, *The Sociology of Teaching*. New York: Wiley, 1932, p. 419.
21. K. McGill, "The School-Teacher Stereotype," *Journal of Educational Sociology*, vol. 9, 1931, pp. 642–51.
22. The difference may be due to the original definition of "status difference"; if it were originally conceived as a difference in the official status, equality would be granted after graduation, but if it were conceived by the professor as a difference in basic competence, it will tend to be withheld.
23. D. M. Schneider and G. C. Homans, "Kinship Terminology and the American Kinship System," *American Anthropologist*, vol. 57, 1955, pp. 1194–1208.
24. Kluckholn, *op. cit.*, p. 115.
25. Sapir, *op. cit.*
26. Cf. L. Coser, *The Functions of Social Conflict*. Glencoe, Ill.: Free Press, 1956, Ch. 6.
27. B. R. Clark, *Educating the Expert Society*. San Francisco: Chandler, 1962, p. 168.
28. E. Z. Friedenberg, *The Vanishing Adolescent*. New York: Dell, 1959, p. 199.
29. Personal communication with Professor R. G. Francis, University of Minnesota.
30. G. P. Stone, *Clothing and Social Relations: A Study of Appearance in the Context of Community Life*. Unpublished Ph.D. dissertation, University of Chicago, 1960.
31. DeFleur, *op. cit.*, pp. 110 and 260.
32. Cf. H. D. Lasswell, "The Structure and Function of Communication in Society," in *The Communication of Ideas*, L. Bryson, ed. Institute for Religious and Social Studies, 1948, p. 37.
33. DeFleur, *op. cit.*, p. 8.
34. R. K. Merton, M. Fiske, and C. Alberta, *Mass Persuasion: The Social Psychology of a War Bond Drive*. New York: Harper, 1946.
35. C. J. Hovland and W. Weiss, "The Influence of Source Credibility on Communication Effectiveness, in *Public Opinon and Propaganda*, D. Katz *et al.*, eds. New York: Dryden Press, 1954, pp. 334–346.
36. H. B. Lewis, "An Experiment on the Operation of Prestige Suggestion," in *Readings in Social Psychology, op. cit.* pp. 18–28.
37. I. and E. Division, "The Effects of Presenting 'One Side' versus 'Both Sides' in Changing Opinions on a Controversial Subject," in *Readings in Social Psychology, Ibid.*, pp. 506–518.
38. I. F. Janis and S. Feshbach, "Effects of Fear-Arousing Communications," *Journal of Abnormal and Social Psychology*, vol. 48, 1953, pp. 78–92.
39. R. F. Bales, "The Equilibrium Problem in Small Groups," in *Working Papers in the Theory of Action*, T. Parsons, R. F. Bales, and E. A. Shils, eds. Glencoe, Ill.: Free Press, 1953, pp. 111–61.
40. G. W. Hartmann, "A Field Experiment on the Comparative Effectiveness of 'Emotional' and 'Rational' Political Leaflets in Determining Election Results," *Journal of Abnormal and Social Psychology*, vol. 31, 1936, pp. 99–114.

41. Merton and Fiske, *op. cit.*
42. Cf. W. J. McKeachie, "Procedures and Techniques of Teaching: Survey of Experimental Studies," in *The American College Today*, N. Sanford, ed. New York: Wiley, 1962, Ch. 8.
43. H. Cantril and G. W. Allport, "Speaker Versus Loudspeaker," in *Readings in Social Psychology, op. cit.*, pp. 103–106.
44. H. J. Leavitt, "Some Effects of Certain Communications Patterns on Group Performance," in *Readings in Social Psychology, Ibid.*
45. J. W. Riley, Jr., and M. W. Riley, "Mass Communication and the Social System," in *Sociology Today*, R. K. Menton, L. Broom and L. S. Cottrell, Jr., eds. New York: Basic Books, 1959, p. 541.
46. E. Katz and P. Lazarsfeld, *Personal Influence*. Glencoe, Ill.: Free Press, 1955, p. 45; see also E. Katz, "The Two-Step Flow of Communication: An Up-To-Date Report on an Hypothesis," *Public Opinion Quarterly*, vol. 21, 1957–58, p. 61.
47. Katz and Lazarsfeld, *Ibid.*, p. 32.
48. *Ibid.*
49. DeFleur, *op. cit.*
50. *Ibid.*, p. 190.
51. P. Lazarsfeld, B. Berelson, and H. Gaudet, "Social Factors in Voting," in *Readings in Social Psychology, op. cit.*, pp. 177–189.
52. Katz and Lazarsfeld, *op. cit.*, p. 53.
53. H. H. Kelley and E. H. Volkhart, "The Resistance to Change of Group Anchored Attitudes," *American Sociological Review*, vol. 17, 1952, pp. 453–465.
54. T. Newcomb, "Attitude Development as a Function of Reference Groups: The Bennington Study," in *Readings in Social Psychology, op. cit.*, pp. 420–429.
55. L. Festinger and J. Thibaut, "Inter-personal Communication in Small Groups," *The Journal of Abnormal and Social Psychology*, vol. 46, 1951, pp. 92–99.
56. W. W. Charters, Jr., and T. M. Newcomb, "Some Attitudinal Effects of Experimentally Increased Salience of a Membership Group," in *Readings in Social Psychology, op. cit.*, pp. 415–419.
57. K. Lewin, "Group Decision and Social Change," in *Readings in Social Psychology, Ibid.*, pp. 459–473.
58. R. L. Schank, "A Study of a Community and Its Groups and Institutions Conceived of as Behaviors of Individuals," *Psychological Monographs*, vol. 43, No. 2, 1932, cited by E. Hartley, in *Fundamentals of Social Behavior*, New York: Knopf, 1952, p. 26.
59. K. Lewin, *op. cit.*
60. Riley and Riley, *op. cit.*, p. 541.
61. H. A. Hyman and P. B. Sheatsley, "Some Reasons Why Information Campaigns Fail," *Public Opinion Quarterly*, vol. 11, 1947, pp. 412–23.
62. *Ibid.*
63. *Ibid.*
64. *Ibid.*
65. *Ibid.*
66. Cited by E. Hartley, *Fundamentals of Social Psychology*. New York: Knopf, 1952, pp. 170–171.
67. *Ibid.*, p. 130.
68. L. Postman, J. S. Bruner, and E. McGinnes, "Personal Values as Selective Factors in Perception," in *Readings in Social Psychology, op. cit.*, pp. 375–383.
69. P. Lazarsfeld, B. Berelson, H. Gaudet, *The People's Choice*. New York: Duell, Sloan, & Pearce, 1944, p. 125.
70. F. C. Bartlett, "Social Factors in Recall," in *Readings in Social Psychology, op. cit.*, pp. 362–368.

71. J. M. Levine and G. Murphy, "The Learning and Forgetting of Controversial Material," in *Readings in Social Psychology, Ibid.,* pp. 402–408.
72. P. F. Lazarsfeld, *Radio and the Printed Page.* New York: Duell, Sloan & Pearce, 1940, p. 134.
73. E. Cooper and M. Jahoda, "The Evasion of Propaganda: How Prejudiced People Respond to Anti-Prejudice Propaganda," *Journal of Psychology,* vol. 23, 1947, pp. 15–25.
74. *Ibid.*
75. *Ibid.*
76. Hyman and Sheatsley, *op. cit.*
77. J. Suttoff, *Administrators Notebook,* Vol. IX, No. 3, University of Chicago, 1960.
78. A. Blome, unpublished doctoral dissertation, University of Iowa, March, 1963, pp. 147–161.
79. This section is based on Parsons' discussion; T. Parsons, "Age and Sex in the Social Structure of the United States," in *Essays in Sociological Theory,* T. Parsons, ed. Glencoe, Ill.: Free Press, 1954, pp. 89–103.
80. Parsons, *Ibid.*
81. F. L. Goodenough, "Semantic Choice and Personality Structure," *Science,* vol. 104, 1946, pp. 451–456; cited by E. Hartley, *op. cit.,* p. 103.
82. M. Mead, *Male and Female.* New York: William Morrow, 1949.
83. R. Centers, "Attitude and Belief in Relation to Occupational Stratification," *Public Opinion and Propaganda,* D. Katz *et al.,* eds. New York: Dryden Press, 1954, pp. 149–150.
84. M. S. MacLean, Jr., and A. L-A. Kao, *Editorial Prediction of Magazine Picture Appeals.* Iowa City: School of Journalism, University of Iowa, 1965, pp. 131–132.
85. *Ibid.,* p. 132.
86. E. Hartley, *op. cit.,* p. 151.
87. R. Centers, *op. cit.,* pp. 149–150.
88. S. A. Stouffer, *et al.,* "Barriers to Understanding Between Officers and Enlisted Men," in *Reader in Bureaucracy,* R. Merton, A. Gray, B. Hockey, and H. Selvin, eds. Glencoe, Ill.: Free Press, 1952, pp. 265–272.
89. Stouffer, *Ibid.*
90. *Ibid.*
91. B. Gardner, *Human Relations in Industry.* Chicago: Irwin, 1946, p. 46.
92. Educational Policies Commission, *Mass Communication and Education.* Washington, D.C.: National Education Association, 1958, p. 120.
93. *Ibid.,* p. 51.
94. *Ibid.,* p. 117.

4

Communication Channels

In light of the increase in public interest, and in
light of the challenges in education which lie ahead
both for the professional and for the citizen, this is
a time which requires that the educator's voice be
heard clearly and with effect in his community.
Likewise, the voices of the people the educator
serves should be heard and understood by him.[1]

FROM THE viewpoint of organizations, there are two distinct
environments of communication channels: (1) Those external, outside the system, and (2) those contained within the system. Each of
these environments, in turn, consists of both natural diffusion processes,
or the informal and spontaneous movement of information throughout the
society or the system, and the explicitly designed formal diffusion channels
through which information is explicitly directed. This chapter deals primarily with channels of mass communication that connect the organization to the outside world, and with other channels of communication internal to the organization itself.

Natural Diffusion

Probably little communication will remain uncontrolled, unintended,
and spontaneous for long. However, in the diffusion of ideas from one
part of society to another there are at least certain phases which create a
natural progression of information. An idea may emanate from a few central sources, spread simultaneously through a variety of channels, and,
after encountering a series of obstacles, it may ultimately arrive at several
terminal points. Depending on the route of the message, an idea may
arrive quickly at some destinations and slowly at others; but for many

types of new information, it will not go very far nor be put to use very quickly. The "circuits" through which information tends to flow in this process are those which offer least resistance to its transmission. They constitute the channels of natural diffusion. The natural diffusion of ideas will be briefly considered first, more or less independently of the routes they take. The remainder of the chapter is devoted to the utilization of the existing communication channels themselves.

DIFFUSION RESEARCH IN EDUCATION

A number of recent studies on diffusion in education have been summarized by Rogers.[2] The early studies of diffusion in education attempted to show the value of local control over the school's financial decisions because of the greater adaptability that was attributed to local control. The capacity of the school to take on new practices and discard outmoded ones approaches an S-shaped curve. That is, at first only a few schools adopt an idea, and then at about the time when the ideas become popular the schools which originated the idea tend to change their practices. This is apparent in the practices of the so-called "laboratory schools" connected with university colleges of education. As Riesman has noted, the laboratory school was one of the first to adopt "progressive" educational practices, but at about the time that these practices were being adopted around the country, many laboratory schools had begun to reassess their curriculum and stress content orientation again. As Riesman puts it, educational innovation moves like a snake, with the head of the progression often turning back closer to the tail-end than to the middle of it.[3]

Until recently the "time lag" required for widespread adoption of new educational ideas has been considerable. It was estimated that the average American school lags twenty-five years behind the most advanced practice. Rogers speculates that this lag in educational practices may be due to the absence of a central scientific source for the spread of innovations, the lack of agents of change to promote the new ideas, and the lack of economic incentive to adopt new ideas.[4] In addition, there has been a general apathy toward change in public education. This apathy can be attributed in part to the fact that public schools are "cultivated," to use Carlson's term;[5] that is, unlike more competitive business organizations, schools are guaranteed a clientele regardless of how outmoded their practices may be.

It also is related to the linkage between schools in locally oriented communities and the rapid changes that are occurring on the national level. Historically, the existing structure of schools has provided a convenient means for indoctrinating each generation with traditional values. On the other hand, as local education has become more central to the economic and national needs of the nation, nonlocal groups such as the federal government, which have less interest in maintaining the local *status quo,* have become more interested in education, and the educational structure has begun to change rapidly.

Compared to the 1930's when Mort and Cornell estimated that it took a practical invention like the kindergarten nearly fifty years to become completely diffused after its introduction, and, typically, fifteen years had elapsed before three per cent of the school systems had adopted an inno-vation; more recently seventeen per cent of the school systems adopted the language laboratory within five years after its introduction; eighteen per cent adopted teachers' aids in the high schools in eight years; twelve per cent adopted team teaching in five years, and twenty per cent adopted Physical Science Study Committee physics in four years. By the earlier formula less than two per cent of the systems would have adopted these innovations within five years.[6]

WHO ADOPTS?

Cocking studied 1,200 schools in the United States regarding their adoption of seven educational ideas, including student work experiences, career conferences, popularized budgets, and radio workshops. He found no significant differences among regions of the United States in their rapidity at adopting new ideas, but he did find that more cosmopolitan schools, located near metropolitan areas, were more likely to adopt new ideas.[7] In addition to the cosmopolitanism of a school, however, there is the very significant factor of wealth which determines how receptive a school is to a new idea. In fact, Rogers reports that educational cost per pupil is the best single predictor of how readily the school adopts new ideas.[8] It would appear that a school must have a certain level of wealth in order to be able to afford experimentation with new ideas. A report by the National Education Association lends support to the significance of economics in the adoption of new ideas. On the basis of a survey of sev-enty of the country's wealthiest communities, adoption of college level courses in humanities and world culture in the secondary schools was found in such wealthy suburban areas as Scarsdale, New York; Beach-wood, Ohio; Riverside, Illinois; University City, Missouri, and Forest Lake, Illinois, have introduced a course in logic. However, economic in-ducements offered by the federal government can offset or reinforce the factor of *community* wealth. Also, per capita expenditure signifies sup-portiveness for education on the part of a community.

Again, in summarizing a large number of studies related to the adoption of innovation carried out by Mort and his students, Ross has concluded that prediction of innovation adoption depends upon response to the question: "How much is spent per pupil?"[9]

Carlson's more recent study challenges this generally accepted view. After studying schools in Pennsylvania and West Virginia, he concluded:

In respect to the power of the variable of expenditure per child to account for *rate* of adoption and *amount* of adoption of new educational practices, Ross' statement summarizing past research . . . is not supported by these data.[10]

Undoubtedly, the increasing activity of the federal government in education, as well as other factors, is having an effect.

VOLUNTARY ASSOCIATIONS AS DIFFUSION CHANNELS

There is some evidence from a study of popular attitudes toward public administration that information tends to flow naturally through voluntary associations—that is, such public service organizations as the PTA, labor unions, and Kiwanis Clubs.[11] In that study, it was found that the citizenry was generally uninformed and had little information about either the practices of public administration or a person's rights and obligations within these agencies. It was found that, with the exception of labor groups, voluntary associations proved to be a structure through which information about the public administration programs was spread.

PERSONAL AND IMPERSONAL CHANNELS

After the death of Senator Robert Taft in July of 1953, researchers compared a university faculty community with a laboring class, interracial community on the rate of diffusion of the information of Taft's death.[12] It was found that the university community learned of the event about three hours prior to the working class, and that the faculty used outside sources of information for details more than did the working class. The faculty community learned of the event through interpersonal communication twice as often as the working class, while the working class received the information through television about five times as often as did the faculty which relied on the radio somewhat more than did the working class.

Thus, it would appear that there is a pattern of natural diffusion whereby information tends to flow more quickly and readily to cosmopolitan, wealthy communities of upper social status. Diffusion is through existing communication structures, such as voluntary associations, interpersonal networks, and the mass media. Attention is now turned to the channels of mass communication which are vital to any direct attempts to spread information and to change the practices and attitudes of members of this society.

Mass Communications

Regarded as a *process,* "communication is communication." The general communication principles outlined in the preceding chapter will generally apply, whether it is administration trying to convey a message to subordinates within the organization or whether the message is aimed at the general public. But, while there are parallels between the "internal" communication processes and the "external" mass communication channels used to communicate with the general public, these channels have their unique characteristics.

THE PRESSURE FOR MASS COMMUNICATION IN EDUCATION

The pressure to keep the local citizenry informed is basic. The local community pays the bill, at least part of it. They must be convinced of increasingly expensive school needs, which in turn requires that they have a thorough knowledge about the reasons behind changing needs—the knowledge explosion, the Cold War, changing vocational structure, and the increased functions assumed by the school and the personnel in it. It is also a stark fact that citizens have a very real control over local education, which they manifest through pressure groups and through their legal representatives on the school board. In the short run at least, the sphere of authority of the chief administrator will extend no further than his school board and his community can be persuaded to permit. Thus, citizens must be informed not only because they "deserve" to be, but because the existence and the expansion of the school program depends on it.

The mass media have created a new perspective for the local citizen. He may have more knowledge about physically remote events than he does about his own local community; citizens of a city may know more about proposed federal aid to education than about a local school bond issue. A good local newspaper can be expected to devote more space to the educational events making news around the country than to local happenings in the home town system. The fact that local school problems may be overshadowed by national issues has enormous implications for the school administrator who is expected to "keep the people informed" about his school program and its needs.

This problem of communicating local problems to the public is aggravated by the layman's suspicion toward experts. This kind of suspicion is apparent, for example, in recent controversies over fluoridation of urban water systems. Despite objective evidence of the health benefits of such a program, laymen are suspicious of experts who try to push such programs in defiance of tradition. The expert implicitly stands for *change*. He uses his public authority, backed by the secrets of his profession, to initiate it, often in the face of public resistance. The layman, on the other hand, cannot adequately judge the expert's knowledge or the full consequences of his recommendations. It is often believed that the expert ignores the "latent" or indirect consequences, although these are often of the greatest importance to the layman.

This kind of suspicion is held against educators in their role as experts in charge of a major public service. Even as the people pay tribute to the educational leader, they may also secretly fear that something will be "put over" on them. Thus, in a complex society the increased efforts of school executives to communicate with those segments of the public which wield control over the schools are confronted by natural barriers of mistrust between the public and its experts. Finding ways to communicate more effectively to the public, and understanding the available mass media, are especially crucial problems for the administrator of today's schools. This was apparent in a recent study in Michigan in which Haak found that people there are less informed about the schools than teachers and administrators generally realize.[13] For example, despite a generally favorable opinion held by large segments of the general public, only forty-four per cent of the citizens of one community could name the superintendent, and thirty-eight per cent gave incorrect replies about salaries.

Carter also found that although the public generally values education they tend to be apathetic and indifferent toward it on specific issues.[14] Even among those most interested in a financial campaign there was the general feeling that they did not understand enough about the schools, and they wanted more information. Almost nine out of ten voters reported that they found newspaper articles helpful in informing them about school affairs. Half of them got information from school bulletins, two-thirds got their information about schools from friends, and one-third mentioned that they had read articles about schools in national magazines.

Haak found that what the public really wants is some direct communication from the school officials themselves. One-half of the public said they would prefer to be informed about the public schools by school officials, but twenty-four per cent said that they were actually informed by newspapers and thirty-six per cent by friends and relatives. It is significant that those voters who found speeches by school officials useful were almost twice as likely to vote favorably for issues as those who found newspaper articles and other mass media useful.

Carter compared two communities in which bond issue campaigns were successful and unsuccessful, respectively. Education was valued allmost equally in the two communities, and the voters in each community were equally informed about the current educational issues and methods. However, a much smaller percentage of the voters in the unsuccessful community participated in any way in the schools, and there was a higher percentage who felt that there was no use in participating.

Who, then, is informed and active in the public schools? Research indicates that it is a highly select segment of the public. Rossi estimates that only fifteen per cent of the citizens of "Bay City" are active in the local schools, twenty-four per cent are moderately active, and sixty-one per cent are inactive. The active public comes from the upper levels of the class system and have above-average education. They tend to be parents of public school children, relatively integrated into the community, and active in community affairs beyond school issues.[15]

In planning his information campaign, it is perhaps more important for the educator to know who, among those active, are *critical* of the schools. Skipton found that the critics of the schools in at least one community had lower than average education. They were persons who were exposed to parochial or private schools, presently without children in the public schools, and who generally lacked contact with personnel in the public school system, especially teachers and principals. They tended to be older persons in manual occupations, frequently first generation citizens of the United States. They appeared to be somewhat frustrated in terms of their own long-term goals.[16]

The above two studies present a striking contrast between the actively interested and the actively critical citizens. If the picture is accurate, it has ironic implications for mass communications in public education. For example, it is quite possible that attempts to reach more citizens, to increase the base of participation in the public schools, will arouse the critics rather than the sympathizers. In a study of voter turnout at bond and tax elections held by 1,054 school districts between 1948 and 1959, the average turnout was only thirty-six per cent of the eligible voters in a district.[17] However, the issues that failed were those which drew larger voter turnout. Turnout declined in large districts and appeared to increase only when the school board was characteristically less responsible to the public. It is patently clear that a groundswell of public "interest" will not necessarily promote the interests of the schools. In fact, if voters are reached indiscriminately, increased communication can be detrimental to a school's program. The effectiveness of an information campaign can be increased by aiming it at segments of the community who are favorably disposed to the schools, and by using personal contacts between school officials and citizens' voluntary organizations.

SIGNIFICANCE AND UTILIZATION OF THE MASS MEDIA

The school's relation to its public cannot be reasonably understood apart from the revolution in the media of mass communication, which has only recently saturated the daily life of most Americans. The mass media has assumed the central place in American life primarily since the turn of the century. Radio and television did not exist then. Between 1904 and 1935 the average week-day circulation of newspapers doubled, and the number of telephones increased twenty-one-fold during that period, while the number of telegrams more than doubled.[18] Today, a single communication may reach as many as 20 million people. An estimated 100 million American citizens look at daily newspapers and over half a billion books are purchased annually. Over ninety-five per cent of homes have one or more radios and more than eighty per cent have television sets.

These media have become so much a part of the American way of life that a failure of any one of them causes hardship, for a substantial number of habitual users. During a newspaper strike, Berelson interviewed sixty newspaper subscribers and found that practically everyone paid tribute to the value of the newspaper.[19] Different reasons were given for the newspaper's importance, however. The necessity of keeping informed was stressed by most respondents, but other evidence indicated that what the majority really missed were the advertisements about radio programs, sales, exchange information, obituary notices, and fashion notes. The newspaper was apparently used also for escape, or psychological relaxation. It provided "conversational pieces" for talk at social gatherings, and it disseminated gossip and human interest stories. For many people, failure to receive their newspaper created personal insecurity.

Habitually used mass communication channels provide potentially useful outlets for communication between school and community. The existence of channels is no advantage, however, unless they are available to the administrator, and unless the messages they report are accurate, sympathetic, effectively presented, and absorbed. From a study of Michigan newspapers, one writer concludes that most of the news stories about the school were routine, concentrated during two or three months of the year, and not among the most attractively written news stories. In fact, he concludes that "School information is one of the least well written portions of the newspaper; absence of significant news is an even more acute problem." [20] Five years after the above study was concluded, one of the authors again analyzed the school content in Michigan newspapers. It was concluded again that the majority of school news was routine and not particularly well written; however, that study did disclose excellent feature article treatment of certain school topics as well as a notable increase in school news devoted to curriculum.[21] It now seems likely that this increased interest was a manifestation of the surge of concern over scholasticism generally resulting from American shock over Soviet space accomplishments. A still more recent study by Haught, using the same categories of content and the same methodology in an analysis of Oklahoma newspapers, found curriculum news accounting for considerably lower percentage of school news though other comparisons between the two studies were strikingly similar.[22]

There is always a possibility that on some occasions the persons in control of the media will be unfavorable toward some aspect of the program and its expenses in both their news reports and editorials. In one sense, newspaper criticism could provide a "check" against folly and extravagance in the schools, and so it could provide protection to the public. However, the persons who decide the content of reports and editorials usually have no special training in education, and perhaps have little interest in it except for its cost, or its effectiveness in teaching the *status quo*.

They have been selected by a special process that emphasizes their personality, their flare for writing, their vocal cords, or their financial capability to purchase the media, rather than their special education and background. One dilemma is that most of those media which *are* sympathetic to the problems of public education (as, for example, educational radio and television stations) have the least audience appeal and have been generally unsuccessful.[23]

Gross surveyed 113 newspapers and 100 school systems in New England and, as a matter of fact, found superintendents to be largely satisfied with newspaper coverage; fifty per cent were *very* satisfied, and fifty-two per cent found them very helpful. Nevertheless, a significant proportion expressed only "mild" satisfaction, and there were a number of specific complaints. Thirty-five per cent thought that the press overemphasized bad or sensational news, thirty-four per cent charged that reporters use only a small proportion of space for educational news, and one-fourth felt that the press does not make education interesting.[24]

Carter likewise found very little overall dissatisfaction with the California papers. expressed by 110 school superintendents there. In fact, twenty-nine per cent said the press does a very complete job in printing news of the school system; fifty per cent agreed that their press is "fairly" complete; ninety per cent said that editors are favorable to the schools; and eighty per cent said that their paper had supported the districts' last school finance request.[25] Yet, despite this relatively favorable review of the press, the California superintendents reported a marked discrepancy between the news they judged the public *needs* to know and what gets into print (as determined from an analysis of four newspapers). Public relations and PTA news were ranked sixth by superintendents as news the public needed to know, but these areas were the most covered, consuming one-third of the nonsports school news space. Educational circulation was judged by seventy per cent of the superintendents as the area most important for public awareness, but it ranked third in space devoted to it.

So it appears that despite the absence of widespread dissatisfaction among school executives with newspaper reporting, what is reported is not what school executives would report, and the relative emphases and attractiveness of stories are sore points of contention. But of even greater importance is the fact that even if there were complete satisfaction with news reports, the method of anonymous "reporting" in papers seldom permits the school executive to present *his own* statements to the public. The paucity of any kind of public contact with school officials was revealed in a survey of two small communities where less than one in twenty residents had "often discussed" school issues with school officials, although one-fourth to one-third of the population said they engage in serious discussions of school issues in their homes.[26] The fact that school executives do not write the stories or in any way control their distribution does not alleviate the fundamental problem which is the lack of communication between the public and school officials. School executives, like most other public officials, have little opportunity to use the mass media themselves for presenting their views and problems to the public. While two out of five Massachusetts superintendents reported a feature column in the local paper written by a student, only three per cent of the papers featured a column by a school official.[27] More attention is given annually to the football coach and to the latest game than to the chief administrator of schools and educational problems. Three-fourths of the Massachusetts superintendents judged that school athletics received very adequate coverage, while only thirty-six per cent said the same of the coverage of superintendents' activities, and only one out of five said that coverage of the school program was adequate.[28] As a result, parents are more likely to learn about a new course in world government from their child than from the persons responsible for providing the course.

CHARACTERISTICS OF THE MASS MEDIA
IN THE UNITED STATES

The relative inaccessibility of the most effective forms of mass communication to most school administrators will perhaps be understood better by reviewing some of the characteristics of the control structure of the American mass media. The consequences of this structure may be inferred from examining the functions of the mass media.

The Control Structure. The limited availability of the mass media to most organizations is a factor of vital importance. Because of concentrated ownership, the mass media are controlled almost exclusively by a relatively small, influential "community" of investors, who are usually in the upper middle class, which tends to be conservative. There is perhaps no more homogeneous grouping than those who are in the "communications" industry, and this homogeneous group differs significantly from all other segments of the society.

The control structure stems from the commercial, profit-making motive behind the media. Unlike many profit organizations, the most salient and basic characteristic of the mass media is that they are commercial ventures which are not supported directly by the consumer; they are financed by brokers and advertisers. Although it is true that the consumer spends billions of dollars annually on mass media, because of the high costs of production consumers do not "pay for" the media. The bankers and the advertisers who do finance the media probably have different sets of values from the artist and the general public.

Concentration. Special agencies within the mass media industry have developed and specialized in preparing most of the communication in standard forms. A handful of advertising agencies prepare one-third to one-half of all television and radio programs. Also ninety-six per cent of all newspaper circulation carries Associated Press stories, and virtually all of the impressions which the average American receives about international affairs, he receives from three major news agencies. This near monopoly of control is the outcome of a highly competitive industry. Between 1930 and 1955 the total number of daily newspapers in the United States was reduced by over 100 per cent, while newspaper circulation during that period rose from 39 million to almost 60 million. Most cities have no more than one newspaper. Furthermore, this same centralization is responsible for mergers between the media. About one-third of radio and television stations (which generally have more outlets per city than newspapers) are owned in part or wholly by newspapers.[29] The communications industry, then, is literally becoming a community owned by special interest groups. While there are other, competing views available on the newsstands, most people are accustomed to the more accessible media and do not trouble themselves with looking at the many specialized magazines.

Standardized Content. The fact that a minority monopolize the media content and/or compete economically is largely responsible for standardization of mass media content. Producers are reluctant to take risks on originality because of their heavy investment. Thus, great cycles of different kinds of movies and television programs result as one producer imitates another whose product has been successful. Acute sensitivity to public criticism has sometimes made television producers reluctant to support frank exchanges of opinion and editorializing on important public issues, such as teaching about Communism, religion, and sex education. Those who do support frank expressions of unpopular ideas do so at their own risk; there is little to encourage it, as everyone disclaims responsibility for the outspoken comments of a courageous commentator. In one large metropolitan city in the midwest, for example, one of the two local daily newspapers refused to accept a paid advertisement supporting the cessation of nuclear testing. The advertising manager was quoted as saying that it is his policy not to give reasons. The following day the group was refused by the other daily in the city. Despite the fact that the newspapers are supposedly independently managed, in both cases it was the same advertising manager who refused the ad; there had been an actual merger at many of the operating levels.

Lazarsfeld and Merton have suggested that since the mass media are commercial ventures supported by a few great business concerns which derive their status from the present social structure, the media are also used to contribute to the maintenance of that structure.[30] Mass media, in other words, tend to support the *status quo*. Social conformity is insured by several procedures: censorship, selective omission, and minimization of economic risk. Censorship is probably the most obvious way in which the mass media support the *status quo*. In one Illinois city, for example, advertisers tried to get rid of a liberal newspaper which supported a strike. In one city, three out of four newspapers at one time refused to accept ads from independent businessmen against one of the major food store chains; the one paper which did accept the ad had no advertising account with the chain in question. Consumers' co-ops have been refused programs on two major networks.

Social conformism is further reinforced by the more subtle processes of selective omission of views and events that are contrary to the dominant views or to those in control of the mass media. This is one of the least noticed, yet most fundamental effects of the control structure. In an international age when most events of major significance are remote from the individual, it is apparent that those things people know about and become aware of are determined for them by what is presented over the mass media, and by a relatively small handful of people, many of whom have distinct, homogeneous values. Reporters, editors, and advertising agencies determine what facts the public will know, and often the particular interpretation to be placed on them as well. What the public knew about the Cuban blockade, the Vietnam conflict, or the race riots in the South depended on the perceptions of reporters and the availability of information to them. Some news items are never heard of, while others are repeated so often that their importance is distorted; relatively infrequent murders are widely publicized, but more frequent and more costly kinds of white collar crimes involving corporate violations of federal antitrust laws, misuse of food and drugs, and violations of weights and standards regulations go relatively unnoticed.

While most reporters probably attempt to remain objective, they work under commercial pressures to find news and report it in such a way that it will sell copy. More important, the attitudes of reporters may be distinctly different from those of other segments of society. Such a discrepancy between the way problems are viewed by the press and by some other observers was true in Massachusetts, for example, where editors and superintendents disagreed on a number of statements regarding educational philosophy. Less than one-fifth of the superintendents, for example, would give more emphasis to teaching subject matter than to developing individual interests, while over half of the press preferred teaching subject matter. Only thirteen per cent of the superintendents advocated grading all students on uniform standards, but forty-one per cent of the press advocated this practice. There were similar differences regarding the place of spontaneity in the classroom, letter grading, and emphasis on the three R's.[31] No one knows how much these differences in attitudes may affect the reporter's perception of a problem and the interpretations of it which his report may suggest.[32] This makes the process of selection and omission of school news extremely significant, a process over which school officials have little control.

The fact that news media operate on the principles of profit and risk has immeasurable implications for the long-range impact that the mass media will have on popular taste and social intelligence. Since the competition is often for "audiences," every listener and reader is presumed to be significant; there is, accordingly, a marked reluctance to deal with complex issues in the media, or to present them in a comprehensive way. There is also constant policing against saying anything or dealing with any topic that might irritate someone. The long-range effects of persistent efforts aimed at a presumably sophomore mentality and designed to entice as many people as possible could be deadening.

Yet, in view of the negative criticism that intellectuals are fond of directing at the popular culture, it is well to maintain a broader perspective. Fourastie provides a refreshing anecdote for undue pessimism:

The intellectual leaders of our time . . . repeat for the length of printed columns that humanity has arrived at the threshold of the apocalypse or else turns without rest in an infernal circle. They find it only too easy to illustrate their theses by some of the frightful adventures into which humanity has recently been thrown.

No one seems to care at all about long-term trends. No one seems to notice the passage of the popular masses from a vegetal life to one that is not so limited. Not a word is said about the disappearance of famines in the Western world. No one is congratulated on the development of intellectual culture, the opportunity of an increasing number of men to enjoy higher education, or the extraordinary increase in the means of aesthetic appreciation.

No one seems to suspect the existence of factors favorable to individuality in the new tertiary civilization. A man who, two centuries ago, would not even have learned to read, if he had survived to maturity, profits by his windows, the central heating of his apartment, and the 300,000 copies of the newspaper for which he writes, to announce that humanity has arrived at the last stage of barbarism.[33]

Undoubtedly, a minority of television and radio programs have a highly educational and stimulating effect on their audiences, and this level of comprehensibility can be expected to improve more with increased education of the American people. But the basic control structure shows no signs of major alteration, short of interference from the federal government.

FUNCTIONS OF THE MASS MEDIA

In view of these unique characteristics of the mass communications industry—that is, near monopoly and standardized content—the media have assumed functions beyond the more obvious informational and entertainment ones. Lazarsfeld and Merton describe some of them: the "status-conferal," "enforcement," and "narcotic" functions.[34] In addition, the well known "escape" function should be included in this list.

Status Conferal. Obviously, "making the headlines" bestows prestige on both the person and the kind of behavior that brought him favorable attention. Those who work in the media have it in their power to "make or break" certain activities, or persons, by selectively publicizing some and ignoring others. This places the school executive in the precarious position of having to solicit the good opinion of those who control the media in order to win recognition for a deserving program. Perhaps the local press and television newscasts, which may devote up to one-fourth of their programs and column inches to athletics, simply reflect the public's established interests. Yet, there is little doubt that the attention itself given to athletics by the media *bestows* status on athletic achievement. By comparison, for example, the scholarship student, the superior senior in art and music, or the school's best writer or scientist receive only token recognition, usually buried in a short column in the back of the society section on a Saturday afternoon. Also by comparison, the athletic coach receives more recognition than do the elementary teachers, the high school algebra or Spanish teacher, and even the superintendent of schools.

One of the relatively unnoticed effects of the status control function of the mass media is that the control structure of the media gives laymen— journalists, columnists, producers, directors, editors, managers of local radio and television stations—authority to speak about issues that are beyond their demonstrated competence to speak or write knowledgably. After one week's study, syndicated news columnists and television commentators will presume to speak about economic, political, religious, or educational issues and social conditions with the authority of a specialist who has devoted his life to any one of these topics.[35] By virtue of this access to the media, Huntley, Brinkley and a handful of other television commentators have received more recognition as "educators" on public issues than most university professors who have spent their lives studying and writing on the issues which news commentators have successfully popularized. A sixty-minute documentary may dismiss a topic that has taken a specialist a lifetime to formulate. However, in the case of several nationwide commentators, the best of such documentaries is remarkably informative, well prepared, and educational. Through the efforts of a large staff of writers and researchers, these commentators can present the material more vividly than most university professors. Nevertheless, the authority to assume the role of public educator is bestowed on a television newsman by the fact that he has access to the media which reaches the public. That access strongly depends on how pleasing is his personality or how dynamic is his voice. His "authority," then, is a function of a monopoly over the media and his special skills as a journalist or newsman trained to gain and hold attention rather than as a specialist in the field of knowledge being reported on. While much of the material is sound and intelligent, this does not change the fact that anyone with the capital to purchase a radio station or a newspaper publishing house can have a public forum for editorializing and deciding which views of others will be heard. Conversely, it provides those in control with the power to exclude any views that are unacceptable to them. These considerations have implications for the significance of a "free press" in a society where only a few are free to exercise that freedom. They have further implications for the discontinuity between the power to control the press and qualifications to use that power.

Largely as a result of the mass media and mass education, educators' roles are dividing into two specialized facets. The "knowing" and "communicating" functions of education are separating. While some subject-matter experts are also effective communicators, there is a vast catalogue of experts who are not skilled communicators; there is likewise developing a battery of skilled communicators who are not experts in many of the particular issues on which they comment. Hence, the status of university professors, and to a lesser extent high school teachers, who have been traditionally expected to perform both the functions of knowing and communicating, is being undermined from both sides—by the specialized experts on the one hand, and by the skilled communicators on the other. The long-range effects of these developments are already in sight. From the teacher's side of the lectern, it is increasingly apparent that students compare teachers with their favorite news commentators and demand an equally exciting and dramatic performance in the classroom from their teachers whose excellence may lie more in the direction of expertise than of entertainment. (How many graduate students have traveled across the country to study under a renowned expert, only to find that he is not an "exciting" teacher?) At the same time, a few teachers are able to build a reputation almost entirely on the basis of their ability to "get the students' interest" and their popularity with students.

Looking at the problem from another perspective, persons employed by the mass media who have the most to say about a subject, who say it most convincingly, who reach the most receptive ears, and who know less about that subject than the experts are very likely to oversimplify. Oversimplification almost always distorts reality. This is not to suggest that there is no need for intelligent explanation which translates the language of the expert into the language of the citizenry at large—this is a role of paramount importance in mass culture, and for that reason the accuracy of the translation is important.

Enforcement. The enforcement function refers to the power of the press and other media to expose immorality and corruption, and to enforce the norms. There has long been a self-righteous, crusading spirit behind many of the mass media, which has made them an invaluable force toward the improvement of society. For, although many people may know privately about certain forms of corruption, they hesitate to take organized action until it is known that they know about the corruption, or until a public proclamation is called for and an agency is ready to exert public leadership.

Indignant newspaper, magazine, and television crusades may be aimed at exposing a complacent, disinterested, penny-pinching public and thus challenge the people to "get out and vote." But at the same time, the wrath of the media is as easily directed against a school bond issue. News media sometimes delight in "exposing" innocuous "offenses" of teachers, such as leaving work early or occasionally using a city car for a private errand. In fact, it is less likely that the media's vindictiveness will be directed at the public, on which it depends for sales, than on the more vulnerable, organized institutions whose unofficial practices make good copy. It is, for example, racketeers and prostitutes who are attacked rather than the customers who make their illicit business so profitable. Similarly, school executives can expect that an alert press is continually on guard for information which would expose conditions in the school that are at variance with the public's sentiment. Indeed, the mass media have played a most prominent role in recent case studies of school-community controversies over textbooks, the introduction of courses in world government, and teaching Communism in the school. Dimly aware of this threat of public exposure, school administrators are easily inclined to become cautious about proposing controversial matters, anxiously screening applicants, and policing any official and private practices of teachers that could possibly create a public disturbance. For example, in one city a superintendent of public schools had been sponsoring social science research with pupils in his system for a number of years. He and the school board were convinced of its usefulness. However, when a complaint of one parent about one of the questions being asked received a barrage of support from the local mass media, he cancelled the entire research program without notice.

The net effect of the enforcement function, then, is to increase caution and conformity in areas that receive publicity. But the dilemma is that no matter how well schoolmen conform to public expectations, their inadequacies and mistakes are more likely to make good copy and receive widespread publicity than are their proficiencies. There is no guarantee that the school will receive "equal time" for its positive and negative aspects. In the absence of such a guarantee, and in view of a crusading news media in some cities, there is a long-range possibility that leadership over the schools will be more inclined toward protecting an innocuous image than toward initiating needed change.

The Narcotic Effect. The "narcotizing dysfunction," as Lazarsfeld and Merton refer to it,[36] is one of the mass media's least noticed and perhaps most important long-term functions. It refers to the tendency of many Americans to spend so much time keeping abreast of world events that they become immune to their significance. Exposure to floods of information may serve "to narcotize rather than to energize the average reader or listener," as Lazarsfeld and Merton put it; "As an increasing need of time is devoted to reading and listening, a decreasing share is available for organized action . . . [the individual] comes to mistake *knowing* about problems of the day for *doing* something about them." [37] Hence, apart from the media's frequent inability to change opinions or behavior, the problem is that mere exposure to the message may inadvertently ease the social conscience of those who hear it, and so provide a basis for rationalizing inaction. Thus, parents attend a PTA meeting, listen to a discussion of the need for better facilities, more teachers, and better paid teachers, and then return home with open minds and closed purses. They are satisfied that they "understand" the problems of public education, but they are still irate over the proposed property tax increase announced in the next morning's paper; they still oppose federal aids to education.

The Escape Function. Another function of the mass media which has been widely recognized, is the "escape" function. "Escapist" communication does not pertain to the content of the communication, but to the *effect* that communication may have on its audience. Escape communication provides an emotional release from personal problems. It may occur when persons identify themselves with the characters in a television program. The person emotionally participates and leaves his own depressed environment and lives, loves, and fights with the characters with whom he identifies. This provides him with a form of compensation; he can be a hero, a villain, or a lover without ever leaving the comfort of his own living room.

The pattern of soap operas is typical of escape communication. In them, the heroine is typically married to a young, rich lawyer or physician. The heroine, who has an exciting, romantic homelife, successfully dominates all of her friends and her family and is capable of solving their problems as well as her own. This image of womanhood provides a tremendous contrast to the listener, the housewife, whose husband comes home in dirty overalls and throws his dinner pail on the floor before he sits down to read the evening paper with a bottle of beer. The housewife, then, may escape her own world momentarily and enjoy another form of being, that of the soap opera heroine.

Escape communication is not necessarily a social problem, and in fact it may have positive functions of relieving boredom and frustration. Only when escape communication is viewed by the audience as a valid source of information does it become a problem. Warner and Henry found that people do tend to regard the solutions that soap operas offer as valid.[38] This solution is usually based on the belief that the difficulties which a person faces can be reduced to a formula based on the existence of *good* and *bad* people. Then, it remains only to change the bad people into good ones (Ma Perkins was good at this), or if one waits long enough the bad will usually destroy itself (bad people invariably fall off bridges, get killed in auto accidents, or are arrested).

The problems presented by this form of communication, then, are usually presented as entirely "personal" ones, and the solutions that are offered are entirely personal, too. They do not challenge the existing social order, nor do they explore the basic causes of problems, which are invariably seen in the personal weaknesses of the characters rather than in the conditions under which they live. Thus, the mass media fosters one of the major fallacies of our time: that social problems are caused by "bad people" rather than by the social order.

IMPLICATIONS FOR EDUCATION

Many of the implications of the foregoing discussion for the role of the teacher should be apparent. The conclusion of one educational commission, however, is worth quoting.

Through the mass media, a whole new set of prestige figures has arisen. The teacher's interpretations of political matters are overshadowed by a host of radio and television commentators; his discussions of the geography and customs of other countries are made pale by the polychrome eye of the motion-picture cameras; his standards of music are obliterated by the assurances of disc jockeys that *everybody* thinks this is a great new recording"; his readings of Shakespeare are made maturish by the professional performance. In essence, among the chief changes in the circumstances of teaching brought about by the rise of the mass media has been the loss of the aura of authority.[39]

The mass media have become impressive, educational, informative, and entertaining aspects of the popular culture. It can also be said they are misinformative and sometimes dull, but in their shadow the teacher has lost much control over what is learned and the way in which it is learned. The mass media have to some extent assumed some of the teacher's former authority. As one result, today's first grader is remarkably well informed about current events, which, as never before, have required him to learn details about the arts, physical science, and politics. School children spend more time with the mass media than they spend in school. Television provides children with larger vocabularies than children who have not experienced television. As the horizons of the younger generation expand, the teachers will have to be intellectually better prepared than ever before to challenge the interested student. Teachers, even at the elementary grades, can no longer afford formless methods-oriented and narrow training. If there is a need anywhere for a combination of liberal arts background and a highly specialized content area, it is in teaching.

Yet, if the mass media can effectively stimulate an interest in current events and provide a general acquaintance with the arts and sciences, there is less certainty that they are as effective as they could be in elevating the popular taste, in critically analyzing the American social structure, in providing information about the rest of the world, or in systematically analyzing a variety of complex issues comprehensively. The image of knowledge fostered by the media is inclined to be a relatively superficial one, a hastily presented summary on a television documentary. These functions—of interpretation, guidance in the formation of taste, critical analysis, and systematic and thorough study of topic—remain the special province of the public school teacher. In fact, if children are not prodded in school to critically and systematically review in depth various views that they have superficially gleaned from the daily newscast, many will have relatively few other opportunities to do so. The classroom is still one of the few antidotes to the narcotizing and escapist effects of the media. But to fulfill these functions, it will require that a teacher become something more than an amateur "Jack-of-all-trades." It will require a curriculum more powerful than the "Jack and Jill" readers and more comprehensive than "Methods 1 and 2," and it will require more intellectual competence than "participation in extracurricular activities," which school administrators often prefer of recent college graduates. Increasing attention to knowledge of the arts and sciences beyond the television documentary, soap opera, and the playhouse is called for if schools are to meet the intellectual competition of the mass media.

CHANGING THE PUBLIC'S OPINION

Each field of mass media is highly concentrated, often consisting of a monopoly in a particular area. Much of what most people know is determined for them by the mass media, and many of its messages are "one-sided." Yet, these features do not determine precisely how effective the mass media are in deliberately forming opinions and influencing behavior. Long-term effects are difficult to assess, but if only specific short-term effects are considered, the mass media are not uniformly influential. They are insignificant or influential only under special conditions; they may sometimes have an effect that is contrary to the intended one; at other times, they may be very influential in the intended direction. The evidence discussed below illustrates these various states of effectiveness and some of the conditions which produce them.

How Influential Are the Mass Media? Generally, the group-anchored character of much personal opinion renders it safe from the relatively impersonal mass media appeals. Lipset concludes as much from a study of opinion formation of a random, representative sample of 480 students and faculty members in a "crisis" situation.[40] He found that opinion formation was largely a product of previous experiences and attitudes. The "crisis" studied was the controversy in the 1950's over a loyalty oath that was mandatory for all faculty members at the University of California. It was found that although Democrats were disproportionately against the oath, the crucial factor was political liberalism which cross-cut the two major political parties. Undergraduates who had more contact with the faculty were more liberal on academic freedom issues than were others. Jews were the most opposed to the oath among religious groups, nonaffiliates were next, and then Protestants; Catholics were the most conventional. The family's religion was an effective determinant of opinion on the issue, even for those who no longer practiced their religion. The higher the socioeconomic status of the parents, the more likely was the respondent to be unfavorable to the oath. Prospective teachers were less opposed than engineers, although this may have been a function of the fact that most of the prospective teachers were liberal arts majors. The point is that it was social background, or group affiliation, and not the message of the mass media which was the major determinant of opinion.

This does not mean that mass media played no role at all, however; for they did play a significant if limited role under certain special conditions. Lipset concludes that the newspaper which people read had little influence on people's opinions about the right of Communists to teach, but with regard to the loyalty oath, persons reading the liberal newspapers tended to have more pro-faculty sentiment than persons reading the conservative papers, even when basic political attitudes were held constant. Thus, the barrage of slanted news stories and editorials during the conflict appeared to have significant effect on student opinion about loyalty oaths. Mass communications, then, are hardly the only determinant of public opinion, but there is reason to believe that they are a *major* one with respect to certain issues, and that they can have an influence over and above so basic a force as underlying political predispositions.

One impressive account of the influence that mass communications can have on stimulating public action deals with one of the stubborn problems that face school administrators; namely, that many sympathetic citizens do not vote on public school bond issues and school board elections. Mass communications have been found to be useful in enticing sympathetic voters to the polls. An experiment on getting out the vote for a city charter revision, for example, showed that only one-third of those not contacted in any way prior to the vote turned out to vote. In comparison, sixty per cent of those who were contacted by mail (and three-fourths of those who were personally contacted) showed up at the polls. There was also evidence that the propaganda either stimulated only those who were favorably disposed to the issue to turn out, or that the propaganda itself made them favorably disposed.[41] Thus, although large turnouts may include a disproportionate number of critics (if the school does not use mass media campaigns), under some conditions mass appeals conducted by the schools may be effective in attracting the school's supporters.

The assumption, however, that mass media messages will change opinion in the intended direction must be scrutinized with caution. As suggested in the previous chapter, there are powerful communication blocks that may prevent or distort intended messages. In fact, the message may boomerang. One of the authors was involved in an experiment on recruiting high school girls into a career of nursing by a direct mail publicity campaign which proved to be a classic illustration of the "boomerang effect." It was found that among prospective nurses (girls who had planned to enter nursing in their junior year of high school), those who received *any* favorable literature developed less favorable attitudes toward nursing than those who received none during the school year—whose images improved markedly. The "altruistic" appeals to nursing (as a way to serve humanity) had the most negative effect on prospective nurses while the more "practical" appeals (about the financial and other employment advantages) had a somewhat more favorable effect, although still not as effective as for those who received no literature. The same message definitely had a different effect on those who were interested and those who were uninterested in nursing as a career, and that effect was contrary to what might have reasonably been expected.[42]

The utility of the mass media for changing opinions seems to be severely limited. One of the chief limitations is the one-way nature of the media. Even if available and sympathetic to the school administration, most mass media permit very little communication from the public to the administrator, a flow of communication that is essential if the administrator is to understand the kinds of reservations and misgivings that the public holds. The process of *inter*action which underlies all effective communication is therefore frustrated by mass communication by virtue of the fact that immediate feedback is impossible.

Strategies for Changing Public Opinion. In view of the highly variable prospects of changing public opinion by mass communication, it is essential to consider *when* mass communications do affect, and when they do not affect public opinion. Drawing liberally upon the preceding discussions, there appears to be three variables that make the difference between successful and unsuccessful efforts to change public opinion: (1) the feasibility of changing the opinions of the opinion leaders who are opposed; (2) the feasibility of undermining the position of the leaders who are opposed; and (3) the feasibility of maximizing what interest the public has in the issue. The role of each of these factors is poignantly illustrated in the account below which describes how one community reversed its opinion against establishing a newly consolidated school in another community.[43]

Prior to the crisis which brought the consolidation issue in "Elm Hollow" to a climax, the majority of the people there said that they would first prefer that the school be located in their own town; but only fifteen per cent said that there was nothing to be said for the other sites. The investigator concluded that only a small proportion of the community, most of them among the fifteen per cent, were intensely concerned about the issue. The three or four extremists who were most vocal and influential in establishing opinion all seemed to be motivated from vested interests: a druggist wanted to conserve his textbook business, a gasoline station operator wanted the fuel trade which a consolidated school would bring into his own community, a carpenter hoped to make the school's desks, a former school board member was angry at the superintendent. Despite years of attempting to crystallize opinion, however, these vocal opinion leaders had been essentially unsuccessful; the community remained apathetic. But then, in an extraordinary move, the state department of education condemned the local school house, which forced the public to make a decision about the location of the new school. At this point, the latent, accumulated effect of the past propaganda opposing other sites crystallized, and the majority came to regard their own community as the only reasonable choice.

The investigator asked, "Why did this crisis lead to a united front of the community as desired by the few extremists, when their propaganda alone could not have this effect?" [44] He concludes that the biased individuals who were vocal created the illusion that there was an extreme community opinion, which may not have in fact corresponded with reality. The continuous advocacy of the minority position led to the belief that there was a consensus in the community. Once it was generally believed that the majority opinion was against locating in any other community, out of community loyalty the majority of the individuals refused to take a position that was contrary to what they believed to be the majority position. The years of preparatory propaganda simply added to the impression that the extreme position had long-standing validity, thus divesting it of the personal interests which motivated its advocates.

Yet, within a few years the community's opinion was completely reversed again by a series of bargaining and co-opting tactics employed by a county politician, whose political position was being embarrassed by the uncompromising position of the community. His first step was to undermine the opposition by supporting its interests in other ways. He supported the druggist for a higher paid political office, promised the carpenter a job collecting taxes, and suggested a school bus franchise to the garage owner. The second step was to destroy the accepted assumption of consensus about the community's opinions. This occurred when few people attended a meeting called for the purpose of deciding the school's location, since most of them had expected that the opinion leaders would protect the community's interest. When no one came forward at the meeting and the opposing town was chosen as the site, there was little movement to reopen the issue; most people came to feel that the decision reflected community opinion. The author concludes, "This technique would, of course, not work where there were genuine interests on the part of each individual in the program. But where public opinion is motivated in many individuals by (1) the impression of universality, (2) conformity to the apparent majority, or illusion of the majority, (3) an illusion created by a vocal minority, then such reorganization is possible. By and large, it seems to the writer that community opinion is generally of this type." [45]

IMPLICATIONS

The case illustrates what may be a typical cleavage between a small but vocal minority which leads opinion, and a. disinterested majority which often simply follows the lead of the most interested and vocal citizens. As one watches public debates over school issues in the newspapers, radio, and television, where the interested minority become easily visible, it is easy to reach the conclusion that a minority represents and reflects the "public" opinion; it is even easier to forget about the less interested majority who are not committed one way or another. In order to effectively change opinion, communication must be directed at precisely this segment—the ambivalents, the neutrals, the undecided, and the mildly committed. The success of a propaganda effort can never be adequately judged by its ability to change the opinions of the interested who have already decided. The success of propaganda must be judged by its ability to reach and affect the middle group.

The above analysis has several implications of immediate utility for predicting the success or failure of an attempt to change public opinion. First, its success depends on the strength of the supporting leaders relative to the strength of the opposing leaders. Second, it depends on the availability of tactics for undermining the positions of the opposing leaders; the use of interpersonal relations seems to be necessary at some stage of the process in order to offset the entirely one-way direction of the mass media which can create a false impression of implied consent among recipients. Third, its success is directly related to the balance between the number of citizens who are neutral or only mildly committed, and the number who intensely favor versus those who are intensely opposed. Often, people who attempt to predict voting behavior and who attempt to change it ignore the most crucial factor, the *intensity* of the views of the persons who are solicited and the stability of their opinions over a period of time. Public opinion polls which do not report intensity, or commitment to an opinion, can provide a misleading picture of the possibility of changing opinion.

The Structure of Internal Communication

Communication within an organization has much in common with the mass communication networks already discussed. Internal communication, however, is complicated by the existence of established communication procedures unique to formal organizations.

The characteristics of a particular internal communication network depend on the number of channels, their overlap and clarity, their ease of access, the normal and variable volume of communication through them, and their form of pattern. Many of these characteristics are difficult to estimate in practice; it is difficult to know, for example, where a statement will end and who, other than the intended, will overhear it, or what type of information will be filtered out of the total message as it is passed on to various parties.

THE POINT OF ENTRY

The point at which information enters an organization will be considered the point of departure in the communication process. "By virtue of specialization," March and Simon observe, "most information enters an organization at highly specific points." [46] The significance of this is that subordinates quite often have more direct acquaintance with the basic organizational functions than do their supervisors, who frequently get their information second-hand. The dependence of supervisors on subordinates for information automatically gives subordinates more influence and discretion over their work than they are legitimately supposed to have. Janowitz and Delaney found that contrary to popular opinion, which presumes that higher officials have a "perspective," in three government agencies in Detroit such officials had less knowledge about their agencies than subordinates (although it was not as true for city agencies where officials had more contacts with local leaders). Significantly enough, the variation in knowledge was not accounted for by the level of the official's education or experience.[47] This finding suggests what effect the delegation of public and personal contacts can have on the chief executive's awareness of his own problems; yet, it is precisely these time-consuming functions that are apt to be delegated in the administrative scheme of things.

INFORMATION LAGS

Once inside the organization, the information can take one of three major routes. It can travel up and down within the hierarchy, it can travel laterally between specialized units, or it might "dead-end"—that is, be forgotten, sometimes permanently. However, the fact that it may be recalled at a later date provides an added dimension to the communication structure: the time lag. Communication moves, as Gardner states, in "fits and starts." [48] The significance of this temporal, rhythmic quality of communication so inherent to human interaction cannot be overlooked. It is responsible for communication delays that could have otherwise changed particular decisions. The fact that relevant information available within the organization might come to light only *after* a decision has been made can be a source of embarrassment and anxiety.

The problem of information lag is part of the larger problem which all subordinates face—how to determine which information is relevant to their supervisor's decisions. Short of requiring indiscriminate communication of every detail upward in the form of a daily log, the only way that a supervisor can be assured of being acquainted with all relevant information is either to tell his subordinates what he wants to know, or else they must be so closely involved with his work and his problems that they can accurately anticipate what is relevant to him. The problem is compounded by the fact that supervisors themselves may not know at the moment precisely what information will become useful to them. Moreover, supervisors will be reluctant to confide in their subordinates sufficiently to depend entirely on the subordinate's judgment of what information is relevant. Not only would this relationship be time consuming, but also it would publicize knowledge of the executives' problems which could frustrate the organization's pursuit of its legitimate goals.

THE COMMUNICATION PYRAMID

Gardner observes a striking difference between kinds of information which go up the hierarchy and kinds which go down.[49] Descriptive information and explanation for failure tend to move up the line, while direct commands move down. Some subordinates are so dependent on their supervisors for recognition that they will try to anticipate his wishes, according to Gardner; perhaps in the process they will read into his words and actions something that is not there. These distortions of communication from the top are duplicated by distortions up the line, emanating from concern for "giving the boss only what he wants." Good news moves up rapidly, but unpleasant information, and information that would reflect negatively on the subordinate's competence, tends to be filtered out. Blau, for example, reports that workers in a government agency consulted with one another rather than with their supervisors, in violation of the official rules which designated the supervisor as a consultant and advisor because the supervisor also evaluated them.[50]

Gardner concludes that because of this distortion process at each communication point, the taller the administrative structure, the more distortion will occur between the top and the bottom and the less informed will be any individual in the organization—including especially the chief executive. Automated procedures of electronic data processing will provide an incentive for even more centralization of the communications structure.

Information seems to be blocked both up and down the hierarchy. Davis reports that *upward* communication tends to be blocked about midway to the top of the organization,[51] while Campbell found that as the size of the group increased, the percentage of workers understanding the payment system in use in an organization decreased; those who did not understand became progressively less satisfied, and their output decreased.[52]

Griffiths, Clark, *et al.* report a study of the organization of one school system in which principals' meetings with the superintendent were monopolized by the superintendent.[53] There was almost no up-the-line communication at such meetings, except to supply specific requests for information. Almost half of the comments in such meetings were made by the superintendent. Most of these comments were directed to the Assistant Superintendent for Instruction. The superintendent spoke almost as often as all the participants combined, and he spoke for a longer period of time than all of the participants combined regardless of the subject discussed. In this particular school, then, the formal system did provide down-the-line communications; and often down-the-line communications were provided by semi-formal organizations, such as the Teachers Association Executive Board. The authors conclude that apparently the administrator's autonomy increased when he limited the formal communication flow to outgoing messages, but as a result his autonomy was jeopardized when incoming messages were blocked. When that happened, the communication flowed outside the bonds of formal organization channels. The result of attempting to block communication up the line stimulated a number of internal pressure groups that operated outside of the formal channels.

Communication between supervisors and their subordinates is further complicated by the differences in their perspectives from the different positions they hold. Roethlisberger states: "The top of the organization is trying to communicate with the bottom in terms of the logical jargon and cold discriminations of the technical specialist, the engineer, the accountant, etc. . . . The bottom, in turn, instead of transmitting successfully its fears to social dislocation, conveys to the top emotional expressions of petty grievances and excessive demands." [54] These demands and grievances may be perceived by the supervisor as normal "griping." Since the gripe characteristically concerns petty grievance, it is easily dismissed. However, the importance of the "gripe" is not the petty grievance that it happens to deal with, but the more fundamental problem at which it is probably aimed. Generally speaking, an increased volume of "griping" is a good indication that subordinates' communication with their supervisors has been blocked in the formal channels.

Department heads, curriculum supervisors, assistant principals, and other line executives each function as mediators between the different perspectives of their subordinates and their supervisors. Because of their intermediate positions, these "middle-men" face built-in dilemmas concerning their own identity and loyalty. The supervisor who must work with his subordinates in order to gain their confidence may become so close to them that he cannot carry out the orders of his own supervisors with full force. If, however, he attempts to identify primarily with his superiors, he alienates himself from his own subordinates. The successful supervisor understands both the formal and the informal communication structure and the channels which are effective.

CHANNEL USAGE

The number of channels of information in an organization tends to be stable. March and Simon propose that a channel used for one purpose will be used for others.[55] Some channels tend to be used for general purpose communication. Formal communication structures, in particular, may be used for communicating personal information and other information irrelevant to the work. One factor which minimizes the number of specialized channels is suggested by Homans, who proposes that every new channel threatens to by-pass those who are in the established channels; new channels are, in other words, status threats.[56]

Whether a formal channel or an informal one (or both) will be used for a particular message depends on a number of considerations. One is the importance of the information for the job relative to its importance for the informal status system; this in turn depends on how well established the informal system is. Another consideration is the amount of time pressure. In periods of crises, the number of channels used by top executives will be reduced and the channels that remain will be overloaded. Information that is relevant to decisions that must be made quickly will probably follow the informal and strictly local channels.[57]

The volume of communication, like the number of channels, also fluctuates with periods of crisis. During a crisis there is a tendency for personnel to withdraw from responsibility by claiming that decisions are beyond their discretion. This withdrawal tendency, or buck-passing, tends to spread up the hierarchy. It fractures the organization into a series of passive, self-contained groups. Thus, while the volume of communication tends to increase during periods of crisis, the number of "links" that must exist between units is expanded so rapidly by this fracturing process and by the reluctance of each group to act, that the total communication process loses effectiveness during such periods.[58]

March and Simon advance several hypotheses concerning the volume of communication within established communication networks. They propose first that less structured and undefined activities place the heaviest burdens on the communication system. Also, the usage of a channel, they propose, is directly related to the channel's efficiency.[59] It may be added that several other conditions determine the rate at which a channel is used besides its efficiency. Organizations which attempt to pursue a number of goals simultaneously, and those which are expected to satisfy demands from the general community, may have a higher volume of communication than organizations with the opposite characteristics. Simpson and Gulley classified over 200 voluntary associations on the basis of these two characteristics into "focused" and "diffuse" (in terms of number of goals), and "internal" and "external" (in terms of involvement of the association with the community).[60] It was found that diffuse-external associations (those with many goals trying to satisfy the community) placed greatest emphasis on maintaining channels of internal communication—that is, educating members as to objectives, keeping members informed, and membership keeping leaders informed. Focused-internal associations placed the least emphasis on maintaining these internal channels. It is also worth noting that diffuse-external associations were less centralized and scored highest in membership involvement.

LATERAL COMMUNICATION LINES

Communication is also structured along lateral lines, especially between specialized communication units. Among such communication units identified by March and Simon are those for transmission (messenger services and switchboard), record-keeping (bookkeeping), research units, and filing sections.[61] The fact that lateral communication lines are usually shorter and often connected directly to the chief executive, directs specialized information *between* each of these specialized communication units; the communication of information to the chief executive is likely to be primarily in one direction.

As mentioned previously, the persons who operate such communication centers have a strategic place of importance beyond their official rank, for they are responsible for determining which messages to send on, their priority, and the most desirable channels to use. These people, curiously, often are not specifically trained to make such decisions, and the fact that they perform these functions may not even be officially recognized.

THE FUNCTIONS OF INTERNAL
COMMUNICATIONS SYSTEMS

Communication within organizations performs a number of recognizable functions. There is, first of all, evidence that the rate of communication in the public schools is positively related to the morale of both teachers and administrators.[62] Also, one study reports that school principals who communicated more with staff members were more effective than those who communicated less.[63]

McCleery's study of administrative changes in a prison indicates that communications systems are bases of power and authority.[64] Traditionally, the prison had been authoritarian; custody had been its major goal. The lines of official communication were all channeled through the custodial office (that is, guards and their immediate supervisors). The reports and recommendations of the custodial staff were approved routinely by the warden's office, which was completely dependent for its information on the custodial staff. This control of the communications system permitted the custodial force to adapt the institution to its convenience and to control the inmate society whose welfare was completely dependent upon the custodial staffs' reports to the warden. The informal hierarchy of the inmate society was also derived from the custodial staffs' monopoly over communication. For, since prison officials operated in secrecy, those inmates who had "connections" with the custodial force could predict where force would fall and provide or withhold warnings. Moreover, since communication was monopolized, newcomers to the inmate society were completely dependent on "old cons" for guidance in "learning the ropes."

Then the prison administration changed. The new administration sought to implement liberal reform and educational policies. By instituting published statements of rules and policy, prisonwide committees, open-door administrative policies, discussion sessions between officials and inmates, and a prison newspaper, communication was increased. Prisoners obtained access to information that had previously been secret, and the monopoly of the custodial staff and of the informal inmate organization was broken. Inmates were less subject to their own informal leaders and to the guards. Guards were obliged to rely on force to control inmates, and newcomers could challenge the position of the "old cons" whose monopoly over the knowledge was also eroded.

Apparently, then, the pattern of communication not only shapes the formal system, but it underlies the informal one as well. As the number of channels of information are increased, the opportunity to exert leadership is broadened and the influence of young persons is increased. Free exchange of information diminishes the significance of "contacts" and undermines persons who have built "special" positions for themselves. In this sense, increasing communication is democratizing. Such changes will noticeably be resisted, not only by the officials who benefit by monopolizing information, but also by subordinates whose positions are dependent on their superiors. From a pragmatic viewpoint, this implies that it is potentially within the power of administrative officials to support or undermine the positions of those below them by manipulating the volume and number of communication channels.

The most obvious function of internal communication is to coordinate the organization's activity. The greater the efficiency of the communication, the more specialization and interdependence can be tolerated. It follows that the extent to which bureaucracy, or centralized authority, can develop is dependent on the efficiency of the communication system. In this sense, the degree of "bureaucracy" is a direct function of the ability to communicate. The early schools in America were forced to decentralize under local control by default, because there was no communication system available to coordinate the many relatively isolated areas within a state or a district. Central city offices, and later state and federal offices, became possible only as the efficiency of communication increased. Thus, the development of educational administration has directly paralleled the development of modern communication devices. For similar reasons, access to communication channels sets the limits of the official hierarchy within a particular school system. The system cannot expand much beyond the limits of the communication facilities between top and bottom.

But while it is obvious that the effectiveness of centralized authority systems depends on the efficiency of communication, it is perhaps less obvious that the effective operation of *decentralized* systems is just as dependent on effective communication. For, in the case of decentralized systems, units that are not otherwise integrated by official rules must still cooperate. That is to say, well-established and routine administrative systems can get by on a minimum of communication, if necessary, because they can fall back on established procedure and rules. But between semi-autonomous, decentralized units this established procedure is not available to fall back on. While decentralization may seem to reduce the need for *official* and directive communication, it does not negate the need for unofficial and informational communication for the purpose of coordination in the system. In fact that need is enhanced in some respects. The decentralization of elementary, junior high, and senior high schools will not mean that there will be less need for communication between them. On the contrary, the preservation of some kind of coordination can be accomplished in a decentralized system only if the self-direction of each unit is based on accurate information transmitted between the units.

And this is the dilemma. For, it is between these semiautonomous units that communication channels seem to be most feeble, and where communication breaks down most easily; school officials are so accustomed to communicating through official lines of authority that they feel little compunction to communicate systematically outside of them. The lack of articulation that can result in decentralized units is evident between high schools and colleges and between junior high and elementary levels, where teachers at each level sometimes refuse to speak to one another about coordinating their efforts. Establishing efficient lines of communication between decentralized units without imposing upon them an official enforcement authority structure that would violate the concept of decentralization is the problem in complex organizations.

SUMMARY

The conditions surrounding the flow of information through a system are extremely complex. As this chapter has pointed out, both formal and informal channels carry information throughout an organization as well as into, and out of it. Moreover, information is always affected in a variety of ways by its source, the culture itself, and the nature of the situation existing at any moment in time.

Today's school administrator is expected to manage an organization in which the quantity and quality of information is continually expanding. His success may indeed depend on his ability to cope with this "information environment." It is certainly true that decision-making, the subject of the following chapter and a process itself dependent on information, is sometimes made more difficult due to the greater speed, and greater numbers of channels now available through which information passes.

BIBLIOGRAPHY AND NOTES

1. Educational Policies Commission, *Mass Communication and Education.* Washington, D.C.: National Education Association, 1958, p. 116.
2. E. M. Rogers, *Diffusion of Innovations.* Glencoe, Ill.: The Free Press, 1961, Ch. 2.
3. D. Riesman, *Constraint and Variety in American Education.* New York: Doubleday Anchor, 1958 (copyright 1956, University of Nebraska Press).
4. Rogers, *op. cit.*
5. M. B. Miles, "Educational Innovation: Resources, Strategies, and Unanswered Questions," *The American Behavioral Scientist,* Vol. 7, 1964, pp. 8–25.
6. R. O. Carlson, *Executive Succession and Organizational Change: Place Bound and Career Bound Superintendents of Schools.* Chicago: Midwest Administration Center, University of Chicago, 1962.
7. Cited by Rogers, *op. cit.*
8. Rogers, *op. cit.*
9. D. H. Ross, *Administration for Adaptability.* New York: Metropolitan School Study Council, Teachers College, Columbia University, 1958, p. 15.
10. R. O. Carlson, *Adoption of Educational Innovations.* Eugene, Ore.: Center for the Advanced Study of Educational Administration, University of Oregon, 1965, p. 63.
11. M. Janowitz, D. Wright, and W. Delaney, "Public Administration and the Public," in *Complex Organizations,* A. Etzioni, ed. New York: Holt, Rinehart & Winston, 1961, pp. 277–85.
12. O. Larsen and R. Hill, "A Mass Media and Interpersonal Communications in the Diffusion of a News Event," *American Sociological Review,* vol. 19, 1954, pp. 426–33.
13. L. A. Haak, "The General Public and the Public Schools," *Administrator's Notebook,* vol. 4, 1956, pp. 1–4.
14. R. F. Carter, *Voters and Their Schools.* Palo Alto, Calif.: Institute for Communication Research, Stanford University, 1960.
15. P. H. Rossi, *The Publics of Local Schools.* Cambridge, Mass.: Graduate School of Education, Harvard University Staff Research Memo No. 2, September, 1954.
16. J. M. Skipton, *Who Are the Critics of the Public Schools?* Cambridge, Mass.: Graduate School of Education, Harvard University, Staff Research Memo, No. 3, September, 1954, p. 96.

17. R. F. Carter and W. G. Savard, *Influence of Voter Turnout on School Board and Tax Elections,* Office of Education, Cooperative Research Monograph No. 5. Washington, D.C.: U.S. Government Printing Office, 1961.

18. W. Albig, *Public Opinion.* New York: McGraw-Hill, 1939, pp. 36, 48.

19. B. Berelson, "What 'Missing the Newspaper' Means," in *Communications Research, 1948–1949,* P. F. Lazarsfeld and F. N. Stanton, eds. New York: Harper, 1949, pp. 111–129.

20. D. J. Luck, *What Michigan Newspapers Tell About the Schools.* East Lansing: Michigan Communications Study, Michigan State College, 1954.

21. W. G. Monahan, "Michigan School News in Michigan Newspapers," *Michigan Journal of Secondary Education,* vol. 5, no. 3, 1964, p. 49.

22. M. S. Haught, "An Analysis of Public School News Content in Oklahoma Newspapers," unpublished doctoral thesis, University of Oklahoma, 1965, pp. 63–66.

23. E. L. Hartley and R. E. Hartley, *Fundamentals of Social Psychology.* New York: Knopf, 1952, p. 189.

24. N. Gross, *The Schools and the Press.* New England School Development Council, January, 1956.

25. R. Carter, "The Press and Public School Superintendents in California," *Journalism Quarterly,* Spring, 1954, pp. 175–185.

26. J. M. Foskett, "Differential Discussions of School Affairs," *Phi Delta Kappan,* vol. 37, 1956, pp. 311–15.

27. Gross, *op. cit.*

28. *Ibid.*

29. Albig, *op. cit.,* pp. 42–46.

30. P. F. Lazarsfeld and R. K. Merton, "Mass Communication, Popular Taste, and Organized Social Action," *The Communication of Ideas,* T. Bryson, ed. New York: Harper, 1948, pp. 95–118; reprinted in *Readings in Social Psychology,* G. Swanson, T. Newcomb and E. Hartley, eds. New York: Holt, 1952.

31. Gross, *op. cit.,* p. 42.

32. Cf. J. T. Klopper and C. Y. Glock, "Trial by Newspaper," and M. Millspough, "Trial by Mass Media" *Public Opinion and Propaganda,* D. Katz, D. Cartwright, S. Eldersveld, and A. M. Lee, eds. New York: Dryden Press, 1954, pp. 105 ff. and 115 ff.

33. J. Fourastie, *The Cause of Wealth* (T. Caplaw, trans.). Glencoe, Ill.: Free Press, 1960, p. 229.

34. Lazarsfeld and Merton, *op. cit.;* this section develops some ideas suggested by their discussion.

35. R. G. Corwin, *A Sociology of Education.* New York: Appleton-Century-Crofts, 1965.

36. *Ibid.*

37. *Ibid.,* pp. 78, 79.

38. W. L. Warner and W. E. Henry, *The Radio Day Time Serial, a Symbolic Analysis.* Provincetown, Mass.: Journal Press, 1948.

39. *Mass Communication and Education, op. cit.,* p. 76.

40. S. M. Lipset, "Opinion Formation in a Crises Situation," *Public Opinion Quarterly,* vol. 17, 1953, pp. 20–46.

41. S. J. Eldersveld and R. W. Dodge, "Personal Contact or Mail Propaganda? An Experiment in Voting Turnout and Attitude Change," *Public Opinion and Propaganda,* D. Katz et al., eds. New York: Dryden Press, 1954, pp. 532–42.

42. M. J. Taves and R. G. Corwin, *Role Conception and Recruiting Appeals; An Experimental Attempt to Change the Image of Nursing of High School Girls,* unpublished research monograph.

43. R. T. Schanck, "Test-Tube for Public Opinion: A Rural Community," *Public*

Opinion and Propaganda, D. Katz *et al.*, eds. New York: Dryden Press, 1954, pp. 598–601.

44. *Ibid.*
45. *Ibid.*
46. J. G. March and H. A. Simon, *Organizations*. New York: Wiley, 1958, p. 185.
47. M. Janowitz and W. Delaney, "The Bureaucrat and the Public: A Study of Informational Perspectives," *Administrative Science Quarterly*, vol. 2, 1957, pp. 141–162.
48. B. B. Gardner, *Human Relations in Industry*. Chicago: Richard D. Irwin, 1945, p. 34.
49. *Ibid.*, pp. 26–27.
50. P. M. Blau, *Dynamics of Bureaucracy*. Chicago: Univ. Chicago Press, 1955.
51. K. Davis, "A Method of Studying Communication Patterns in Organizations," *Personnel Psychology*, vol. 6, 1953, pp. 301–312.
52. H. Campbell, "Group Incentive Pay Schemes," *Occupational Psychology*, vol. 26, 1952, pp. 15–21.
53. D. Griffiths, D. L. Clark *et al.*, *Organizing Schools for Effective Education*. Danville, Ill.: Interstate Printers & Publishers, 1963.
54. F. J. Roethlisberger, *Management and Morale*. Cambridge, Mass.: Harvard Univ. Press, 1941, p. 63.
55. March and Simon, *op. cit.*, p. 169; cf. also C. F. Hermann, "Some Consequences of Crises Which Limit the Viability of Organizations," *Administrative Science Quarterly*, vol. 8, 1962, pp. 61–82.
56. G. C. Homans, *The Human Group*. New York: Harcourt, Brace, 1950, p. 461.
57. March and Simon, *op. cit.*
58. Hermann, *op. cit.*
59. March and Simon, *op. cit.*, pp. 164, 167.
60. R. T. Simpson and W. H. Gulley, "Goals, Environmental Pressures and Organizational Characteristics," *American Sociological Review*, vol. 27, 1962, pp. 344–51.
61. March and Simon, *op. cit.*, p. 167.
62. D. L. Arnold, "Morale as Influence by Participation in Group Planning and Action," *Educational Research Bulletin*, vol. 32, 1953, pp. 202–211; also F. S. Barry and R. Lonsdale, "Influences Upon Administrative Morale," *The School Executive*, October, 1956, pp. 76–77.
63. D. O. Clark, "Critical Areas in the Administrative Behavior of High School Principals," unpublished doctoral dissertation, Ohio State University, 1956.
64. R. McCleery, "Communication Patterns as Bases of Systems of Authority and Power," Theoretical Studies in Social Organization of the Prison, Pamphlet 15. New York: Social Science Council, March, 1960.

CHAPTER

5

Characteristics of the Decision-Making Process

> . . . No administrator can simultaneously plan the textbooks, invent the television monitor, and design the classroom seats. But he can make his influence felt in the shaping of ways in which education is to proceed to a greater degree than it has been felt in the past. For the key decisions which make development real instead of oratorical have to be made by the educational administrator.[1]

THE DECISION process is a crucial part of any organization. From one viewpoint "organization" *is* a program of decisions made recurrently and concurrently at all levels and within the confines of past decisions; "leadership" is the act of making and implementing decisions; the "character" of the organization is a symptom of the nature of the decision-making process; finally internal strains are largely a result of discrepancies in authority and power to make decisions which often occur between professionals and administrators, between line and staff, and between community and organization.

The Formal Process of Decision-Making

Decisions do not occur in a vacuum. There is an orderly process to decision making. Griffiths states that, "Decision making is the process which one goes through in order to be able to pass judgment and terminate a controversy." [2]

INDECISION

Not making decisions is often as important as making them. There are probably many more reasons why an issue does not get decided than why it does. As Barnard suggests, the question may not be pertinent; or if it is it may not be pertinent now; or if it is pertinent now it may be delayed while awaiting further information; or the person asked to consider it is not competent or has not the authority to decide.[3]

Barnard suggests that questions posed by superiors to subordinates are more likely to be decided than questions posed by subordinates to superiors. But questions which the executive poses for himself to decide are the most likely to be ignored, for when questions are pressed from below or above, others have granted the administrator the authority to decide; but decisions which he initiates may be questioned.[4]

THE LOGIC OF DECISION-MAKING

In defining the decision-making process, several writers have described the process as a series of steps. Griffiths presents the steps as: "(1) Recognize, define, and limit the problem. (2) Analyze and evaluate the problem. (3) Establish criteria or standards by which a solution will be evaluated or judged as acceptable and adequate to the need. (4) Collect data. (5) Formulate and select the preferred solution or solutions. (6) Put into effect the preferred solution."[5]

This mechanically defined step procedure breaks down in practice, however, because administrators are not all equally adept at recognizing the need for decision. A problem to one administrator is not regarded as a problem to another. In addition, the perception of problems is related to one's knowledge regarding the area of the problem. A superintendent with a limited perception of his role and little or poor communication may fail to realize that things "aren't going well" until the teachers threaten to strike. In contrast, the superintendent who is concerned about good staff relations and communications is continually alert for problems of conflict and makes many decisions to correct situations which may lead to internal strife. According to Griffiths this is the reason why it is not possible to develop skill in decision-making *per se;* instead, ". . . one must develop skill in making decisions about something in particular."[6]

According to Griffiths the second step (analyzing and evaluating a problem) is where the problem is "sized up." This is the point at which such questions are asked as: What does this problem mean to me? What does this problem mean to the school system? What can I do about it? What do I want to do about it? or, Is this a problem on which no decision should be made?

At this point it is evident that the solution to a problem will be in terms of the decision-maker's perception, knowledge, and value system.

Griffiths regards the value system of the decision-maker as especially significant in determining the degree and nature of the action taken on a problem.[7] For instance, some people in a community may be very vocal in expressing their desire for an expanded vocational program in their high school. The final decision depends to a great extent on how the superintendent and board of education view those who are making the request, the need in relation to the existing program, the desires of the student body, the factors connected with facilities and finances, the future development of the community, and so on. These would all be tempered by the professional background and experience of the board of education members as well.

The ability to analyze potential conflict situations is an especially important skill for which all administrators will find repeated use. One source provides guidelines for the analysis and evaluation of differences of opinion. First, it is necessary to identify the nature of the differences of opinion as they develop among segments of the staff; the differences may be attributed to differences of facts, or to differences of goals, methods, and values. Second, the underlying cause of the difference may be investigated; it may be due to differential access to information, different perceptions of the same information, or different interests due to special roles which the disputants occupy within the organization. Finally, the stage of evolution of the conflict needs to be evaluated. Among the several possible stages are: (1) anticipation of conflict as proposals are advocated; (2) conscious but unexpressed differences, as small clusters of persons talk about the proposal openly among themselves; (3) open discussion where information is sought and decisions are implicitly challenged; (4) open dispute; and (5) open conflict where people become committed and identified with a position.[8]

The nature, cause, and stage of the dispute, in turn, influence the action that can be effectively taken toward it. For example, an "information campaign" would be effective only where the difference is a factual one caused by differential access to information, and where the dispute has not yet reached the stage of open conflict. When the cause stems from the disputant's different roles in the organization, perhaps the conflict can be alleviated only by redistributing scarce resources or decision-making power. If the conflict has reached the open stage, reassignment of personnel and functions may be one of the few available alternatives.

This third step of establishing the criteria by which the solutions will be evaluated is quite crucial. It is here where the value systems of the individual or the organization are again brought into play. Decision-makers always function in a framework of variegated values; personal values, cultural values, and the values of the organization itself add subtle but complex dimensions to the conflict. Decisions aimed toward settling disputes between teachers and parents, or among teachers, or between supervisors and subordinates, are rendered difficult by virtue of the values which anchor the disputants' positions. And, of course, the values themselves may be in conflict. But where some institutions may develop quite irrelevant procedures for dealing with conflicts so that fundamental value issues can either be obscured or somehow evaded, schools are uniquely unable to employ such gambits effectively. Broudy has expressed this unique difficulty succinctly:

". . . the administrator of the educational institution is not in quite the same position as the administrator of other social institutions. The business administrator can fall back on the principle: business is business, and the politician can fall back on the principle that good politics is what keeps the party in power. The educator, however, deals with nothing but values—human beings who are clusters and constellations of value potentials. Nothing human is really alien to the educational enterprise and there is, therefore, something incongruous about educational administrators evading fundamental value conflicts. A lapse in moral integrity that in a businessman or a politician or a lawyer is merely deplored in an educator becomes intolerable. The public will never quite permit the educational administrator the moral latitude that it affords some of its other servants. For to statesmen and soldiers men entrust their lives and fortunes, but to the schools they entrust their precarious hold on humanity itself.[9]

In deciding about important problems—curriculum planning, personnel, school, and community relations—legal and social values must be viewed before coming to the final decision. Griffiths states, "In a sense, a decision on criteria and standards must be made prior to the major decision."[10] This substantiates the fact that the decision-making process is a sequential one.

After a problem has been defined as to its workable limits, relevant data upon which the decision can be made must be made available. These data come from a variety of sources, and at times more are collected than can be used. However, the situation is often such that time will not allow data to be collected. For example, when a breakdown occurs in the central heating system of a school building, ideally there should be an investigation followed by a report and possibly, if the cost of repairs will be quite high, the work should be let on a bid basis. However, this procedure would take time which can be costly by affecting the unity of the school system through dismissing pupils in just one school. Furthermore, additional damage could result to the building as a result of lack of heat. This means that shortage of time will not allow the proper data to be collected. The course of action often taken in a problem of this nature is to call the first available repairman and give him the instructions, "Fix it as quickly as possible." Also, some problems in a complex organization are so technical that participation in making decisions is automatically limited, even though there is ample time and the decision will affect everyone.

Also, some decisions may revolve around a new situation in which there has been little experience and for which data are not available. Here again the situation is such that the final decision may have to be delayed for a while. The collection of relevant data also may vary from an exact step procedure inasmuch as those involved may not recognize which data are relevant.

The decision-making process involves considering several alternative solutions and predicting the results of each. Dubin says, "A central problem for organizational decision-makers is to choose between maintaining the systems of action 'as is,' or changing them in desirable and feasible directions by desirable and feasible amounts. This may be called the 'context facet' of organization decision-making." [11] It would be ideal if all possible solutions could be analyzed in terms of predicting the results. However, the factors bearing on decisions of schools are so varied and complex that it is difficult to anticipate the results of all alternatives at the present stage of administrative science. This is illustrated by a problem which plagues many school administrators today: where should new school buildings be located? Since the life of a school building exceeds fifty years, predictions must be made regarding birth rate, mobility of population, housing development, and industrial and business development. Many factors affecting each one of these categories can alter the predicted pattern upon which the final decision was made. The gross underestimations of population growth made by demographers during the early forties is enough reason for caution in making such decisions.

One alternative already mentioned is the decision to do nothing, or not to make a decision. Likewise, Griffiths points out that multiple solutions may be satisfactory at times. In speaking of the decision-maker, Griffiths states, "He predicts the consequences on the basis of what he knows of the solution's probabilities of success. Some of these probabilities can be stated mathematically, but more often they must be approximated. This is certainly true in school administration, where the superintendent can only approximate in a very rough way the probable success of a chosen path of action." [12]

The selection of the one preferred solution logically follows the step of analyzing several alternatives. This is not an isolated process, for the final selection comes about only as a result of several subdecisions. To illustrate, prior to making the final decision whether to establish a new program in a school, such as remedial reading, many factors would need to be considered and decided upon. Some of the considerations would be: Is there a need for this service? How will this service be coordinated with the new program? Is there any community bias which would affect the success of the program? What qualifications will be required of the teachers? How many teachers would be needed? Is the financial aspect of the school such that the program can be adopted? Will there be a classroom problem? These constitute just some, but not all, of the considerations which would involve making subdecisions prior to the final decision.

The matter of how one decision is selected from several alternatives is not yet understood. One nonstatistical approach has been presented by Cartwright and Festinger where the valence concept is theorized as the basis of decision-making.[13]

The final step in the process of decision-making is anticipating the consequences of the decision. This usually calls for numerous additional minor decisions. Griffiths points out that this further emphasizes the sequential nature of the decision process.[14]

Decisions are formulated to guide the activities of the school. To bring this action about, an administrator must introduce, define, and gain teacher support. The communication of decisions is often ignored or poorly performed. "All too often," Simon says, "plans are 'ordered' into effect without any consideration of the manner in which they can be brought to influence the behavior of the individual members of the group."[15]

Although organizations attempt to secure authority for their executives (through titles, salary differential, control of resources, and so on), it is partially true that, "executive decisions carry authority only when the subordinate accepts them and permits them to influence his activities."[16] People generally like to have some part in the decision which affects them, and therefore it is more effective when domination is reduced to a minimum.[17] If subordinates must comply, they prefer complying to a co-operatively developed rule. Since this is less impersonal, the feeling of being subservient is not so great. This is not to say, however, that subordinates generally reject decisions of their superiors. Subordinates often want the system clarified and will subscribe to the decisions of superiors if they do not seriously distort their own basic roles.

The Decision Environment

The actual decision process, however, should not be confused with the *logic* of making decisions. These logical phases do not, in themselves, entirely capture the essential characteristics of decision-making. The logic of ends-means relationships is, of course, one basis of many decisions. But most decisions are probably as immediately determined by the exigencies of the external environment as they are by calculating logic; for the daily pressures of the environment impinges on leaders as realistically and often more effectively than logical relations between means and ends. It is true that such questions as definition of purpose, clarity of lines of authority, and the relation of actions to goals are logical parts of the decision process. But the basic decision often concerns the question of which of these logics are to be *compromised* in the face of uncontrollable or unforeseen circumstances.

Even where logic *is* stressed consistently (rather than expediency, the force of circumstances, irrational emotions, or blind faith), it is difficult for the executive to be completely "logical," because the consequences of a decision often cannot be assessed beforehand. The outcome of a decision is so involved with other decisions, the decisions of other organizations and others in the outside environment, uncontrollable changes, and long time-spans required to assess the eventual outcome, that it may be virtually impossible to evaluate the reasonableness of one choice over another.

With reference to this problem, Bennis has pointed out that an executive is almost literally forced to resort to informal communication in order to assess a decision. He states: "The decision-maker . . . faced with no operable means for evaluating a decision—as is often the case—and with limited data, has no other recourse than to utilize a group, both as a security operation and as a validity tester." [18] He goes on to say that such a method may not be the most effective but it is psychologically functional. Decisions about which courses to add to the curriculum have been necessarily based on many of these factors.

There are at least five types of commitments which influence any decision: (1) internal traditions, (2) formal commitments to outside organizations, (3) pressures from the outside, (4) past decisions, and (5) existing relationships between personnel. The first three of these have been or will be discussed elsewhere. It should be sufficient to recall that the alternatives available to an organization are sharply delimited by the values of the community, competition for limited resources, delegation practices, conceptions of organizational justice, and commitments to the public and to personnel.

COMMITMENTS TO THE OUTSIDE

Decisions that affect the organization's relations with the external environment are often more important than those concerning problems of internal coordination, because they extend the scope of the organization's commitments beyond its sphere of control and affect its external support. For this reason the administrator's importance is much less dependent on his internal coordinating functions than on how his decisions commit the organization to outsiders. However, for similar reasons, any personnel whose relations with outsiders are such that their decisions either commit the organization or provide it with outside support are important within the organization.

PAST DECISIONS

Each decision involves the selection of an alternative. Once made, the decision sets a precedent and necessitates an entire chain of other decisions, which commit the organization to an irrevocable line of action which further limits future alternatives.[19] To help prevent this restrictive aspect of decisions, they are sometimes purposely repeated to avoid any long-term commitments. For example, contracts may be signed annually even when teachers are seldom released, and teaching schedules are often rearranged each semester despite obvious regularity of assignments in classes, hours, and rooms in most cases. Reconsideration of the schedule at frequent intervals maintains the option of change in favor of the organization which then maintains control over favorable assignments and, therefore, the informal reward system.

Even after an organization's purposes have changed, its former commitments may handicap the fulfillment of its new goals. For example, in a community where teachers were frequently hired on the basis of their personal character and connections and their loyalty to community traditions rather than on training and teaching competence, a new superintendent's efforts to stress impersonal hiring criteria in order to raise teaching standards may be resisted by the board and staff as well as by the local Teachers College. The decisions that are currently feasible, in other words, are severely circumscribed by previous decisions. In the same way it can be expected that earlier decisions of public school educators to stress limited goals of literacy and the "three R's," and, more recently, social adjustment, will handicap current efforts to reorient public schools toward more strenuous scholastic goals.

EXISTING PERSONNEL RELATIONS

Because subordinates are personally affected by their superiors' decisions, they seek to influence them. For example, Kingsley reports that after a change in political party in England, top-line governmental subordinates made proposals to top officials which were primarily designed to maintain the stability of their own departments and their positions within them.[20] They were able to convince the cabinet officials that those proposed changes which threatened their status were too difficult, impractical, or impossible to implement. The resistance of civil service subordinates to proposed changes delayed reforms. In turn, the longer the new government delayed making policy changes, the more it became responsible for the old practices, which made it even more difficult to reverse policy.

Similarly, a school system is not likely to implement basic changes simply by electing a new school board or appointing a new superintendent. Administrative subordinates and teachers have a great deal of power to sabotage any program they do not approve, regardless of whether it is explicitly "democratically" administered. In one school system, for example, a principal sought repeatedly to institute a "half-day curriculum" of four-hour courses once a week, which would give teachers time to take classes on field trips and cover subject matter in a period other than the traditional fifty-minute time segments. He was successfully resisted by teachers because it threatened to increase their workload, to upset their organization of time, and to increase their administrative chores.[21]

School personnel are in some respects competitors seeking recognition for their ideas and skills. As Bryson aptly observes, "In practical matters, the question almost always gets settled, but it is a man and not an opinion that wins . . . the administrator is not only choosing among alternatives; he is inescapably choosing among advocates as well." [22] In this setting, administrative decisions are not simply "rational" in the narrow sense of that term; the decisions that are made are not compelled by the most "efficient" means to an end.

The fact that the existing personnel relations are normally structured along hierarchical lines presents an even more fundamental dilemma for decision-making. The problem is that the characteristics of the hierarchy which make it useful for coordination tend to restrict the opportunities for group consultation in decision-making. As Blau and Scott state, "But the very mechanism through which hierarchical differentiation improves coordination—restricting and directing the flow of communication—is what impedes problem-solving." [23] Democracy, Blau has observed elsewhere, is based on the principle of "freedom of dissent" which is inimical to the principle of efficiency on which bureaucracy is based. All attempts to rely on the participation of those closest to the problems reverses the normal subordinate-superior relationship. It requires interaction between superiors and subordinates on a colleague basis, which the social barriers normally preclude, and it places the superior in the position of receiving advice from his subordinates, which reverses the normal process. And yet, Pelz reports evidence that consultation with persons whose orientation differs from one's own is associated with the most effective problem-solving.[24] The need for internal coordination and the maintenance of the authority system both prohibit excessive communication and argument among persons who disagree, but disagreement may contribute to problem-solving.

Decision-Making as a Bargaining Process

There is more than one locus of decision-making power. In an illuminating discussion, Cert and March repeat what should not need repeating, that others besides the executives in an organization have goals and demands.[25] They suggest that the decision process be reviewed as a *bargaining* process (rather than a series of steps exercised by a single locus of authority). In the bargaining process, both sides make demands which require modification of basic organizational policy and, perhaps eventually, modification of its goals. Thus, it is clear that many decisions are not made with an eye on the official goals, but rather they are made in order to pacify elements within the organization who have goals of their own.

Cert and March further emphasize that these decisions do not occur within a static environment where the goals are fixed, but they take place in a changing context. The concept "organizational slack" which they introduce suggests the nature of the change: one part of the organization changes at a different rate than other parts, creating "lag" or "slack." For example, they ask, what happens when the rate of expansion in an organization outruns the current level of aspiration? More top positions become available than there are people to fill them. The decision is whether to retain the present operation and incur a staff shortage or whether to increase the rewards for the position, and perhaps eliminate other functions (For example, athletics or drivers' education) in order to do this. Thus, the real decision is which goal to sacrifice. It is not entirely clear what "goals" the administrator will use in making that decision or, indeed, whether he has the *power* to make it. For example, in a time of shortage of physics teachers, they are being paid on a uniform salary schedule around the nation at a rate equivalent to the drivers' education and Latin teachers, despite the fact that physics teachers can command a much higher market price outside education than many other teachers who are being "overpaid," according to demand for their skills elsewhere. Does the decision to pay teachers at a uniform rate imply that all educational functions are of equivalent value? Or were the official goals actually taken into account? Can the administrator, in fact, change the decision, or is he forced to abide by it by other than logical concerns—for example, the power of teachers' unions?

Cert and March see each member of the organization with a "disorganized file case full of demands," only a small number of which are stressed at a point in time.[26] This raises the question: what causes certain goals of members and officials to be stressed at a point in time? And what events shift the demands—for example, for salary as opposed to tenure and autonomy? They conclude that because no one set of demands is stressed uniformly, inconsistent goals can exist simultaneously by stressing each goal at different times and limiting attention to one at a time. If there are inconsistent goals, it is by no means apparent that decisions can or will be consistent over time. Consistency of decisions can be achieved only by eliminating some of the goals, many of which the organization may be reluctant to give up. Thus, schools have been able to retain a multitude of goals—from scholarship and critical thinking to character training, citizenship, vocational training, and social adjustment—by stressing each at various times and places and by alternating negligence of goals with their emphasis at appropriate periods of time. Thus, for a while social adjustment is stressed, until the pendulum swings toward scholarship, and then ultimately to another aspect of the program. Decision-making takes on a cyclical, rotary character, which is to be expected in the complex, inconsistent world with which the modern school system must cope.

Involving the Staff

One of the prevalent myths about decision-making is that the decisions are made by "the executive." On the contrary, all levels of personnel participate in the process to some degree.

THE COMMITTEE SYSTEM

In complex organizations, committees usually play a prominent part of the decision-making process. Hunter points out that the great faith in committees is founded on the belief that if people can just "get together" in a meeting, most, if not all, problems will be solved.[27] There is similar faith in school boards as well.

Despite the functional necessity of committees and official boards and people's abiding faith in them, the committee is usually not the place where major problems are *resolved*. The important issues are usually discussed and compromised in advance of the meeting in off-stage, behind-the-scenes private conferences. In fact, one of the most frequent complaints of newspapermen is that in public meetings the members of school boards show unanimity which is the outcome of debate that often took place in private meetings preceding the official one. The official committee meeting is more usually the place where minor issues are discussed and where preformed conclusions are finalized. The committee is the scene of important conflicts and resolutions only where there is an indeterminate or a shifting power structure.

Functions of the Committee. However, committees have several functions. In the first place, a committee provides a stable structure for introducing problems. It provides both a place and a relevant membership to consider the problem. Second, it is a testing ground on which to assess potential interest and support for certain proposals. A small nucleus of committee members provides advance evidence of the amount of support on hand; often this is the place where issues are discarded before they are raised in more public and embarrassing ways. Third, it is an arena for testing out justifications of action. The semipublic nature of the committee forces individuals to disguise their selfish interests or illogical reasons under ideologies which legitimate their actions to the public. Fourth, committee meetings provide a communications link between dominant leaders and subleaders. They provide a setting for top leaders to solicit personal support for their programs. This communication is normally from top leaders to subleaders. The views, problems, and proposals of top leaders dominate the meetings. Subleaders are expected to lend support, and newcomers and neutrals are expected to remain silent or raise harmless questions. Excessive participation by subleaders interferes with this communications function and threatens the dominant leaders' control. If a persistent subordinate fails to recognize that committees have these public relations and status maintenance functions he will be ostracized.

This does not mean that the committee meeting serves no function for subordinates. On the contrary, in the committee meeting subordinates have an opportunity to demonstrate special skills, knowledge, and, above all, their loyalties to their superiors.

Then, committees function as semipublic arenas where a network of private contests are exposed to the final tests after preliminary bouts. Here the lines of contest are laid down, and dominant leaders publicly display to the doubtful the strength of their loyal supporters. The committee is not merely the forum for "free discussion," but it is sanctuary where free-flowing power is exercised and meets the final test without too much embarrassment.

DECENTRALIZED AUTHORITY

Within this partially hostile decision-making environment, the chief administrator can hardly afford to be a man of leisure who sits back dreaming up new ideas and issuing arbitrary directives. He is more accurately viewed as an arbitrator of interest groups that are seeking to dominate the issues and perhaps to circumscribe the powers of his own office. In this setting, as Bryson stresses, the ability to administer is not equivalent to the ability to create new ideas.[28] On the contrary, in order to be innovative, administrators must overcome these inherent constraints of the administrative position.

Informal leaders are often in a better position to be "creative," precisely because they are less constrained, and their energy is less consumed by conflicting pressures. The administrator is *forced* to rely on the participation of his subordinates. Administrative skill rests to a great extent simply on the ability to see the value and consequences of ideas suggested by subordinates. It is this fact which prompts Bryson to assert that there is more inventiveness for sale on the market than there is first-rate administrative capacity.[29]

In one sense, the question of whether there should be decentralized participation of subordinates in decision-making is a moot point—organizations are in fact decentralized, informally if not officially. However, the causes and the extent of decentralization as well as the advantages and disadvantages, remain open to analysis.

Causes of Decentralization. First, decentralization must occur whenever administrators supervise personnel who are so highly specialized that the administrator lacks power or competence to make many of their decisions.[30] Many teachers of science feel that they are better prepared than their principal to determine what curriculum science students need in high school; similarly, some teachers trained in psychology of learning probably feel more prepared to teach than the department head who "supervises" them. For these reasons, the analytical distinction between technical and policy matters is increasingly difficult to maintain as the staff becomes specialized, for high level technical decisions do affect policy and policy limits the discretion of technical decisions. Clearly, the teacher's treatment of the gifted child or the problem child is at the same time a technical matter of the psychology of learning, and a matter of school policy. It is difficult to separate the two spheres. Similarly, the selection of textbooks and teaching materials are technical matters which nevertheless reflect school policy. To the extent that teachers make these technical decisions, in effect policy decision has also been decentralized.

Second, most administrators could not handle all of the decision processes if they tried. Under the daily pressures of official and unofficial obligations, the administrator is forced to review decisions already made by his subordinates and to *select* from among alternatives that have been proposed from below. It is partially because principals have other problems that they tend to discourage teachers from sending discipline problems to the main office. Consequently, decentralization is enforced by requiring teachers to make decisions about discipline problems.

Third, subordinates must make decisions in order to adapt their work to unique or local circumstances. Policy is normally designed to regulate the standard situation in common to the system and cannot encompass the variety of circumstances encountered by individuals and suborganizations, circumstances which force the policy to be compromised. For example, strict requirements of punctuality and regular attendance normally expected of middle class schools do not seem to be as rigidly enforced in some lower class school districts where children are regularly absent without excuse and are customarily tardy. Failing to receive cooperation from the homes, being understaffed and facing possible losses in state aid, such schools tend to informally adopt rather lax attendance-taking and truant policies. Wherever standard policies are difficult to maintain under local conditions, decentralization of decisions tends to occur in practice.[31] Also, the need of local districts for the support of community influentials may force the school board to adopt hiring practices that are opposed to the official policy of the system.

Fourth, decentralization is sometimes necessitated by internal power arrangements. For example, in situations where a subordinate receives direct commands from two or more bosses, he is essentially forced to make the decision. His own decision power is enhanced by this "overlapping authority." In a study of a surgical ward, one observer notes that many important decisions about patient care were essentially left to the discretion of the head nurse because the surgeon and interns from whom she took orders did not agree. In these cases, the subordinate is forced to decide on the priority and feasibility of conflicting demands.[32] The child is caught in this situation of "overlapping authority" in conflicts between parents and teachers. Children are also under a system of overlapping authority with respect to parents, and the clever child learns to utilize this situation by playing one parent off against the other when one denies his requests. Decentralization is, then, partly an outcome of nonunilateral and overlapping lines of authority which flourish in complex organizations.

Fifth, participation of subordinates in the decision process may be initiated by the superior as a *tactical* play. Participation, for example, is used as a form of cooperation in which subordinates are absorbed into the leadership in order to secure their support for the decision and to throttle opposition. Coch and French found in their study of the Harwood Manufacturing Corporation that participation of workers in executive decisions increased their motivation.[33] It was initially observed that after transfer to a new job, a worker became negative, his work became substandard, and he relearned the new job very slowly or quit while relearning. Apparently, resistance to transfer was a product of the amount of incentive provided to relearn the new job as opposed to the amount of group resistance to change. Group resistance to change was considered to be a form of aggression against management for removing workers from a job on which they had demonstrated competence, and for their temporary displacement as inferior novices on new jobs. Such displaced groups usually restricted production on the new job to such an extent that an individual operator's productivity dropped 50 to 100 per cent after change.

The problem of motivation, under the circumstances, was not of motivating individuals, but of dealing with group pressures. In the experiment, group pressure was controlled under three conditions. First, some workers were allowed no participation in decisions made in the transfer or production procedures. Second, some participation was allowed by providing representatives on the decision committee who were told the reasons for change. Finally, total participation was given to all transfers who were given the opportunity to make suggestions and participate directly in the design of their new jobs. The recovery rate on the new job was found to be directly related to the amount of participation, and rates of turnover and aggression toward management were inversely related to the amount of participation.

Lewin explains the effectiveness of participation this way. An individual can be changed either by adding forces in the desired direction—that is, incentives offered by management—or by reducing opposing forces or group resistance. The second procedure creates less total tension on the system. He concludes that "it is possible that the success of group decision, and particularly the permanence of the effect is, in part, due to the attempt to bring about a favorable decision by removing counter-forces within the individual than by applying outside pressure." [34] Some of the problems associated with deliberate co-optation of subordinates will be considered in a succeeding chapter.

The Subordinates' Responsibility. These pressures for decentralization assure some participation, but they do not assure that the subordinates will have any *significant* degree of responsibility for the decisions in which they participate. Four basic aspects of the decision process have been identified by Bryson: policy decision, execution, advice, and interpretation. [35] These functions provide the dimensions along which it is possible to determine the *degree* to which a bureaucracy is "representative" or punishment-centered. The chief executive will frequently try to retain at least the first function and delegate the others. School boards, for example, are expected to deal only with major policy and assign superintendents and their subordinates the responsibility for the technical decisions of execution.

However, there are several problems created by this division of labor. One problem is that because it is the responsibility of subordinates to execute policy, they are in a position to wreck it. The chief executive officer is usually rather effectively isolated from dissent and is relatively unacquainted with the daily execution of his policy; he is, consequently, not in a position to discover whether or not his policies are being enforced. [36] Another problem is that subordinates do *interpret* policy daily as they deal with the public and their clients, and as they organize their work routine. Even when they agree with the basic policy formulation, subordinates must constantly choose to stress one or another aspect of it. Deciding what to omit, what to spend time on "today," and what to postpone constitutes an interpretation of policy. There is no doubt that subordinates do assume these functions; the only question is whether the chief executive requests and encourages it, and whether they are allowed a significant degree of authority to implement their decisions officially, or whether they must act informally.

Another problem is that the minor decisions which subordinates are permitted to make tend to react upon major decisions. The actions of subordinates, even technical ones, may commit the organization to practices which interfere with major policy. For example, in delegating to department heads decisions about hiring teachers, the principal denies himself the choice of a staff that would support his policies. Moreover, as Weber has observed, the control of bureaucracy is possible only in a limited degree for persons who are not technical specialists. [37] The trained specialists, such as English teachers, are more likely to get their ways in the long run (for example, about freedom to read certain books), than the policy-making school board, because in controlling the technique the specialist controls the daily affairs of the organization.

Whether subordinates are authorized to participate in decisions will depend on such conditions as the urgency of the decision, the cost of participation, and the threat of participation to the administration's power. When a subordinate is called upon to give advice, the superior-subordinate relation is reversed temporarily. Most important, the threat of exposing secret operations and strategies circumscribes the extent to which subordinates can participate. Organizations are jealous of their top-secret information, which may be used against them in a competitive situation. For example, a subordinate's participation makes him aware of plans which threaten his own security—that he may be demoted, or the functions of his job reduced.[38] Moreover, participation by subordinates increases the possibility of information "leaks" which start rumors.

RESISTANCE TO DECENTRALIZATION

Tannenbaum lists three steps in the decision process—recognition of alternatives, consideration of the consequences of each alternative, and choice between alternatives. Subordinates may be implicated in the first stage, and there are reasons why they may participate in the second stage; but authority to participate in the third stage, especially when it concerns policy, is often denied.

Administrative Resistance. Subordinates must participate, but they must not control—that seems to be the administrator's dream. Because there is always the possibility that participants may gain control, these two requirements are a source of tension. Although administrators may make every effort to secure participation of their subordinates, they also are cautious to institute measures which guarantee that the subordinate will not gain control or affect policy. These precautions easily create a superficial situation in which subordinates participate in only a token way. This is true of most student governments and many teacher committees which in fact have no power, which is the major reason these agencies usually have little popular support.

The hierarchical pattern of decision-making often obscures ideologies which support the right of professionals to influence the decision process. Lefton, Dinitz, Pasamanick, and their colleagues found in a psychiatric hospital that the ideological emphasis on "team" decisions contrasted with the fact that decisions were actually made by those who had the most authority within the hospital's hierarchy.[39] The "participation" of various professionals in committees did not provide them with any power to make decisions, even in their special spheres of competence. It is significant that it was precisely the personnel who operated on wards that most vocally espoused democratic participation who were most dissatisfied with the system. Thus, merely assigning more authority to subordinates does not guarantee that they will be more satisfied if discrepancies remain between the power to implement their professional role conception and their employee status.

Employee Resistance. Teachers seem to be ambivalent about the amount of decision-making responsibility they actually wish to assume. On the one hand, Hoppock found that the most frequent single suggestion by teachers for the improvement of administration is that teachers be given more important roles in determining school policy.[40] Also, from a study of thirty-five activities in twenty school systems, Sharma reports that in most cases the percentage of teachers desiring participation of groups of teachers in decisions were considerably larger than the percentage reporting such participation. Teachers especially wanted responsibility for decisions relating to instruction and curriculum.[41] It was also concluded that teachers' satisfaction with their school was directly related to the correspondence between desired and actual decision-making practices among teachers.

However, while it is commonly assumed that subordinates are eager to participate in management, there are reasons why this is risky for them. It is quite possible that the boss will receive suggestions as personal criticisms. Moreover, a suggestion may affect co-workers adversely.[42] Any suggestion which might create unemployment or endanger the advancement opportunities of co-workers will be vigorously resisted by subordinates. Also, since proposed changes in official duties may jeopardize unofficial practices in *unanticipated* ways, subordinates may be reluctant to propose official changes on those grounds.

It is paradoxical, Drucker observes, that at one time, employees' representatives demanded the right for their employees to make decisions against employers' resistance, but today the process is almost reversed. Employers now demand that employees contribute to decisions, sometimes against the resistance of employees. Incentive plans and suggestion boxes are two widely practiced ways by which administrators encourage employees to participate in management. Drucker reports that in 1944, the 400,000 employees of General Motors made more than 115,000 written suggestions for improvements. But the fact that three-quarters of the suggestions could not be used suggests that the overt purpose of the program was nearly frustrated.[43]

Gross reports that the majority of school superintendents and school boards want their teachers to participate in major policy decisions, and forty per cent of the teachers in that study feel that their part in policy formation should be increased.[44] But in practice, for example, in only ten per cent of the systems do staff actually consult with the superintendent about filling a vacant teaching position,[45] and from other studies there is little evidence that school teachers are eager to actually assume the responsibility for added decision-making authority. Seeman found that on four out of ten items designed to elicit opinions as to the type of leadership that teachers preferred, a majority favored a direct "authoritative" leadership style which afforded them little opportunity to participate.[46] On some items, teachers demanded that the administrator take more responsibility than he was willing to assume. Seeman concludes that one of the limitations of "democratic administration" is that teachers do not want to participate a great deal because of the increased responsibility and work that such participation entails. The dilemma is that while teachers may dislike being "bossed," they often prefer that someone else make the decisions. In one 1945 survey by the NEA, over half of the rural and urban teachers interviewed did not feel that their participation in policy-forming bodies should be increased.[47]

It is significant that participation of subordinates may be associated with quality of the educational program. In a study of academic freedom, for example, it was found that the proportion of faculty reporting meetings with the administration in determining administrative policy on academic freedom increased directly with the quality of the college. In colleges rated as "high quality," two-thirds of the faculty reported such meetings, compared to less than half of the faculty in low quality schools.[48]

The paradox is that currently *participation* in decisions and delegation of *minor* decisions is being enforced by administrators while they jealously guard decisions that directly affect policy. On the other hand, subordinates are resisting some of the decision responsibility while seeming to prefer more power to determine policy which affects their own work.

THE CENTRAL FUNCTION OF INFORMATION

Although policy decisions are more far-reaching in that such decisions are more likely to concern the total system, the importance of wider participation in the development of such policies is valuable because of the need for increased amounts of more accurate information rather than any considerations of "democratic administration." *Consent* to decision is obviously important, but *conferral* may be even more so. The *confer-and-consent* paradigm (Figure 2) of the decision environment is representative of both the *real*, or actual, process by which decisions are arrived at in school organizations as well as a *prescribed* process—that is, a deliberate method for organizing decision-making.

This particular representation postulates that decision-making is dependent upon (1) information and (2) the communication of it. In addition, it assumes that decisions are purposeful. By purposeful, we simply mean that decisions—*all* decisions—are related ultimately to the ends of the organization even though such goals may only be dimly perceived by some particular decision-maker.

It has now been established that decisions which affect personnel in an organization are more effective when such personnel either participate in the decision process or willingly consent to be governed by such decisions. Although this fact is axiomatic it is still ignored by many administrators. The disruptive aspects of such apparently deliberate ignorance are not necessarily the consequences of "autocratic" administrators; rather, the danger to the general well-being of the organization is the consequence of either the lack or the distortion of information.

This is not a startling revelation, to be sure. Modern organizations are more dependent than anything else upon mechanisms and procedures for the efficient flow and utilization of information. As organizations become

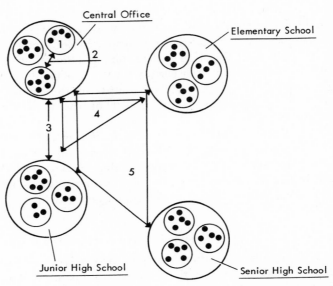

FIGURE 2. "Confer and consent": The decision environment. A school may be conceived as a system—that is, a set of interacting components and subcomponents, each one of which engages in in-put and out-put behaviors. In the above scheme—oversimplified to be sure—a school system is depicted as including four basic elements: a central office structure, a high school, a junior high school, and an elementary school. Each of these elements is composed of subelements of subcomponents. Accordingly, there are five levels of decision funtions depicted: (1) decisions within subcomponents; (2) decisions between subcomponents; (3) decisions between two components; (4) decisions between more than two components; and (5) policy decisions which involve aspects of all components.

more segmented, their information needs not only increase quantitatively, but available channels naturally become somewhat short-circuited.

The benign and affable administrator is just as likely to be the victim of such an information stricture as is the overbearing autocrat. *Who* is empowered to make a decision is sometimes less important than simply *knowing* that it was made. In relatively small school systems, the informal or natural interaction process provides this knowledge, but as the system increases its scope these natural interaction patterns become more confined within the boundaries of various subsystem units. This decreased interaction between units distorts the flow of vital information, and the system must resort to the superimposition of some form of communication between its various components. Traditionally, the committee, which has been discussed previously in this chapter, has been a popular device for this purpose, but, as has been pointed out, the committee does not always solve the problem.

The paradigm (Figure 1) becomes deliberate when administrators rec-·ognize the consequence of constricted information flow to the decision-making process, and are also *willing* to provide both the climate and the opportunity for conferral within and between organizational units. Deliberateness in the establishment of a "confer-and-consent" decision environment is a method for maintaining "openness" in the system, because otherwise the tendency toward a collectivity of closed subsystem units is a natural consequence of increasing size in organizations.

It is important, of course, that spheres of administrative and professional decisions be carefully distinguished, but the *same* information may be vital to both kinds of decisions.

PROFESSIONAL-EMPLOYEES IN THE DECISION PROCESS

The professional characteristics of teaching make the administration of teachers a special case of the problem under consideration. One study of professional physicians working in hospital bureaucracies is instructive of the procedures used by administration in dealing with professionals in the decision process.[49] Three conditions reduced the conflict that was incipient between these professionals and their supervisors.

First, spheres of administrative and professional decisions were rigidly distinguished by both the professionals and their supervisors. Physicians were willing to grant the supervisors the right to make purely administrative decisions, such as those regarding schedules, since this released them from onerous chores. Complying with such administrative requests did not imply a loss of professional dignity. At the same time, physicians retained freedom to make decisions about professional matters such as those directly affecting patient care. This distinction between professional and administrative decisions is not equivalent to the distinction often made between policy and technical decisions, for decisions about patient care involve both policy and technique.

Second, decision-making was distinguished from advice. When the administrators did attempt to interfere in spheres of professional decisions, or when their administrative decisions impinged on the professional authority, they handled the situation by offering advice and left the actual decision to the professionals. The bureaucratic model of organization was reconciled with professional norms in this way. Since advice is a form of control by which responsibility for the final decision is avoided, this procedure was of some advantage to the administration as well. Presumably, the roles of advice and authority would be reversed with respect to administrative problems. The separation of professional and administrative authority within an organization performs a valuable function. It provides strong support for both spheres, the professional and the administrative, and makes it less difficult for any official to unduly sacrifice either function for the sake of the other. Conversely, if authority for both professional and administrative functions is vested in one administrative office, there is always a danger that the administrator will be tempted to strengthen his administrative position by bargaining away professional principles. For example, a superintendent may be tempted to restrict academic freedom for the sake of good public relations and the support of community influentials.

Third, the supervisors were themselves highly trained physicians. Conflict seems to be avoided by assigning supervisory duties only to those who also have gained professional respect from their subordinates.

The above three points have special relevance for educational administration. Delegating professional decisions which essentially involve the teacher's relationship to the student reduces a certain amount of strain between teachers and administrators. At the same time, increased respect of teachers for administrators will be achieved only if administrators maintain professional training requirements. Some of these considerations will be examined further in the last chapter.

SUMMARY

Although decision-making may be defined as the reduction of alternatives, this chapter has attempted to demonstrate that such a definition grossly oversimplifies a highly complex process.

Effective decision-making is the product of considerably more than intuitive "feelings" of sensitive administrators; it is based on knowledge, experience, and dependable information. Moreover, decision-making in educational organizations demands an understanding of the legal aspects of the organization's structure, the problems involved in maintaining internal stability, and the relationships between school and society which affect the value-systems of school personnel. These various factors comprise the organizational context of school administration and are considered in the following section.

BIBLIOGRAPHY AND NOTES

1. Educational Policies Commission, *Mass Communication and Education*, Washington, D.C.: National Education Association, 1958, p. 124. Several authors propose a decision-making theory which is central to the organizational process. For example, the critical role of decisions in organizations is reflected in the character of

Griffiths' propositions: "Major propositions—The organization of an institution is determined by the structure of its decision-making process; if the formal and informal organization approach congruency, the institution will approach maximum achievement. Minor propositions—A rank of an individual in an institution is determined by his control over decision making; the effectiveness of an administrator in an institution is inversely proportional to the number of final decisions which he must make as an individual; the inter-relation of an individual to another in an institution is inversely proportional to the number of final decisions which he must make as an individual. Sub-propositions related to organization— The less the emphasis on centralization in the organization of an institution, the greater will be the number of decisions made at the source of action, and the more effective will be the decision-making process." (See: D. Griffiths, "Administration As Decision-making," in: A. Halpin (ed.). *Administrative Theory in Education.* Chicago: Midwest Administration Center, 1958. pp. 148–149).

2. D. Griffiths, *Administrative Theory.* New York: Appleton-Century-Crofts, 1959, p. 202.

3. C. L. Barnard, *The Functions of the Executive.* Cambridge, Mass.: Harvard Univ. Press, 1938, pp. 195–199.

4. *Ibid.*

5. D. Griffiths, *Administrative Theory in Education.* A. W. Halpin, ed. Chicago: Midwest Administration Center, Univ. of Chicago, 1958, p. 132.

6. *Ibid.*, p. 134.

7. *Ibid.*, p. 135.

8. W. H. Schmidt and R. Tannenbaum, "The Management of Differences," *Harvard Business Review*, vol. 38, 1960, pp. 107–115.

9. H. S. Broudy, "Conflicts in Values" in: R. E. Ohm and W. G. Monahan, eds., *Educational Administration—Philosophy in Action.* Norman: College of Education, Univ. Oklahoma, 1965, p. 52.

10. Griffiths, in Halpin, *op. cit.*, p. 136.

11. R. Dubin, "Stability of Human Organizations," in *Modern Organization Theory.* Mason Haire, ed. New York: Wiley, 1959, pp. 218 ff.

12. Griffiths, in Halpin, *op. cit.*, p. 137.

13. Cited by Griffiths in Halpin *op. cit.*, p. 138.

14. Griffiths, in Halpin, *op. cit.*, p. 139.

15. H. A. Simon, *Administrative Behavior* New York: Macmillan, 1947 p. 108.

16. *Ibid.*, p. 21.

17. *Ibid.*, p. 22.

18. W. G. Bennis, "Leadership Theory and Administrative Behavior," in W.G. Bennis, K. D. Benne and R. Chin, *The Planning of Change.* New York: Holt, Rinehart & Winston, 1961, p. 440.

19. Barnard, *op. cit.*

20. J. D. Kingsley, "The Execution of Policy," reprinted in *Reader in Bureaucracy.* R. K. Merton *et al.*, eds. Glencoe, Ill.: Free Press, 1952, pp. 216–221.

21. "Changing the Curriculum at Southside," in *Administrative-Relationships: A Case Book.*, J. Culbertson *et al.*, eds. Englewood Cliffs, N. J.: Prentice-Hall, 1960, pp. 346–366.

22. L. Bryson, "Notes on a Theory of Advice," reprinted in *Reader in Bureaucracy, op. cit.*, p. 210.

23. P. Blau and W. R. Scott, *Formal Organization.* San Francisco: Chandler, 1962, p. 244.

24. D. C. Pelz, "Some Social Factors Related to Performance in a Research Organization," *Administrative Science Quarterly*, vol. 1, 1956, pp. 310–335.

25. R. M. Cert and J. G. March, " A Behavioral Theory of Organizational Objectives"

in *Modern Organization Theory*, Mason Haire, ed. New York: Wiley, 1959, pp. 80 ff.

26. *Ibid.*
27. F. Hunter, *Community Power Structure*. Chapel Hill: Univ. North Carolina Press, 1953.
28. Bryson, *op. cit.*
29. *Ibid.*
30. T. Parsons, "Suggestions for a Sociological Approach to the Theory of Organizations," *Administrative Science Quarterly*, vol. 1, 1956, pp. 77–78.
31. Cf. M. Dalton, *Men Who Manage*. New York: Wiley, 1958, Ch. 5.
32. R. L. Coser, "Authority and Decision-Making in a Hospital: A Comparative Analysis," *American Sociological Review*, Feb., 1958.
33. L. Coch and J. French, "Overcoming Resistance to Change," in *Readings in Social Psychology*, G. Swanson, T. Newcomb, and E. Hartley, eds. New York: Holt, 1952, pp. 474–490.
34. K. Lewin, "Group Decision and Social Change," in *Readings in Social Psychology*, *op. cit.*, p. 471.
35. Bryson, *op. cit.*
36. Cf. *From Max Weber*, H. Gerth and C. W. Mills, eds. New York: Oxford Univ. Press, 1958, p. 234.
37. *Ibid.*
38. R. Tannenbaum, "Managerial Decision-Making," *The Journal of Business*, vol. 23, 1950, pp. 33–38.
39. M. Lefton, S. Dinitz, and B. Pasamanick, "Decision-Making in a Mental Hospital," *American Sociological Review*, vol. 24, 1959, pp. 882–892.
40. R. Hoppock, "What Teachers Think of School Administrators," *School Executive*, vol. 69, 1949, pp. 40–42.
41. C. L. Sharma, "Who Should Make Decisions?", *Administrator's Notebook*, vol. 3, 1955, pp. 1–4.
42. P. Drucker, *Concept of the Corporation*. Boston: Beacon Press, 1960, p. 193.
43. *Ibid.*, p. 190.
44. N. Gross, *Explorations in Role Analysis: Studies of the School Superintendency Role*. New York: Wiley, 1958.
45. *Ibid.*
46. M. Seeman, *Social Status and Leadership: The Case of the School Executive*. Columbus: Bureau off Educational Research, Ohio State Univ., 1960.
47. NEA Research Bulletin, *The Teacher Looks at Personnel Administration*, Dec. 1945, p. 123; NEA Research Bulletin, *Teacher Personnel Procedures: Employment Conditions in Service*, May, 1942, pp. 110–112.
48. P. Lazarsfeld and W. Thielens, *The Academic Mind*. Glencoe, Ill.: Free Press, 1958, p. 170.
49. M. E. W. Goss, "Influence and Authority Among Physicians in an Out-Patient Clinic," *American Sociological Review*, vol. 26, 1961, pp. 39–50.

The Organizational Context of Educational Administration

6

The Legal and Structural
Setting of Education

In each society—the Nation, the City, the business, or the University—someone must make rules to govern the conduct of and the relations among those who are banded together—thus each maintains order and certainty among the group and facilitates the achievement of whatever it is established to do. But like other governments, neither can afford order if a certainty of it is achieved at the cost of the freedom of those who are governed.[1]

EDUCATION in this country has a definite legal structure, or a body of laws. The law of any phase of government is found in constitutions, statutes, and judicial proceedings. School law is no exception. It is through constitutions, statutes, and the courts that the people have attempted to set up the rules by which "we play the game." These rules become one basis for determining what can and cannot be sanctioned in order for the culture to survive. The rules, the regulations, the statutes, and the courts are the tools of social control which dictate what human behavior *ought* to be. But the extent to which the law *can* control behavior depends upon how willing the people are to accept the law. For instance, one of the authors lived in Oklahoma when liquor was prohibited in that state. Yet, without any question a lot of people bought and drank whiskey in Oklahoma. Although the law did not sanction the purchase and drinking of whiskey, social custom allowed it.

Laws, court decisions, statutes, rules, and regulations make up a large part of the formal structure of a social organization. Although this codified apparatus does not describe the informal structure, the student must understand the legal structure which sets the formal dimensions of the organization, as well as the many informal forces which are at play within the organization. Because the administrator must spend much of his time making reports and checking on laws and legal procedures in order to administer the school system, it is appropriate to briefly review the legal and governmental controls on education and their history. The historical development of our legal body of rules provides insight into many of the issues and beliefs held in educational administration today.

The Early Historical-Legal Setting

In 1919 Elwood Cubberley wrote:

The road that man has traveled since the days when might made right and children had no rights which even parents were bound to respect, to a time when the child is regarded as of first importance and adults represented in the state declare by law that the child shall be cared for and educated for the welfare of the state, is a long road and at times a very crooked one.[2]

The above quotation from Cubberley is startling even today. Nearly fifty years after Cubberley wrote his famous book, *Public Education in the United States,* we still find an amazing number of people who do not understand or even believe that education is a function of the state. As this book is being written, the world is engaged in an unprecedented struggle of ideologies. "Might still makes right," but now as never before the welfare of the state (here the word "state" is used in the broader sense of the nation) is dependent on an educated populace.

The present legal and governmental structure in this country has a long history and has evolved out of a fundamental commitment to the belief that the individual is the single most important unit in government. The individual was and still is considered the controlling factor in government. He shall control government and shall have some part in the making of the laws by which he lives.

The structure for education evolved during an era when centralized government was feared. Many people had come to this country to escape the consequences of strong central governments. The early American settler felt that in order to guard against the possibility of government becoming too strong, it should be close to the people so that it could be controlled by the people.

THE INFLUENCE OF THE COLONIAL PERIOD

The first attempts to organize education date back over 300 years to the colony of Massachusetts. At that time the education of children was a responsibility of the family. The kind and quality of education that children received, if any, was determined by the parents and the church.

Perhaps the Puritans had as much of a hand in shaping the beginning of the present American school system as any group. They settled along the New England coast in little congregations and set up a civil-religious form of government which became the New England Town. The "meeting house" was always located in the center of town. It was here that they worshipped and carried on governmental affairs.

Education was left to the voluntary efforts of the parents. Instruction in the home and apprenticeship training were the means by which children would be taught enough to participate in religious services and to earn a living. Education in America at this time was truly local in character, and it was voluntary.

The religious town governments volunteered to establish Latin grammar schools to prepare boys for Harvard, which had been established by the colonial government in 1636 primarily to prepare young men for the ministry. Here, then, was a voluntary apprentice system of education carried on by the home (a form of private instruction in reading and religion) and by Latin grammar schools located in large towns.

The voluntary educational system evidently did not work too well. Parents did not assume their personal obligation to educate their young. Apprentices were to learn from masters of apprentices, but the masters proved negligent too. As a result a group of leaders in the Puritan Church asked the Massachusetts colonial legislature to assist them in compelling parents and masters to teach the children.

Massachusetts Law of 1642. Consequently, the legislature declared a mandate stating that the town officials should "ascertain from time to time if parents and masters were attending to their educational duties; if all children were being trained in learning and labor and other employments profitable to the commonwealth; and if the children were being taught to read and understand the principles of religion and the capital laws of the country." The law supplied village officers with the right to impose fines on those who failed to provide proper instruction. According to Cubberly [3] this was the first time in the English-speaking world that a legislative body representing the state ordered that all children should be taught to read and write.

Interestingly enough, the behavior of the early settler in his reaction to laws in 1642 bears considerable resemblance to that of the twentieth-century citizen. The law was clear, but he did not follow it. The 1642 law demanded that parents educate their children, but it did not provide for the establishment of schools. It may have been that the early pioneer could not have followed the law, even had he wanted to, because of the personal hardships he was facing. It may have been that the importance of education was not considered great enough by many individuals to compel them to do what the law so clearly stated had to be done. Whatever the reason, the law proved unsatisfactory.

The Massachusetts Law of 1647. Five years after the passage of the first law in Massachusetts, the colonial government noted that education was still inadequate in the colonies. It then passed the famous "Old Deluder Act." The act received its name from a sentence in its preamble which stated:

It being one cheife proiect of ye ould deluder, Satan, to keepe men from the knowledge of ye Scriptures, as in form^r times by keeping y^m in an unknowne tongue, so in these latt^r times by perswading from ye use of tongues, y^t so at least ye true sence & meaning of ye originall might be clouded by false glosses of saint seeming deceivers, y^t learning may not be buried in ye grave of o^r fath^{rs} in ye church and commonwealth, the Lord assisting o^r endeavors.

This law ordered that every town of fifty householders should at once appoint a teacher of reading and writing, and provide for his wages in a manner to be determined by the town; and every town of 100 householders must provide a (Latin) grammar school to prepare youths for the university. There was a fine of five pounds for failure to comply with this law.

MASSACHUSETTS LAWS SET A PRECEDENT

The Massachusetts law said in effect that if the Commonwealth of Massachusetts was to survive, the children must be educated. George H. Martin,[4] an early historian of Massachusetts, wrote in 1894 that the following principles could be drawn from the laws of 1642 and 1647:

(1. The universal education of youth is essential to the well-being of the state.

(2. The obligation rests upon the parent.

(3. The state has a right to enforce this obligation.

(4. The state may fix a standard which shall determine the kind of education and the amount.

(5. Public money raised by a tax may be used to provide education as the state requires. This tax may be general, though the school attendance is not.

(6. Education higher than rudiments may be supplied by the state.

Opportunity must be provided, at public expense, for youths who wish to prepare for the university.

Since that time, Martin continued, these principles have been borne out in court decisions and form the basis for state concern for education today. "The idea underlying all this legislation was neither paternalistic nor socialistic. The child is to be educated, *not* to advance his personal interests, but because the state will suffer if he is not educated." [5]

Accordingly, the primary function of the public school, as it is viewed in legal theory today, is not to confer benefits upon individuals as such; [6] the school exists as a state institution because the very existence of civil society demands it.[7] The student of administration is often confronted with two meanings of the statement "Education is a function of the state." First, it can be interpreted as either the United States, or in relation to a state in the United States. If it is defined as a function of an organized society, or of the body politic, or of any organized sovereign body of people, then education can be construed as the means by which an organized society attempts to insure its perpetuation. The survival of the United States depends upon an intelligent, informed, and educated citizenry. The education of youth is of such vital importance to a democratic society that the state has been granted much power in limiting the control of the parent over the education of his child.[8]

Another meaning of the statement "Education is a function of the state" is dependent upon the fact that education is not mentioned in the Constitution of the United States. Therefore, it becomes a power reserved for the states through the tenth amendment which states: "The powers not delegated to the United States by the Constitution, nor prohibited by it to the states, are reserved to the states respectively or to the people." As will be shown later, although the right of the state to operate school systems is a reserved right, the state, of course, cannot violate the Constitution of the United States as it pertains to the rights of the individual.

THE ORIGIN OF SCHOOL DISTRICTS

The New England town with the meeting house in the center was the only form of government in the colonial era. Beyond that, of course, the people were governed by the King of England. Religious faith became the primary social tie among the people. The civil and ecclesiastical governments were, in fact, one. The meeting house was the place where both civil and church matters were settled. When they met to discuss church affairs, it was a parish meeting; when roads, schools, or bridges were discussed, it was a town meeting.

Through its power to enact laws which affected the township, the town meeting became a semilegislative body, and it also was the unit of representation to the colonial legislature (the general court). However, the town meeting soon became a place where far more than local issues, either church or civil, were discussed. Cubberley points out that it reached its greatest importance in the years prior to the Revolution which he credits to the "initiative and superiority of the masses of the people." [9]

By the end of the seventeenth century the New England town had begun to decline. The early New England town had been the epitome of religious intolerance, settled by people of the same faith and organized to keep other faiths out; but the religious fervor which held the town together had begun to wane. The need for a close union dwindled after the war. Cooperation and defense became less important, and individual interest rather than township interest became the center of concern. New settlements established throughout all parts of the town rendered former laws requiring all dwellings to be located within a half mile of the parish church obsolete and unenforceable. As people settled away from the meeting house, attendance at church, town meetings, and the town school became major undertakings.

The disintegration of town control arose from a demand for more individual control by the people in the towns. A demand for subdividing the town into parishes arose, wherein each township or parish established machinery for civil government. By 1700 there were as many as twenty parishes within the eighty towns in existence. Each had the right to establish full legal and civil machinery for carrying out parish business. The parish meeting soon became a place where the assertion of parish rights was made. Interestingly enough, parish rights, rather than church matters, became the main concern. [10]

The parish, which was the result of efforts to decentralize the local government, increased district, or area, consciousness. People in each district wanted complete control of everything and full local benefit from all taxes paid; taxes for purposes outside of the parish were scorned. Towns were subdivided into highway districts. Dame schools were instituted in the parishes and were operated on a private tuition basis. Town schools, which were often dependent upon a tax levied on the parents whose children attended them, were becoming short of money because the people were sending their children to the dame school rather than the central town school. In fact, in many cases in order to gain support, the town school had to be located in certain parishes because of refusals to levy taxes unless the school were to be located in a given parish for a given length of time. The next step was to allow the parish to build and operate its own schools. Soon schools were built wherever needed, and the present district form of government evolved.

It is important to note that because the parishes derived their power from the town, the new school districts did *not* emerge with any powers; they were not independent corporate bodies with power to tax. These powers came later. Early school districts in New England were activated wherever there were enough people for a school. However, district boundaries were planned. This was the basis for the spread of the district concept from the east to the west.

The District System Was Unsatisfactory. As early as 1837 Horace Mann, secretary of the Massachusetts State Board of Education, began working for the abolition of the existing district system and for centralizing school government into larger units. Students of educational administration today should be aware of the fact that the fight to reorganize school districts into more effective and efficient units has a long history. Scholars, planners, and researchers in school administration today point out that there is justification for a total of about 5,000 school districts in the United States. Table 2 summarizes what is happening in the United

TABLE 2.

Number of School Districts in United States *

YEARS	NO. OF SCHOOL DISTRICTS
1931–1932	127,531
1947–1948	94,926
1949–1950	83,718
1951–1952	71,094
1953–1954	63,057
1955–1956	54,859
1957–1958	47,594
1958–1960 †	40,605
1964–1965 ‡	28,814

* Biennial Survey of Education in the United States 1956–1958, Statistics of State School Systems 1957–1958, U.S. Office of Education, OE-200020-58.
  Number of local basic administrative units (school districts), 1931–1932 to 1957–1958, in the United States (forty-eight states and Washington, D.C.)
† Data for 1959–1960: N.E.A., Research Division, "Estimates of School Statistics," 1959–1960 Research Report 1959-R23, Dec., 1959, p. 18.
‡ Data for 1964–1965: N.E.A., Research Division, *N.E.A. Research Bulletin,* vol. 43, No. 1, Feb., 1965, p. 5.

States in regard to reorganizing school districts into larger units. This will be discussed in greater detail later in this chapter.

THE EARLY STATES AND EDUCATION

The pattern of the New England colonies had advanced both the concept of education as a state function and the pattern of district control. The Declaration of Independence which held that "All men are created equal" and that they are "endowed by their Creator with certain inalienable rights," no doubt expressed another underlying directive for education.

Although scholars will disagree about why the Constitution of the United States makes no mention of education, it seems clear that the following conditions had some bearing on the fact of this omission: (1)

most of the 13 original states had some constitutional or statutory provision relating to education before the adoption of the federal Constitution; this could have been a major reason for the "hands off" policy of the convention delegates; (2) the concept that it was a local (that is, state) function carried out in the colonies was firmly implanted in the minds of the writers; (3) religion and education at the time were not separate, and thus to support schools governmentally was to support religion; (4) education was more or less an individual matter best handled at the local level; and (5) it was not a significant national problem. Whatever the reason, education was not mentioned in the United States Constitution; nor can any record be found in the debates of the Convention that education was ever considered to be of little more than remote concern to the federal government.

With few exceptions, as each of the states came into existence their constitutions made it obligatory for the state legislature to provide for the establishment and maintenance of efficient public school systems. At an early stage, forms of state regulation over education were initiated when grants of land were made by the federal government for school purposes and state school funds were made available for use by local schools. "The receipt of aids from the state was accompanied by the necessity of making reports to the state and this in turn evolved into compliance with other state requirements." [11]

As Keesecher comments, many states in the early days made the mistake of supposing that state political officials, who were subject to political pressures and partisan sentiments, make good state school officials.[12] Over the years states have tended to overcome these mistakes, and the trend is to remove schools from state and local politics by declaring them to be "nonpartisan." Most states now have men who are appointed on a nonpartisan basis as chief state school officers.

The Present-Day Relationship of the State and Education

State school codes are a collection of legislative statutes which establish ways and means for conducting the affairs of education in the state. Law libraries contain a legion of court cases pertaining to school issues decided by high state courts. Almost every state department of education has issued bulletins, guides, and statistics on education ranging from comprehensive curriculum guides to specifications for buildings, buses, and school equipment. These are pertinent to the day-to-day work of every teacher, principal, superintendent, and board of education.

STATE CONSTITUTIONS

It is evident by now that education as a state function is no accident; it predates the federal Constitution. Every state in the union has, by constitution, statute, or practice, assumed that education is a function of the state, and court decisions have held this to be true. The provisions of state constitutions embody the basic laws of the state just as the federal Constitution is the law of the land. The state, of course, cannot enact legislation which is contrary to, or in conflict with, the federal Constitution. The Congress of the United States may not enact legislation which is in derogation of the United States Constitution, nor can a state legislature enact laws which are in derogation of the state Constitution or the federal Constitution.

State statutes can be divided into two basic groups: (1) mandatory laws which, in effect, establish the minimum program of education, and (2) permissive laws which enumerate the functions that are delegated to the district under the appropriate conditions. Some school codes grant extremely wide powers to local school districts.

THE COURTS

Public school systems over the years have been involved in extensive conflicts between individuals, the school districts, and the state. Courts have been called upon to settle these disputes and to provide directives for action. Courts have repeatedly stated that education is a state function. Newton Edwards has written: "Whatever vagaries may have been entertained by educational reformers or others, the courts have been forced by necessity to formulate a theory of education based upon what they deem to be fundamental principles of public policy." [13] The Supreme Court of Minnesota states it this way: "This court so frequently has affirmed the doctrine that the maintenance of the public school is a matter of state, not local, concern that it is unnecessary to further review the authorities at this date." [14]

In a chapter entitled "The School and the State," Newton Edwards cites thirty-one separate cases in which courts have spoken and enunciated the following principles in regard to the relationship of the state to education:

1. Public education is not merely a function of government; it is of government as is police power or the power to administer justice.

2. The state finds it right to tax for the maintenance of public schools in its duty to promote the public welfare.

3. The primary function of the public school, in legal theory, is not to confer benefits upon the individual as such; the school exists as a state institution because the very existence of civil society demands it.

4. The state may go "very far indeed," by way of limiting the control of the parent over the education of his child.

5. The state cannot prohibit private schools.

6. The state can prohibit the teaching of doctrines which challenge the existence of the state and the well being of society.

7. The state may require that children be educated in schools which

meet substantially the same standards as the state requires of its own schools.[15]

SCHOOL DISTRICTS OPERATE UNDER DELEGATED POWERS

By and large, state legislatures have delegated much of their power with reference to schools to local districts. The local board of education and, therefore, the school district are in reality arms of the state. Local boards of education have been delegated the expressed or implied authority and power to employ, dismiss, and pay teachers, to determine the curriculum, to levy taxes, construct buildings, transport children, provide meals, determine fitness of children to attend school, enforce attendance, and all other duties necessary to operate a school system. Each state has laws which regulate the boards. These laws are usually considered the minimum essentials to guarantee equal opportunity of education to all children. In fact, state minimums are often so low that many authorities believe that schools which meet only these minimums should be liquidated. While state laws and curriculum requirements are usually minimal, local educational leadership is expected to raise local schools above the minimum.

The State Department of Education

The role and function of the State Department of Education is still an emerging one. Although all states today have a chief state school officer and a state department of education, the fact that education in this country originated as a local function far back in the New England towns has handicapped movement toward any kind of centralization. Home rule, which has been the doctrine of public school control in this country, is still used as an argument against school district reorganization, in spite of the fact that today the citizen who cares about exercising his right to vote on issues or to protest to his school board can live fifty miles from his board office and reach it more easily than could his grandfather who lived only five miles away. Fears of graft and corruption often lie behind the resistance to centralization at the state level, despite the fact that it is harder in most states to misuse funds at the state level than it is at the local level. City governments are notoriously more corrupt than state governments.

FUNCTIONS OF STATE DEPARTMENTS OF EDUCATION

Every state education official today and every state department employee recognizes that education functions best when it is close to the people. What, then, is the main function of the state department? While they have several functions, all educational authorities have defined the primary function of the state department as a "leadership function." In other words it is supposed to develop a state-local partnership to help schools do a better job of education by providing expert help, stimulation, guidance, and vision to local school authorities. There are, of course, other functions which the state department must perform. Important among these is a regulatory function; for the most part, this means enforcement of the law with regard to state minimum standards in education. Thurston and Roe list the following categories as part of the regulatory function of state departments of education:

1. Program—assuming minimum program in both quality and scope and assuring that proper procedures are used in their accomplishment.

2. Personnel—determining whether teachers and other school employees are properly qualified.

3. Plant—proper observance of rules of health and safety, both in construction and maintenance.

4. Child accounting—assuring that minimal educational opportunities are provided through enforcement of compulsory attendance laws, child labor laws, pupil accounting, and personnel services.

5. Finance—employment of proper safeguarding, accounting, and economy.

6. Structure—insuring that basic requirements of the law are followed.

7. Administration—assuring that basic procedural and administration duties are performed in compliance with the law.[16]

"Service" constitutes another function of the state department. Thurston and Roe divided service into two facets: (1) service performed for the state as a whole, and (2) service provided to local school districts.[17] Such services will vary from state to state. In some states service to the state as a whole is rendered by the State Department of Education acting as an educational information center for interpreting education in the state to the chief executive of the state, the state legislature, and the people, through comparative studies, statistical information, advice, clarification of laws, statutes and regulations. In other states the state department may be responsible for operating special schools (for the blind, deaf, and so on), archives, libraries, teacher placement agencies, teacher retirement funds, controlling interscholastic athletics, programs of rehabilitation for the handicapped, and many other activities.

In many states schools may receive special service in school district planning, school house construction, curriculum planning, special educational program development, in-service education for teachers, and technical advice on almost any problem regarding school organization and operation. The extent of services rendered varies from state to state and depends upon the perceptions of the people of the state as to the role of the state department with regard to local schools. It also partly depends on the skill of the state department's personnel in initiating a dynamic program which sets forth a cooperative team approach to solving state educational problems.

Unfortunately, the relative status of the department of education in state government has not been subjected to the study necessary to effect significant advances and improvement in state education agencies.

APOLITICAL ADMINISTRATION

Educational control in this country is supposed to be apolitical—that is, neither nonpolitical nor political. Every legal effort is made to keep the issue of education out of partisan politics. The argument—a sound one—is that public schools are for all the people of any party, working class, or religion. The public school is not supposed to teach political doctrine; but it is a place where all such doctrines can come under objective analytical scrutiny. The public school is to develop in children the ability to think critically and to evaluate and understand the world around them. However, there are two unanticipated consequences of this value position: politicians are generally indifferent to the support of public education, and educators have not had immediate access to and influence over the political machinery that could potentially aid and support education more than it has.

INTERGOVERNMENTAL PROBLEMS

State departments of education in this country are usually organized apart from the ongoing political government, but there is generally an overall policy-making body (State Board of Education). The membership of such bodies is determined in a number of ways. In some states its members are appointed by the governor, with or without the approval of the legislature. In other states the state board may be elected from districts by the people. In still other cases, the membership may come from school board members at the local level. In any case, it is usually recommended that the terms of office be staggered so that any one change in parties at the state level could not put into effect strictly partisan policies in a short time. Staggered terms also provide for continuous operation.

The state board of education appoints a chief executive officer who shall provide leadership and carry out the policies of the board. As the highest educational office of the state, this position should be filled by a professional educator whose career has been one of proven and *outstanding* leadership. Wherever this office is subject to popular election, however, as is the case in a number of states, leadership is not predictable.

FORMAL POLITICAL CONTROLS

State boards of education face real difficulty in attracting highly qualified individuals to the position of chief state school officer. For one reason, education at the state level is part of the internal organization of state government. The chief executive officer of the state school system *is* a professional educator and should be treated as such, which means employing a qualified professional from the ranks of professionals, one who is *not* related to present partisan politics. In most cases this means that the remuneration for the position ought to be adequate enough to attract an outstanding professional. But state boards have found that the position of chief state school administrator is looked upon within the state government as a post equivalent to that of other departments such as highways, health, taxation, and so on. These ranks, although technically equivalent to that of the chief state school officer, are usually filled by appointment of the governor and may change with administration; in general they are not comparable in salary to those of local school superintendents. State legislatures are reluctant to treat the position of the chief state school officer, and his salary, any differently than other chief state administrative offices. Consequently, state boards of education must seek applicants for the position of chief state school officer at a lower salary than a well-qualified candidate could receive as a district superintendent. The present Commissioner of Education in Minnesota is a case in point; the man sought by the State Board of Education and highly recommended by his colleagues had to take a substantial salary reduction to accept the position of Commissioner of Education for the state. There are cities within the state of Minnesota that pay the local superintendent of schools as much as $10,000 more than the Chief State School Officer. Yet, the future of education in the state is more dependent upon state level leadership than local level leadership.

Of course, state government employees are generally paid at a lower salary rate than equivalent workers outside state government. As is true with many governmental officials, persons at the state level in education, many of them extremely capable and outstanding leaders, serve with a sense of duty and a commitment to the task; their monetary compensation is seldom commensurate with their contribution.

CIVIL SERVICE

Another problem concerns relations between state departments of education and state civil service organizations which have been established to (a) protect professionals in government from partisan politics, and (b) guarantee justice in the administration of salary schedules and working conditions. These two functions may conflict. Usually the heads of departments change with changes of political party control, but professional employees such as doctors, statisticians, accountants, clerks, and secretarial help are protected by civil service regulations.

However, the salary problems and personnel needs within the state department of education are somewhat different from those in other government agencies. Assistant state superintendencies, directorships of divisions, coordinators, and supervisors in education require professional personnel of a calibre high enough to gain the respect of local school administrators, principals, supervisors, and teachers. Such personnel are expected to provide leadership to local schools; but in many states civil service specifications and classifications ignore the leadership function of these positions as well as the range of responsibilities involved. Usually civil service salary minimums and maximums are determined in relation to the salary of the chief of the department. The salary maximum of the second-echelon employee must be a certain number of points below that of the highest ranking employee in the department; consequently, when the salary of the Chief State School Officer is fixed by law, the problem of recruiting state department personnel becomes critically maximized. In some states the salaries of state department personnel are not equivalent to the salary of classroom teachers.

The authors can cite two states where civil service is an issue. In one state all education department employees below the Chief and Assistant Chief State School Officer are governed by civil service regulations. A majority of employees within that state department want the state department of education to be removed from the civil service classification. The argument is that the state civil service classifications do not provide salaries commensurate with what the employees are actually doing. These employees argue that if they performed only what the civil service job descriptions call for, the department would not and could not function. This state has no job classifications which even approximate those actually performed by state department of education employees. Most of these people could teach in a classroom for more money than they receive at the state level.

The State Department of Education in a second state does not come under the civil service regulation, and the employees want to be included in it. They want protection from arbitrary political dismissals and more job security. There are states in which the role and function of the state department of education has been so defined that civil service positions reflect the role of the state department in providing leadership, service, and research to the state schools, but in general such harmony is rare.

MULTIPLE CONTROL OVER STATE DEPARTMENTS

The work of the state department of education is dependent on other governmental departments. Some examples of other agencies which exercise some control over state departments are:

1. *Departments of Justice.* In most states only the attorney general or the court can make an interpretation of the constitutionality of a particular act in a particular school. A wise attorney general may seek the advice of the state department before ruling on the legality of an act, but it is out of the hands of the department. A legal division within the depart-

ment may aid the schools within the state, but within the bounds of the authority and prerogatives of the attorney general and courts.

2. *Departments of Administration.* These departments, set up within the state government to make it more efficient, usually provide for centralized purchasing, internal accounting, and auditing, and may set the policy for utilization of data processing equipment, centralized publication facilities, and so on. This department has, in many states, great power and control over all governmental departments.

3. *State Fire Marshall's Office.* In many states school building plans must be approved by this office before local districts may proceed. In some states the school construction section of the state department works closely with the fire marshall; it must.

4. *Department of Public Safety.* This office is most often concerned with school bus and transportation problems, safety of equipment, licensing of drivers, and other related problems.

The number of other governmental agencies which influence state department operating efficiency varies from state to state. Too often public school administrators, board members, and teachers assume that the state education department is a relatively autonomous agency that can determine its needs for internal operation. This is not the case. As part of the internal administration within state government, the state department of education is coordinated with other departments, sometimes to its advantage and other times not.

Recommended Principles for the Reorganization of State Departments of Education

Thurston and Roe [18] suggest twenty-one principles for the proper organizational structure of state departments of education. Among these, the following are particularly important:

1. The education function is so complex that it can only be carried out through a number of institutions, agencies, and activities. Cooperation, coordination, and unification of other educational and social agencies for more effective educational operation are essential activities of the state department of education.

2. An effective organization will emphasize and continuously utilize in proper balance the four constituent elements of administrative activities: (1) planning, (2) execution, (3) appraisal, and (4) interpretation.

3. The state legal plan should provide mandatory rules and regulations for minimum socially essential educational requirements and broad legal powers to enable local educational authorities to expand educational effort in accordance with needs and allow experimentation in unexplored areas.

4. The educational functions of the state should be exercised through

an adequate state educational authority that includes not only a representative state board of education to determine policy but also competent professional specialists selected on the basis of merit.

5. Administration is to facilitate the accomplishment of the purposes of the state department of education. Administrative personnel should provide leadership in the achievement of these purposes and should see that members of the staff have the necessary time, materials, and working conditions for the performance of their functions.

6. The prominence of the state department of education will be achieved by the work performed and by the excellence of its personnel as they work individually and coordinately. To achieve such excellence, provision must be made for staff members to avail themselves of opportunities to make significant contributions locally, nationally, and internationally.

However, the student of educational administration must do more than understand the principles of organization recommended by competent authorities. The real problem lies in the fact that administrative organization for education attempts to place itself beyond the spheres of politics in the state, but is completely surrounded by the political organization and is subject to controls by it. The nature of political control is crucial. How can states develop programs in education without first finding the way to introduce these programs into the policy-making stream of politics?

EDUCATIONAL ADMINISTRATION AND STATE POLITICAL STRUCTURE

School administrators and state department personnel have a major problem during political elections determining how politicians stand on educational matters, and how to introduce educational matters into the state decision-making machinery. Moneypenny, a political scientist, points out that the "executive in state governments is the principle determiner of programs which come before the legislature—and programs which are introduced into the legislature without his support are very unlikely to secure serious legislative support." [19] Moneypenny distinguishes between the problems of securing legislative support at the federal and at the state level. The governor's veto power is ordinarily more absolute than that of the President of the United States, since the legislature is rarely in session to override a veto once it has been given, and the governor's power over his own party is apt to be considerably greater than that of the President. Nor are state legislators generally likely to have the degree of independence from the governor that members of Congress have from the President. Thus, the inevitable conclusion is that at the state level the governor's position is enormously important in formulating state educational plans and policy.[20]

In most states, educational matters are introduced to the legislature through legislative interim committees or standing committees. These committees, which constitute only a small part of the legislative membership, negotiate directly with educational spokesmen. Whatever legislation introduced is likely to be the result of bargaining among school groups, interim committee members, and the governor. As Moneypenny observes, interim committees are very unlikely to introduce legislation which does not have some assurance of approval by the governor.[21] As the members of the legislature have little time to study bills, there is a tendency to follow the recommendations of party leaders, the recommendations of the interim committee, and/or the recommendations of spokesmen who are self-appointed educational critics.

According to Moneypenny, state departments of education do not play a key role in the resolution of educational issues.[22] State department staff members usually work with interim commissions, though in some states the chief executive officer of the department has more access to the governor's council than do elected officials in state government. The formulation of state educational policy and plans is often frustrated by two main problems: first, in some states the state department of education is looked upon as an agency that threatens local autonomy; thus there is a tendency for local school administrators to join together for a program which they take to the legislature, by-passing the state education department; second, there is disagreement within and among various professional organizations in education about the direction that education *ought* to take in a given state. In many states interim committee members receive requests for contradictory legislation from two or more educational organizations. It is not unusual, for example, for the American Federation of Teachers and the State Education Association to ask for directly contradictory legislation. Legislators in one such state came to the conclusion that no one in education knew what he was talking about; they probably thought that inaction or no action was the better course to follow.

Students of educational administration will disagree about whether state departments should engage in active programs for education and be prepared to advocate and seek support for them from the state legislature. In many states, the state department of education apparently sees its function as that of supplying data to the legislature with no attempt to develop a comprehensive long-range program for education in the state. In many cases local superintendents of schools and local board members would not support such activity. Consequently, very seldom do educational issues concerning the program, curriculum organization, or intraschool organization get discussed in state legislatures. The areas most apt to become issues in partisan politics are the extent of state financial support and school district reorganization. In regard to financial support, political commitments to hold down state spending or to provide a different distribution of funds among competing state agencies become issues. Rural legislators are reluctant to support laws which would eliminate school districts in local areas back home. Recent fruitful effort to reapportion legislatures may effectively change this situation, but it remains to be seen.

It is our contention that education is a part of the political arena, and that education at the state level can best be promoted by state departments and local educational authorities working together to develop programs. The advantage of its being apolitical is that the department of education and the local school systems can focus their attention on the problems of teaching children independently of any political party line. But the challenge is to manipulate all sides of the political picture, rather than to stay out of politics altogether.

The Local School District

ITS LEGAL STATUS

The separation of education from political government has been more successfully achieved at the local level than at the state and federal levels. At the local level it is the local board of education which decides educational and fiscal policy. The local school board is an arm of state government created for the purpose of implementing educational programs which insure the survival of the state. This board is relatively autonomous with respect to educational matters, and it is not required to balance education with street improvement, sewers, police protection, and other agencies of local government.

School districts have been legally defined as quasi-corporations rather than full municipal corporations such as cities or towns. A municipal corporation is usually considered a city or town established for the purpose of local government. While a city or town is in part an agency of the state designed to assist in the affairs of civil government, its main concern is advancing the local interest. Thus the powers granted to a municipal corporation for legislating its own ordinances and regulating its own affairs are broad and extensive. School districts, on the other hand, are instruments of the state intended primarily to facilitate the administration of state government. The local school district executes state educational policy.[23] Although the powers of the board of education are great, these are delegated powers.

Newton Edwards points out, however, that when the general powers and obligations of the school district are discussed they are definitely considered quasi-corporations, but for purposes of constitutional and statutory interpretations they are often held to be municipal corporations.[24] In Iowa, municipal corporations are authorized to issue bonds. The courts have held that this applied to school districts. Edwards suggested that the term "municipal corporation" is often used in a genetic sense or in such a broad sense as to include quasi-corporations.

The functions of school boards are defined as policy-making, legislation, and evaluation. The school board is responsible for implementing state law, developing policy where necessary to implement the law, and, in the absence of specific law, to serve as a legislative body. It is also supposed to evaluate (1) the administration of the schools, (2) the employed personnel, (3) the educational program, (4) the financial program, (5) the school plant, (6) pupil personnel, (7) the public relations program, and (8) cooperative programs with other community agencies which have a bearing on the educational program. In other words, boards of education have been delegated powers and duties with the purpose of assuring that the schools of the community are properly operated in all respects. This nation's 159,000 local school board members are public servants selected to carry out the wishes of their constituents in accordance with the laws of the state.

THE SCHOOL BOARD

Authorities in educational administration usually advocate that board members be elected at large on nonpartisan ballots. In fact, most state statutes prescribe a popular vote on a nonpartisan ticket. Terms of office are overlapping and usually run for four years.

Studies reveal that the trend is toward smaller school boards.[25,26] Board membership has decreased from an average of 14.2 members in 1902 to 8.2 members in 1927 to an average of about 5 members at the present time.[27] The literature in educational administration tends to recommend that the number of board members should not exceed 9. This is necessary, because it is more difficult for larger boards to arrive at intelligent decisions.

In cities, board members tend to come from business and professional groups. A study by the NEA revealed that forty-two per cent of the board members in smaller towns were farmers.[28] Generally, however, it can be said that board members come from the managerial or professional classes rather than from laboring or working classes.

The NEA study reveals that the amount of formal education of board members is increasing and is greater than that of the average citizen. In 1946, for example, seven out of ten board members had a high school education and one out of three had graduated from college.[29] Whalen studied over 1,800 board members in the midwest and found that the average number of years of formal education was about fifteen.[30]

Criteria for Board Membership. Although most states set some qualifications regarding residency and age, no state sets educational qualifications for board membership. The question of qualifications is left up to the individual voter and his fellow citizens. Ward G. Reeder suggests that the criteria for evaluation of suitability for board membership should be the following: (1) success in vocation, (2) sufficient time to devote to school board business, (3) good judgment, (4) willingness to cooperate with other board members and with the superintendent, (5) good acquaintance with the local school system, (6) deep interest in child welfare and education, and (7) honesty and other characteristics of good citizenship.[31]

The problem of determining who should be on the school board is a difficult one for voters today. In large cities the individual voter often relies on endorsement by particular groups or organizations that he respects. Individuals in large cities are often encouraged by organizations or groups of citizens to "throw their hat into the ring." In many instances groups which have a sincere interest in the schools are formed, and these groups urge individuals to run for the board of education. In some instances groups are formed which have an "ax to grind," and these groups also sponsor individuals for the board of education. However, interestingly enough, many times the person who has run on a platform which is extremely critical of the present school operation finds that the operation of the enterprise has been sound and alters his critical views after his election.

Very seldom are *educational* issues the platform of a school board candidate, beyond that of determining a "good program for all children in the district." It is claimed that matters pertaining to subject matter content, method, and organization are better left to board study and decision and to the expertise of professionals. These matters need careful study and consideration by a board which has available the best consultant help and data that it can receive through the administrative staff of the schools. Citizens are more apt to elect board members on their commitments in terms of tax rates. By and large the voter is probably not well *enough* informed about what constitutes a sound educational program, or what differentiates an excellent school system from a poor or mediocre one. The quality of a given school system is dependent upon the expectations of citizens' groups, the insight, understanding, and quality of the state and local board of education and the understanding, commitment, insight, quality, and ability of the local superintendent of schools and his staff.

Geographic Basis of Representation. Frequently a criterion for board membership becomes a matter of geography beyond that of living in the school district. In some cities board members are elected by ward or other subdivision of the city. The precept behind geographic representation is that people and children in each ward or division will have representation on the board. However, nearly all writers in educational administration advocate that board members be elected at large, for the following reasons: (1) ward or area representation does not follow populations; (2) ward or area representatives are expected to represent their own areas rather than the total system, making it extremely difficult to have the board function as a policy making organization; (3) ward or area representatives will tend to substitute their judgment for the professional judgment of the administrator on what is needed in the school system, which tends to make the board an executive board rather than a policy board; (4) a board established to represent geographic areas assumes that each board member is equally strong and equally demanding, which is most often not true, and (5) the school systems should be headed by a strong, professionally trained educator who is given the responsibility and necessary authority to provide the best possible educational experiences for all children in the district. A board based on area or ward representation can make it impossible for an administrator to operate, if it is inclined toward the idea that ward areas are more important than the district as a whole.

In the process of urbanization and school district reorganization which is taking place in most states, there is considerable reason to believe that geographic representation is increasing as school districts reorganize and join urban centers. In many Iowa cities of 2,500 or more all school board members were from the central urban area until school district organization. Informal agreements were reached which more or less guaranteed the rural area at least one or two representatives on the board of education. This is taking place because in many communities the school district boundary had been co-terminous with the city boundary until reorganization. In many cases where there are two rural representatives on a five-member board, the rural area has more representation per citizen and per school child than does the urban center.

The concept of a board elected at large guided by a competent superintendent of schools to administer fairly and equitably an educational program for *all* children is not fully accepted or understood in school control.

Superintendent-Board Relationships. All educational writers agree that the most important single responsibility that a school board has is that of appointing a competent superintendent of schools. The superintendent of schools is the executive officer of the board. His realm is the executive function, while the board is the legislative policy-making body. One of the chief functions of the superintendent is to obtain, organize, and present data and information relevant to problems at hand so that the board can make intelligent policy decisions. It is recommended practice that the board refuse to enact legislation or make policy without the recommendation of the superintendent of schools. Policy execution is the responsibility of the professional experts on the staff. The board, however, has the power, authority, and responsibility to evaluate how well policy has been executed.

In actual practice, however, many boards of education do not have written policies, and as a result boards frequently spend much time in administrative or executive functions. The larger the community, the more likely is the board of education to have written policies, and the less inclined it is to become involved in administrative or executive functions. The ability of a board of education to function intelligently and effectively is dependent upon (1) the intelligence, understanding, ability, and ethical commitment of individual board members, and (2) the intelligence, ability, understanding, and ethical commitments of the professional chief executive of the board. The relationship between a board of education and the superintendent of schools must be one of absolute mutual respect and trust. If this mutual respect does not exist, as it often does not, the relationship will be less than effective.

INTERNAL DISTRICT ORGANIZATION

Authorities on educational administration agree that there should be only one executive of the school system who is responsible to the board of education for all aspects of the school district operations. However, some school districts in the United States do have a unit system of organization where more than one person is directly responsible to the board for the operation of the school district.

School organization within a district is usually portrayed in the form of an organizational chart as illustrated in Figure 3. Individual school dis-

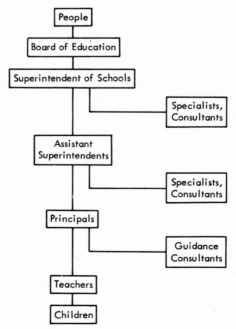

FIGURE 3. A typical school organizational structure as depicted in organizational charts.

tricts vary from this basic chart in terms of the magnitude of the operation. In most texts in educational administration, and in most school systems, a differentiation is made between line and staff functions. The "line" refers to the line of authority from the board of education to the child." The line personnel in school organizations are considered to be, in most cases, the board of education, the superintendent of schools, certain assistant superintendents of schools, principals, teachers, and children. These persons have authority that decreases from the top down. Staff officers officially do not have authority to make decisions for the line officers. Instead they serve as specialists in prescribed areas and provide help and information to line officers so that intelligent decisions can be made by them.

School districts can be further divided into administrative units, attendance units, and fiscal units. The administrative unit is a geographic area over which a given board of education has responsibility for administering the schools therein. The attendance unit is a geographic area from which children attend a given elementary or secondary school. Usually the elementary attendance unit is smaller than the administrative unit, or the high school attendance units; it can, however, be co-terminous with any of them. Local boards of education have the legal right to establish attendance units within the district insofar as it is done without discrimination. The fiscal unit is the area within which the board can levy taxes for the support of the schools.

NUMBER OF SCHOOL DISTRICTS

School district organization in the United States makes little sense governmentally or educationally. In 1957 there were 50,446 school districts compared with 17,198 townships and towns, 17,183 municipalities, 14,405 special districts, and 3,047 counties. Over half of the governmental units in this country in 1957 were local school districts.[32] In 1953 one school district in the United States (New York City) enrolled more children than the total enrollment in each of forty states.[33] Using the 1953 enrollment figure, there were 956,549 children enrolled in the New York City public schools. This one district enrolled more children than were enrolled in all the 2,600 school districts in Minnesota in 1958–1959,[34] or the 2,052 school districts in Iowa, the 2,585 Kansas school districts, or Nebraska with 3,800 school districts. It has changed but little since that time.

School districts have become so fragmented that Iowa, Nebraska, North Dakota, and South Dakota which educate about four per cent of the children in the nation have about twenty-five per cent of the school districts in the nation.

Urbanization Problems. When one speaks of the number of school districts in the United States today, the term has little significance in regard to the numbers of children educated. Within most states large numbers of children are educated in relatively few school districts. For example, in 1960, within the rural state of Iowa, the eleven largest districts enrolled twenty-six per cent of all the children. The five largest districts in Iowa enroll approximately 110,000 children, while 308 of the smallest school districts enroll approximately 106,700 children. The city of Des Moines enrolls 45,221 children, which is equivalent to the combined enrollment of 165 of the smallest school districts.

The relative influence of the seven board members in Des Moines, with 45,221 children, is considerably less than the approximately 795 board members from the 159 small rural districts in regard to the solution of school problems confronting the children of Iowa. The problem of the urban community, which now educates and will continue to educate an ever increasing majority of the children in the state, is becoming increasingly crucial. Urban communities in most states are being discriminated against in state legislatures by their failure to approve reapportionment. The relative advantage that small districts have is magnified by the simple quantity of school board members who can (and do) place political pressure on legislators, and can similarly dominate state school board association matters.

SCHOOL DISTRICT REORGANIZATION

The graph (Figure 4) summarizes the recent history of school district reorganization.

Since 1930 the number of school districts in the U.S. has decreased by 77.4 per cent. Mississippi eliminated 97.3 per cent of its school districts. Illinois and New York reduced the number of school districts 8,000 and 10,000 respectively. This picture, however, is somewhat misleading because a huge majority of the closed districts were one-room rural school districts, many of which were not operating schools during the past few years anyway. As of 1964–1965 there were 28,814 districts, 3,158 of which were nonoperating districts. Thus, eleven per cent of all the total number of districts in 1964–1965 were making arrangements for the instruction of their pupils with some other operating district.[35]

Reorganization of school districts in terms of satisfactory secondary schools has not been accomplished. A great majority of the reorganized school districts are still too small to provide a comprehensive educational program and adequate specialized personnel to meet the needs of all children from kindergarten through twelfth grade.

Burton Krietlow identifies several factors which hinder proper reorganization of school districts: (1) ownership of school property; (2) fiscal control and title of property which rests with a city rather than a district; (3) complacency; (4) fear of having no effective part in the operation and control of the new district; (5) concern over the needs of a new building and the location of the school when reorganization takes place;

(6) concern over changes in tax rates.[36] Other reasons that school district reorganization has been slow include competitive athletics, fear of superintendents and teachers that they may lose their jobs, anxiety of merchants over loss of business, and so on.

Most state legislators and state department of education officials recognize that present school district organization is poor and inefficient. The problem is that rural dominated legislators are under such extreme pressure from local groups that when legislation is passed, it is usually so cumbersome or so constructed that it is extremely difficult to obtain a favorable vote for reorganization. Only a very few state legislatures have

Number of Units

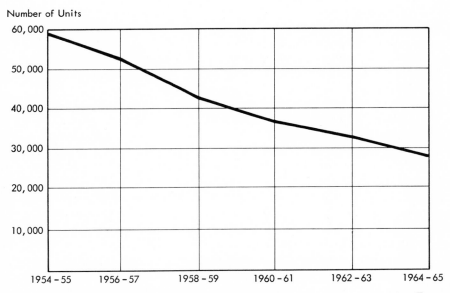

FIGURE 4. Number of local school administrative units (1954–55 to 1964–65). (From NEA, Research Division, *Research Bulletin*, vol. 43, no. 1. 1965, p. 4. Used by permission.)

reorganized districts by law; most of them have devised means by which local citizens can determine whether they wish to organize a new district by referendum.

CRITERIA OF AN EFFECTIVE SCHOOL DISTRICT

When considering the problem of determining what the characteristics of a good school district are, students of administration have concluded that present efforts in school district organization are far from approaching any semblance of effectiveness. School districts of the future are going to be much larger than almost all of the present reorganized districts. Latest thinking on the subject suggests that within the next two decades about 5,000 school districts are all that will be needed in the entire United States.

As early as 1934 Dawson made a careful study of practices in city and county systems and found that at least thirty-one persons are needed to provide the necessary administrative and supervisory functions in a standard administrative unit.[37] He concluded that a school district would have to enroll about 12,000 pupils to justify a staff of this size if the school instructional costs were to bear a reasonable relationship to the total cost of the educational program. Dawson was roundly criticized by many because it was thought a district this size was unattainable and impractical. Today it seems quite reasonable. In fact, in terms of the future, 12,000 pupils may be too few.

Most authorities agree that a good school district should have the following characteristics and functions:

1. Offer a program of education that is comprehensive and includes sound general education and vocational education from kindergarten through adult education.

2. Have a wide enough and large enough district to assume an ever-increasing educational load placed on schools by technology and an increasingly complex society.

3. Have enough children (10,000 for example) to justify offering every service and program necessary to meet modern educational requirements.

4. Have enough attendance units with adequate equipment so that long bus rides can be eliminated (one hour each way for high school children and one-half hour each way for elementary children as maximums).

5. Be as geographically homogeneous as possible.

6. Consider sociological aspects of the community. Ideally a good school district ought to be large enough to insure inclusion of a substantial number of people who are well educated and have high aspirations for schools.

Many of the most critical decisions on educational quality are presently made at the local level. Districts differ greatly in their ability to support education and in the level and quality of education that is provided. Local control is unique to American education. However, it has in some cases been badly abused. In other cases districts have no control over quality because they are too poor, or have so few students that only marginal education is the best that can be offered.

Education at the Federal Level

The federal government has been concerned with education, and has participated in promoting it since 1785 when Colonel Timothy Pickering proposed to Congress that the new state of Ohio have reserved Lot No.

16 of every township for the maintenance of public schools within the township. This was known as the Ordinance of 1785. The famous Ordinance of 1787 set a policy without implementing it for the Northwest Territory. This Ordinance declared that "religion, morality, and knowledge being necessary to good government and the happiness of mankind, schools and the means of education shall forever be encouraged." The federal government later adopted the policy of reserving land for each of the new states as they entered the union. The famous Morrill Acts during the term of President Lincoln provided land and monies which established and promoted the land grant colleges.

Through the general welfare clause of the Constitution, the federal government has been an active partner in education for 177 years. However, with the exception of the federal land grants, the activities of the federal government have been selective. That is, until 1965, it has tended over the years to provide monies for selected parts of education rather than grant general aid to support education. The Morrill Acts in 1869 and 1890 grew out of the Civil War and the need for advancing agriculture and the mechanical arts. Later, in the early 1900's, the Smith-Hughes Act provided support for vocational training at the secondary level.

The two decades immediately following World War II witnessed persistent campaigns on the part of public school personnel for greater participation by the federal government in the support of education. Two major issues inhibited this participation: (1) the fear of loss of local and state control of educational policy-making, and (2) the question of whether funds could or should be made available to private and parochial schools.

Following the Soviet Union's first successful launching of a man-made satellite, interest in the quality of public education provided a new dimension of arguments to proponents of federal aid. Using the national welfare as a motive for its passage, the National Defense Education Act was passed in 1958. The effect was almost immediate. In 1950, for example, approximately $32,000,000 was appropriated to the U.S. Office of Education; by 1960, this had increased to $464,000,000.[38] In a ten-year period, the amount of financial assistance to education through the U.S. Office of Education had increased fourteen times.

When the 1965 Congress convened, education constituted one of its major commitments. The 1964 Congress passed more than twenty different measures concerning education, but in the following year Congress enacted the largest aid-to-education bill ever proposed, the Elementary and Secondary Education Act of 1965.

There are ten major federal programs today which constitute the bulk of the federal government's role in education. These include the Elementary and Secondary Education Act of 1965; the National Defense Education Act; the Vocational Education Act; the Economic Opportunity Act; the Civil Rights Act; the Library Services and Construction Act; School

Assistance to Federally Affected Areas (the familiar "impacted" legislation); the Manpower Development and Training Act; and educational television assistance through the Federal Communications Act.[39]

The key agency in administering the bulk of new federal funds to education is the U.S. Office of Education.

THE UNITED STATES OFFICE OF EDUCATION

The U.S. Office of Education was established in 1867. For about three-quarters of a century the office performed as an agency for the collection and dissemination of information on education. In more recent years the office has assumed responsibility for analyzing and interpreting the information which it collects. As a result of these responsibilities, the office became a source of professional consultative help to organized education. Literature in educational administration has generally regarded the functions of the U.S. Office as those of data collection, dissemination, and interpretation. The original act stated:

There should be established—a department of Education, for the purpose of collecting such statistics and facts as shall show the condition and progress of education in the several States and Territories, and of diffusing such information reporting and organization and management of schools and school systems and methods of teaching as shall aid the people of the United States in the establishment and maintenance of efficient school systems, and otherwise promote the cause of education throughout the country.[40]

Until 1964–1965 little emphasis had been given to the last sentence—"to promote the cause of education throughout the country." Within the past two years, however, the potential power of the office of education has become especially visible through its efforts to withhold Federal monies from states and cities suspected of racial discrimination. The office, however, appears to have been unsuccessful in a recent political clash with the city of Chicago over this issue.

In the document, "Federal Education Agency For the Future," the writers state that the basic mission of the Office is to "promote the cause of education." [41] There appears to be little question that there is a need for some federal agency which can aid in the formulation of federal policy. The United States Office of Education is not yet staffed or equipped to provide assistance to all of the various facets of the federal government which are concerned with education. Mobility of population, national defense and survival needs, international relations, educational research, dissemination and interpretation of information about education in the United States are examples of areas of education which cannot be handled by individual states. Some agency is needed to provide coordination, or establish federal-state policy so that education in the United

States collectively meets these problems. Although legislation enacted in 1964 and 1965 provides for some of this, it is still not entirely effective.

SUMMARY

The school administrator of the 1960's and 1970's will occupy a position in which he will face national-state-local conflicts, and power will play an important role. He is living and working at a time when the basic legal and philosophical structures of education are being rapidly modified. He will play a part in these changes. His job will be one which will include far more than local or state conflict. He will be watched by national power groups of all kinds. His actions will have implications for America's position in international affairs.

While the legal setting of education must reflect broad changes in the society and its cultural values, the pattern of the past suggests that the nature and structure of the school organization itself—both formal and informal aspects—will respond to change more rapidly. The following three chapters consider aspects of schools as formal organizations and explore in greater detail, some characteristics of organizational structure, and internal control.

BIBLIOGRAPHY AND NOTES

1. J. J. Corson, *Governance of Colleges and Universities*. New York: McGraw-Hill, 1960, pp. 7–8.
2. E. P. Cubberley, *Public Education in the United States*. New York: Houghton Mifflin, 1919, p. 1.
3. E. P. Cubberley, *Readings in Public Education in the U. S.* Cambridge, Mass.· Houghton Mifflin, 1934, pp. 18–19.
4. G. H. Martin, *The Evolution of the Massachusetts Public School System*. New' York: Appleton, 1894, p. 284.
5. *Ibid.*, p. 284.
6. *Bissell vs. Bavison*, 65 Conn. 183, 32 Atl. 348.
7. *Meyer vs. State of Nebraska*, 262 U.A. 390.
8. E. P. Cubberley, *State School Administration*. New York: Houghton Mifflin, 1927. p. 143.
9. *Ibid.*, pp. 144–145.
10. W. W. Keesecher, *State Boards of Education and Chief State School Officers*. U. S. Office of Education, Federal Security Agency, Bulletin 1950, No. 12, p. 5.
11. *Ibid.*
12. *Ibid.*
13. N. Edwards, *The Courts and the Public Schools*, rev. ed. Chicago: Univ. Chicago Press, 1955, p. 23.
14. *State Board of Education of Minneapolis vs. Erickson*, 190 Minn. 216, 251 N. W. 519.
15. Edwards, *op. cit.*, pp. 23–4.
16. L. M. Thurston and W. H. Roe, *State School Administration*. New York: Harper, 1947, p. 79.
17. *Ibid.*, p. 80.

18. *Ibid.*, pp. 84–86.
19. P. Moneypenny, *A Political Analysis of Structures for Educational Policy Making,* "Government of Public Education for Adequate Policy Making" (papers of 4th Career Development Seminar, University Council on Educational Administration, November, 1959). Bureau of Educational Research, University of Illinois College of Education, Urbana, 1960, p. 6.
20. *Ibid.*, p. 7.
21. *Ibid.*
22. *Ibid.*, p. 8.
23. For a full discussion, see N. Edwards, *op. cit.*, Ch. IV.
24. *Ibid.*, p. 55.
25. W. S. Diffenbaugh, *Certain Practices in City School Administration.* U. S. Bureau of Education Leaflet No. 29, G. P. O. 1927.
26. NEA Research Division, *Status and Practices of Boards of Education,* Research Bulletin No. 24, April, 1946, pp. 47–83.
27. M. M. Hull, *Provisions Governing Membership on Local Boards of Education.* U. S. Office of Education Bulletin No. 13, G. P. O. 1957, p. 66.
28. NEA Research Division, *op. cit.*
29. *Ibid.*
30. R. E. Whalen, *Effectiveness of Elective and Appointed School Board Members,* doctoral thesis, Indiana University.
31. W. G. Reeder, *Fundamentals of Public School Administration,* 4th ed. New York: Macmillan, 1958, p. 67.
32. American Association of School Administrators, *School District Organization,* National Education Association, 1958, p. 81.
33. *Ibid.*
34. U. S. Office of Education, Biennial Survey, *Statistics of State School Systems,* 1957–58, U. S. Department of Health, Education, and Welfare. G. P. O. 1958, p. 36.
35. NEA Research Bulletin, Vol. 43, No. 1, 1965, p. 5.
36. B. W. Krietlow, "Factors Limiting School Organization," *The Nation's Schools,* vol. 51, 1953, pp. 81–84.
37. H. A. Dawson, *Satisfactory Local School Units,* Field Study No. 7, Division of Surveys and Field Studies, George Peabody College for Teachers, Nashville, Tenn., 1934, p. 39.
38. U. S. Office of Education, Department of Health, Education, and Welfare, *A Federal Education Agency for the Future,* G. P. O. April, 1961.
39. For a complete résumé of federal legislation enacted as of 1965 which pertains to education, see *School Management Magazine,* June, 1965.
40. U. S. Department of Health, *op. cit.*, G. P. O., p. 1.
41. *Ibid.*, p. 56.

7

The Essentials of Bureaucracy

> The technique of civilized labor requires for its perfection a hierarchical structure of society "one mind for a thousand hands," a system of leaders and executors.[1]
>
> In any society the establishment of an educational program calls for a plan and an organization for carrying out the program. In primitive groups the organization was usually relatively simple, but as society became more and more complex and schools were developed the need for an appropriate organization to carry out the purposes of education had to be developed.[2]

Bureaucracy as an Ideal Type

SPECIALIZATION

SCHOOL systems have a bureaucratic organization. Bureaucracy refers to a method of organizing administrative functions. The method consists or essentially two principles, coordination and specialization. Specialization, the process of breaking work down into standard components, is accomplished through a hierarchy of *offices* which establish spheres of delegated responsibility. Officials are appointed, rather than elected to office, and they should qualify on the basis of skill rather than personality characteristics alone. Thus, the basis of official superiority is supposed to rest on competence and knowledge. Specialization permits the economy of training skilled experts in a relatively short period, thus cutting personnel training costs and raising work standards. Spheres of jurisdiction are prescribed to offices, and duties of office should be performed by dedicated workers for whom the job constitutes a career. Figure 3 (Chapter 6) is a simple example of specialization in a school organization.

Since work constitutes only one of the employee's interests, bureaucratic principles are contrived to (1) secure personal, long-term attachment to the organization, and (2) assure compliance with the requirements of office.[3] The first problem is met by guarantees of security in the career in the form of advancement opportunities, pensions, and seniority. The second problem is handled through penalties set for deviation, by principles intended to exclude the total personality from the work situation, and by in-service training.

COORDINATION

Specialization sets in motion a counter-process, *coordination;* the work is coordinated from *central offices* responsible for reintegrating specialized activities into a consistent whole. Central offices are rooted in three principles: centralized graded authority, a system of rules, and impersonality.

Centralization. Centralization gives bureaucracy its rational character. For in the central office resides ultimate authority for final decisions concerning the ends of the organization, decisions on the functions of each specialty, responsibility for delegated duties, the formulation of policy, and the regulation of affairs of subordinate officers. Every official is accountable to his superior for discharging the special duties of his office, a condition which is often referred to as "the chain of command"—an elaborate ritual designed to maintain consistency among well-defined spheres of competence.[4] Referring a problem to a responsible department helps prevent inconsistent decisions between interdependent parts of the organization.

Rules. Rules represent the extension of central authority into the routine work situation.[5] Much of the administrator's daily routine consists of applying rules to particular cases. This persistent reference to rules routinizes even the most dramatic work problems which confront the organization by classifying them and prescribing standard solutions. An irate parent who approaches the superintendent of schools with a problem which seems uniquely tragic (as, for example, her child's failure in a subject) may resent the routine detached way she is treated by the superintendent's office. Nevertheless, at the same time it is precisely this ability to routinize problems—whether problems of illness in the hospital, death in the morgue, or failure in school—which increases the public's confidence in the professional bureaucrat. As a matter of fact, the parent would have little confidence in a superintendent who did not see something of the routine even in the tragic; it permits rationality to rule emotion-ridden situations. In addition, this bureaucratic detachment enables the organization to more "exactly" pursue its fundamental purposes (see Chapter 1).

However, what appears rational for the individual specialist may violate the rationality of the organization. For example, although a teacher may find a seventy-minute class period is the most efficient working time for her classes, extending her class periods would, of course, disrupt the co-ordination of the entire school and consequently reduce rather than increase its overall efficiency. In this way, rules, objectionable though they may seem in particular cases, are ideally patterned after a model of overall organizational rationality.

Impersonality. The principle of impersonality promotes discipline by separating office from person, thus minimizing the significance of the total personality while illuminating the job requirements. The broad out-lines of job performance are standardized, and office holders are expected to divorce their personal preferences, property and friendships from the performance of their duties. Thus, official relationships among offices and clients are impersonal and contractual. This is particularly important since organizations normally recruit personnel with a variety of interests, training, and background who are frequently political enemies.[6] By suppressing external distinctions, organizations attempt to build reliance on their own systems of evaluation. The "democratic" atmosphere is thus only an unintended consequence of minimizing social class, ethnic, family, and other social distinctions for purposes of efficiency.

The impersonal character of bureaucracy is protected by (1) elaborate record-keeping procedures and (2) handbooks which make knowledge the property of the organization rather than of particular persons, thereby rendering individuals expendable to the organization. Record files constitute the organization's memory, just as rules establish its division of labor. It is such principles which also permit personnel turnover without seriously disrupting the work routine.

School bureaucracy often violates the usual elaborate record-keeping of bureaucracy. Knowledge in the form of teacher-made curriculum materials, work sheets, and study guides often remain the exclusive property of the teacher. Most higher echelon school bureaucrats, however, actively seek to control teacher-made materials. Handbooks set forth certain principles, often stated as rules, regulations, and policies for personnel to follow. The handbook is impersonal; all personnel are treated as though they were alike. However, it is less threatening to receive a handbook with rules and regulations laid out for everyone than it is to be told individually what must be done, and it creates less personal resentment. The reader of the handbook may not *personally* care for some or all of the regulations, but he is comforted by the fact that he has not been singled out for special attention. The handbook tells him, in effect, that he can expect to be treated the same as everyone else.

It is curious that while the threat of possible penalty is usually inferred, most of the time no special penalties are listed if the teacher fails to follow the rules. For instance it would be interesting to speculate what the penalty would be if a teacher failed to empty his mailbox as specified in the sample pages of a teacher's handbook as follows:

Hours of Duty

All teachers are to be in their rooms by 8:20 A.M. and no later than five minutes before the homeroom takes up at 1:32 P.M. All are requested to remain after dismissal until after 4:30 P.M. Teachers should plan to be available for student and parent conferences within those time limits. Your being in the building someplace will not serve this purpose if you cannot be found. Develop the habit of encouraging students to visit you before school as well as after school. If it is necessary to leave earlier than 4:30 P.M., please obtain permission from the principal.

Hall Duty

It is the common responsibility of each member of the faculty to control the movements and the behavior of the students at all times throughout the day. Each teacher is expected to be on duty outside the classroom door after 8:30 A.M. and when classes are passing. Men teachers should assume the responsibility for the supervision of the boys' restrooms; the ladies the same responsibility for the girls' restrooms.

Daily Announcements

Any and all material for the Daily Bulletin must be turned into the Office of the Principal by 4:30 P.M. of the previous day. All materials must be approved by the principal. The Daily Bulletin will be in each teacher's box by 8 A.M. each day and must be read at the beginning of the first period.

Only in cases of extreme emergency will special bulletins or verbal announcements be sent to rooms, and these only with the approval of the principal.

Weekly Calendar

Each Friday a calendar for the next week will be prepared and placed in your mailbox on Monday morning. This calendar will include as nearly as possible the scheduled events of the week. Each Thursday all sponsors are asked to hand into the office the information about any special meeting planned for the next week such as the place, day, hour, and purpose.

Teachers' Mailboxes.

Each teacher has a mailbox in the principal's office and should come in before school in the morning and during the noon hour to receive any letters, communications, or bulletins which may have been placed there. Teachers must not allow things to accumulate in the mailboxes. They should be emptied daily.

IMPLICATIONS

Thus, these two principles—specialization of work and the coordination of tasks and their derivatives (hierarchy of offices, delegation of authority, professional career, centralized authority, a system of rules, impersonality and files)—constitute the division of labor which is bureaucracy. Specialization and coordination present a picture of bureaucracy as a simultaneous expansion and contraction of responsibility, a constant *process* of delegation and recentralization. In general, the greater the specialization, the greater will be the centralizing tendencies since greater specialization demands greater coordination.

The socially significant consequences of modern bureaucracy are the centralization of control and standardization of work performance. The former permits rationality but, significantly, does so by removing the decisions from the individual worker and the local community. The latter provides the foundation of the regularity of our society as well as increasing its efficiency but at the same time imposes on the individual rigid work routines and pressures to conform to the organization, reducing opportunity for self-expression or deviation.

This constitutes a very brief description of the ideal conception of bureaucracy as it has been imagined by theorists of our time. This is the conceptualization, implicit in descriptions of school systems found in traditional administration textbooks. While the term "bureaucracy" is often used in a derogatory sense by the layman, it is, as a matter of technical usage described above, simply a style of organization.[7] There is no question that school systems are bureaucracies. The questions that ought to be raised, however, pertain to the extent that the school bureaucracies function in the ideal terms often used to describe its organization. These questions will be explored subsequently and in the chapters which follow.

Evaluation of the "Ideal Type" Bureaucracy

ITS NONDESCRIPTIVE FUNCTION

The foregoing statements are typical of descriptions of modern large-scale organization. Most statements of this kind are directly or indirectly derived from the ideas of Max Weber and his followers. Because of his overwhelming influence on the development of ideal-type descriptions, the work of Weber and the assumptions implicit in derivative descriptions of large-scale organizations deserve closer attention.

Weber's work owes a great debt to the *ideal type*, a tool which was originally used to lend precision to cross-cultural comparisons. The ideal type is not an average of existing attributes—that is, it is not an empirical generalization based on observations—but rather it is a "pure" type derived by abstracting the most logically characteristic aspects implicit in a concept. Its purpose is not to describe reality. Far from it. It specifies a general perspective to evaluate specific factors observed. It alerts the observer of bureaucratic organizations to certain characteristics—their rules, hierarchy, specialization, and so on. The ideal type, in itself, is not to be compared with reality; rather it provides the *criteria* by which to compare different parts of the real world. Consequently, while it is a guide to research, it is not a substitute for it.[8] Whether bureaucracies actually exist in the form specified by the ideal type is to be decided by empirical investigation, not by referring to Weber or other theorists.

However, scholars following Weber's leads have chosen to ignore their historical antecedents. Some investigators have interpreted ideal characterizations of organizations as empirical descriptions of bureaucracies, with resulting misconceptions about their nature. Others, who have found empirical situations out of harmony with the ideal description, became unnecessarily disillusioned.[9]

CONFUSION OVER ITS IDEAL AND DESCRIPTIVE MEANINGS

Weber's own use of the ideal type also contributes to the confusion. While he objected to the notion that ideal types are empirical laws or hypotheses, his bureaucracy is in fact not simply a conceptual scheme, but a series of hypotheses as well.[10] For example, Weber states, ". . . it is held that the members of the corporate group, insofar as they obey a person in authority, do not owe this obedience to him as an individual, but to the impersonal order. Hence, it follows that there is an obligation to obedience only within the sphere of the rationally delimited authority . . ." [11] Whether a subordinate may in fact be "obligated" to perform personal services for superiors is a matter for investigation. And if investigated, the statement as an hypothesis would undoubtedly be rejected in many instances.

Francis and Stone find three meanings of bureaucracy as Weber uses it, two of which are relevant for this discussion. One is for the purpose of making cross-cultural comparisons. In this connection, bureaucracy is a fixed jurisdiction, a graded system of authority, a system of central files, a set of special skills called office management, official activities which demand the full time of personnel, systematic and general rules which specify procedure. This set of criteria permits the classification of particular organizations as bureaucratic or nonbureaucratic. Another meaning of bureaucracy is found in Weber's ideal type analyses, which are statements about the *nature* of organization, in contrast to historical comparison. The three major characteristics of this meaning, according to Francis and Stone, are rationality, impersonality, and routinization.[12] (Weber has also used the term as embodying a set of testable hypotheses rather than as a type.)

STRESS ON POLAR SITUATIONS

A major disadvantage of the use of the ideal type is that it seems to stress the extreme situation.[13] It thus shifts attention from variability to the polar conditions. Weber's stress on rationality, for example, tends to obscure the facts of irrationality; the emphasis on rules directs the observations away from conflict; the emphasis on the public goals of efficiency has led to the assumption that efficiency is the only goal of bureaucracy; and prophecies about the inevitable "bureaucratization," or rationalization, of the modern world persuades observers to ignore conditions of the modern world which prevent bureaucratization. For these reasons, widespread use of the ideal type has fostered a number of myths about organization, which will be considered in the next chapter.

IDEAL TYPES OF BUREAUCRACY IN
SCHOOL ADMINISTRATION

It must be concluded that the popularity of ideal type descriptions of bureaucracy which are found in much of the literature of educational administration may easily lead the student to misconceptions of existing administrative situations.

The persistent reliance of administrators on the ideal conception of organization is most evident in the widespread use of organization charts. When asked to describe his organization, the administrator will invariably point to his organization chart. A notable trend away from dogmatic reliance upon ideal organizational charts and prescriptive lists of administrative duties can be noted in the texts written in 1940. In that year Moehlman in his standard work in the field, *School Administration*, recommended that the autocratic, inflexible school organizations of that time be replaced by flexible democratic organizations, a popular theme of the period.[14] Nonetheless, even Moehlman accompanied his appeal for improvement in current practice with an idealized table of organization and prescriptive lists of duties, which were certain to maintain the *status quo* he disliked.

Moehlman's organizational chart was entitled "General Administrative Positions and Personnel" (Figure 5). Superintendents are to facilitate the instructional process by (1) maintaining the adopted educational policies of the state; (2) appraising the policies in accordance with executive needs; (3) supplying the board of education with the means for informing the agents and the people of the conditions in the schools; (4) furnishing creative leadership to the teaching profession and the board; (5) acting as professional advisor to the board of education. However, in the later (1951) edition of *School Administration*, Moehlman precedes his discussion of a democratic school organization with *empirical* generalizations about organizations typically found in cities of various sizes.[15]

A decade ago the *Thirtieth Yearbook* of the American Association of School Administrators noted that organization lends itself to graphic analysis, so far as the lines of authority are concerned.[16] The Yearbook provided two organizational charts referred to as "practical but not necessarily ideal patterns" for differing types of school systems. They stressed the various tasks to be performed. The exact jobs, they cautioned, would vary from community to community depending on community size and the situation.

Yet, as late as 1958, in discussing the superintendent's relation to the school board, Reeder provided a sample organizational chart for a school

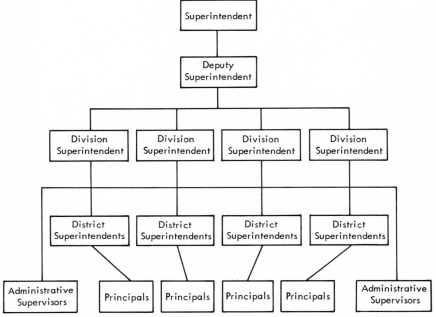

FIGURE 5. General administrative positions and personnel. (From Moehlman, A. B., *School Administration*. Used by permission of Houghton Mifflin, Boston, 1940, p. 287.)

system (Figure 6). A detailed explanation of the chart is not to be found. The design of the chart implies a misleading division of authority. In this figure, for example, the high school principals and assistant superintendents are placed on equal levels in the hierarchy. Assistant principals in this organization are given authoritative responsibility over department heads. Block outlines representing the stockroom man and the truck man are much larger than the single block to represent all high school teachers or all grade school teachers. There is some doubt raised over this outline: is this sample an ideal type or an empirical generalization about administration? [17]

More recently, Knezevich provided a formal chart of school organization which he clearly labels an idealized version.[18] Criticizing such line and staff charts, he submits that they are no more than idealized pictures of the school operation, that they do nothing to reveal the informal organization, and that seldom is the chain of command limited to the paths of relationships indicated.

The disturbing element in the ideal type is that while it need never refer to concrete situations, it gives the appearance of an empirical de-

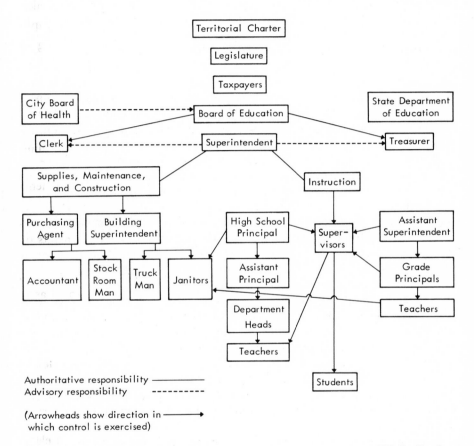

FIGURE 6. Sample organization chart for a school system. (From W. G. Reeder, *The Fundamentals of Public School Administration*, 4th ed. New York: MacMillan, 1958, p. 82.)

scription. Thus, unless care is taken, logically derived formal statements may be confused with descriptive accounts, which creates a stage for disastrous misinterpretations. For this reason the ideal type must be used with discrimination. At best it is meaningful when used as a standard to compare observed situations. As a practical expedient, it might be well to disregard it in favor of either hypotheses or concrete descriptions or organizations as they operate.

Blueprint Organization. "Analysis" of organization trouble spots may amount to little more than an analysis of the organization chart, and "reorganization" may consist of little more than reordering it. A survey conducted for a school district in one of the states bordering the Great Lakes disclosed the tendency of organizational charts to be not only oversimplified but inaccurate when compared with what is actually happening in the district. Figure 7 outlines the organization as envisioned by the superintendent. Following weeks of analysis the survey team presented their interpretation of actual practice in Figure 8. The superintendent's chart was neat, simple, almost a textbook sample, but utterly worthless as a picture of the organization as it functioned. On the other hand, Figure 8 pinpoints trouble spots, such as the large number of employees dealing directly with the board of education without going through the superintendent of schools. Figure 8, while less flattering to the superintendent, provides a bench mark to measure proposals for future reorganization.

The term "blueprint" organization has been coined to describe the character of organization charts, for they are supposedly the blueprints of the structure of the organization. (see Figure 9). They provide a temptingly concise summary of the functional relations between parts of the organization. However, like blueprints, they specify only the model as it is supposed to exist. And also like blueprints, they omit most of the vital operating details. Undue reliance on organization charts may easily lead to misconceptions about the way the organization functions.

A peculiarity of organization charts is that they become less precise at the lower echelons of the organizational hierarchy. The arrangement of the chart assumes that one is looking down from the top.[19] Since they are usually intended primarily to picture the organization of management, its specialization and interrelations, the rank and file specializations and elaborations are blurred or omitted. At best, each administrative position is pictured independently, while workers, clerks, principals, and teachers are pictured as groups. This is demonstrated in the organizational chart in Figure 9.

Prior to a study and subsequent recommendations for reorganization, the organizational chart for an Upper Plains State school system revealed a number of inconsistencies in lines of authority and policy execution (see Figure 10). Among these were the following:

1. The chart clearly shows that teachers are responsible to principals. Yet, according to the chart, the superintendent is responsible for supervision of teachers and teaching, a primary responsibility of principals in a good organization. The teacher is automatically caught between the principal and superintendent, if one is to follow the chart.

2. The teachers are further caught between the principals and the

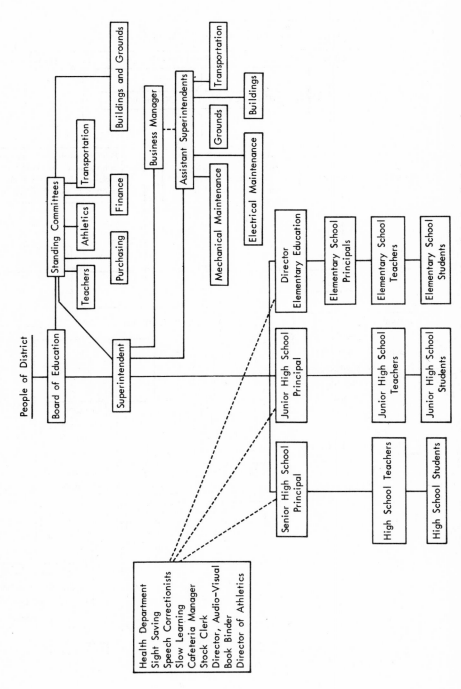

People of District

FIGURE 7. The structure of one school system as the superintendent described it to a university survey team.

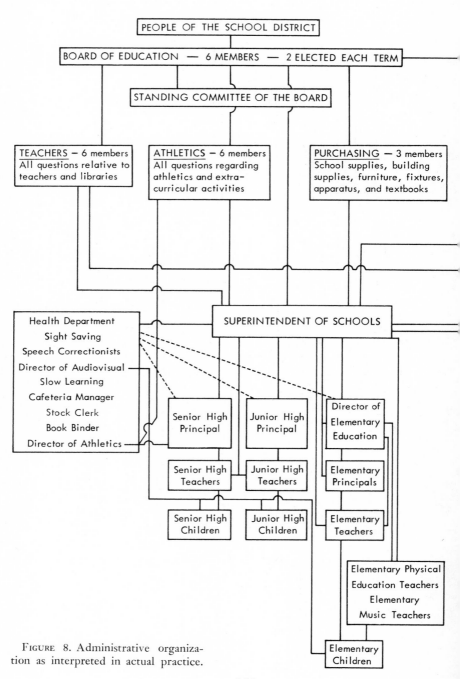

FIGURE 8. Administrative organization as interpreted in actual practice.

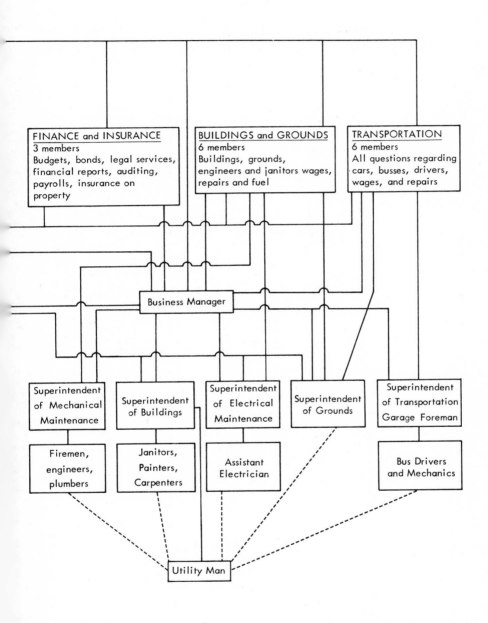

FINANCE and INSURANCE
3 members
Budgets, bonds, legal services,
financial reports, auditing,
payrolls, insurance on
property

BUILDINGS and GROUNDS
6 members
Buildings, grounds,
engineers and janitors wages,
repairs and fuel

TRANSPORTATION
6 members
All questions regarding
cars, busses, drivers,
wages, and repairs

Business Manager

Superintendent
of Mechanical
Maintenance

Superintendent
of Buildings

Superintendent
of Electrical
Maintenance

Superintendent
of Grounds

Superintendent
of Transportation
Garage Foreman

Firemen,
engineers,
plumbers

Janitors,
Painters,
Carpenters

Assistant
Electrician

Bus Drivers
and Mechanics

Utility Man

Solid lines represent lines of authority
Broken lines represent lines of cooperation

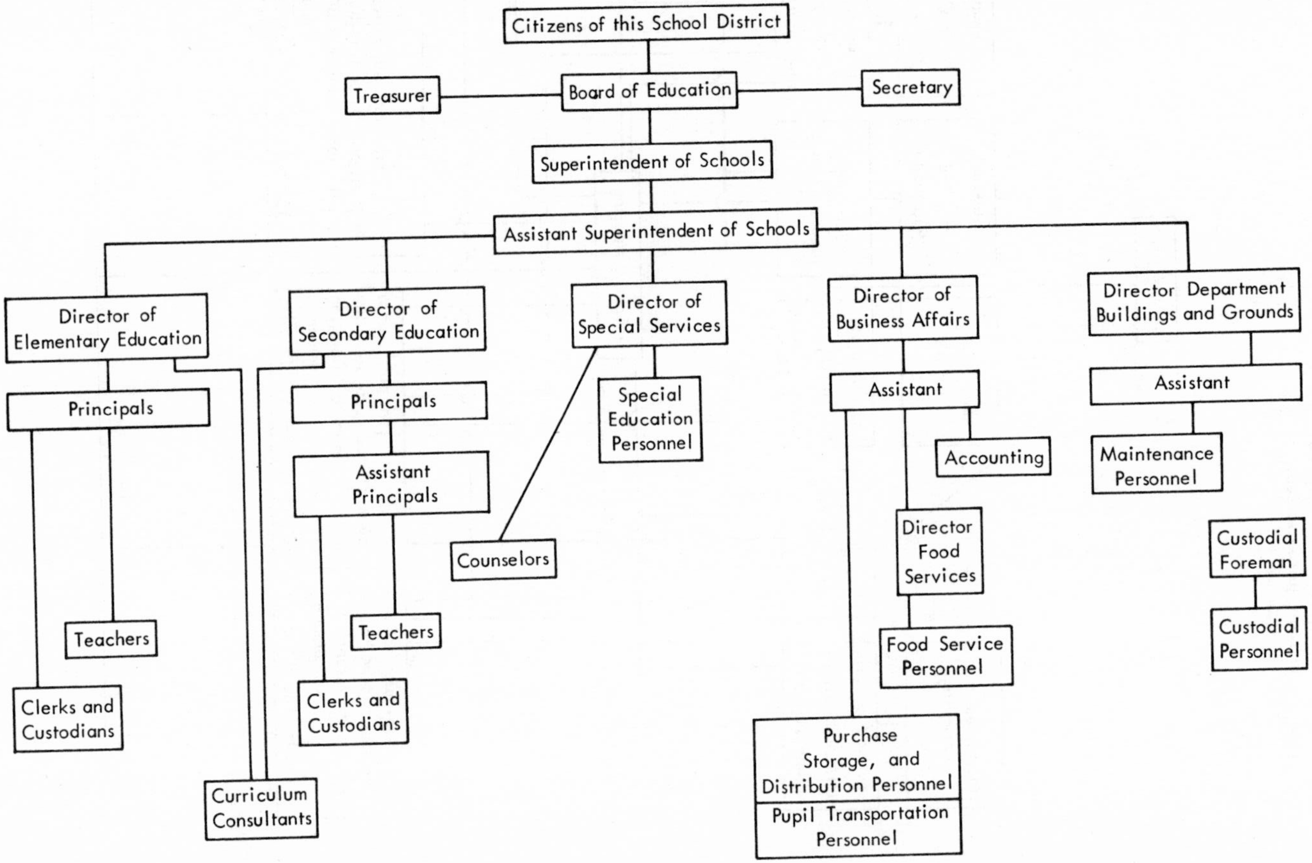

FIGURE 9. Administrative Organization Chart for system.

196

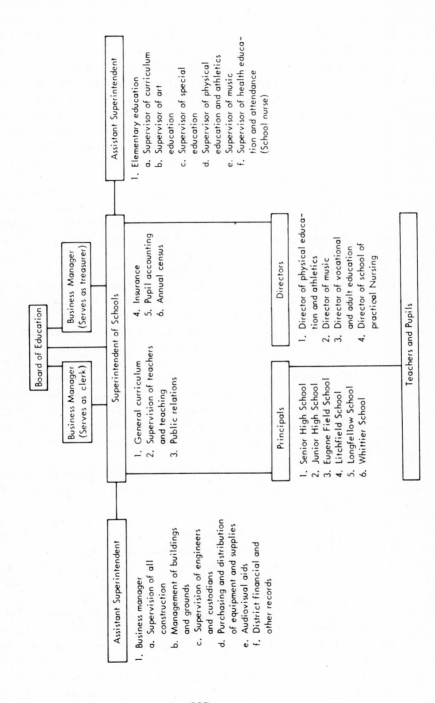

FIGURE 10. Organization Chart of Administrative Responsibilities. Upper Plains School District. (Used with permission.)

197

assistant superintendent (in charge of elementary education), whose position serves as an arm of the superintendent's office and is responsible for elementary education and supervision of curriculum.

3. According to the chart there are several division heads who are directly responsible to the superintendent; a director of physical education and athletics is directly responsible to the superintendent even though athletics is primarily a secondary school function. Physical education and athletics are also found as a part of the responsibility of the assistant superintendent of elementary education. A director of music education is found reporting to the superintendent while supervisors of music are under the assistant superintendent.

4. The chart shows the assistant superintendent (in charge of elementary education) responsible for elementary education, supervision of curriculum, art, special education, physical education and athletics, music, health education, and attendance. The chart fails to show who is responsible for these activities at the secondary level. Conceivably it could be the principals, the directors, or the superintendent.

5. The position of business manager as assistant superintendent is baffling. It shows this assistant superintendent in two cases reporting directly to the board of education (via the clerk and treasurer); in these roles the chart can be interpreted to mean that the position supersedes the superintendent and, according to the chart, the superintendent seems responsible to the business manager. In the role of business manager, the assistant superintendent serves as a staff officer to the superintendent responsible for operating the building program, purchasing and distribution of supplies, audiovisual aids, and keeping financial records. This type of organization for business has many potential dangers, among them the conflict of interest and authority between the assistant superintendent of business affairs and the superintendent.

Following the study of this school district's functional organization, a more appropriate structure was proposed and adopted by the board of education (see Figure 11).

Even on technical grounds organization charts are not precise. For example, they indicate the vertical echelons of authority more clearly than they do horizontal divisions of labor and interdepartmental relations.[20] Also "identical" organization charts do not assure that two organizations are in fact equivalent with respect to centralization of authority, conformity to rules, or degrees of specialization. They also convey the misleading impression that personnel are interchangeable among parts. While equivalent parts are interchangeable, personnel seldom are; in fact personnel tend to rather jealously guard the identity of their positions. As pointed out early in this chapter, one important function of bureaucracy is to insure personal, long-term attachment to the organization. If personnel can be shuffled about, this particular bureaucratic strength is mini-

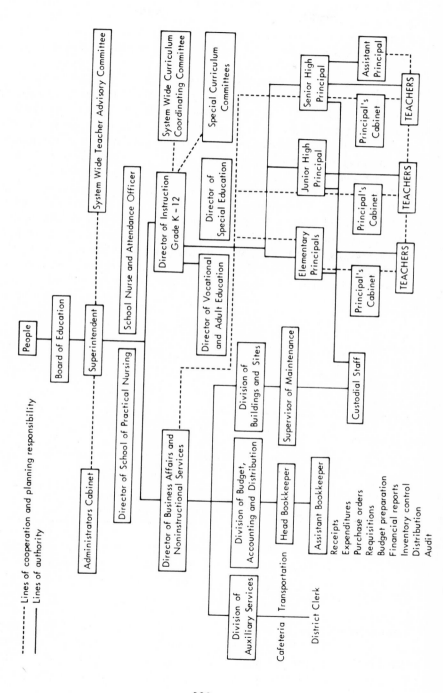

------- Lines of cooperation and planning responsibility
——— Lines of authority

FIGURE 11. A proposed organizational chart for the Upper Plains School District. (Used with permission.)

mized. Obviously, the organization chart should not be interpreted so literally, but frequently it is. Job specifications and professional specialization requirements are frequently based on precisely the assumption that all schools in the system are identical and that personnel are interchangeable.

Thus, by conveying the impression that organizations are identical and their personnel are interchangeable, the blueprint conception or organization contributes to the myth of rationality. It provides a framework of organization which gives the impression that personnel management depends entirely on the discretion of rational consideration of the administration. This impression of personnel is derived largely from the assumption that persons filling formal positions of an organization chart are incidental to the rational consideration of organization—that is, the paradoxical assumption of "impersonal personnel relations."

The Pyramid Structure. One cannot escape the convincing logic of the blueprint organization. The image of organizational structure that it portrays seems to be reasonable enough; and if the blueprint organization is accurate, the conclusion that its form assumes the nice symmetry of a pyramid seems unavoidable (See Figure 12). The pyramid is intended to

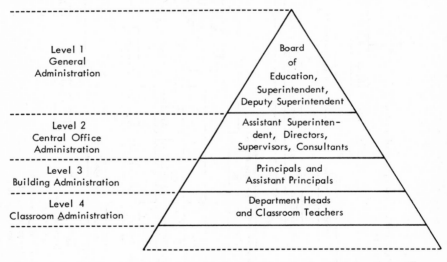

FIGURE 12. An organizational pyramid for public school administration. (From S. J. Knezevich, *Administration of Public Education.* (Used by permission of Harper & Row, New York, 1962, p. 63.)

symbolically represent the official ranking of authority of the organization's offices. This stratification of authority is popularly described as the "chain of command." Within the school system the chain of command extends from the superintendent through his assistants to principals, department heads, teachers, and ultimately to the students and secretarial staff and custodians.

But like the blueprint organization from which it is derived, the pyramid organizational form does not necessarily describe the actual distribution of power, however logically it portrays the ideal system of authority. While it suggests the broad limits of authority to issue orders and command obedience, it does not portray actual practice. For example, the pyramid does not represent the degree of independence that a subordinate has established with respect to his superiors; nor does it indicate the fact that subordinates can control their superiors through a variety of tactics, such as work slow-downs, disloyalty, possession of secret knowledge, and so on.[21] The pyramid does not portray the amount of participation which personnel actually exercise in the management of the organization. Finally, it does not identify the extent to which a staff member *represents* the organization to the public. This last point alters the power distribution, because members who represent the organization to the public have it in their power to bind the organization to commitments, which invariably affects its scopes of power.

Administrators in rural communities have often been powerless to change the scope of financial support of vocational agriculture programs in the face of opposition by agriculture instructors who have strong support from local agricultural pressure groups. Farmers may concede that fewer opportunities exist for boys in farming today, but the services and contacts of the local vocational teacher in many instances echo the farmers' continued and highly vocal support.

In other words, the pyramidal structure represents an official conception of *authority*, but it does not depict the actual distribution of *power*. To understand organizational functioning, it is necessary to understand the implications of this distinction.

Power and Authority

Part of the confusion between ideal and actual conceptions of bureaucracy stems from a tendency to confuse power with authority. Power is the capacity to use force, and authority is the legitimate right to power. But neither power nor authority imply the actual demonstration of force; they refer to its *potential*. For this reason the right to use force does not imply that it can always be used. For example, the high school principal may be authorized by the community and its board to require the teachers to take on "extracurricular activities" as a condition of employment. But if their union resists, his power is severely curtailed; his official obligation to retain his teaching staff significantly reduces the available alternatives. At the same time, as the illustration suggests, subordinates are exercising power without necessarily having the authority to do so. Similarly, a superintendent or school board member may use unauthorized power to have teachers fired for personal reasons.

These disparities between power and authority constitute one of the major dilemmas of modern organization. Indeed, the relationship between power and authority itself is somewhat of a dilemma. Although power is directly dependent on the number of available alternatives, the conditions of legitimacy may impose such restraint on the use of power that it is severely reduced.

While authority remains an exclusive property of the office, power is neither a property of office nor is it exclusively a personality characteristic. Rather, power is created out of certain situations and is available to persons favorably situated who have access to the conditions which generate power. These specific situations are found in the official and unofficial characteristics of the organization itself. The official organization makes power more accessible to some personnel than to others. For example, the secretary of a superintendent in a large school system sometimes controls the mailing list. This duty potentially provides her with power to control dissemination of certain kinds of information to certain teachers. In fact, because it affords direct contact with the chief executive, the position of secretary can be a very powerful position with its thorough access to the chief executive's personal correspondence and its other opportunities to gain his personal confidence.

One analysis suggests that any organizational "status" located in a managerial structure which provides strategic access to the control, or influence upon the control of information, assumes significant dimensions of potential power.[22] Hence, under some conditions, even a janitor may capture a position of power. Waller tells of a janitor to whom the superintendent often came for advice on major policy decisions.[23] Not only may such a worker interact with most of the school personnel, but if he has been in the system longer than many of the faculty, or if he is a long-time resident of a small community, he may have an important influence on public opinion.

Power may be used for either "good" or "bad" purposes. Power, like money, is simply a medium of exchange.[24] Its utility is measured by what it will enable the person to achieve that could not be achieved without it. And its value must be assessed in terms of the purpose for which it is used. Of course, like money, power is sometime desired for itself but, also like money, only in exceptional cases.

From a democratic point of view, perhaps the ultimate basis of authority is the agreement which citizens have reached on the assignment of certain powers to particular offices. Considering this democratic ideal almost exclusively, one author proposes that the authority of an order is determined by whether or not it is accepted by members of the organization.[25] This, for instance, might mean that the superintendent has a right to judge teaching competence and discharge poor teachers only so long as other members of the community and/or the organization agree. The consensus of organizational members seems to clearly imply authorization; and conversely, the resistance of subordinates seems to challenge the right to perform these functions. It is to this condition that Jaques has devoted some rigorous analysis and to which he refers as "the sanctioning of authority."[26]

Authorization from the majority of subordinates, in effect, permits the administrator access not only to existing rules but also, more important, some influence over the rule-making machinery. Thus power evolves from this control over rules. Merely by applying or withholding application of rules tends to encourage those conformity behaviors which affect consensus. Through such a process, one comes to understand the structural bases behind the cliché that "power begets power."

But however democratic, it cannot be presumed that authorization is the exclusive prerogative of the members of the organization or of the local community. In the first place, the members may disagree among themselves, in which case some other party will assume the right to grant or withhold authority. Also, even if counted, every person's opinion is not counted equally; is the opinion of the principal equivalent to that of the janitor or the teacher? Another reservation arises from the fact that organizations themselves may rest on other than representative bases—they may be authoritarian. But there is a major restriction of the democratic concept of authority: if the distinguishing feature of authority is a sense of legitimacy, this legitimacy may be derived from sources *outside* the organization. Social traditions and other agencies, such as the legislature, religious bodies, professional organizations, local school boards, and the State Department of Education, can *bestow* legitimacy on the functions of an office even when subordinates within the organization or residents of a particular community object.

In fact, it is characteristic of an administrative society that authority *is* bestowed by outside agencies. A good example of this occurs in many communities in relation to civil defense. The writers know of two cases where either the school system or an administrator in the school system was authorized by agencies outside of the system to assume civil defense functions. In the first case, the city council decided that since the school system had the only shelter facilities in the city, the school board was the logical agency to assume the responsibilities for civil defense. The local newspaper carried the story and several service organizations in the community backed the idea before the board of education had been contacted. At a special meeting the board issued a statement in which it said that the school system would cooperate with civil defense officials in whatever way it could, but that civil defense was a community problem rather than a school problem. They raised serious questions about the use of school buildings for shelters. They also pointed out that as new buildings were constructed any additional construction for shelter purpose would increase building costs, and they protested any attempt to make the school district assume financial obligations beyond that of providing personnel and facilities for teaching. Nevertheless, the political pressure was such that the superintendent of schools became the local director of civil defense, a job he did not want. His authority rested on the community power structure rather than the consensus of subordinates. Largely because the school system refused to provide for shelter space in the new building, a vote on a bond issue was defeated.

In a second case the superintendent of schools was approached by a committee to take on the responsibility of educational director for civil defense in a medium-sized city. He suggested to the committee that they approach a top-notch young junior high school principal for the job. The young principal conferred with the superintendent and took the job. He had two interesting experiences. The first experience occurred while he was in the process of organizing a plan for the evacuation of children in the public school system. He had no problem with the junior high school teachers who saw him as their principal, but when he met with the elementary and senior high school teachers to explain the plan and elicit their support, he found that they would not cooperate with him. He finally accomplished the job by working through the superintendent and "borrowing the colonel's eagles." In other words, he had to borrow the prestige power and authority of the superintendent of schools. The staffs of the elementary senior high schools accepted him on one basis of authority—that bestowed as an agent of the superintendent—but not on the other as junior high school principal. To ask whether he had "authority" is to miss the point; he had several types of authority—bestowed by subordinates and by superordinates—which had differential value before different audiences.

Because of the variety of authorities that can be appealed to in modern society, there is a persistent tendency for dissent to arise among groups bestowing various sources of authority. Power is always in the process of becoming authorized, and persons who are authorized to use power persistently tend to overstep their offices and use it in more questionable ways. Consequently, in practice it is often difficult to distinguish between power and authority—that is, to know when power is being utilized legitimately. Under these conditions the legitimacy of official acts is difficult to establish. For example, does a principal have the authority to withhold a student's grades because he is in trouble with the law? In cases where there is dissent among the public it is often not even clear who has the right to *decide* the issues. It is power itself that looms large in the solution of these conflicts. For whenever two groups support different conceptions of what is proper, they each attempt to accumulate enough power to have their point of view accepted. This was true of the Crusades and continues to stimulate the zeal behind missionary work. It is true on a lesser scale of most differences of opinion. In such cases, the establishment of authority itself often represents the outcome of a power strugggle. Just as the North's authority to make federal laws which the South opposed was decided by the Civil War, so the question of whether the public or the professional teacher has the ultimate authority to pass judgment on the selection of textbooks will be decided by the outcome of that struggle.

In short, the problem of authority is regressively based on power; curiously, in marginal situations the right to use power may be bestowed only by those who have the power to bestow it.

REASONS FOR THE SEPARATION OF POWER AND AUTHORITY

When disparities do arise between power and authority, the dissent threatens the "we" aspect of the organization. But they typically do not occur in the daily routine of activities. There are, according to Barnard, several reasons why authority is seldom challenged by subordinates.[27] First, most administrators take care to issue only those orders which they know will be obeyed. For the same reason, many rules which are resisted are not enforced in practice. Second, most persons are indifferent to the legitimacy of most orders. Most orders are irrelevant either to their moral codes or to their way of life. It seems to make little difference to many teachers whether they drive on the right-hand or the left-hand side of the road, or whether one text or another is used. Constant concern with such questions leads to "moral exhaustion." In fact, persons are disposed to grant authority rather than question it precisely because they are unwilling to take the time, effort, and abuse necessary to resist it. Finally, organizations often develop a sense of community which discourages outright dispute of authority. In these situations, the violation of an order by an individual seems to constitute an attack on the entire organization, including one's co-workers whose positions or very job may be threatened when their colleague "stirs up trouble."

It is, however, a mistake to judge the importance of an event by its infrequency of occurrence. A single unauthorized act of power can create an organizational crisis which becomes the source of deep-seated organizational tensions which in turn have the capacity to modify the total character of the organization. The sources of the disjunction between power and authority, when they occur, can often be traced to the nature of organization itself.

There are several reasons why the organization generates many of its own dilemmas. The first of these reasons is related to the fact that specialization tends to develop beyond official limits. An official will tend to devote most of his time and energy selectively to a few of a complex of duties which constitute his office. For example, the vice-principal in a school system may specialize in purchasing because he knows how to calculate the percentage of waste and breakage, knows how to estimate needs, knows the "right people" to buy from and where to get a "good deal"; he may find himself buying increasingly more for the entire system, even though he is not specifically authorized to do so. The very fact that he may know more about the details of the job than anyone else further enhances his control over the job.

As another example, the school typist is not ordinarily authorized to command teachers, but in fact she may have power over them because she can control the work schedule. While she cannot refuse to type authorized work, the teacher who does not treat the typist properly may find that her work is finished later than she had wished, and only the typist knows whether the time taken was reasonable.

Second, the tendency for delegation to develop beyond official limits separates power and authority. The duties of an official may be sloughed off or assumed by subordinates. In this way, the "dirty work" of the higher rank is absorbed into the lower ranks, bestowing power in the process.[28] The addition of duties from a higher rank tends to increase the subordinates relative power. For example, while the administrator concentrates on purchasing, the budget, or curriculum development, his secretary assumes more responsibility for preparing reports to the State Department of Education, which in turn gives her reason to gradually exercise control over principals and others by prescribing proper reporting form, establishing deadlines, specifying the number of copies required, and so on.

Third, organizations have only partial control over the assignment of power because a person's power is also directly associated with the number and importance of his contacts outside the school. Teachers who have the support of many influential parents are valuable to the school, and they are in a position to get their own way. For example, the principal may be reluctant to refuse a pay increase to a teacher who is a good friend of an influential school board member. Within the organization as well power in excess of authority can be gained from personal contacts, which in turn are more easily made in some positions than others. The principal's secretary may be showered with the good will of his teachers because of her ability to delay or modify their messages to her superior, and because she has the opportunity to pass along her personal report on the teacher as well.

There are still other reasons why the school cannot completely control power. The power of personnel is, for example, partially an independent function of their chief executive's authority and power: the superintendent's secretary tends to claim prestige over the high school secretaries. Similarly, teachers working for an influential principal might claim status over other teachers in the system. The official position also determines which members have access to information. High school students sometimes have jobs which allow them private access to records, which bestows on them a position of power over their peers. In short, discrepancies between power and authority may develop because the official position places persons in differential access to power.

Finally, power becomes disassociated from authority whenever areas of jurisdiction are not clearly prescribed. In any organization there are jobs which are "no one's" particular sphere of authority, and which anyone may claim as his if he performs them well or frequently. In the process of adding unclaimed jobs to a position, the sphere of control is expanded. While these may eventually become authorized functions of the position, the transition creates ambiguous discontinuities between power and authority and constitutes the kind of dynamic element that gives an organization its distinctive character. Moreover, the simple fact of having difficulty in communicating with some officials can result in subordinates affecting changes in the authority structure. For example, the custodian may be reminded repeatedly that he must channel his requests through the principal, but if the principal is frequently "tied-up" it is much easier to merely call the Director of Buildings and Grounds. A pattern that is effective is difficult to change.

It is apparent, then, that power and authority diverge in practice. This divergence corresponds to the discrepancy between the official and unofficial structure: the official structure is safeguarded by authority, while the unofficial structure is largely a function of power and nonauthorized relationships. The multiple bases of authority and the role of power help to stablize organizations in the face of dissent. Consensus is only one of the characteristics which account for the organization's stability and is not a necessary condition. The role of power wielded by the informal organization in maintaining organizational stability has still not been completely assessed, but stabilization seems to be a fundamental function of power in modern organizations.

SUMMARY

Bureaucracy is, then, a means of organizing work which permits—even encourages—specialization of talent and effort. Specialization creates a need for coordination, which is achieved in a hierarchy of graded authority regulated by rules and other standardizing, depersonalizing mechanisms. A net result is a highly specialized, standardized, and centralized set of offices bound by depersonalizing rules. From a purely personal viewpoint, this system may at times appear as a solemn system of red tape managed by indifferent personnel whose primary skills seem to be the application of forbidding rules and "buck-passing." Such a characterization, however, even if it were true (which will be discussed in Chapter 9), does not describe bureaucracy, but rather characterizes its presumed consequences for the *individual;* bureaucracy is not designed for the pleasure of individuals so much as it is engineered to institutionalize work. There are other consequences, mainly the efficient and effective uses of specialists.

However, the logically derived portrayal or the pyramidal structure is partly mythical, rooted in stereotypes of blueprint organizations which have become traditional. While it portrays an ideal conceptualization of the authority system from the viewpoint of management, it seldom if ever depicts the actual use of power in many facets of operation. So long as it is clearly understood that it reflects the ideal, the pyramidal image of the organization has some utility. However, the temptation to convertly fuse the ideal and descriptive leave it susceptible to subtle transformations, wherein the ideal is represented as fact. When this occurs, the pyramidal image, like other features of the blueprint organization and indeed every feature of the ideal type, contributes to a mythology of organizations which is clearly detrimental to the understanding of conduct in organizations. That mythology is considered in the following chapter.

BIBLIOGRAPHY AND NOTES

1. G. Simmel, *The Sociology of George Simmel,* trans. by K. H. Wolff. Glencoe, Ill.: Free Press, 1950.
2. E. L. Morphet, R. L. Johns, and T. L. Reller, *Educational Administration: Concepts, Practices and Issues.* Englewood Cliffs, N. J.: Prentice-Hall, 1959, p. 8.
3. R. Dubin, "Technical Characteristics of a Bureaucracy," in *Human Relations in Administration,* R. Dubin, ed. Englewood Cliffs, N. J.: Prentice-Hall, 1951, pp. 156 ff.; for a short summary of the concept of bureaucracy, see Max Weber's discussion in *From Max Weber's Essays in Sociology,* H. Gerth and C. W. Mills, eds., pp. 214 ff. New York: Oxford Univ. Press, 1958. For a description of formal positions in public school, see D. E. Griffiths, D. L. Clarke, D. R. Wynn, and L. Innaccone, *Organizing Schools for Effective Education.* Danville, Ill.: Interstate Printers & Publishers, 1962, Chs. 10–13.
4. P. M. Blau, *Bureaucracy in Modern Society.* New York: Random House, 1956, p. 88.
5. *Ibid.*
6. W. E. Moore, *Industrial Relations and the Social Order.* New York: Macmillan, 1951, p. 88.
7. Technically speaking, the term "bureaucracy" refers only to a special way of organizing *administrative* functions; but since it does reach into all levels of large-scale organization (through rules, its principles of impersonality, and delegated authority and the standardization of all work), generally speaking the entire organization can be considered within the bureaucratic context.
8. Blau, *Ibid.,* p. 34.
9. For example, Friedrich complains that bureaucracy is neither "ideal" nor a "type," since types derive their significance from the empirical reality that they typify;

he criticizes Weber for not doing what he explicitly tried to avoid, i.e., derive types from empirical observations.

10. Blau, *Ibid.*, p. 34.

11. M. Weber, *The Theory of Social and Economic Organization*, trans. by A.M. Henderson and Talcott Parsons. Oxford Univ. Press, 1947, pp. 329–340.

12. R. G. Francis and R. C. Stone, *Service and Procedure in Bureaucracy: A Case Study*. Minneapolis: Univ. of Minnesota Press, 1956.

13. T. Parsons, "The Professions and Social Structure," *Social Forces*, May, 1939. See also D. Martindale, "Sociological Theory and the Ideal Type," in *Symposium on Sociological Theory*, L. Gross, ed., Evanston, Ill.: Row, Peterson, 1959, Ch. 2.

14. A.B. Moehlman, *School Administration*. New York: Houghton, Mifflin, 1940, p. 287. A discernible trend away from dogmatic reliance on ideal charts and prescriptive lists of administrative duties can be generally noted in the texts written since 1940, but there are few texts that do not at least pay lip service to them.

15. A. Moehlman, *School Administration*. (Boston: Houghton-Mifflin, 1951. pp. 188–192.

16. A.A.S.A., *The American School Superintendency*, Thirtieth Yearbook, 1952, National Education Association, Washington, D.C., p. 87.

17. W. G. Reeder, *The Fundamentals of Public School Administration*, 4th ed. New York: Macmillan, 1958, p. 32.

18. S. J. Knezevich, *Administration of Public Education*. New York: Harper, 1962, p. 74.

19. Moore, *op. cit.*, p. 96.

20. *Ibid.*, p. 274.

21. C. Dreyfus, "Prestige Grading: A Mechanism of Control," in *Reader in Bureaucracy*, R. K. Merton, A. Gray, B. Hockey, and H. Selvin, eds. Glencoe, Ill.: Free Press, 1952, pp. 258–64.

22. W. G. Monahan and W. J. Foley, "Control of Information as a Source of Power in Organizations," unpublished working paper, Iowa Center for Research in School Administration, Univ. Iowa, 1966.

23. W. Waller, *The Sociology of Teaching*. New York: Wiley, 1932, pp. 80–81.

24. Moore, *op. cit.*, pp. 262–263.

25. C.I. Barnard, *The Functions of the Executive*. Cambridge, Mass.: Harvard Univ. Press, 1938, p. 163.

26. E. Jaques, *The Changing Culture of the Factory*. London: Tavistock, 1951. For an excellent essay on Power, see D. Cartwright, "Power: A Neglected Variable in Social Psychology," Studies in Social Power, Univ. Michigan, Research Center for Group Dynamics, 1959, pp. 2–14.

27. The following discussion is based on Barnard, *op. cit.*, pp. 168–169.

28. E. C. Hughes, "Work and the Self," in *Social Psychology at the Crossroads*, J.H. Rohrer and Mazafer Sherif, eds. New York: Harper, 1951, p. 319.

CHAPTER

8

Five Myths of Organization

We are currently so busy hiding conflict that we quake when we must simultaneously deal with it and pretend it does not exist.[1]

THE APPEAL of the ideal, the formal, and the public aspects of large-scale organizations for theorists has contributed to a series of popular myths about organizations which sociologists are fond of challenging. They are less widely used today than a decade ago, yet they persist. These myths are sometimes unwittingly used as theoretical assumptions about the nature of administration. They include assumptions about (a) the rationality of modern organization, (b) impersonality of work relations, (c) infallibility of rules, (d) unity of ends, and (e) the existence of a single bureaucratic form.

The mythical character of these propositions does not stem from naïve *belief* in them. Certainly anyone who has worked in school systems is familiar with their frequent lack of logic, extensive rule evasion, personal favoritism, internal conflicts, and contrasts of customs between schools. Rather, the propositions take on their mythical character because they tend to be perceived sometimes as implicit *theoretical* assumptions about organizations, and these may remain virtually unquestioned at theoretical levels of analysis. Thus, like myths, they are denied in particular and believed in general.

Not only have some organizational theories failed to systematically account for the characteristics which refute the ideal type, but when irrationality, rule evasion, favoritism or similar conditions are recognized, the tendency has been to dismiss them as "exceptions," irrelevant to the main organizational character. Indeed, the mythical qualities of the organization have sometimes been accepted as the "normal" perspective, and differences, no matter how frequent, have been explained in terms of "deviations" or the familiar "unintended consequences" which plagued some theorists (see Chapter 1). The keynote of this chapter is, however, that the pivotal character of modern organization is precisely the result of the contradictions of the mythical characteristics listed above.

Rationality

PERSONAL PERSONNEL

In the long run, personnel management is effective only when the inevitability of personal relationships is incontestably assumed. Yet, when personnel policies forbid conversation between students and teachers and require indiscriminate reassignment of teachers to jobs, the social foundation of organization is being disregarded. To assume that the relations between a teacher and the janitor are adequately characterized by their official duties, that their "personalities" are irrelevant, and that the stated relationship is exactly comparable wherever there is a similar formal division of labor is a common but fundamental error of interpretation.[2]

However matter-of-fact the administrator may view relationships among his personnel, the personal element does play a fundamental part in the thinking and action of school men. Since the formal organization is, after all, not specifically designed to satisfy personal desires of workers, they will take steps to achieve their desires through informal procedures.

INFORMAL ORGANIZATION

Beginning with a series of already classic studies carried on in the 1930's at Western Electric Corporation's Hawthorne Works in Chicago, by a group of Harvard social scientists (Elton Mayo, F. J. Roethlesberger, and Western Electric's W. J. Dickson), the influence that primary groups have on work performance has been repeatedly reported over the past thirty years. The Mayo group initiated their studies with little appreciation of the significance of the work group on productivity.[3] They soon observed that many experimental changes in the physical working conditions, variations in lighting, introduction of rest periods and refreshments, and changes in length of working days did not result in the expected reduced output of a group of girls isolated from the rest of the plant in a special observation room. Moreover, upon returning to the original working conditions, productivity often reached a new high. The investigators began to realize that other factors are more important than the physical working conditions, which led them finally to identify these other factors affecting productivity. It became apparent that productivity was not a function of the physical conditions, but was due to the fact that these girls were taking considerable pride in their part in the program and shared the distinction of being singled out for the experiment. They had been consulted about the experiments and asked to contribute suggestions, which made them feel important and appreciated, and they were allowed freer interaction than their counterparts who were not participating. The conclusion was obvious: the performance of people depends on their own values and personal relationships.

The discovery of these now rather obvious facts challenged prevailing assumptions that a man in the work setting is economically motivated and individually responds to official incentives. The findings accentuated the "irrational"—that is, the noneconomic motives of workers. But this finding also had an unexpected consequence. Since then studies have been sponsored by management which emphasize irrationalities of workers; the implication seemed to be that the rank and file workers are irrational, motivated by their sentiments, while management remained logical, motivated by rational economic considerations. The irrationalties of the management system have been systematically studied only recently. Some of these studies will be considered subsequently; but at least initially the educational bureaucracy may be considered in the perspective of Page's observations about the Navy's unofficial or "other face." [4]

Bureaucracy's "Other Face." Page reports several instances which demonstrate that the intent of the official naval bureaucracy is frequently modified by the personal qualities of those within it. The fact that many pressing problems develop for which efficient solutions are not possible within the official framework itself evokes extralegal methods. For example, official communications in most cases must go through the "chain of command," clearly an indispensable requirement from the viewpoint of the authority structure of the military organization. Yet when a pressing problem needs immediate solution, the chain of command is circumvented. Although such informal procedures are never officially sanctioned, they are nevertheless privately tolerated because they are necessary for the organization's effectiveness. Page concludes that bureaucracy has "another face," one submerged from the public, yet vital to its character.

One of the writers is acquainted with a superintendent of a medium-sized midwestern school system who is publicly noted for his insistence on official chains of communication. Yet, this administrator is also an active Rotarian, as are key persons in each department of the secondary school. By tacit agreement among department heads, any of the group whose department needs help is allowed to walk back to the office from the weekly noon luncheon with the superintendent. Other department heads stall a few minutes and return as a group. These five-minute walks are "off-the-cuff," never mentioned at school, and produce results. Any other direct approach by a department head is rebuffed by the question, "Have you talked to your building principal?"

ADMINISTRATIVE REACTIONS TO
INFORMAL ORGANIZATION

It can hardly be contended that administrators have failed to realize that "workers are people," which is, after all, an elementary fact. But the problem is created by the particular interpretation which administrators are likely to place on this fact. There is a tendency to regard personal relations as either (a) *irrelevant* or (b) evidence of *subversion*.

Irrelevance of Personal Relations. Management's implicit assumption that personal relationships are irrelevant to administrative decisions is no more evident than in the extensive transfer of teachers in many organizations. Arbitrarily assigning and transferring teachers according to logical need disregards a basic human problem. Workers derive rewards and recognition from membership in their work groups. It takes time and energy to gain acceptance as the "idea man," or the "inside dopester," or the "clown" of the group. Because persons form their identities partially in terms of their memberships in work groups, transferring these memberships may extract price in their identity, and so may be resented.

There is a reciprocal relationship between the organization of work and patterns of personal relations. The job itself is often the *basis* of membership in cliques; for example, language and humanities teachers may stand off socially from science and shop teachers. Attitudes which develop in these cliques may affect the job performance of those involved; the teaching performance of a new teacher, for example, may be affected if she is rejected by her co-workers. These personal relationships also help to shape the *official* standards. Unofficial "initiation" ceremonies which exist in every organization help the new member to learn the expected work procedures. The new teacher, for example, will remain an outsider in the school until loyalty is proved to co-workers, which will include demonstrated attitudes toward the administration or its policies and special ways of covertly getting around certain rules, regulations, and official responsibilities. The newcomer may be expected not to volunteer for "hall duty," but to willingly chaperone the school dance, to "pass" a certain percentage of students, to use certain pedagogical techniques in the classroom, to regard certain topics (such as sex) as taboo, and to demonstrate willingness to criticize some persons or to joke about them without restraint (such as the principal's wife). In short, the initiation period tests the newcomer where it counts, to discover the teacher's definition of his work roles. Official responsibilities often get defined in this way by peer group standards and procedures.

The significant fact about personal relationships is that they are a basis of stratification and reward just as surely as are official rewards. They are not irrelevant. It is largely the prestige values of *workers* that make the work of men more important than women, that determine whether the senior worker is more esteemed, that make school secretarial work more important than janitorial work. Of course, none of these things are detectable from organization charts, and, even more significant, they are not normally subject to the control of the administration. It is widely recognized that persons who work together have personal sentiments, form friendships, express dislikes, and view one another beyond their professional capacities. But the significance of these facts must still be systematically incorporated into the discipline of administration.

Subversive Aspects of the Informal Organization. The view that personal relations are subversive is probably even more prevalent, and certainly more important for a theory of administration, than the view that they are irrelevant. The view emphasizes the fact that cliques of subordinates often hold values which differ from those of the administration, and that these groups collaborate to restrict output. Teachers, like industrial work groups, agree on standards of work performance which often limit possible work output. They may implicitly agree on the proper number of "unauthorized" days to take off each year, the maximum number of hours to spend each month on "outside activities," and the proper time to leave work each day; principals may agree informally among themselves to reduce their monthly work load by accepting only a limited number of outside speaking engagements, or by taking longer lunch periods. Sarcasm, ridicule, personal threats, "dirty glances," and unfriendly attitudes from co-workers are normally used on "rate busters" who work beyond the informal expectations.

For these reasons, the informal work group may appear as essentially subversive. Reactions of administrators to perceived subversion from this source takes one of two forms. On the one hand, the situation may be defined as abnormal due to "poor organization." Subversive work groups are then considered to be an accidental result of the formal organization. The remedy is to "reorganize," which may include developing more regulations, closer supervision, or redistributing managerial responsibilities. On the other hand, the situation may be declared the result of "misunderstanding" on the part of workers about the pressing need for their cooperation, the restricted budget, and so on. Then the remedy is to change either the worker's attitudes or his knowledge; this requires the use of either "supervisors strong in human relations" in the second case, or "efficiency experts" in the other. In either case, the tacit assumption is that subversive workers want to cooperate, or at least that they can be persuaded to so do if they are provided with encouragement.

CHARACTERISTICS OF INFORMAL ORGANIZATION

Although it is partially correct, the "subversive" conception of work groups is not a completely adequate account of their origin and persistence, for informal work groups do not always undermine the organization. As a matter of fact, the informal organization is often a bulwark of the organization's effectiveness. An example of how informal relations may increase the effectiveness of organization is illustrated in the following hypothetical case:

A State Department of Education received funds to hire two new typists immediately. According to regulations, a request for applicants had to be typed on special forms and approved by two superior officers before the state civil service inspected the proposed classifications. The civil service would then send at least three applicants to be interviewed by the employing department head. These procedures normally required several weeks, especially since personnel would not likely even receive the request for several weeks while it circulated through higher echelon officers for approval. Therefore to expedite the request the department head violated official procedures by telephoning the personnel officer directly to state his request before it had been officially forwarded. This enabled the department to interview and actually hire the requested typists before personnel received the written request.

This case demonstrates an informal relation which actually increased the organization's level of performance over that which would have resulted from following the official policies. The informal relation supported the organization's goals even though it violated official means.

Informal Structure. Informal organization consists of two conceptually distinct parts: (1) a *group* of persons and (2) a set of expected *relations* among them, or a *structure*. A group is founded in personal sentiments which develop over time among particular individuals; when these individuals leave, the "group" is dissolved. Structure, on the other hand, exists over a period of time independently of the particular persons who comprise the membership; turnover of membership does not greatly alter the structure.

It is important to realize that the existence of the informal relations described above does not depend on a *group* of particular personalities—that is, it does not depend on who the persons are. The use of informal telephone relations has probably existed for some time; that is, the newcomer to the state department of education probably had to learn the informal telephone relationships with the civil service officer just as certainly as he had to learn his official duties and rules.

When particular informal *relations*, such as the one described above, constitute a part of a system of relations, it is proper to speak of an informal *structure*. An example of how informal structures operate is provided by the military experiences of one of the authors who served as an army battalion supply sergeant.

From the first week on the job, the writer was systematically introduced to depot personnel who would be processing battalion supply requests. It was apparent that building friendships with strategic personnel at the depot was expected. In fact, procedures for doing so were built into the job itself. On several occasions, arrangements were made by superior officers for the writer to travel thirty to fifty miles to depot headquarters to pick up supplies which were normally shipped by truck for the only apparent reason of meeting depot clerks in order to build an acquaintanceship with them. While at the depot, battalion supply personnel were encouraged to take official time to join informal work groups there, to use first names, have coffee together, and develop "understandings" of standard work procedures. On one occasion the sergeant who was being replaced advised that "it helps to have contacts" at depot headquarters.

The reasons for instituting these personal relationships were soon obvious. When any strategic equipment, such as an antiaircraft gun or radar, was out of action for longer than three days, for any reason, it had to be reported to command headquarters, which in turn initiated pressure on the battalion officers to get the equipment back into action under any circumstances. Under these conditions, supply could not wait for formal requisitions to be processed by depot when a major piece was out of action as a result of lack of replacement parts. Against regulations, the request was phoned in to a depot contact who shipped out the part immediately, often several days in advance of official paperwork.

Occasionally depot contacts could not be reached. When it was then necessary to carry out the emergency transaction with depot employees with whom prior informal contacts had not been established, the depot clerk tended to question the justification for the requisition and often enforced official procedures. This was because each depot clerk had "preferred" units which were supplied with scarce strategic parts first. Thus, whether or not units received parts immediately depended almost entirely upon informal contacts with depot personnel who handled the requests. The power of low status personnel at depot headquarters to dispense valuable supplies gave them influence far beyond that merited by their official rank, and in some cases they were even "courted" by the top battalion supply officer himself.

Not only do such informal systems frequently function effectively, but they provide an avenue of countervailance to the formal structure. In this regard, Anderson has stated:

. . . it would be expected that where attempts are made to highly structure behavior and to impersonalize relationships within an organization, there will arise informal systems based on personal relationships to countermand the formal, rigid, impersonal system, to allow the individual to maintain some control over his working environment, and to maintain his self-respect.[5]

It is imperative to note that although the informal structure depended on *personal* relations, these relations were institutionalized and highly stable; the pattern would have existed regardless of the contact's name, for the relationship rested on mutual work interests rather than purely personal sentiments. It should also be noted that there was nothing particularly subversive about the informal structure. Indeed, it is apparent that the informal relationships expedited requests and provided a principal mean of distributing scarce goods when no more logical means was available.

While the illustrations concern military experience, informal work requirements are found in school systems as well. What may appear to the principal to be an idle conversation between his secretary and the superintendent's secretary may, in fact, be the potential basis of valuable informal cooperation between his office and that of his superior.

The Informal Group. The preceding illustrations pertain to an informal structure. It was demonstrated that such relationships are part of an institutionalized pattern that is as much a part of the job as are official relationships, and that they are *expected* to be cultivated regardless of the actual sentiments of whomever happens to be involved. In addition, however, there are in every organization "primary relations," or cliques of people who gather together to eat lunch, drink coffee, or travel to and from work. In contrast to the informal structure, *group* relations are purely personal, existing only for personal reasons and only for the duration of contact among the individuals involved. These groups of people, however, do normally discuss their jobs, and they may also arrive at a common understanding about their respective work. They may develop sufficient solidarity to control their members and make distinct contributions to the organization. Gross lists several of these contributions.[6]

First, when groups are composed of persons from different departments, having different jobs, they tend to cut across specialties, which helps to promote coordination and cooperation among separate parts of the organization. Members of such groups will be encouraged to go out of their way to help members of other departments for personal reasons on the basis of their mutual friendships even when they are not officially rewarded for doing so. Thus, such groups may reduce conflict among specialties.

Second, the influences of informal cliques may compensate for lack of official controls. There are, in fact, times when the official bureaucracy is invoked solely to legitimize decisions made on informal bases. The cliques may, for example, decide how to get the task accomplished in the absence of formal direction from designated offices which may be buried in paperwork and problems of their own. When such cliques include superiors, they provide a direct channel of communication which may reduce or increase friction between echelons. For example, Gross suggests that the subordinates may be informally cautioned by their immediate superiors about inadequacies in their reports, before the reports go on to higher echelons. Also, such sessions provide subordinates with an opportunity to elaborate on their excuses for inadequate performance, which do not appear on the reports, and which their superiors may relay to higher echelons.

The fact that supervisors (as well as subordinates) make intentional use of informal personal relations to enhance their control over subordinates should not be overlooked. In a sample he examined, Carlson noted school superintendents acted impersonally with their own administrative staff, but they spent a great deal of time and effort cultivating very personal relations with teachers. The reason for the difference in treatment of teachers and treatment of the superintendent's own staff, he conjectured, is the relative invulnerability of teachers to rules because of the fact that they work behind closed doors where rules are difficult to enforce. Superintendents were, therefore, forced to rely on relatively time consuming and emotionally tiring "particularistic" relations with teachers to build personal loyalties to accomplish what the rules could not.[7]

Third, Gross points out that it is often in primary groups where specific job definitions, a specific division of responsibility, and crystallization of loyalties are ultimately decided. The primary group provides a kind of social security against conflicting demands of dual loyalties, a group rationale for doing things a certain way, and a crystallization of the organization's division of labor.

Finally, it can be added that the primary group functions to retain members and curb absenteeism. The prospect of social relations and friendships undoubtedly attracts many housewives from their kitchens into the classrooms and compels otherwise reluctant students to return to school day after day—their friends are there, and there is lunch, the coffee break, the school play rehearsal. Absenteeism is unquestionably one consequence of poor social relations at work.

Group and Structure.   Because any specific group of people contains both personal and structural aspects, group and structure are best conceived as types of relationships rather than types of actual collectivities. If the relation arises primarily because of work interests and pressures and expectations, and if the expectations between parties are standardized and passed on to newcomers, the informal grouping may be said to be primarily "structured." If, on the other hand, it arises out of purely personal sentiments for individual and spontaneous reasons and changes as members change, the relation primarily constitutes a social collectivity. It is in this latter fashion that "group" is usually defined. The relative predominance of group and structural relations endows a specific grouping of people with its unique character. Group and informal structure, in combination, constitute what is commonly known as "informal organization," which may consist primarily of the group relations or of the structural relations, depending on the particular case. But in any case, informal structural and group relations may both contribute to more effective pursuit of the formal organizational goals.

It may be concluded that informal work organizations do not necessarily arise as a means of sabotage; they occur when the security of the work group is jeopardized by official policies. Administrators who recognize this fact can frequently design policies in such a way that the informal work group will support rather than sabotage their basic intent. Instead of work groups being either irrelevant accidents of organization to be ignored or subversive elements to be corrected, it may be assumed that informal work standards and procedures are an inevitable consequence of formal organization. For not only does formal organization exclude the needs and values of personnel, but no official system can anticipate all possible contingencies which the organization will encounter. The informal organization is a built-in system of flexibility through which the organization may adapt to extenuating circumstances.

It should be clear, then, that informal organization has at least two functions. First, to the extent that formal organization is not designed to achieve the interests and values of personnel, their security will be provided by their own organization. Second, because of changes in the external environment and because no administration can predict that future perfectly, a system of rules that anticipates all of the problem that an organization may confront is impossible; the informal organization provides flexibility within a relatively rigid authority pattern. One of the fundamental dilemmas of bureaucracy is created by conflicts between these two functions: guaranteeing the security of personnel and insuring flexibility of the organization. In some cases it is precisely the proposed changes in the organization which threaten the security of the employees and lead to an informal pattern of subversion and conformity.

However, regardless of these incipient problems, it is certain that informal organization is an indispensable element of large organizations. As one writer has observed, the very irrationality management now seeks to remove is an essential foundation of effective organization.[8]

Infallibility of Rules

FUNCTIONS OF RULES

A tendency toward rule proliferation which is characteristic of rational organizations, fosters a faith in them, or at the least a sanctity which makes them enviable. Indeed, the growth of bureaucracy itself is largely an expression of western man's faith in the infallibility of rules. This seems to be justified to the extent that they contribute to the predictability of work performance and increase standards of work. For, as Gouldner points out, rules do serve several valuable functions. First, rules function as explications of policy, in that they provide a definitive statement of the job, limiting the subordinate's options.[9] Second, rules are a form of communication, substituting for personal repetition of orders; they are, moreover, a superior form of communication insofar as rules are more carefully expressed than verbal orders and so less ambiguous than hastily worded commands. Third, Gouldner suggests that rules have a "screening" function, in the sense that they provide a buffer between superiors and subordinates; because of rules there is not only less need for the superintendent to give direct orders to his subordinates (that is, to "order everyone around"), but also the principal can remain on good standing with everyone by "passing the buck" upward ("It's not my idea, I just enforce the rules around here"). In this way, the impersonality of rules obscures the existence of power discrepancies by bolstering the superior's position without implying that he may feel personally superior. Personal relationships are maintained precisely because a government by rules is a government by "no one."

Fourth, rules establish public evaluation standards which facilitate what Gouldner describes as their "remote control function." The public character of rules enables deviations to be detected by remote superiors through the use of "spot checks." If each school were to operate on a unique basis, there would be no standards for judging and therefore improving operations. But because of rules even the layman has a basis for evaluating the effectiveness of school systems. Attendance rules, for example, are supposed to be applied uniformly throughout a school district. It is common practice to expect a call from the parents when a child must be absent because of illness. If no call is received from the parents of an absent child by 10 or 11 A.M., the principal or attendance officer calls the home. Despite the general application of this procedure in many systems, some principals are considered "tough" on absences simply because they do call the home. Knowing the rule, parents consider principals who do not call the home "easy" on absences, or even "lax."

Finally, rules provide a sense of legitimacy for punishing offenders. Punishment invoked without warning is illegitimate, but rules constitute explicit warnings concerning the kind of behavior which will be punished. Since punishment is usually also circumscribed by rules, punishment is not likely to be interpreted as a form of personal aggression; instead it constitutes further warning—that is, warning to potential offenders. Thus, parents will acknowledge the right of principals to punish their children if they are truant, even though they themselves may feel that an occasional truancy is not especially important.

FALLIBILITY OF RULES

While rules perform several crucial functions, it should be equally clear that they do not always work. This inherent fallibility of rules is precisely the quality that is overlooked when strict compliance to them is demanded. The tacit assumption of strict enforcement seems to be that the rationality of organization can be increased *only* by rule compliance, when in practice rationality often requires the evasion of rules. Rules are fallible for several reasons: they require interpretation, they encounter organized resistance, and humane considerations require their violation; and rules validate tradition and preserve apathy.

INTERPRETATION

There are several reasons why the application of rules requires *interpretation*. First, rules are by nature abstract, functioning only as general guides to specific situations. A principal who docks the pay of a teacher who has spent hundreds of hours of his own time improving the curriculum because he leaves school during his free period is ignoring the general expectancy that rules must be interpreted before application. Second, they are often intentionally formulated only in the most general terms at the top of the hierarchy to be made increasingly specific as they are passed down the line. Because situations are different, no set of rules anticipates all consequences, and decisions must be made to determine the situations under which rules are applicable.

Also, even after the appropriate rule is selected, values and situational factors determine its application. Francis and Stone describe a typical case where interpretation of rules is necessary involving a Federal Employment Security investigator and a client who claimed that she should receive compensation because she was fired unjustly. The woman claimed that she had been fired from the housekeeping department of a large hospital because she had been late to work three times. From the way she told her story and acted, the interviewer believed her and decided she was eligible. But in a similar case the same investigator decided against the client because he seemed to be "covering up." Francis and Stone conclude that in unambiguous cases interviewers followed the rules closely. But some cases required interpretation of the rules, and in those cases the most crucial factor in arriving at decisions seemed to be the investigator's moral attitude toward clients. They tended to enforce rules where it was felt that clients did not morally deserve compensation. Thus, literal interpretations of rules were used to support intuitive conclusions.[10]

Other tactical uses of rules are described by Gouldner who points to their "leeway" function, or a rhythmic relaxation and tightening of rule enforcement.[11] Occasionally the plant guard in the factory observed by Gouldner would carefully examine packages which workers brought out of the plant, while at other times he would make only a cursory inspection. Also, sometimes punctual "punching-in" would be rigorously enforced, while at other times it was treated casually. Enforcement seemed to be most rigorous when small tensions between workers and supervisors began to coalesce into definite rifts. A certain public school system had a set of rules for teachers to follow regarding the use of the teacher's lounge, time for reporting for duty, time for leaving the building, and so on. When the faculty was cooperative and things were going well, the rules were "stretched." Teachers could report at 8:40 rather than 8:30 and could leave early. However, if the group as a whole was felt to be wasting time or acting defiantly, the rules were more likely to be enforced. Thus, formal rules were used by the principal to bargain for the cooperation of teachers. Gouldner would describe such rules as one type of "chips" to which the board of education staked the superintendent and principals.

In view of their tactical function, it is apparent that rules are not as essential for rational decision as is often supposed; they are used instead as weapons in supporting essentially nonrational decisions. This explains why rules which are normally overlooked may be invoked in particular cases. For example, in one urban school system it was common practice for school teachers to take time off for certain personal reasons when they were in fact released to attend professional meetings. However, one teacher was caught attending a religious convention in another state when she was supposed to be at a school convention and was fired. Apparently, she appeared to be abusing a lax situation for illegal purposes related to the church-state issue. Tactical application of student rules provides a further illustration. The boy who is a constant behavior problem probably has some justification when he complains to the principal, "The teachers are picking on me." Because of his record of misconduct and nuisance, each school and classroom rule become peculiarly inflexible in his case. If he whispers in class, runs in the halls, or eats candy in the library, a reprimand is certain. Yet he may notice that the same minor infractions by classmates are overlooked.

Finally, rules are subject to interpretation because of inherent conflicts that normally arise between the authority system and systems of rules. Organizations utilize both direct orders from officers and the rules to command. When these do not coincide, the employee is forced to interpret the meaning and relevance of the rule with respect to the orders he received. Turner, for example, observed that naval officers give unauthorized orders to subordinate dispersing officers, and suggests that because officers normally have powers beyond what their actual authority warrants, a lesser officer may be afraid even to suggest to his superior that his request is inconsistent with regulations. The existing organization is a compromise between the two forms of control, and administrative orders themselves are sometimes a cause of rule evasion.[12]

RESISTANCE TO RULES

From the above illustration it is clear that it is not only the meaning of rules but their relevance which is subject to interpretation. When interpreted in certain ways, employees will resist rules for several reasons: (1) because they do not seem to be in the best interest of the organization, (2) because they violate the security and autonomy of the employee, or (3) because they are contrary to fundamental traditions of the organization and community.

In the Organization's Interest. This point is of particular importance. On the one hand, undoubtedly many persons who violate the rules of the organization do not have its best interests at heart, but their own instead. There are, however, numerous instances where (1) no particular benefit accrues from the rule, (2) when its disadvantages outweigh its advantages, or (3) when its application would be to the total detriment of the long-range task of the organization. Although particular examples are always debatable, an example of the first instance is a rule that "messy attendance reports" will not be accepted from teachers by the attendance office. There may be some benefit in the rule to the official image it gives to the attendance office, but it would be difficult to defend many such rules as contributing anything to the organization's effectiveness. Perhaps rules standardizing modes of dress or students and teachers are in a similar category—the motive for these rules is based on considerations other than organizational effectiveness. The second instance is sometimes found in policies which call for lower salaries for married women teachers and which forbid tenure to them. Thus teachers have been known to keep their marriages a secret until they were ready to leave the system. A blanket exclusion of teachers who happen to be married may be a detriment to the school's long-range effectiveness, particularly in an era of teacher shortages. It is also sometimes questionable whether the time teachers spend enforcing "hall duty" rules, cafeteria rules, or even attendance-taking rules best contributes to the overall effectiveness of public school education compared to possibly more efficient uses of their talent. Finally, an example of a rule which is completely detrimental to universal education might be one like this: "Only students with an 'A' average may have access to the library." Such rules exist for undergraduates in several large universities. What should a librarian do with an "ineligible" undergraduate who is bold enough to sneak into the library stacks for an afternoon's browsing. Perhaps he should be trying to squeeze into a telephone booth like a good college undergraduate. The point is that violation of rules does not necessarily imply that the goals have geen sabotaged; on the contrary, the intent may have been to uphold them.

Personal Considerations. Workers may prevail upon one another's sense of sympathy or humanity to corrupt the rules for one another's mutual interests. Turner borrows Aristotle's typology of friendship to illustrate three reasons for rule violations which enable workers to secure control over their work: (1) friendship patterns, (2) simulated friendship, and (3) the exchange system. (1) Persons will sometimes break rules for friends which they would not otherwise break; a teacher, for example, may prevail upon his friend to teach his classes while he is absent for an unauthorized reason. (2) Less enduring "simulated" friendships may have similar effects; by simulating friendship with the principal through compliments, a teacher attempts to be defined as a "friend." The teacher may dislike him, but, by simulating friendship, he feels that he may get certain related privileges, including the right to ask for special favors. (3) While both of the first two patterns have in common the exchange system, simple exchange, or bargain, does not require friendship to be operative. *Any* person who is "human" is expected to find technical loopholes which will assist a person in distress, regardless of his rank.[13] It is imperative to note that far from feeling guilty about their part in the exchange system, personnel morally justify the practice of violating rules to help a friend. According to Turner, the individual who puts a legal technicality ahead of doing favors for others is regarded as reprehensible. If rules violate a basic cultural value of helping a friend, they may be violated.

Violation of tradition. Every new rule creates the risk that some hallowed, traditional way of doing things will be suddenly transformed into a "violation." Gouldner's account of "no smoking" regulations in an industrial plant demonstrates how rules may be evaded when they violate basic traditions of employees. The rule violated the workers' traditional right to smoke, which was supported by a belief that they would become nervous and irritable if they did not smoke. The rule also threatened traditional status relations by establishing distinctions between plant and office workers who were allowed to smoke.[14] In this case, because the "no smoking" rule was imposed from the outside by insurance companies, management and workers jointly violated the "no smoking" policy as a cooperative venture.

Another source of trouble arises when the administration attempts to legislate "equality" in situations where employees are not willing to accept it. For example, the promotion of women to positions in which they command men can be a constant sorespot in many organizations. Males can be expected to resist female supervisors as long as they are raised in a culture which stresses male superiority. Thus, women superintendents, principals, and guidance directors may expect to face personal value conflicts. Experiences of childhood and as students and classroom teachers condition women educators to expect male leadership. Given a position of authority, they frequently have some self-doubt as to the propriety of their new role. Further, women in public school administration report resistance to their leadership from mothers of students and women subordinates in addition to resistance from men. As the percentage of men teachers has increased in public schools, women superintendents have become increasingly rare.

Rules themselves form a heritage which creates still other problems.

They accumulate in the files even after they have become outdated. It is not clear why outdated rules are allowed to remain in the books (for any reason other than indifference). But the fact that rules, though stated categorically, are used *conditionally* may have some bearing. For although the outdated rule is no longer relevant in most occasions in its stated form, it may be still appropriate in some *extreme* situations should they arise. Complete discard of generally outmoded rules would leave the extreme situations unregulated.

PRESERVATION OF APATHY

Another reason that rules are inherently fallible is related to their function of establishing work standards. Because standards specify only the minimum level of performance, in one sense rules determine how little the worker needs to do. Gouldner calls this their "apathy-preserving" function.[15] The fact that conforming to the *letter* of the law is a form of sabotage provides an insight into this function of rules. As Gouldner expresses it, the rules do not modify *attitudes* toward work, but are used as guide-lines for *behavior;* they seem to signify management's "surrender in the battle for the worker's motivation." Thus, rules serve to stabilize work apathy, the very problem they are often supposed to reduce.[16]

IMPLICATIONS

These inadequacies of rules have in common an underlying dilemma: while rules are designed to account for the routine and the typical, the world of fact is not entirely foreseeable. Events invariably arise that have not been accounted for by the rules, or are inconsistent with their intent. The situation is responsible for both flexibility in the interpretation of rules and organized resistance to them.

It may be concluded that the violation of rules are inevitable because of their nature, their place in the organization, and because of the nature of organizations themselves. The interests of an organization and its employees and the value of traditions all underlie the resistance to rules. Violation is not primarily due to negativism, stubbornness, personality deviation, or ignorance of the law. It is much too prevalent to be attributed to these personal sources. Rather, violation represents a natural compromise of impossible situations posed by the administrative structure itself. Deviation has its source partially in conflicts among rules and conflicts between rules and values; thus, deviation from one rule may simply represent loyalty to an opposite principle.

Because of the complex interdependence between formal and informal procedures, extension of rules may be expected to increase, not decrease, informal organization. Similarly, the sphere of interpretation increases, as does resistance, as rules proliferate to standardize work performance. Reasonably, rules could be designed to secure certain aspects of the informal system rather than to diminish it. They might be engineered to pro-mote what contribution the informal organization is making to the organization's purposes. Perhaps rules are needed most and are most effec-tive in the absence of informal procedures for handling the situation rather than where there is too much informality. Because of the resistance and resentment rules may create, the total effectiveness of the organiza-tion may be reduced by an indiscriminate proliferation of rules designed solely to resist the informal organization.

One fact is clear: informal organization has a direct bearing on the principles of administration. Not only must administrative principles deal with the informal organization, but also some existing informal relations must be systematically incorporated into organizational policy and proce-dures before they can be completely effective. Yet, while administrators know that informal organization exists, they have perhaps been too re-luctant to admit its inevitable relevance to the official organization and to planning. Indeed, by starting with the ideal conception of bureaucracy which endorses impersonal rationality, deviations appear as "violations" to be corrected, or accidents of imperfect organization. Instead of advo-cating administrative principles which assume social reality, adminis-trators appear to have frequently designed their rules independently of it, or have intended to actually prohibit "socializing" on the job, violation of procedural techniques, misuses of office, and "cutting channels," all of which can result in a pathological proliferation of rules and sanctions. The paradox is that although these policies are designed to increase obedi-ence, the organization's total effectiveness may be ultimately reduced.

Unity of Ends

COMMON GOALS IMPLICIT IN DEFINITIONS OF ORGANIZATION

The assumption that there is a single organizational purpose is no more apparent than in the ways the term "organization" has been defined. For example, one writer states that "organization in the social sense refers to either the patterns or structure of relations among a number of persons oriented to a set of goals or objectives, or to the group as a whole viewed as a unity." [17] Workers are assumed to be oriented to a *set* of goals and objectives, and the whole is viewed as a *unity*. Although such a charac-terization may apply to the most abstract dimensions of an organization, the actual existence of contradictory sets of goals and objectives within the organization is precluded by definition, as are the resulting internal resistances and compromises among goals.

COORDINATED UNITS

Barnard's definition of formal organization as a system of consciously *coordinated* activities or forces of two or more persons avoids imputing to workers common motives and the acceptance of common goals. Coordination does not require agreement or personal involvement with organizational ends—only some incentive to conform (a commitment) as a means of control. As Barnard suggests, ". . . an organizational purpose has directly no meaning for the individual. What has meaning for him is the organization's relation to him—what burdens it imposes, what benefits it confers." [18] It is apparent that the essential bond between organization and the individual is contractual; the worker exchanges services for economic, religious, political, and emotional rewards. While the worker's loyalty may be sought, it is not necessary, not even characteristic, for the organization's existence. Only a small minority of employees are acutely loyal to all of the organizational goals at any one time.

FUNCTIONAL AUTONOMY

Even Barnard's definition suffers from a compulsive logic. While the organization's parts are *logically* interdependent and subordinate to the general ends of the organization, in fact the parts often develop "functional autonomy," which in practice reduces the possibility of complete coordination.[19] Since it is often possible for subdivisions of an organization to obtain independent financing from outside sources, logically subordinate divisions (vocational schools, vocational departments, and to some extent other federally subsidized divisions) may develop autonomy and power over superior divisions. In these cases, department goals may be more operative than the goals set by the board of education and the superintendent, statutes, or the organization's logical function.

The so-called independent financing of school activities provides a classic example of functional autonomy. Funds raised by students in special interest clubs, football gate receipts, and band boosters' donations all promote the autonomy of the various subdivisions that collect the money. Illustrative of the extremes of such autonomy is the case of a high school athletic director who purchased a fancy used motor coach for team trips. He reasoned that since the football team could "afford" the expenditure, why bother paying mileage for an ordinary school bus. His financial autonomy also extended his influence over decisions outside the strictly athletic realm; he was, for example, able to expedite the rate of promotion of his staff and, to some extent, the salary schedules in his department.

Argyris' definition of organization is one of the few that explicitly accounts for the vital influence of functional autonomy. The definition includes several aspects: (a) plurality of parts, (b) each part achieving specific objectives, (c) each maintaining themselves through their interrelatedness, and (d) simultaneously adapting to the external environment, thereby (e) maintaining the interrelated state of the parts. He concludes that the essence of organization is not found in its goals or structure, but in the patterning (and, it might be added, conflict) between semiautonomous but interdependent parts.[20] He proposes that the number of such "linkages" between the parts of an organization determine its stability: the more interrelations that must be maintained the greater the likelihood it will break down at some point. Thus, the potential for conflict among units is a function of their number.[21]

OFFICIAL OBJECTIVES

When it does not refer to some logical function that the organization performs for society the organizational "goal" may refer to the more limited objectives of a part of the *administration*. In this sense, organizational goals usually represent the interests and aims of a small minority of the personnel, sometimes only a minority of the administration. Gouldner's question implies this: What do the general rules make predictable, and for whom is it being made predictable?[22] It is instructive that certain things are *not* made more predictable by rules—for example, the right of chief executives to be tardy or their obligations to work for salary increases for subordinates. In matters of most concern to the rank and file of teachers, such as merit rating, the rules are designed to minimize the teacher's ability to predict his future income, partially because school boards assume that people are motivated by anxiety and insecurity as a result of traditional reliance on carrot-and-stick values. In general, the rules that get implemented and enforced are probably of greatest benefit to top-level officials whose aims not only represent the official ends but also represent their personal interests and unique perspective of those ends.

One of the major problems with official educational policy statements is that even the chief executives have little consensus on the primacy of various goals. Schools, probably more than most other organizations, are plagued with a conflicting and confusing variety of ends. Religious philosophies, experimentalism, rational humanism, social reconstruction, social mobility, community service, intellectual training, and character development are goals that are attributed to education. Indeed, the Educational Policies Commission at one time listed forty-three educational objectives ranging from the inquiring mind to homemaking, and from occupational efficiency and adjustment to social justice and devotion to democracy. This multiplicity of goals constitutes one of the basic complexities and sources of conflict within the school as an organization. Attempts to achieve even a few of these major goals with current resources must lead only to frustration.

Perhaps more than any other single occupational group, educators have been unable to make a consistent choice among highly regarded but often difficult aims. The attempt to achieve such a multiplicity of goals guarantees that none will be achieved sufficiently and leaves the educator open to criticism from the outside and unable to resist other functions that are placed on the school by every group that has a criticism to voice. It is precisely at the point of resources, or in general the means to carry out the end, that selections must be made. As Lieberman points out, critical thinking may be an admirable goal, but critical thinking cannot be developed without criticizing something that is important, a price which many educators and citizens are not willing to pay.[23] Also many persons favor fulfilling a variety of goals, but the community is unwilling to pay the cost. The educator's most difficult task is not choosing between "good" and "bad" alternatives, but choosing among highly regarded but competing values.

INTERNAL CONFLICT

Resistance to official goals has already been noted; it was suggested that one function of informal organization is to control the conditions of work and to maintain work group goals where these conflict with formal policies. Resistance to rules was also noted to be a normal reaction to formalization which violates the organization's goals, flexibility, and traditions.

Types of Conflict. Organized internal conflicts occur among the various parts of the organization: subdivisions, echelons, mutual interest groups, line, and staff. From the standpoint of the organization, conflicts fall into three general classifications. First, "jurisdictional" disputes may arise between *echelons*. In this case, persons of similar rank develop interests *across* official divisional lines. For example, teachers may resist policies or practices of the "downtown administration" regardless of which school they are in or their specialty within it. This tendency for subordinates to identify with one another and unite against their superiors is, however, partially offset by an opposing tendency to identify with superiors in order to elevate personal status. One study found that the resentment which factory workers usually expressed toward their own immediate supervisors was not generalized to the managerial class as a whole because the workers had secret hopes that, by a stroke of luck, they might become supervisors themselves in the future.[24] Because of a tendency to personalize antagonisms, most subordinates do not become generally hostile to the class of administrators, but rather are best characterized as being in an unstable state of ambivalence. Thus, even while uniting against superiors on occasions, subordinates may support them against outside opponents attacking the entire organization.

Because subordinates may identify with even those superiors whom they resent, there is a recurring tendency for leaders of subordinate groups to be absorbed into the superordinate group without relinquishing their leadership over the subordinates. This is noticeable among union leaders, for example, whose social status and activities more closely resemble those of management than labor. A similar development occurs among leaders of professional movements who may be more compatible with their opposition than with the rank and file of their own organization. A comparison of the views of national officers in educational associations with the rank and file and with organized business would, for example, be enlightening on this point. Certainly, the promotion of presidents of local teachers' associations to principalships is a familiar story. Given this compatibility between leaders of superior and subordinate groups, the superior group has an immediate advantage if it co-opts the leaders of subordinates, and they will usually tend to betray their followers precisely because of their privileged relationship with the superior group.[25] School administrators also make use of this principle by persuading student leaders to go along with their point of view. Student leaders may, in fact, become more loyal to the administration than to the other students' interests.

Second, clashes of interest may arise among official *subdivisions* of a single echelon of the formal organization. For example, when specially trained counselors and teacher-counselors became generally available in the fifties many conflicts developed between them and the unspecialized "homeroom" teachers who had enjoyed directing the homeroom guidance programs begun in the 1930's and 1940's. Some homeroom teachers who had traditionally provided certain advice and services to the homeroom group resented the "intrusions" of the specialist. Although subdivisions logically are integrated components of an organization, in fact specific units often have a history of growth and development and personal interest and loyalty which is independent of their logical place in the organization. This is because an organization usually expands from the bottom up, growing by the addition of subunits. The complex organization is a series of smaller organizations integrated through coordinating offices.[26] Each segment is in competition for its survival and rewards with other departments.

Third, disputes are constantly arising among *special interest groups* that form within specific divisions. The tendency for functionally related groups to segment into nuclei of special interests is a distinguishing feature of the modern large-scale organization.[27] The specialists that run school systems join distinctly different professional associations and unions, each having different interests and values. There are separate associations of principals and of superintendents; separate unions and professions for teachers and for subject-matter areas; there are janitors' unions, guidance directors associations, and many others within a single school "system." There are over 500 such national, regional, and local educational organizations listed in the Education Dictionary. It is this web of interest groups that in fact constitutes the "organization." They splinter its unity and strength. Recently principals and superintendents have been deluged by separate segments of teachers advocating "modern" algebra and special approaches to chemistry, physics, and foreign language, all clamoring for immediate implementation of their respective programs. Each group maintains that its approach is imperative for a modern curriculum and should be introduced as soon as materials can be purchased. As a net effect of these conflicting pressures, many administrators have developed a cautious "wait and see" attitude. Departments of educational administration are not immune to conflicts of special interest either. The 1960 AASA yearbook proposes that one-half-day blocks of time be allotted specifically for preparation in theory and techniques of general administration.[28] Professors of educational administration have encountered difficulty in convincing their professional colleagues and deans that such a change is necessary and feasible.

Alliances may follow along specialty rather than departmental lines and form among persons stationed throughout the system. For example, teachers with similar specialties stationed throughout the system tend to identify on the basis of their specialties rather than their departments. Studies have found that high school teachers often go into teaching because of an identification with their area of specialization, such as mathematics, rather than with their particular school system.[29] They may have more in common with mathematicians throughout the state than with most of the other teachers in their own school. Similarly, teachers of literature throughout a system may resist the vocational program, while shop teachers resist efforts to increase the strength of the academic types of programs.

Other types of alliances develop around age and sex groups, ethnic and racial backgrounds, mobile and nonmobile employees, and a number of other categories. That these seemingly congenial gatherings are in fact alliances is not always immediately apparent. Persons in the informal work groups studied by Gross said that they associated with certain cliques because of similar backgrounds, or because they were persons whom the respondent liked. Yet, that explanation was insufficient, for Gross found that not one clique member was a competitor of any other member of his clique, and this fact of noncompetitiveness was more of a determinant of friendship patterns than was personal background. The reason that competitors were excluded, as it appeared to Gross, is that competition is a serious obstacle to approachability. Every cohesive group, according to Gross, strikes a bargain: it will accept him if he is approachable; but he will be approachable only if it is guaranteed that nothing he reveals will be used against him. The admission of competitors would threaten that guarantee and thus the very basis of the clique.[30]

Finally, internal cleavages develop among members who are dependent on different *publics* in their work. An employee's work may primarily involve relationships with (1) the public or (2) with clients, or (3) with internal supervisors only. These three types of personnel tend to develop different work goals. For example, Francis and Stone suggest that persons who directly work with clients sustain an ideal of service to the client more readily than persons who are isolated from the client, who tend to be oriented to procedure and enforcement of official rules.[31] Similarly, staff officers who must deal with the public much of the time (such as principals, school nurses, truant officers, or vocational agriculture teachers) may be expected to develop more sensitivity to public opinion than do teachers and the clerical staff who do not deal with the public so directly.

The Natural Role of Conflict.   Despite their prevalence, the vital place that these conflicts occupy in organizations is systemically ignored in theoretical statements of the administrative processes. In fact, one investigator finds relatively few references to conflict by American social scientists.[32] Failure to deal with conflict is in part due to the fact that the audience of the social scientist is not his professional colleagues but the laymen who requested the research. Social scientists investigate problems engineered by laymen who control research funds. These are the very persons to whom an analysis of power is most threatening. Many of the persons most interested in problems of school administration are administrators and school boards, who are among those most constrained to avoid threatening anyone with embarrassing questions about power.

Nor does the tendency to rely on official stereotypes prompt questions about conflict. There is little indication of its existence in the disguise of formal policy statements, organization charts, and other statements of ideals. Studies of administration in concrete situations are needed—the actual "happenings and goings on." But these studies need a firm conceptual foundation which permits conflict to be observed. Toward this end, the administration of schools may be conceptualized as a matter of coping with organized *groups* in various states of tension. Although it is natural to assume that human relationships are between individuals, "conflict" also implies *groups* in conflict. Group conflict may overshadow the relationship between even potentially compatible persons if they represent opposing groups. An exclusive focus on individuals obscures important community and national characteristics and ethnic, racial, and family prejudices which are transported into the organization by its members and which greatly affect the work climate setting the stage for internal conflicts.

Organized conflicts create underlying tensions which often threaten to break down the established ways of doing things. Far from providing a stable, predictable setting, in this image an "organization" provides only a minimum foundation of established relationships which does little more than establish the limits on an arena of strategies among special interest segments. This creative and dynamic character of most organizations presents a serious challenge to hopes of complete predictability and planning. Included in the administrative process is occasional resort to experimental use of strategies for dealing with and compromising group conflicts.

INSTITUTIONAL DRIFT

Institutional drift is a natural reaction to an environment over which no party has complete control. The term "institutional drift" refers to a discrepancy between the *official* purposes of an organization and the *operating* goals which actually govern the organization in its day-to-day routine. Institutional drift is less a matter of design than an inescapable necessity to compromise which is forced on administrators at all levels by the special daily pressures they must take into consideration.

Causes. There are several causes of institutional drift. First, one authority suggests that because the abstract policy statements are not particularly helpful in solving daily problems, daily problems and short-range aims are substituted for professed goals.[33]

Abstractness is especially characteristic of educational goals, as the following communiqué from a principal to his teachers illustrates:

Circular #28
Please keep all circulars on file, in their order
Topic: Maximal Goals
To develop deeper understanding of the special functions of secondary education and to enlarge the teacher's concept of the meaning of education in our democracy; to ascertain and bring about needed changes that will facilitate the improvement of techniques of teaching and coordination; to direct experimentation in purposeful and concomitant learnings; to make use of all ancillary agencies available to school and community; to measure the results of teachers' activities in terms of pupil growth toward approved ideals [34]

Long-range policies may, in fact, interfere with the organization's effectiveness in day-to-day operations. Under pressures to find immediate solutions to pressing problems long-range goals are easily ignored.

Second, policies tend to be formed without explicit recognition of all of the emerging outside pressures impinging on the organization or, indeed, without prior knowledge of what they will be. Daily decisions, however, are made within a competitive context. The competitive nature of the situation may force officials to compromise some basic goals in order that others may be fulfilled. It is interesting to observe the effect of athletic success on long-standing policies concerning pep rallies, impromptu demonstrations, and release from class. Under the pressures exerted when a school's team becomes a contender for the state champion-ship, policies to keep athletics in proper perspective during an ordinary season suddenly become inadequate with the approach of closing weeks of successful competition. A few years ago the administration of a "Big Ten" university was forced by such pressures to grant an "official" holi-day at the close of a winning football season when a Rose Bowl bid was announced. At the same time, a resident poet was awarded the Pulitzer Prize, but this more academic accomplishment was allowed to pass almost unnoticed. In such cases, the drift from goals more acutely reflects a sacrifice than willful violation of them.

Third, social changes are normally responsible for a certain degree of institutional drift. There tends to be a lag between formal policy state-ments and the contemporary social reality which an organization faces. For example, the formal educational goal of preparing children to be good Christians, formulated by the Puritans, remained a formal policy long after it had been essentially replaced by vocational training. Simi-larly, in some areas agricultural training remains an official goal despite changes which have occurred in the community.

As important as social change is, the internal change which organiza-tions themselves naturally undergo is limited in the course of their career. If the organization is too successful, for example, its goals may be achieved, in which case new goals must be created if it is to continue to survive. This is the peculiar fate of certain limited purpose organizations such as the "March of Dimes" which was momentarily left without a goal when polio was conquered. This, however, is extremely unlikely to hap-pen in schools, but may happen in certain departments within a school in which the objectives are limited.

The sacrifice of some goals and the emergence of others not formally intended may occur either because of a realistic, rational appraisal con-cerning which goals can best be achieved in the situation, or because of a less rational tendency over a period of time for minor decisions to cul-minate into an operating policy different from the formal one. In any case, institutional drift is responsible for operational goals and purposes which are not identical with the formal ones. It contributes to conflicts of goals within the public schools.

The Single Bureaucratic Form

When combined, the fallacies discussed previously in this chapter—impersonality, rationality, fallibility of rules, and unitary ends—create still another fallacy: that bureaucracy has one characteristic form which has a compelling and irresistible existence due to its efficiency and effec-tiveness. The popular model which looms in the background of most dis-cussions of bureaucracy is the military establishment, with its emphasis on compliance in conduct and the crucial role of discipline. This image is nurtured by a widely accepted "ideal type" (discussed in the preceding chapter) which casts all bureaucratic organizations into one structural form, in which all major decisions are ascribed to central offices and imposed on disciplined ranks, and in which rules and rigid disciplinary measures for control are emphasized.

DUAL BASIS OF AUTHORITY

There are two bases of bureaucratic authority. Some rules are established by *agreement,* and others are established by *imposition.* Parsons and Gouldner suggest that Weber apparently confused these two bases. On the one hand, Weber attributed bureaucratic authority to "knowledge"; on the other hand, he asserted that, above all, bureaucracy rests on "discipline." The first principle presumes obedience to be a means to an end, while in the second, obedience is an end in itself, and the morality and rationality of the order are ignored in favor of the authority of the chief executive.[35] Under the first principle, the individual obeys because of his feelings; under the second, he obeys regardless of his feelings. Gouldner concludes that Weber was describing not one, but two types of bureaucracy which Gouldner terms "representative" (based on technically justified rules established by consent) and "punishment-centered," which imposes obedience to rules as the criteria of performance. The vital character of any particular organization will vary depending on whether it emphasizes imposition or agreement. It is instructive to consider the conditions under which each rises.

AUTHORITARIAN AND REPRESENTATIVE BUREAUCRACY

Bendix describes a discipline-centered, authoritarian administration which is similar to the "punishment-centered" concept—that is, one in which the official's obedience is exclusively to his superiors. Because his obligation is to prevailing authority, he develops a feeling of solidarity against the public which he confronts as a representative of higher authority rather than as a "public employee." Since the measure of his loyalty and performance is his conformity to rules, the administration becomes suspicious of a subordinate who disobeys rules or attempts to evade responsibility as it is officially defined.[36] Under "representative" or democratic administration, the official has more authority, which is limited only by diffuse forms of supervision, and that authority rests on a spirit of public service. Because the democratic administrator stands ambivalently between his superiors and the public, his compliance to orders is conditioned by his sense of responsibility to the public; because his behavior is checked constantly by the public and because public pressures invade all levels of the operation, he is evaluated on his *initiative* as well as his *compliance.*

Bendix insists that these types differ, not because one is more efficient but arbitrary and the other representative but inefficient; on the contrary, the distinction rests on the way obedience and efficiency are combined with *initiative*. Perhaps it is not possible to direct every activity in any organization, as some reliance must be placed on initiative of personnel to implement the overall policies. But the democratic form will encourage initiative by appealing to the employee's sense of responsibility rather than by setting up elaborate systems of control.

However, Bendix's analysis ignores the fact that there are other reasons for initiative besides public service. For example, professional standards promote the initiative of professionals, and they are not always completely coincidental with either administrative goals or public sentiment. Witness, for example, physicians' strikes and opposition to publicly supported health care plans. Moreover, the public pressures which influence the bureaucrat's decisions can be illegitimate as well as legitimate ones.

The gypsum plant which Gouldner studied was divided into two productions places, the mine and the surface.[37] The miners were able to restrict hierarchical administration and placed less emphasis on specialized spheres of competence than did surface workers. They expressed a hostile orientation to rules and displayed relatively little "impersonalization" in supervisor-worker relations. In short, surface workers were more "disciplined" than miners. These differences arose for several reasons. First, managers of the surface force perceived their personnel to be less motivated than did mine management. The latter believed that miners "worked hard" under severely dangerous conditions, while by contrast, surface management anticipated that their subordinates would "goldbrick" at the first opportunity. Second, management of the two divisions had different conceptions of the *effectiveness* of discipline-centered bureaucracy. Miners had traditionally been "their own bosses" and exhibited high, informal social cohesion, bolstered by a tradition of resistance to outside authority and justified by the dangerous conditions under which they worked. Their physical isolation from the central offices also enabled them to resist disciplinary bureaucracy and substitute their own form of permissive bureaucracy. The physical dispersion of schools may be likewise important.

Punishment-centered bureaucracy was initiated when workers were perceived to be failing in their role obligations and opposed to the official system. The fact that it arose as a reaction to opposition suggests that conflict in organizations may be a primary explanation of the emergence of different bureaucratic forms. If conflict can be responsible for punishment-centered bureaucracy, it seems entirely premature to assume that bureaucracies exist solely because of their efficiencies—which is the image conveyed when bureaucracy is conceived as operating and developing "without the intervention of interested groups," as Gouldner puts it.[38] It is possible that a variety of organizational types are efficient and effective and that neither is essential for bureaucratic growth. Actually, the company Gouldner studied had never worked out any way of measuring the effectiveness of its program. On the contrary, the discipline-oriented bureaucracy seemed to be less a way of achieving efficient organization than it was a response to threatened breakdown in social relationships—that is, it was a defense against perceived opposition. Such bureaucracies are monocratic and, as shown by Gouldner's study, are dominated by a production ideology. In such cases, of course, there is a necessity for organizational control to be connected directly to extrinsic rewards. Such a reward system is connected primarily either to a number of status positions (promotion) or to wages. In modern organizations there are not enough of these "rewards"; even well-developed wage and salary systems apparently do not significantly motivate very high performance.[39]

The philosophy of extrinsic rewards still persists even with educational organizations which have been forced, due to inadequate salary structures, to depend much more on vertical mobility within the hierarchy. On this point, Thompson observes:

> With enormous expansion of knowledge flooding the organization with specialists of all kinds and with the organization increasingly dependent on them, this reward system is facing a crisis. With all his pre-entry training, the specialist finds that he can "succeed" only by giving up work for which he is trained and entering management—work for which he has had no training.[40]

Although the teacher must receive training in administration before entering "management," the pattern is the same. However, one of the real weaknesses of the extrinsic reward system is, as Thompson further asserts, that it ". . . stimulates conformity rather than innovation." [41]

When administration and employees do not have mutually threatening perceptions of one another, bureaucracy will develop in a different way. For example, the safety program in the same factory Gouldner studied was characterized by a large number of rules with several agencies established to enforce them. But it provoked little hostility from the workers, for it was designed particularly for their benefit, and it reinforced middle-class attitudes toward drunkenness on the job, being clean-shaven, and so on. In fact it was the *workers* who sought to formalize management safety obligations whenever they perceived management to be negligent in fulfilling their obligations to care for employees. Workers initiated punishment-centered bureaucracy when they perceived management in opposition to the official goals.

Implications: A Reassessment of the "Informal Organization"

The popularity of the term "informal organization," which is currently in widespread usage, is due largely to a growing awareness that the popular myths discussed in this chapter are inadequate to explain organization. However, since it is primarily a *reaction* to idealistic conceptions of official organization, the term has been assigned a multitude of meanings which encompass most of the ideas discussed in this chapter, and whose only common element is one of a variety of "differences" from the official model of organization. Oddly enough, the term has the peculiar distinction of being a category applied to a range of "exceptions" from an ideal type that does not normally exist in the first place.

Specifically, the term has been used in conjunction with three models, all of which concern forms of behavior that regularly occur, but which are not formally prescribed in written job requirements or administrative codes. The first meaning is derived from a legal model of organization. It applies to all *illegal* and *unofficial* acts. The "illegal" connotation refers to organized resistance to laws and statutes and may be illustrated by the implicit expectation in some schools that teachers will "wink" at troublesome truants who leave school before the legal age. The "unofficial" meaning pertains to all behavior that violates codified policies and rules of the organization endorsed by the administration—for example, unofficial norms of work restriction and the practice of ignoring violations of administration sponsored "no smoking" rules.

NONOFFICIAL SOCIAL MODELS

The second usage of "informal organization" is derived from a social model of organization which incorporates *nonofficial* behavior. Nonofficial conduct has four principal components: customs, ideologies, norms, and sentiments. *Customs* are often aspects of the broader society which include rules of etiquette regulating interpersonal conduct, rules concerning violence, freedom of speech, and attitudes toward the opposite sex, and old age. There are also customs peculiar to an organization, such as weekly informal gatherings of the faculty. Customs are normally justified by ideologies—that is, values stated as facts; they, too, may be either reflections of the larger society or peculiar to the organization. An example of the former (societal reflection) is the proposition that administrators are personally superior to their subordinates; instances of the latter (purely local) might include a belief that teachers of former eras had two-hour lunch periods. These traditions and ideologies form the organization's *culture*.

Social *norms* include the expectations which govern nonofficial relationships. They constitute the informal organizational structure. They may include common understandings that only "local" teachers will be hired or that rural people will have more representatives on the school board than the town people. Together, customs and norms constitute a network of customary social *relationships* which persons are expected to fulfill as surely as their official roles.

The impersonal quality of the informal organization contrasts with the very personal character of the fourth meaning derived from the social model, *sentiment*. Unlike the other meanings, which refer to the relationships that exist independent of personalities, sentiment is the exclusive property of *groups* of *individuals*. It is this sense of informal organization that is implied with the term "informal group," or clique. Personal group relationships include friendships, personal animosities, romances, and intrigues. While traditions and norms both specify the standard, expected forms of behavior, the distinctive quality of sentiment is its focus on the unique grouping that occurs because of purely personal interest. Of course, both culture and structure are carried out by persons, but "sentiment" calls attention to the purely personal element in certain groupings. Unlike the other meanings of informal organization, the group is dissolved when its members leave. These distinctions raise several important problems, such as how do "groups" influence "structures?" When is cooperation provided by the "structure" and when is it served through the "group?"

THEORETICAL MODELS

The first two meanings of informal organization encompass all of the extralegal, the illegal, and nonlegal social patterns of behavior, including the cultural traditions and normative structures and group sentiments. Opposed to both the legal and the social models is a third use of the term which refers to deviations from a theoretical specification of ideal bureaucracies. This use of the term is understood only in conjunction with the official administrative model. It refers to all observed conduct that cannot be explicitly derived from the logical forms specified in the official model. About the only question that can be raised is, why does "deviation" from a conceptual ideal occur? Compared as it is to an *ideal*, the questions that are raised are misleading if interpreted in terms of reality. It may be more meaningful to ask how the ideal, formal organization can ever exist.

The factors responsible for discrepancies between the model and reality may be the same factors that are responsible for illegal, unofficial, and nonofficial conduct. But in addition, one writer proposes that the ideal model of bureaucracy itself confounds two distinctly opposed characteristics—bureaucracy and rationality.[42] Bureaucracy consists of (1) a hierarchical authority structure, (2) a specialized administrative staff, and (3) differentiated rewards according to office. The rationality concept includes (1) limited objectives, (2) performance emphasis, (3) segmental participation, and (4) compensatory rewards in return for participation. Bureaucracy is related to the authoritarian basis of bureaucratic authority, while competence is the basis of rationality. While these are not logically incompatible concepts, Udy's evidence, gathered from cross-cultural area files, suggests that they can be at least empirically inconsistent within the same organization. Indeed, Udy proposes that there is an inverse relationship between rationality and bureaucracy.

If there are two submodels within the single ideal model of bureaucracy, discrepancies between the ideal model and informal organization are partially due to inconsistencies within the model itself. This would help to explain the laymen's charge that "bureaucracy" (the authoritarian basis) is inefficient "red tape," in view of an ideal description of "bureaucracy" (rationality) as a system which stresses efficiency. The proposal also provides for the possibility that many forms of organization may lead to efficiency and that, conversely, increasing authoritarian controls does not necessarily increase the efficiency of a bureaucracy. This explanation poses a major dilemma of organizations: employees are expected to act both rationally *and* bureaucratically.

SUMMARY

The first two meanings of the concept "informal organization" direct attention to the culture and the structure in which the organization actually exists and the persons that comprise it. However, the third general usage directs attention to the incompatibilities within the ideal model of organization itself as a source of nonrational conduct. When the official culture and structure are added to the picture, the complexity of organization reaches perplexing degrees. But the full drama of organization must be considered if the nature of administration is to be fully understood.

In this chapter, we have tried to demonstrate that there is a tendency to assume that bureaucratic structures possess certain qualities which do not in fact characterize such structures in the real world. These qualities are: (1) rationality; (2) impersonality of work relations; (3) infallibility of rules; (4) unity of ends; and (5) existence of a single bureaucratic form. Such assumptions are mythical by virtue of the fact that they seem to survive in the face of empirical and logical evidence to the contrary.

The consequences of these and other factors which complicate the tasks of internal organizational management will be considered in the following chapter.

BIBLIOGRAPHY AND NOTES

1. M. Dalton, *Men Who Manage*. New York: Wiley, p. 263.
2. W. E. Moore, *Industrial Relations and the Social Order*. New York: Macmillan, 1951, p. 271.
3. See, for example, F. J. Roethlesberger and W. J. Dickson, *Management and the Worker*, Cambridge, Mass.: Harvard Univ. Press, 1938; for descriptions of the school system as an informal organization, see L. Iannaccone, *The Social System of a School Staff*, unpublished Ed. D. thesis, Teachers College, Columbia University, 1958; and N. J. Boyan, *A Study of the Formal and Informal Organization of a Junior High School Faculty*, unpublished Ph.D. thesis, Harvard University, Cambridge, 1951.
4. C. H. Page, "Bureaucracy's Other Face," *Social Forces*, vol. 25, 1946, pp. 88–94.
5. J. G. Anderson, "Bureaucratic Rules: Bearers of Organizational Authority," *Educational Administration Quarterly*, Vol. II, No. 1, 1966, p. 30.
6. E. Gross, "Some Functional Consequences of Primary Controls in Formal Work Organizations," *American Sociological Review*, vol. 18, 1953, pp. 368–73.
7. R. O. Carlson, *Executive Succession and Organizational Change: Place-Bound and Career-Bound Superintendents of Schools*. Chicago: Midwest Administration Center, Univ. Chicago, 1962, pp. 30–35.
8. R. Bendix, "Bureaucracy: The Problem and Its Setting," *American Sociological Review*, vol. 12, 1942, pp. 502–4.
9. The following discussion is based on A. W. Gouldner's *Patterns of Industrial Bureaucracy*, Glencoe, Ill.: Free Press, 1954, pp. 162–168.
10. R. G. Francis and R. Stone, *Service and Procedure in Bureaucracy: A Case Study*. Minneapolis: Univ. Minnesota Press, 1956, pp. 42–44.
11. Gouldner, *op. cit.*, pp. 172 ff.
12. R. H. Turner, "The Navy Disbursing Officer as a Bureaucrat," *American Sociological Review*, vol. 2, 1947, pp. 342–48.
13. *Ibid.*
14. Gouldner, *op. cit.*, p. 182.
15. *Ibid.*, p. 174.
16. For a concise discussion of the dysfunctional effects of bureaucratic rules, see Anderson, *op. cit.*, pp. 7–34.
17. Moore, *op. cit.*, p. 72.
18. C. Barnard, *The Functions of the Executive*. Cambridge, Mass.: Harvard Univ. Press, 1938, p. 88.
19. A. Gouldner, "Organizational Analysis," in *Sociology Today*, R. K. Merton, L. Broom and L. S. Cottrell, Jr., eds. Glencoe, Ill.: Free Press, 1959, pp. 400–429.
20. C. Argyris, "Understanding Human Behavior in Organizations: One Viewpoint," in *Modern Organization Theory*, M. Haire, ed. New York: Wiley, 1959, p. 125.
21. *Ibid.*
22. A. W. Gouldner, "On Weber's Analysis of Bureaucratic Rules," in *Reader in Bureaucracy*, R. Merton, A. Gray, B. Hockey, and H. Selvin, eds. Glencoe, Ill.: Free Press, 1952, pp. 48 ff.
23. M. Lieberman, *Teaching as a Profession*. Englewood Cliffs, N. J.: Prentice Hall, 1956, p. 34. *Cf.* Educational Policies Commission, *The Purposes of Education in American Democracy*, NEA, 1938. A more recent statement of objectives by the same group, however, lists only one major goal: critical thinking. The American public does not seem to agree on what is the most important benefit that children should receive from this education, according to a 1944 survey. One-third men-

tioned regular subjects and character education first, one-fourth listed vocational training, citizenship was mentioned first by fourteen per cent, and eleven per cent mentioned social adjustment. National Opinion Research Center, "The Public Looks at Education," Report No. 21, Univ. Denver, 1944.

24. K. Archibald, "Status Orientations Among Shipyard Workers," in *Class States and Power: A Reader in Social Stratification*, R. Bendix and S. M. Lipset, eds. Glencoe, Ill.: Free Press, 1953, pp. 395–403.

25. G. Simmel, *The Sociology of Georg Simmel*, trans. by K. Wolff. Glencoe, Ill.: Free Press, 1950, p. 280. See also Ch. 6, "Cooptation."

26. C. Barnard, *op. cit.*, pp. 101–106.

27. D. C. Miller and W. H. Form, *Industrial Sociology: An Introduction to the Sociology of Work Relations*. New York: Harper, 1951, p. 839.

28. American Association of School Administrators, 38th Yearbook, *Professional Administrators for America's Schools*, Washington, D. C., NEA, 1960.

29. E. L. Jones and M. V. Halmon, "Why People Become Teachers," in *The Teachers in American Society*, L. J. Stiles, ed. New York: Harper, 1957, pp. 236–37.

30. E. Gross, "Social Integration and the Control of Competition," *The American Journal of Sociology*, vol. 67, 1961, pp. 270–71.

31. Francis and Stone, *op. cit.*, pp. 158 ff.

32. L. A. Coser, *The Function of Social Conflict*. Glencoe, Ill.: Free Press, 1956, Ch. 1.

33. P. Selznick, "Foundations of the Theory of Organization," *American Sociological Review*, vol. 13, 1948, pp. 25–35; much of the following is based on Selznick's discussion.

34. B. Kaufman, "From a Teacher's Wastebasket," *Saturday Review*, Nov. 17, 1962, p. 59.

35. A. W. Gouldner, *Patterns of Industrial Bureaucracy*. Glencoe, Ill.: Free Press, 1954, pp. 19 ff.

36. R. Bendix, "Bureaucracy: The Problem and Its Setting," *American Sociological Review*, vol. 12, 1942, pp. 498–502.

37. Gouldner, *Patterns of Industrial Bureaucracy*, supra.

38. *Ibid.*

39. See F. Herzberg, B. Mausner, and B. Snyderman, *The Motivation of Work*. New York: Wiley, 1959.

40. V. A. Thompson, "Bureaucracy and Innovation," *Administrative Science Quarterly*, June, 1965, p. 5.

41. *Ibid.*

42. S. H. Udy, Jr., "Bureaucracy and Rationality in Weber's Theory," *American Sociological Review*, vol. 24, 1959, pp. 791–95.

CHAPTER

9

The Problems of Internal Organizational Control

[Bureaucracy] . . . is not some foreign substance which has been infused into the life-blood
of an institution; it is merely the accentuation of
characteristics found in all.[1]

THERE is a series of dilemmas which runs through institutional life
and which creates the central problems of bureaucracy. Consider
the following:

Clear organizational lines are essential to administrative
efficiency, but if they become too fixed they tend toward inflexibility.

Well-defined goals increase the striking power of the enterprise, but they often harden the mold.

Definite levels of authority, or the hierarchy itself, assure effective command, but the hierarchy is another factor which
encourages inflexibility.

Rules defining appropriate methods and procedures increase
the organization's efficiency, but they stifle the creativity of
individuals in it.

Efficiency requires specialization of knowledge and function,
but specialization narrows the individual and leads him dangerously close to a rut.

In order to reward employee loyalty and performance older
employees are promoted, and yet seniority is not always associated with competence.

Many of these familiar problems which confront nearly all educational

243

administrators stem from the school system's hierarchy of offices or, in other words, the "chain of command." The chain of command functions on the principle of delegated authority, which involves the separation of responsibility from control, and the separation of authority from power. It is often responsible for an imbalance between effort and reward. The preoccupation with rank, which is commonly associated with the chain of command, and its symptoms will be considered below.

Preoccupation with Rank

Teachers are expected to be simultaneously oriented toward their own work, to the children they teach, and to the administration. In view of this range of authority levels to which teachers are simultaneously responsible, the delegation of functions to them understandably creates a mildly schizoid preoccupation with rank simultaneously up and down the hierarchy.

SUBSERVIENCE TOWARD SUPERIORS

For the subordinate, preoccupation with rank is manifested by subservience to superiors. Since superiors control the important rewards, subordinates are often inclined to be responsive to their bosses' slightest whims and often model their own work habits around those of their boss. New teachers may be tempted to rely on a course syllabus preferred by their department head or principal rather than developing plans of their own. Indeed, they may become so sensitive to their superior's comments that his most casual suggestions are made the basis for revising the course or teaching methods. But because subordinates are often unable to distinguish the mandatory from the permissive facets of a superior's behavior, subordinates' conformity may be even greater than the superior himself would demand, or prefer.

INDIFFERENCE TO SUBORDINATES

In contrast to the subservience of their subordinates, superiors are often indifferent toward them. Of this, one writer says, "While each boss is thus the center of attention from the subordinate, he in turn is busy watching his own boss and wondering about him. As a result, he tends to look upon his subordinates in quite a different way. He rarely worries about their opinions of him; he does not lie awake at night wondering if his acts make him look like a fool in front of them . . . he does not even remember that he is not supposed to be annoyed with them if they are upset by his indifference or demand a lot of his time." [2]

Consequently, the superior-subordinate relationship is "lop-sided," each stressing different characteristics of the relationship; the subordinate accentuates the personal, the superior the contractual aspects. As a result, superiors and subordinates are predisposed to evaluate one another in different ways. While principals will be inclined to evaluate teachers in terms of their performance, teachers are more concerned with the personalities of their superiors; the teacher appears to the principal as "competent" or "incompetent" or as "a good disciplinarian," but to teachers the principal is "a nice guy," or "a real bear." In general, then, a "good boss" is a considerate one, while a "good worker" is a productive one. Such imbalances between the personal subservience of the subordinate and indifference of the superior to employees' personal feelings is ultimately a source of tension between the ranks, for potential misunderstanding is built into the relationship.

OFFICIAL "PARANOIA"

Just as surely as *evaluation* by superiors increases the dependence of subordinates on them, *delegation* of responsibility to subordinates creates a delicate situation wherein the superior's success is dependent upon the performance of his subordinates. This fact is manifest in the nagging fear of superiors that their subordinates will fail. Largely for this reason the superior's general mode of indifference toward subordinates is colored by a gentle "paranoia" about subordinates which occasionally pervades the mind of even the most self-confident administrator.

These paranoid dimensions arise from a characteristic of delegation itself—a conflict of interest that naturally arises between the superior and his agent because of the fact that the agent's motivation is dependent upon his relationship to his superior rather than upon his direct interest in the goals. The superior's commands to subordinates are more likely to be related to his own personal goals than to those of his subordinates, so he is normally more concerned with quick, thorough achievement of his commands than are his subordinates. This is typical of attendance reports which teachers are supposed to submit on time; these reports are more directly related to the administrator's work than to that of the teachers, and so require close supervisory checks.

Furthermore, under delegation rewards are often independent of effort; a vague injustice may be sensed by the subordinates who "do the work" while their boss "gets all the credit for it." It is often true that persons such as coal miners, who do the most tedious, boring, and exhausting work, receive the least compensation and honor; similarly in the professions, a lawyer's fame rests on the essential assistance of his clerk; and the superintendent's reputation rests upon the bookkeeping efficiency of his accounting officer and the skill of his teachers. This tendency for some to benefit from the work of others not only dampens subordinates' ambitions, but is at least one cause of the superiors' suspicion of them. Criticism and fault-finding of subordinates is inherent in this situation, where the reputation of a superior depends on the performance of his subordinates. As a consequence, the actions of superiors have an extraordinarily internal reference to the mechanics of controlling their own subordinates in order to protect their position, which deflects their attention from policy-making functions and the general goals of the organization.

INCOMPETENCE

Under these conditions, it is not surprising that superiors seek to retain control over functions they have delegated. To the extent that a principal retains active control over delegated responsibilities, it creates a disparity between subordinates' responsibility for a task and their authority to perform it, and this in turn contributes to the incompetence of subordinates. For example, the teacher may pursue her own course outline with reluctance until she receives some kind of endorsement from the principal or supervisor. Thus constrained to get approval for every action, subordinates are severely handicapped in achieving their tasks.

Retaining authority at the upper levels also restricts the subordinate's competence by eroding his authority over other parties. It may be difficult, for example, for the superintendent to understand why one of his teachers has had so much trouble getting the janitor to clean the blackboard when the superintendent himself gets such good cooperation. Yet, the teacher cannot be expected to secure cooperation without some authority to affect the janitor's positional security.

EVASION OF SUPERIORS

Administrators are expected to help personnel with their personal and professional problems. Nevertheless, subordinates often deliberately avoid requesting advice of their superiors; there seems to be an ideology that successful teachers have no problems. Consequently, many serious problems are not brought to the attention of administrators. This was found to be the case in one federal law enforcement agency.[3] When agents encountered problems, they were supposed to consult only with their supervisors, but since their supervisors rated them and controlled their promotions they were reluctant to reveal their problems to the supervisor. Instead, agents consulted with one another in violation of official rules. However, since repeated requests for advice also undermined the agent's professional standing among his colleagues, agents were constrained to consult only with those other agents with whom they were friendly, regardless of their ability; this may have reduced the overall quality of advice given.[4]

Causes. There are several reasons why subordinates might not wish to reveal their problems. In the first place, the admission by a subordinate that he is unable to solve problems often appears to be a confession of his own incompetence. Even if he is expected to have problems in his present position, it is nevertheless an indication that his ability warrants no greater responsibility. There is, at the same time, a natural reluctance to create extra work for superiors by bringing one's problems to them. However, this reluctance varies with the nature of the problem itself, and a subordinate can gain favorable recognition by reporting an especially serious situation, particularly if he has had no direct responsibility for its occurrence. Thus, teachers are not reluctant to relay gossip concerning widespread unrest among parents in the community or a growing movement to defeat an urgent bond issue. (Also, they will seek advice which flatters the boss, such as asking personal opinions about the best route to work or the best restaurant in town.)

In the process of calling the administrator's attention to his problems, the subordinate also calls attention to himself. Gordon observed that teachers were reluctant to send discipline problems to the principal's office because it would advertise their own inability to handle problems.[5] Since bureaucracies use care in evaluating the qualifications of personnel and classifying them at the time of hiring, they are normally assumed to be competent until demonstrated otherwise. Single salary schedules based solely on training and experience typify the assumption that competence exists. In view of this assumption, the subordinate has little to gain, and possibly much to lose, by calling attention to himself.

Subordinates are also reluctant to reveal problems which might embarrass their superiors with respect to co-workers or the public. In learning of a problem situation, the superior may be forced to take action that he would prefer to avoid and be forced to investigate people whom he otherwise supports. A teacher who complains to a principal, who happens to be a personal friend of the drama teacher, that the drama coach requests her students to be absent too frequently challenges the principal's own judgments and jeopardizes his staff relationships. Because the subordinate seldom knows precisely how his problems will be perceived by his superior, he is inclined to avoid unnecessary issues.

Finally, calling a problem to the attention of superiors may expose embarrassing, unofficial, and illegitimate practices of one's colleagues. Teachers leave the undesirable chores, such as monitoring halls, chaperoning dances, taking tickets at athletic events, and heavy teaching loads, to new teachers, but new teachers seldom file official complaints as this would interfere with the informal organization and create even greater problems for both the subordinate and the principal, who is forced to reassess the traditions of his entire organization. Reluctant to interfere with the informal practice of his subordinates, the principal may simply decide that the teacher who bothers him with problems of this kind demonstrates an incompetence to "handle herself."

TENSIONS BETWEEN SUBORDINATES AND INDIRECT SUPERIORS

The disparity between authority and responsibility which delegation creates also arouses in superiors a jealous inclination to control *indirect* subordinates (that is, the subordinates of an immediate subordinate, such as the relation between superintendents and teachers). Anxiety over indirect subordinates creates "short circuits" in the chain of command.

However, the practice is usually resisted by intermediate administrators because, when a remote superior gives commands directly to another's subordinates, it provides them with more information than their supervisor himself possesses and places the latter in a position of receiving instructions from his own subordinates. Subordinates also tend to resist meddling by their remote superior if he is interfering with the work for which they are responsible. Besides, the intervention of indirect superiors creates "overlapping authority," which places the subordinate in the awkward position of having to satisfy two bosses at once. Nevertheless, these occasions do provide an ambitious subordinate with the opportunity to impress top officials, which also enhances his position with his own supervisor.

If subordinates do resist their remote superiors' efforts to control them, these superiors may resent them for it. Yet, a stubborn subordinate can probably count on his own immediate supervisor to come to his defense, because the employees who refuse to cooperate with their remote superior are the very ones who are most cooperative with their direct supervisor.

When high-ranking officials meddle in the internal affairs of their subordinate units, their actions modify the hierarchy in unintended ways. For example, if the chief executive shows more interest in the operation of one section of his organization than in the others, his interest will tend to modify the organization. Because school boards normally stress finance, the superintendent may spend most of his effort on the financial aspects of administration; the business manager may achieve a control over the financial program which enables him to influence educational policy far in excess of his official authority. In this sense, organization is best understood in terms of the relationships that its officials have with their chief executives.

TENSIONS WITHIN THE RANKS

Not only does delegation contribute to ideological disputes *between* echelons, but because delegating authority to a subordinate thereby distinguishes him from his co-workers, it also breaks up the homogeneity of the employees. To the extent that this prevents them from confronting the boss as a group, it is often to the superior's advantage that his subordinates are delegated unequal, rather than equal, types of work.[6] The differentiation resulting from delegation creates sufficient conflict of interest to keep the subordinates more loyal to their superiors than to their own group interests.[7] In fact, one author proposes that employee policies are specifically designed to split the strength of subordinates by giving them differential ranks.[8] Positions such as athletic director, the "teaching principal" in an elementary school, or appointed department heads responsible to the principal have this effect. To that extent, it is apparent that the official division of labor is not determined entirely by the functional needs of the organization. When superintendents or principals delegate important work to a few select teachers, they are not only building a loyal nucleus of subordinates, but they are also dividing the subordinate group among themselves. However, while this reduces their ability to resist the executive's wishes, the resulting feuds and jealousies may also disrupt the informal organization and prevent whatever positive functions it normally performs.

In their effort to maintain an appearance of superiority to one another, employees create increasingly finer distinctions, which promotes an artificial separation among themselves and creates an informal hierarchy which is usually far more complex than the formal requirements of their work would demand.[9] Dryfess explains the tendency for organizations to become bureaucratically "rigid" in terms of the threat that change poses to this *artificial* basis of rank rather than to the "rational needs" of administration.

This "artificial" (that is, nontechnical) stratification is obviously a fundamental element of work. It develops in its most complex form whenever large numbers of persons are engaged in the same functional activities. "Teachers," for example, may use a range of status symbols to differentiate themselves from their co-workers, including favorite classroom locations, use of name plates, access to telephones or dictaphones, smoking privileges, private radios, private offices, carpeting on the office floor, special parking places, and numerous other privileges. Changes which threaten this artificial hierarchy may be resisted.

An administrator may have more control over the informal symbols than some official symbols, such as salary schedules. This same artificial hierarchy within the school system is often reflected in the salary schedules of teachers; often minor salary differences are of fundamental importance for prestige. Rewarding the discontented influentials with informal devices may be a more effective strategy than attempting to use formal rewards.

In a large suburban school system which was growing in size, the superintendent felt that he now needed a director of secondary education to coordinate the work of the growing number of secondary school principals. One of the authors, who served as a consultant to the system, found that although all principals acknowledged that they could not get enough time from the superintendent's busy schedule to discuss their problems, the secondary principals were resisting the establishment of the new position for several reasons: (1) the new director would no doubt be selected from among the ranks (which had been announced), and the principals felt that they now had a team which could work together; (2) the director would usurp too many decisions now made by the principals; (3) they objected to the director's office being located in the central administration building; they felt if a new director were employed, he should be housed in a secondary school where he would be close to secondary teachers and principals, and where he would be less likely to "consider himself big brass"; (4) they also felt that the public's perception of the director would be such that he, rather than the principals themselves, would be expected to speak for secondary education. Here is a case where resistance to change was motivated by its threat to the existing status structure.

CEREMONIALISM

"Ceremonialism" is a term used to refer to pompous displays of status symbols that accrue from positions of authority. Its function is to provide persons in positions of authority with sufficient public recognition to validate their positions. However, ceremonialism tends to be used personally for the conspicuous consumption of prestige far in excess of any logical need.[10] Pompous costumes, formal modes of address, and other ritualistic signs of deference, which are to be found at school assemblies, graduation ceremonies, and in some PTA functions, tend to exaggerate the social distance between school administrators and their students and parents.

A distinctive feature of the ceremony is that it is an attempt to bestow high community status on officials whose main source of authority resides within organizations. That is, on ceremonial occasions the rank customarily confined within organization is introduced into social spheres and recognized by groups outside the organization. Partly for this reason ceremonies are usually held outside of the work area during nonworking hours.

In summary, bureaucratic organization is initially conceived of as a means to a socially approved end, and often continues to be so regarded by the public. But the personnel who staff bureaucracy, whose careers depend on its survival and its program, are predisposed in practice to defend organizational means over idealized purposes. The maintenance of one's own position becomes important in itself. Rifts develop among levels of supervision, social status considerations undermine official prescriptions, and important problems are obscured. The concern with rank that pervades modern organization is expressed in a variety of different ways by persons at different levels of authority who, because they develop different, often incompatible interests, perceive the organization from various perspectives. Conflicts and misunderstandings are natural outcomes.

"Buck-Passing"

A second set of problems are generic to another principle of delegation which is commonly known as "passing the buck." Buck-passing differs from the normal process of delegation in two ways. First, while the normal act of delegation is intended to fix responsibility, buck-passing is designed to evade it. Second, while delegation is normally from superiors to subordinates, buck-passing is more typically the delegation of responsibility upward from subordinates to their superiors, or out to other units. Buck-passing has several functions in school systems: counteracting excessive delegation, defense against unrewarded effort, face-saving, and friction reduction.

COUNTERACTING EXCESSIVE DELEGATION

Buck-passing is a socially acceptable way of resisting assignments which are difficult to carry out under certain conditions at a certain level of authority. By referring the problem to his superiors, a subordinate can avoid responsibility for jobs which he cannot do. Shunting responsibility upward represents a way of counteracting the extreme effects of the separation between authority and responsibility that occurs upon delegation.

DEFENSES AGAINST UNREWARDED EFFORT

Buck-passing is also a way to avoid work that might go unrewarded. Systems of justice are never perfect. This is particularly true in large organizations, whose "impersonality and interchangeability" are poor guarantees that additional efforts will be rewarded. In fact, zeal in assuming authority can bring undesired consequences as often as not. One observer of the U.S. Navy reports that an "eager beaver" might be retained overseas or in rank longer than a less valuable person who could be released; or a valuable person might suddenly be transferred to units which are in greatest demand of his services, thus depriving him of his friends. On the other hand, unearned rewards often accrue to undeserving persons. Military officials who jeopardized their positions by unnecessarily assuming added responsibility increased their chances of failure without necessarily increasing their reward.[11] Evasion of responsibility is normal under such circumstances where there is no particular advantage in assuming a responsibility.

FRICTION REDUCTION

Buck-passing insulates persons in the chain of command who know one another personally in the sense that it is easier for one person to accept orders from another if the orders are claimed to have originated from a higher, impersonal source; the supervisor can deny responsibility for the orders he must enforce. The commands of the principal are easier to take when he stresses that he is only following the directives of the superintendent's office or the State Department of Education. If he can maintain that he did not originate the order and does not personally believe in its value, he is protected from charges of being an imprudent autocrat, which is a suspicion to which administrators in a democracy are particularly subject. Subordinates are therefore forced to turn their resentment toward more remote top executives whom they are not in a position to effectively sabotage. At the same time, buck-passing also protects the subordinate from being placed in the derogatory position of being personally subject to his immediate supervisor.

"FACE-SAVING"

Subordinates are reluctant to commit themselves to decisions which their superiors might not support. The persistent possibility that a subordinate's decision might be reversed by his superiors is a special threat to face and another cause of buck-passing. Shunting responsibility upward is a way of preventing embarrassment from this source with one's own subordinates.

A special cause of buck-passing occurs due to normal discrepancies that arise between authority and special competence. Officials who are authorized to make decisions because of their rank may lack specialized knowledge to do so competently. Avoiding responsibility in these cases is a way of "saving face." It avoids embarrassing displays of ignorance.

Specialists use a unique form of buck-passing, which is implicit in the concept of limited "sphere of responsibility." [12] When the professional claims a sphere of competence, he is in effect disclaiming responsibility for the unintended consequences of his acts which happen to fall outside the immediate sphere of his ethical responsibility. In this way, the philosophy of specialism provides a convenient rationale for buck-passing.[13] Each party can claim that he did a competent job even while admitting the production of an inferior total product. The inability to trace responsibility for the quality of English or reading, or juvenile delinquency, to a particular administrator or teaching level, for example, provides each individual educator with an impeccable defense against public criticisms of education. Each level assigns responsibility for considering the "broader issues" of policy to the next level. Up and down the hierarchy personnel tend to become passively addicted to doing their "job" while disclaiming responsibility for overall social consequences of their organization. The public does not know precisely where to attack, for the final product appears to be nobody's concern through default. This is one of the significant problems of an atomic era in which specialists develop weapons capable of destroying civilization under the cloak of limited responsibility and buck-passing.

JUSTICE IN ORGANIZATIONS

Buck-passing supports a unique brand of *justice* within complex organizations. It is a way of distributing the blame over so many offices that no one office is severely damaged by public criticism. Consequently, blame takes a special meaning in complex organizations. Although blame appears to apply to individuals, it is used as a defense of the organization's respectability. Blame can be assigned in a way which prevents serious damage to the organization's reputation, rather than as a way of administering justice to employees. Sometimes the behavior of subordinates reflects less on the integrity of the organization than does the conduct of a high-ranking official. In such cases, subordinates may be expected to gracefully accept blame in order to protect the reputations of their superiors. Principals can blame teachers for late reports in order to save face with the superintendent's office, while the superintendent can blame his principal's tardiness when his own reports are not completed in time for the school board meeting. However, by the same token, the conduct of teachers represents the moral fibre of the school in some cases; then blame can be shifted upward. The principal may be expected to accept the blame for his teachers, for example, when an irate parent complains about the way a teacher has treated her child.

Evidence that it is the organization's reputation and not personal fault that is often on trial in public education is reported in the study of academic freedom in American universities. College social science teachers expressed apprehension that public institutions provide little protection for a professor whose views have been warped and publicized by a student. When the school's reputation was at stake, the administration usually acted as though the teacher were guilty of the charge, without investigating it.[14] One respondent reported that the president of his college reprimanded him for using a questionnaire containing items on the United Nations and government ownership without an attempt to ascertain why he had used them.[15] In another case, a botanist who admitted that he was at one time a member of the Communist party was fired despite the fact that a questionnaire completed by his students revealed that he had not expressed his views in teaching.[16] The vast majority of all charges ended in dismissal, suspension, unpromotability, or other official repercussions, usually without the benefit of an investigation.

Blame is used strategically to obscure scandals that arise within organizations. Despite principles of impersonality, there is a close connection among persons and their offices. An official's unofficial conduct casts its shadow over the integrity of his office and of the organization. For this reason, organizations are reluctant to dismiss officers for misconduct, as it would reflect on the organization; often the incompetent and unethical are shunted off to more isolated positions where they will receive less publicity. However, for the same reasons, when the official's misconduct becomes publicized, organizations are compelled to take action to avoid complicity.

The fact that organizations have the power to condemn a man but seldom the power to pardon him from an incensed public, greatly affects the concept of justice. To avoid notoriety, in some cases guilty persons may be spared blame, while in other cases blame will be placed on innocent persons. In neither case is blame assigned solely out of concern for individual justice, for what often seems to be at stake is the image of the organization. The influence of large-scale organization is having an unfathomed influence on the concept of personal justice and is creating an urgently fascinating problem that will become increasingly urgent as the administrative society matures.

"Red Tape"

A third problem area concerns the extensive use of written forms in complex organizations, a practice commonly labeled as "red tape." Red tape represents another effort of the administration to retain control over delegated responsibilities. Formal reports provide a way of checking that the task was performed properly. They also prevent subordinates from monopolizing information. The derogatory connotations of the term concern a series of fundamental complaints against modern organization. Some of these problems may be exposed by examining the meanings that underlie complaints which laymen commonly make about "red tape."

INVASION OF PRIVACY

The popular resentment of red tape reflects a conflict between the principle of service to clients and the best interests of organizational efficiency. Written forms are for the convenience of the organization but are of great inconvenience to the persons who must fill them out; they see the task as unnecessary or at least irrelevant to them. However, the term is indicative of even more fundamental problems between organizations and clients. From a study of one hundred and twenty-four respondents, Gouldner concludes that in objecting to the "unnecessary" work which red tape entails, people are actually expressing discontent about the invasion of privacy it entails; in other words red tape seems to violate the principle that everyone is privileged to withhold certain facts about himself.[17]

Most school systems require job applicants to complete standard personnel forms and batteries of personality tests. Questions about family income, history of mental illness in the family, race, religion, and other personal questions are standard. The organization can use and interpret this information according to its own interests and perspectives, but the individual has no corresponding right to gain access to and utilize private information about the organization or its officers. Nor do they have detailed understanding of how their responses will be interpreted by the authorities. The right of organizations to ask questions which even a personal acquaintance would have no right to ask is indicative of the moral authority which complex organizations are assuming in contemporary society.

POWERLESSNESS

Gouldner suggests that the public's objections to red tape above all reveal a sense of personal powerlessness in the face of arbitrary and even malicious power of bureaucracies. In this respect complaints against red tape are voiced by persons who feel overwhelmed by the demands of the modern rational economy. But the complaints are aimed at clerks and secretaries in the superintendent's office rather than against the system itself, which is the real source of irritation. The complaints are socially accepted, if ineffective, forms of aggression against the administrative economy. Criticisms of the system's procedures (red tape) substitute for aggression against the higher echelons of the organization and the general principles of bureaucracy. As such, the charge of "red tape" seems to register the complaints of political conservatives rather than a demand for more radical reform.[18]

The Conservative Basis of Organization

Conservatism is a common ingredient of the foregoing problems; it lends a unitary significance to them. Ceremonial preoccupation with maintaining and increasing rank, face-saving and impression management for the benefit of administrators, entrenchment of power, avoidance of responsibility, red tape as a weak complaint against means, displacement of goals, the conserving effects of encumbering social traditions, and a pervading climate hostile to change all contribute to the conservation of the *status quo*. In addition to these problems, conservatism takes special forms, forms generic to the nature of organization itself. Precedent and the routinization of work, after all, constitute the basis of organization. It is in this sense that one writer describes bureaucracy as the "composite of institutional manifestations which tend toward inflexibility and impersonalization . . . it is institutionalization writ large." [19]

The dilemma is that the internal features of organization may become so highly valued that its socially prescribed goals are neglected. Inflexibility penetrates the organization, and, in view of the rapidly changing society, this is often detrimental to its effectiveness. Consequently, an understanding of the causes of the conservative basis of organization is theoretically imperative. These are reviewed below.

GROWTH OF TRADITIONS

Traditions normally permeate an organization, imbuing it with a sacred quality which defies change. One writer observes:

> . . . they [the institutions] seem to have a life of their own after they have been in existence for some time; it is as though they were the collective embodiment of all those devoted souls who have gone before . . . an all-consuming smugness settles down over the landscape, like a London fog which stops traffic and permeates every keyhole. The institution is stronger than men. The executive must conform with becoming propriety or be politely but effectively shunted aside.[20]

This pervading sense of propriety and respectability which overshadows bureaucracy thus may force overemphasis on an organization as an end unto itself rather than as a means for achieving ends.

DEPENDENCE ON THE ENVIRONMENT

Because any organization is dependent on its environment to some extent, it is prompted to enroll the greatest possible number of outside supporters. To do so often requires concessions to the demands of outside groups and cautions against alienating any possible outside supporters. The most conservative are appeased in order to appeal to the widest possible base. This may be witnessed in the effort and publicity which some State Departments of Education spend on developing relatively innocuous "curriculum guides." While the activity may be justified within the framework of its goals, it is significant that it is an activity which draws less public criticism and which alienates no one, compared to more controversial forms of leadership such as raising certification standards, teachers' salaries, and the consolidation movement which are pursued less rigorously and with less publicity.

The tendency to "play it safe" stifles innovations, particularly since the organization usually knows what its sponsors like from past experience but are uncertain about which future innovations would upset them. Because the failure of innovations may have serious repercussions on the person's career and the organization's reputation, the activities which receive approval and endorsement are those most likely to succeed. Failure is minimized by ignoring, postponing, or dropping projects that do not have strong initial support. This contributes to a follow-the-leader, middle-of-the-road philosophy characteristic of many organizations.

EVALUATION PRACTICES

Evaluation practices used in complex organizations also contribute to the conservatism. The use of seniority as a basis for promotion has a particularly deadening effect on initiative, for extolling the virtues of experience favors old age. In most school systems today, the way to the superintendency is up through "the ranks," a long process. Top-level responsibility is left to the aged who are naturally reluctant to dismiss procedures which proved so instrumental for their own success.

Other evaluation practices are also responsible for conservatism. When subordinates are lauded for their conformity to specific operating rules, these practices become transformed into sacred rituals by employees who, having once mastered them, resist their modification.[21] Some teachers are reluctant to adapt to new techniques and procedures; for example, to what extent does educational television threaten teachers at the level of their classroom techniques instead of the educational goals so often talked about? On the other hand, when employees are evaluated in terms of *results* rather than the techniques they have mastered, the use of initiative and experimentation with alternative methods is encouraged to a greater extent.

Rigid adherence to routine can be used as a defense against superiors in the face of the insecurity feelings provoked by incompetence. In one federal agency, for example, public investigators who were less confident resisted changes in routines because they used routine as a substitute for inadequate knowledge to handle a task. However, investigators who were judged to be competent did not object to changes.[22] In general, officials who feel competent to handle their responsibilities probably do not worry as much about consequences of change as do less secure officials.

PROPRIETY

Codes of propriety restrict the time and place at which innovations are successfully proposed. Again, the sanctity of age is important. The right to propose a significant departure from the established ways is the prerogative of precisely those least likely to use it—the senior staff members who have a vested interest in the organization. Junior members who seriously propose any appreciable innovation are considered presumptuous, for the ideas of the young are generally regarded as less valid than those expressed by their elders.

This dubious attitude toward youthful advocates of change can be detrimental to an organization's potential effectiveness. Although he may be often naïve, a new member is in a position to contribute effective new ideas for he has the advantage of an original, cosmopolitan perspective freed from the bondage of ineffectual local traditions. Moreover, in a competitive situation, seeking the recognition that has already been granted to his seniors, the young person is *stimulated* to contribute new ideas. Of course there are ways in which youth does not have to wait its turn to speak. Private endorsement from a senior member who will introduce the idea in his name is an effective tactic. The technique is illustrated in the comments of a young factory employee concerning his superintendent: "I never tell him anything. . . . It doesn't pay to. I hint at something . . . Then he'll come around in a week or so and tell me the same damn thing in different words and ask me how I like it . . . We both pretend it's his idea but we both know it's not." [23] Such collaboration benefits the senior as well, for he reaps the imagination and effort of his juniors, and the situation affords the senior staff the opportunity to throttle threatening ideas of impetuous members. The fact that the organization can control even the right to speak out provides it with a powerful reward for senior members of the organization and the ability to throttle disrupting changes of newcomers.

SUCCESSION

The drama by which organizations settle into an atmosphere of conservatism is revealed in the customary ways in which they handle recurrent organizational crises, particularly the succession of chief executives. On the one hand, as "outsiders," new administrators are motivated to make changes. Not only have they been instructed about the predecessor's faults by their superiors, but, under pressure to "make good," the new executive is *compelled* to make changes in order to demonstrate that he is contributing something.[24] Thus sensitized, he is quick to perceive any informal privileges of workers as impediments to efficiency, and his proposed revisions in turn threaten their status. Yet, subordinates hold the newcomer morally responsible for the promises and obligations which he has inherited from his predecessor, but they will soon realize that many of their former privileges are completely misunderstood by the successor. The fact that an outsider was promoted over them simply aggravates their resentment.

"Bureaucratic sabotage" is a normal reaction. This term refers to subordinates' use of their powerful informal positions to mobilize sentiments against the plans of their executive. Not only are they in a position to withhold information from their new superior, but being an outsider, the newcomer cannot even benefit from the informal communication network. The successor, in turn, reacts to his employees' resistance by mobilizing another form of conservatism—proliferation of bureaucratic rules and red tape. The successor is compelled to organize bureaucratically, not because he wants to, but because the threat posed by his noncompliant subordinates may compel him to. Thus, paradoxically, a situation which would logically seem to encourage change—the succession of executives—provokes a conservative reaction from subordinates.[25]

SUMMARY

Problems of internal control are products of the system of rank and delegated authority—that is, the separation of authority and responsibility.

It raises four central problems: preoccupation with rank, buck-passing, red tape, and a strain toward conservation of means.

Preoccupation with rank produces an ambivalence in subordinates toward superiors which is manifested at once as subservience and resistance to them; this ambivalence is also expressed by superiors as general indifference to subordinates mixed with occasional pangs of fear (which may assume paranoid-like dimensions) about their irresponsibility and their ability to sabotage goals.

Because their own welfare is dependent upon the way their superior uses his power, subordinates stress the personal qualities of a boss in evaluating him—that is, his humaneness, compassion, and fairness; but since the boss's career in turn depends upon the way his subordinates perform, he is predisposed to evaluate them in terms of their technical competence and loyalty. This differential emphasis on personal relations and technical competence by subordinates and superiors provides a somewhat inconsistent basis for mutual expectations.

Preoccupation with rank at the higher echelons leads to "short circuits" in the chain of command because indirect superiors attempt to retain control over spheres of authority officially delegated to intermediates. The practice threatens to undermine the authority of intermediates and jeopardizes any special informal understandings which may have arisen between direct supervisors and their subordinates. To the extent that superiors maintain control over work after it has been delegated, the practice encourages a degree of incompetence in subordinates. In these cases the subordinate is constrained in his actions by fear of possible reprisal from a superior or reversal of his decisions from above, thus limiting his alternatives and effective influence.

The principles of hierarchy exaggerate tensions between superiors and their remote subordinates in three ways: (1) The concept of hierarchy supports noninterference with indirect subordinates, but at the same time the remote superior is dependent on their performance. (2) This situation may reduce the effectiveness of the organization since the official that is most concerned with the accomplishment of delegated work is not in a position to directly command those who are doing the work. (3) The situation encourages adjacent ranks to unite against nonadjacent levels. Much can be understood about the relationship among ranks by observing reactions to "short circuits" in the chain of command.

Finally, preoccupation with rank is a source of tension among subordinates. Minute differentiations among ranks create conflicts among personnel. This situation prevents a united front against the boss, but it promotes bureaucratic rigidity because rational changes tend to threaten the informal status system; at the same time informal differentiations proliferate the bureaucracy.

Buck-passing is a common reaction of subordinates to normal processes of delegation by which they evade responsibility by passing it back upwards, to other units. It is a strategy for resisting responsibilities for which there is no clear-cut authority, to avoid work for which there is no guaranteed reward, to avoid responsibility for decisions which one is incompetent to make, and to escape the moral consequences for one's own activities. Where buck-passing is utilized, blame often cannot be fixed on particular offices and seldom on persons, which makes it possible to assign blame on the basis of expediency or the organization's reputation; this represents a modification in the concept of justice, which traditionally has been applied to the individual.

While buck-passing is a reaction of *subordinates* to delegation, *red tape* represents the efforts of *superiors* to maintain control over delegated authority. Public attitudes toward it reveal a sense of powerlessness engendered by the developing administrative society and resentment toward invasion of privacy and other offenses of organizations against individualism.

Efforts to preserve rank and status encourage *conservatism*. There are also several other reasons that organizations grow conservative, including the following: the tendency for techniques to become infused with value, transforming them into hallowed traditions; the pressures on organizations to avoid alienating anyone, to prevent outside interference, and to gain support from outside; the practices of rewarding seniority and evaluating personnel on the basis of their techniques rather than the results they produce; and codes of propriety which throttle youth. Even changes of leadership can arouse conservative responses, especially in subordinates who have the power to sabotage proposed changes, and in the successor who is forced to react conservatively. Although strategic replacement is one of the few effective ways of combating conservatism of an organization, the practice violates norms of the broader society concerning "fairness" to loyal members of the organization.

Since these are, by selection, the *problems* of organizations, there is no implication in this chapter that they represent the normal conditions within school systems. But if they are present at all, it is necessary to understand the conditions of their occurrence. In order to understand complex organizations, there is a need to study in greater detail the prevalence and causes of suggestions which have been only outlined here. For although educators have become aware of the influences of outside forces on education, and although they have been concerned with developing a philosophy by which societal change can be incorporated in the curriculum, surprisingly little attention has been paid to the effects of the internal hierarchy on the performance of school personnel. It may be speculated that the quality of performance is inversely related to the degree of hierarchy.

Conditions in the environment external to the organization—the broader society—contribute additional dimensions of complexity to problems of internal control; the following chapter examines facets of the society's relationship to the management of schools.

BIBLIOGRAPHY AND NOTES

1. M. E. Dimock, "Bureaucracy Self Examined," *Public Administration Review*, vol. 4, 1944, p. 198.
2. B. Gardner and D. G. Moore, *Human Relations in Industry*, rev. ed. Chicago: R. D. Irwin, 1950, p. 9.
3. P. Blau, *The Dynamics of Bureaucracy*. Chicago: Univ. Chicago Press, 1955.
4. For an interesting and relevant study concerning the institutionalization of a due-process norm as a device for settling superior-subordinate conflicts, see W. M. Evans, "Superior-Subordinate Conflicts in Research Organizations." *Administrative Science Quarterly*, June, 1965, pp. 52–64.
5. W. Gordon, *The Social System of the High School*. Glencoe, Ill.: Free Press, 1957, p. 44.
6. G. Simmel, *The Sociology of George Simmel*, trans. by K. Wolff. Glencoe, Ill.: Free Press, 1950.
7. *Ibid.*
8. C. Dryfess, "Prestige Grading: A Mechanism of Control," in *Reader in Bureaucracy*, R. K. Merton *et al.*, eds. Glencoe, Ill.: Free Press, 1952, pp. 258–264.
9. *Ibid.*
10. A. K. Davis, "Bureaucratic Patterns in the Navy Officer Corps," *Social Forces*, vol. 27, 1948, pp. 143–153.
11. *Ibid.*
12. R. K. Merton, "The Machine, the Worker and Engineers," *Science*, vol. 105, 1947, pp. 79–81.
13. *Ibid.*
14. P. Lazarsfeld and W. Thielens, *The Academic Mind*. Glencoe, Ill.: Free Press, 1958, p. 206.
15. *Ibid.*, p. 288.
16. *Ibid.*, p. 52.
17. A. W. Gouldner, "Red Tape as a Social Problem," in *Reader in Bureaucracy*, R. Merton, A. Gray, B. Hockey and H. Selvin, eds. Glencoe, Ill.: Free Press, 1952, pp. 410–418.
18. *Ibid.*
19. Dimock, *op. cit.*
20. *Ibid.*
21. Blau, *op. cit.*
22. *Ibid.*
23. M. Dalton, *Men Who Manage*. New York: Wiley, 1959.
24. A. W. Gouldner, *Patterns of Industrial Bureaucracy*. Glencoe, Ill.: Free Press, 1954.
25. The problem of succession is treated more fully in Chapter 10. In a study in progress, Corwin has found that the rate of conflict in twenty-eight public high schools is directly associated with the number of staff additions as well as several structural characteristics of schools—notably the participation of teachers in routine decision making, standardization, and the sociability of a faculty. (R. G. Corwin, *Staff Conflicts in the Public Schools*, Phase II, forthcoming.) Whether the executive comes from inside or outside the organization makes a difference in his ability to overcome this resistance. (See R. O. Carlson, *Succession and Organizational Change*, Chicago: Midwest Administration Center, Univ. Chicago, 1962.)

IO

Work and Society

Another bifurcation of problems arises from the fact that the problems and interests which impel men to organize are of a quite different kind from those which occur in running the organization. . . . Actions are taken, policies adopted, with an eye more to the effect of the action or policy on the power-relations *inside* the organization than to the achievement of its professed goals.[1]

Institutionalization

THE PROBLEMS discussed in the preceding chapter are almost exclusively the result of inconsistencies among internal principles of organization. These problems are compounded by incompatibilities between internal principles and ideologies of the broader society. Inconsistencies between social values and principles of the organization force compromises in both. These contrasts between organizations and their surrounding society arise partly, as one writer states it, from the persistent fact that the problems which compel men to organize are different from the problems and interests of running an organization.[2] The process by which practices initially established as means are infused with value is called *institutionalization*. The original goals which gave rise to the organization as a means are modified in order to maintain the organization itself, a situation which is responsible for the series of administrative dilemmas outlined below.

Logically, the ultimate justification of any action of a member of an organization is the contribution of that action to the goals of the organization. Nevertheless, officials usually have more interest in maintaining or enhancing their positions than the general public has in restraining them, and the sheer occupancy of a position provides its own defenses against opposition.

DISPLACEMENT OF GOALS

Frequently administrators become so closely identified with their offices that their personal interests are indistinguishable from their official responsibilities to society. Conversely, any action of such administrators is *prima facie* assumed to be in the best interests of the organization, and opposition to the chief executive's program implies to some people opposition to the organization itself. For this reason subordinates who publicly criticize administrators often run the risk of censure and other controls on the mistaken precept that disloyalty to the chief administrator is equivalent to disloyalty to the organization.

Administrators live with the persistent threat that their internal opponents will openly criticize them and publicly expose the idea that administrative policy does not represent the aims of all levels of the organization. They may utilize *position-maintenance* tactics to secure their position. The principle of position maintenance and the need for loyalty tends to turn administrative attention inward to the problem of morale, which deflects attention from the main institutional goals to which the organization is supposed to be attending.

DEPARTMENTAL AUTONOMY

Levels of supervision are presumed to depend upon one another and are coordinated in terms of overall goals. However, because entire departments as well as individuals seek to secure their positions, *levels* of supervision are in fact inclined to become somewhat independent. Their success in achieving independence depends on their relations outside the organization. In many school systems the hiring of all personnel, for example, is coordinated through the central office; principals must "clear" personnel and they may be prohibited from hiring their own substitute teachers. However, clearance takes time and creates complicating delays in their own program. Principals are sometimes predisposed to use devious hiring procedures which give them more independence from the main office than they are supposed to have.

On each supervisory level the kind of pressures to act independently are described in a study of the military. The unit commander's prestige, both within the unit and locally, depends on his ability to "get things done," but he is often frustrated by what seems to be the unresponsive decisions of headquarters. As a result, he tends to rely on his own initiative to solve those problems which were supposed to be "cleared" by a higher authority.[3] Consequently, some of the most pressing problems never come to the attention of the top officers. Parallel cases exist in school systems. Clearing with higher officials detracts from the principal's competence to accomplish things. For example, a principal may wish to give a deserving teacher a week's leave of absence to care for sick relatives, but he has inadequate time to get his request and his substitute teacher cleared with the main office. One recourse is to hire someone informally and pay her under the permanent teacher's name without bothering to inform the higher office.

As one writer warns, it is erroneous to view the responsibilities of subordinates as "delegated" from top levels because the functions of each level are essentially different.[4] It is not merely a matter of superintendents and principals telling teachers what to do, for teachers maintain spheres of authority of their own even when they are not officially recognized as such. No executive has supreme authority over any matter. Differential access to outside support, both moral and financial, gives individuals and departments a point of leverage.[5] It is largely because of the different time pressures and different bases of reputation at each level of authority that these "breaks," or discontinuities, in any line of authority arise.

This tendency for subordinates to take matters into their own hands has several consequences. First, it can give top officials an over-optimistic and inaccurate view of the organization's problems. Second, a subordinate's actions commit the entire organization to a line of action which may be embarrassingly inconsistent with official policies. The principal in the previous illustration may have violated official policy and established a precedent, which later may embarrass other parts of the system.

Another possible effect is that subordinates assume duties beyond their staff capacity, which creates a subtle, often unrecognized transfer of authority from one office to another and perhaps neglect of logically important duties. For example, in a certain school system, a dynamic and personable principal who had come up through the vocational route had in operation one of the best vocational programs in the state. Other aspects of the school program were not as finished and were somewhat weak. This school was located in an upper middle class section of town, and a majority of the children from the school went on to college. In spite of a stated system-wide educational policy calling for a diversified curriculum meeting the needs of the children in the communities served by the school, this man literally "sold" his community on a vocationally-oriented program. Any attempt to modify the program was met with what appeared to be strong community action against it. This school operated for fifteen years before community pressure was brought to bear on the central office. When careful investigation was made, it was found that over the years several attempts had been made by local citizens' groups to change the emphasis of the program, but all of these attempts had been put down successfully at the community level by the principal and loyal patrons of the school.

Finally, when unauthorized autonomy is discovered by higher authority, there tends to be a stiffening of regulations and controls—principally paper reports—designed to return control to the central office. The burden of additional reports increases the trivial work of subordinate units without necessarily altering their behavior, because technical requirements can always be fulfilled without achieving the basic goals; this "red-tape" orientation stresses fulfillment of *minimum* requirements rather than the ends it is designed to implement. To pursue the above illustration, regulations designed to prevent the hiring of unauthorized substitutes challenge the staff to develop clever procedures for falsifying reports and evading responsibilities not required in the report. Paper controls direct subordinates' attention from the work to be controlled toward the controls themselves.

SUMMARY

Since each supervisory level operates under different environmental pressures, what is urgent at one level is a matter of routine at the next. The tendency for each supervisory level to develop unofficial ways of handling problems not officially within their jurisdiction provides adaptability to a variety of problems, but it also frustrates the efforts of top-level administrators to develop a consistent overall policy. Yet, elaboration of formal controls diverts the organization's attention to the controls themselves and deflects it from its official obligations to society.

Influences of Social Status on Office

The preceding problems of goal displacements and departmental autonomy represent subversions of societal values by the self-interests of members of the organization. However, from another perspective societal values often compromise official norms. The actions of officials are greatly modified by their social statuses, and, in fact, it is probably fair to say that behavior in organizations is as much a result of social status as of official duties.

RACE

Strains among the races within the schools result in the compromise of official policies. For example, for many years the concept of the community elementary school has been advocated. Most school administrators embrace the concept of organizing the public school system so that elementary schools serve neighborhoods. This has been an established practice in this country for many years. In large cities such as Chicago, St. Louis, and Philadelphia the neighborhood elementary school served as the main link between the large school organization and the individual members of the community. If a particular neighborhood had a peculiar problem, or if it was made up of a large percentage of foreign-born people who had problems with the language, the local elementary school curriculum was altered to provide specialized help. This often required the establishing of specialized curricula and specialized staff to meet the needs of the people in the neighborhood. In city after city in this country official board policy adopted the concept of the elementary school serving a neighborhood and being geographically close to the home of the child.

In recent years, however, the concept of the neighborhood school has been contested on the grounds that it tends to discriminate against residentially segregated races. In a large eastern city, for instance, the school board had approved construction of a new building to replace an old one on the same site for a neighborhood, but it was being fought by the very neighborhood for which it was intended. The people claimed that the school system was discriminating against them because of their race; they pointed to the fact that there were vacant rooms in elementary schools in other parts of the city. The school system was finally forced to abandon its policy of neighborhood schools for these children and adopt a policy of transporting them to other schools. Although discrimination violates bureaucratic norms, the new policy caused loss of efficiency and increased cost of services, the very antithesis of bureaucratic organization.

AGE

Official authority is further compromised by special cultural attitudes toward age. Although younger people with advanced education may be more technically qualified than older persons who have not kept up with technical advances, seniority is the commonly used method of promotion within school systems. Because of Americans' preference for experience, the sheer persistence and loyalty of older workers is deemed worthy of reward. The young who do find themselves in command of their seniors are embarrassed by their own lack of achievement. The "boy wonder" brought in from the outside is suspect of the oldtimers who expect far more of him than they would of their peers. Young executives must somehow temper their official authority with respect for their elders or else appear pretentious. One solution is to grant the elder subordinates more autonomy than younger subordinates are permitted.

Thus, the official bureaucratic policy of rewarding people on the basis of their competence violates the cultural axiom that authority and age must correspond. The use of seniority reflects a cultural value as well as an official bureaucratic value. School boards and administrators reinforce these cultural expectations in their official and unofficial evaluation practices. Although experience may only ingrain irrational mistakes handed down over time, teaching and administrative "experience" tends to be regarded as value in itself, almost without regard for the type or quality of experience or the degree of thoughtless and uneventful experience it may have included.

SEX

Social relations between the sexes also modify the official norms. One writer describes two central themes which regulate the sexes of our culture: ". . . (1) that it is disgraceful for a man to be directly subordinate to a woman, except in family or sexual relationships; (2) that intimate groups, except those based on family or sexual ties, should be composed of either sex but never both." [6] The first theme expresses male resistance to female dominance, which is reinforced by a pattern of sexual behavior stressing male dominance. The second theme also represents a form of antifemininism. Since women have traditionally represented the official morality system, male groups have usually excluded them. That men and women cannot completely accept one another is evident in the popular ridicule of the "sissy" and the "tomboy" and in the confinement of tabooed words, obscene stories, and the like to unmixed male (and female) groups. As a consequence of this strain, mixed male and female work groups are potentially less cohesive than unmixed work groups.

Caplow observes that most women who are in positions of authority over men are in staff jobs which require little supervision or in temporary situations, such as training sessions, where relationships with subordinate males are temporary. When women do directly command men it is difficult for them to exercise their authority completely; they usually make concessions and show leniency which modify the official relations. A study of countermen and waitresses in restaurants is suggestive of the influence which relations between the sexes have on the official structure. Although countermen usually have higher job statuses than waitresses, in practice waitresses actually command countermen in the process of relaying customers' orders to them. Countermen resent taking orders from waitresses.[7] However, in one restaurant it was learned that waitresses wrote out order slips and placed them on a spindle for countermen to fill in sequence. The procedure depersonalized the relationship and minimized status conflicts; men did not have to directly face the fact that women were giving them orders. Attempts to resolve cultural tensions between the sexes were responsible for modifications in the work pattern.

Female executives not only have less authority within the organization, but sex also affects relationships with parties outside the organization. Because of its predominantly female character, the prestige of teaching fluctuates with the status of women in the society. The female teacher is probably less able to deal authoritatively with adult males and students than are males (although women do have the advantage of being the objects of chivalry when dealing with men).

In view of these considerations, the brutal fact is that women executives erode the authority structure and jeopardize the prestige of the organization. Women seldom hold important administrative positions in school systems. Even though women constitute over fifty per cent of the high school teachers, men hold over ninety per cent of high school principalships. Proportionately more women are principals in elementary schools because of the low proportion of male teachers there. But in recent years men are rapidly replacing women in the elementary principalships as well.

Of course, the scarcity of females in positions of authority is also due to competing demands of marriage and motherhood. Social pressures on women to get married and have children reflect attitudes developed during this nation's rural experience when children were an economic necessity and when women had to be married for economic support. The pressures to marry and have children are less functional in an economy where women may have their own careers and in a world which is overpopulated, but the pressures persist and prevent most women from seriously considering a career as a realistic alternative to marriage and children.

Despite prejudices against her and her own ambivalence to her career, the career woman is not without defenses in a male world. Many women have developed tactics for using their female status to their advantage in official relationships. Caplow suggests that although males have learned to derive satisfaction from economic competition with their peers, both sexes have been taught from childhood to avoid competition with each other.[8] The male's inadequate experience in competing with women may be used to advantage by women who do choose to compete.

The Compromise Nature of Organization

In view of the inconsistencies among the internal principles or organizations, it is not surprising that the actual operation of an organization represents a delicate compromise of personal values, social traditions, and official and informal norms. While these compromises disturb the fulfillment of many laudable ideals, they nevertheless manifest the creative element of organization that enables it to adapt and develop.

The compromising nature of organization mainly has its basis in two types of incompatibilities: conflicts among positions (interstatus conflict) and conflicts within positions, or "role" conflicts. The former will be dealt with in this chapter; role conflict is the subject of Chapter 15.

MANAGEMENT-EMPLOYEE CONFLICT

In a study conducted by Evan in which management-employee conflict was investigated in two types of research organizations, it was concluded that there is a tendency for *technical* conflicts (for example, disagreements over work) to decrease with higher status, while *administrative* conflicts (for example, disagreements over policies and procedures) tend to increase with higher status.[9] This may indicate that there is higher frequency of conflict among persons in the same status than among different statuses.

At any rate, while interstatus conflicts take a variety of forms, the two case studies briefly described below will provide the reader with a sense of the compromising process characteristic of all organizations. One study of unofficial management-union relations demonstrates conditions which may be generally true of management and employee relationships.[10] Dalton learned that the national company-union agreement, which was logical enough, was not being applied in practice at the local level; agreements at the national level could not be applied because of interfering informal understandings which had previously been arrived at on the local level. Because national union contracts were too inflexible and standardized to meet the needs of local union and management, a tacit agreement developed locally between both parties to evade important clauses of the national agreement. Official top-level policies were compromised in the face of these informal commitments, with mutual benefits accruing to both low-ranking company officials and their subordinates. Private dealings between representatives of labor and management were widespread. In one case, the unions went on strike because their nonunion foreman was not promoted.

Several of the dilemmas described in this and the preceding chapter are illustrated in the findings of the Dalton study. For example, foremen and grievance chairmen compromised their official relationship as well as their relationship with subordinates in order to preserve their own prestige; foremen often reclassified workers into higher pay grades without requiring them to take necessary tests in exchange for the word of grievance chairmen not to process certain grievances that would put the foreman in an unfavorable position with superiors. In general, fewer grievances were processed each year by the grievance officer, not because there were fewer grievances to be settled, but because grievances were increasingly settled informally; belligerent grievance committee men were not successful.

One notable compromise designed to prevent conflict between middle management and workers was devised when top management, suspecting that their program of close supervision over maintenance costs was being sabotaged, requested division heads to make personal plant inspections. This placed division heads in a position of overt conflict with workers upon whom they depended to meet work quotas and so on. Inspection also threatened to provide division heads with knowledge of tabooed practices, which on the one hand would require them to take punitive action, and yet on the other hand would embarrass them to their own superiors if it were learned that the practices were taking place in their department. Moreover, punitive action would merely increase worker resistance and create new problems. As a face-saving tactic, division heads publicized the date of their planned inspection and its route beforehand. In this way, they saved the dignity of their official position without placing their subordinates in an awkward position. Official demands were compromised by unofficial demands of supervision through this simple face-saving tactic.

Strategic leniency was also used as a basis for compromise. Because their decisions had been reversed by their own superiors in previous grievances, foremen refrained from using formal channels in settling grievances. This practice turned out to be an effective weapon in controlling troublesome employees, for by delaying a reclassification test for a period of time, the foreman used the threat of a "tough" test as a way of settling a grievance issue.

Also, social status considerations modified official conduct. Better income, preferred vacations, and so on, were obtained for special workers by grievance committee men in collusion with the department superintendent; family status was especially important. In one case, a grievance officer allowed a foreman to give his brother regular salary increases in exchange for his signature permitting bonus-increasing factors for some of the workers in the department.

Similar collusion can be expected in the public schools among administration, teachers, and students. In some schools where it is illegal for students to give gifts to their teachers, the practice occurs with regularity because teachers, administrators, and students agree to "know nothing about it."

STAFF-LINE CONFLICTS

Relationships between staff and line personnel are also commonly fraught with underlying status frictions that modify the organization. The staff, consisting of specialists who serve in an advisory capacity to the chief executive, normally exists without much formal authority. In a school system, the school nurse, guidance director, probation officer, treasurer, curriculum coordinator, and so on are commonly staff positions. The staff's function is not to command nor to engage in the principle work, but to make suggestions which are supposedly welcome and provide help in improving work. On the other hand, the line consists of the direct chain of command involved in the principle work—that is, the superintendent, the principal, teachers, and students.

Again, Dalton's studies of three industrial plants are illuminating. Dalton points out that staff-line relationships generally are based on the assumption that (1) the staff is content to function without authority over the line; (2) contributions of the staff will be welcomed by the line; (3) contributions of the staff will be accepted by the line.[11] However, the actual relationship between staff and line reported by Dalton was often precisely the opposite of these formal conditions. Staff and line personnel were separated by several tension-producing cultural factors. For example, the staff men and line men were of notably different ages. Staff men were younger and displayed conspicuous ambition. Probably they were less secure and less resigned to their present status. However, since there were fewer levels of hierarchy in the staff sections, chance for advancement was systematically restricted. But they could increase their sphere of authority by increasing the number of subordinates under their direction and by gaining power over the line. Partially for this reason, staff departments increased at a faster rate than did line departments.

The tendency for staff budgets to increase at a faster rate than line budgets seems to be a general characteristic of modern large-scale organization.[12] Although the expenditures for administering public schools remained constant from 1929 to 1952, fluctuating between 3.5 and 4.5 per cent of total expenditures (auxiliary *staff* services considered separately) increased from 4.4 per cent to 7.8 per cent over the same period.

The age difference was also responsible for a disparity between the social status and the official rank of line and staff officers. Older line officers resented receiving instructions (which often appeared as orders) from the younger, less experienced staff. To compensate for their embarrassment about receiving suggestions from younger men, line officers received staff ideas with exaggerated amusement.

The line and staff differed in formal education. A high proportion of staff personnel were college graduates who had little direct work experience. While at college, these future staffers had not foreseen the resistance they were to encounter. Once on the job they soon learned that although they had been prepared to fill their logical role, their freedom to work was restricted by a complex of informal snares to which they had to defer if their ideas were to be accepted at all. Those who did adapt to the informal organization found a comfortable niche for themselves, but they did not contribute as much as their superiors. Those who did not adapt, left, producing a high turnover rate among staff officers.[13]

Besides age and educational differences, staff-line relations were aggravated by the competitive natures of their formal offices. Since they were the official agents of top management and were well educated, the staff felt somewhat superior to the line officers. Also, their chief means of advancement involved criticizing the line officers' work. Line officers naturally resented being criticized by the staff, for suggested revisions implied that the line men had been stupidly wrong all these years. Also the staff officer was regarded as an "outsider" in the work area who provided a channel of communication upward over which the line had little control. Staff innovations were feared not only because they threatened to "show up" line officers, but also because proposed changes threatened to expose forbidden practices. The staff man's interest in activities of the line was therefore perceived as a potential threat to the informal organization.

On the other hand, because top line officers did have some authority to evaluate staff officers who were being considered for advancement, the staff was cautious about pressing ideas which were opposed. Anyway, it was relatively simple for line officers to sabotage proposals which they privately opposed, even though they could be forced to adopt them by their superior officers. Confronted with this official and informal power of line officers, the staff often compromised their own position by cooperating with the line in evading rules in order to secure their cooperation informally. For example, a staff chemist responsible for maintaining production standards let the standards slide occasionally in exchange for a "good word" to the big boss from the line officer. Also, the staff would occasionally transfer money over from its budget to the line in exchange for the acceptance of new staff proposals. Delays in applying proposed changes were frequently granted to the line officers as well.[14]

The evasion of rules by subordinates is not only tolerated by superiors, it is sometimes encouraged for the purpose of achieving conformity behaviors. Gouldner has characterized this state of affairs in organizations with a concept that he calls "reciprocity-multipliers." [15] Postulating that increasing bureaucratization is accompanied by perceptions of increasing pressure for conformity behaviors from *rules*, Gouldner holds that administrators use "indulgency" to reinforce their authority. He states:

> . . . Administrators may voluntarily withhold application of certain formal rules, even though they have a right to apply them. Non-application of a rule, when it is not imposed upon, or obligatory for the actor, constitutes a "favor" and multiplies the other person's tendency to reciprocate, thus recharging the informal system and making the formal rules less necessary for organizational operation.[16]

This tends, therefore, to encourage "voluntary" conformity rather than conformity through formal rules.

Similar compromises between status and office probably occur among line and staff in school systems. Line-staff conflicts in the public schools sometimes occur when the curriculum director or the finance officer is given dual authority with the principal to determine the school's program on finances. When either of these positions are indirectly responsible to the main office, or the principal's head, an incipient conflict is in the making. Their decisions will undoubtedly affect the kind of decisions that the principal and his faculty will be able to carry out effectively. In this sense their authority undermines his. Also, in at least one lower class school known to one of the authors, teachers covertly collaborated with the attendance office to conceal from the State Department of Education the large number of unexcused absences which the truant officer was unable to control. A system of "careless" attendance-taking characterized the entire school.

The problem of line and staff represents a larger problem inherent in all organizations: the parallel dilemmas of combining social status backgrounds with official roles and of combining change and habit. Whenever some personnel stand to gain from change, others stand to lose from it; cleavages develop among groups of different age, education, sex, or ethnicity and cosmopolitanism around this issue of change.

EXPLOITATION OF OFFICE

Outside social pressures that weigh on officials and their personal interests tempt them to compromise the very principles that underlie their own office. A number of cases reported by NEA investigations reveal the powerful influences that educators' other social roles, obligations, and personal ambitions occasionally may have on corrupting their office.[17] For example, one study found that there was a payment of $2,500 by a prominent high school principal to another official for the purpose of passing a principal's examination. There have been payments of money to politicians to secure night school and summer school appointments, contributions to political funds on the basis of goods or services sold to schools by certain firms or because of nepotism, favoritism, religious affiliation, and other reasons for hiring unrelated to competence. In one case it was found that teachers paid a "kickback" of part of their salaries to secure a position, to hold it, or to be promoted. In still another case it was found that a superintendent had written twenty-three textbooks which were adopted by his system, many of the books about a field in which he had no training or experience. These and other cases of corruption suggest that the compromises of office may be very fundamental and are derived from the same kind of pressures as other types of white collar crimes.

The preceding studies illustrate the characteristic conflicts among offices that occur because of uncalculated internal pressures arising from institutionalization of means, social status considerations, private interests, and other social considerations that contribute to displacement of organizational goals. There is still another kind of conflict which is just as compromising, a conflict inherent to positions themselves. It is referred to as "role conflict." The discussion of this problem is reserved for a later chapter.

Toward a Theory of Organizational Process

THE IDEAL IMAGE

To stress the compromise nature of organization is to stress its dynamic quality. The foregoing discussions of common fallacies about organization, the conflicting organizational principles, the status friction that is so characteristic of complex organizations, and the persistent process of change and role conflict that underlies it presents one conclusion: the most fundamental facts of organization are obscured when organizational *structure* is the exclusive concern, as it tends to be. While conflict, and the compromise nature of organizations, are hardly *unknown*, these characteristics are seldom *systematically* incorporated into the crucial theoretical premises about organization, or about the nature of administration and supervision. Far from finding a central place within such theoretical descriptions, change and conflict are regarded as unfortunate accidents, the result of "poor" leadership, or situations which must soon be "corrected" rather than as essential elements of organization.

The conventional system of organizational analysis, which often consists of a series of job descriptions and rules, is focused almost exclusively on two characteristics: the ideal and the routine.

Stress on the ideal in turn is manifest as (1) institutional favoritism, (2) instrumental bias, and (3) extensive reliance on structural concepts.

Institutional Favoritism. "Institutional favoritism" refers to exaggerated attention given to the ideals that dominate the organization. In the case of school systems, educational and business *institutions* are stressed, for example, ideals of efficiency, quality, scholarship, and character formation. This is a natural result of abstracting the *logically* important aspects of schools for description. However, the logical importance of an ideal does not assure that it is in fact important in the operating organization, and the logical importance of each ideal does not describe the way the full range of organizational values and practices are integrated. More attention needs to be paid to the way educational values are actually compromised by religious, family, social class, leisure, and other institutions.

Instrumental Bias. Besides the pressures of institutional favoritism, ideal views of organization reflect the biases of persons who interest themselves in organizational analyses and administration. Students of administration are inclined to view all behavior in terms of its instrumental contributions to general organizational ends. Because the administrator is perhaps more likely than anyone in the organization to see the "complete" picture, or the way components of the organization match, there is a natural tendency for him to consider each act in its logical relation to other parts of the organization. This imparts a rational bias to the analysis and distracts attention from nonrational elements. Since consultants are hired *by* the administration, they are imbued with the same perspective—a perspective which is implicit in the problems for study which the administrators set before them.

Structural Concepts. The idealistic view of organization also depends largely on the *concepts* used, which are invariably *structural* ones. The institutional-instrumental framework obscures conflicts within the official formal organization itself and creates a static image of organization which seldom exists. Analyses are usually at the abstract level of *positions,* and consequently less systematic attention has been given to the components of these positions, the role conflicts. It is reasonable to presuppose that organizations are "organized," but this preference for the organizing facets obscures the disorganizing, unstructured elements of organization which are sometimes irritating to administrators and theorists alike.

ROUTINE

These factors responsible for ideal conceptualizations of organization occur partially because analyses are unempirical; they may be very *selective* empirically. There is a tendency to select out the *routine.* "Routine," according to Burns, is completely reciprocal activity in which the action of one is reinforced by the return action of another.[18] In its simplest form it includes exchanges of greeting, remarks about the weather, mutual compliments, and so on, all of which are designed to reaffirm one another. In these cases the function of the act is to promote consensus. "Role," as traditionally conceived, has this air of routine consensus about it, in the sense that one person's obligations are presumed to be another's right; this view makes role performance appear to be a mutually reinforcing activity rather than a conflict-provoking one.

It is unfortunate that because the daily routine constitutes the bulk of the organizational behavior it is also assumed to be the important theoretical component of organizations. The principles on which an organization is based are most clearly revealed at precisely the *non*routine points of departure where decisions between contrasting alternatives must be made. Indeed, this is so important that one author proposes that it might be more fruitful to regard routines as substitutes for the normal process of change, rather than regarding routine as the "natural" aspect of organization.[19] Routine, as a matter of fact, is never a perfect control over a continually fluctuating environment. Burns proposes that what is recognized as "social change" is actually the failure of routine substitutes; in these cases, action reverts to its *natural* state of spontaneity. What is usually dealt with as an unnatural consequence of the "main" business of organization—change—is so widespread that it is more reasonably regarded as an inherent part of organization itself.

CHANGE

If the important organizational process is not just the acting out of structural impositions; if, on the contrary, structure is a temporary curtailment of a more fluid and variable process, then there is an evident need for a conceptual framework that accounts for conflict and change as central themes of organizations. The embryo of such a framework would include two concepts, reciprocity and interplay.

Reciprocity. "Reciprocity" refers to the norms that govern exchanges of favors. It occurs where the actions of one person or group commit another to a future obligation. There are two normative components: (1) people should help those who have helped them, and (2) people should not ignore those who have helped them elsewhere.[20] The norm exists partially for reasons of expediency; if the person wants to be helped by others, he usually must help them in return. But it has a moral basis as well; people believe they *should* help those who have helped them. For example, when a principal agrees to hire the school board member's unqualified daughter to teach, his action commits the school board member to support some aspect of his program in the future, such as a proposed salary increase for the faculty. Both parties are engaged in reciprocal favors which, even though in violation of the legal norms, are regulated by the cultural norm.

Since the norm is comparatively indeterminate, it also helps to account for the instability of organizations. For the specification of duties and highly uniform performances is precluded by the norm which is sufficiently broad and yet demanding enough that it can be applied to countless numbers of ambiguous situations which are not otherwise regulated by any specific status obligations. For example, in some schools where there is no explicit regulation permitting teachers to substitute for one another, principals may informally permit some of them to do so as an unstated exchange for their cooperation in carrying out extra duties not called for in their contracts. What may appear to the outsider as immoral "favoritism" on the part of the principal is part of a broader moral reciprocal relationship.

Reciprocity also gives *official* obligations a sense of righteousness which adds personal meaning to work.[21] For example, a principal may give a teacher a salary increase not only because he is obligated to do so, but because she is otherwise a considerate teacher who has earned it. In this way, the norm prevents power relationships from disintegrating into complete exploitation and safeguards the status system; the person in power is morally obligated to repay benefits even when he is not obligated to do so officially.

Although analyses of organization usually assume that organization is established and ongoing, a dynamic view requires some such explanation of how certain forms of organizational practices develop. Unpaid obligations provide the parties involved with an excuse for interacting, an excuse which is often absolved upon repayment. Their relationship is guaranteed at least for the period of the unpaid favor. For this reason, repayment of favors is sometimes avoided by one or both parties. The norm also often acts as a "starting mechanism" whereby social interaction is integrated and initiated. It is possible that an original favor will establish an informal relationship, which becomes part of the informal organization.[22]

Interplay. The term describes strategic forms of interaction where, as Burns puts it, the acts of one party depend upon what the opposing party does.[23] Far from reinforcing one another, acts of interplay are *strategically* opposed to one another. The concept focuses on the tactical nature of organization in which parties competitively try to outbid one another. It is characteristic of debate, commercial bargaining, and all types of conflict. The fascination of all forms of interplay is that, because the subsequent conduct of the person is dependent upon his success or failure in resisting the designs of the opposition, it is often difficult to predict. In the interest of strategy, the actions of persons or organizations are often intentionally designed to be unpredictable, misleading, and flexible. This dramatic element of strategy lends a fluid quality to the nature of organization, and is as much the "stuff" of organization as is routine, roles, and offices. If so, behavior is not entirely predictable either from the logic of social structure or from personality attributes.

SUMMARY

In summary, organizations must be understood in more comprehensive terms than those provided by idealized conceptions of the institutional, instrumental, and routine elements of the office. Norms of reciprocity and interplay forms of action provide notable clues to the significant aspects of the processes that are inherent to the ongoing organization.

The end-means schema by which organizations are viewed as a means of achieving cultural values has obscured an important fact—action has no ultimate end. For every act there are innumerable consequences, each in turn creating new actions. Thus, action cannot be foretold with certainty simply by considering how well actors conform to expectations; strategy must also be considered, and in much of what is strategic, the ramifications of action can only create more action. The desire to identify the ends of action leads those who study administration to concentrate on one consequence of organization—the *established*, institutional, and routine ways of doing things. This is to ignore its dynamic quality. Systematic examination of the leads suggested by such concepts as "interplay" and "reciprocity" provides a more comprehensive and ultimately more fruitful view of organization.

We have pointed out in this chapter that motivations generated by a societal concern (in this case, the education of the young) and culminating in an organized effort designed to relieve that concern, are obfuscated by the subsequent development of new goals unique to the created organization. Paramount to a highly articulated arrangement of individuals, values, and tasks is the problem of *survival* as an arrangement. It is by virtue of interaction between the organization's unique ends and the larger sociocultural purposes it is constructed to serve that it defines its functions. The following section is devoted to analysis of this functional context of educational administration.

BIBLIOGRAPHY AND NOTES

1. P. Selznick, "An Approach to a Theory of Bureaucracy," *American Sociological Review*, vol. 8, 1943, pp. 51–52.
2. *Ibid.*
3. R. J. Braibante, "Administration of Military Government in Japan at the Prefectural Level," *American Political Science Review*, vol. 43, 1949, pp. 250–274.
4. T. Parsons, "Suggestions for a Sociological Approach to the Theory of Organizations, I, II," *Administrative Science Quarterly*, vol. 1, 1956, pp. 63–85 and 225–239.
5. *Ibid.*
6. T. Caplow, *The Sociology of Work*. Minneapolis: Univ. Minnesota Press, 1954, p. 238.
7. W. F. Whyte, "The Social Structure of the Restaurant," *American Journal of Sociology*, vol. 54, 1949, pp. 302–308.
8. Caplow, *op. cit.*, p. 243. This is not entirely accurate, since middle class males and females compete with each other for grades and other school rewards throughout their school career, but it is nevertheless true that males are accustomed to dominate rather than to compete with women in work situations.
9. W. M. Evan, "Superior-Subordinate Conflict," *Administrative Science Quarterly*, June, 1965, pp. 52–64.
10. M. Dalton, "Unofficial Union-Management Relations," *American Sociological Review*, vol. 15 1950, pp. 611–619.
11. M. Dalton, "Conflict Between Staff and Line Managerial Officers," *American Sociological Review*, 15, 1950, pp. 342–351.
12. C. N. Parkinson, *Parkinson's Law*. Boston: Houghton, Mifflin, 1957, p. 7.
13. Dalton, "Conflict Between Staff and Line Managerial Officers," *op. cit.*, pp. 342–351.
14. *Ibid.*
15. A. W. Gouldner, "Organizational Analysis," in *Sociology Today*, in R. K. Merton, *et al.*, eds. New York: Basic Books, 1959, pp. 423 ff.
16. *Ibid.*, p. 426.
17. O. H. Dalke, *Values in Culture and Classroom*. New York: Harper, 1958, pp. 447–448.
18. T. Burns, "The Forms of Conduct," *The American Journal of Sociology*, vol. 64, 1958, pp. 137–151.
19. *Ibid.*
20. A. W. Gouldner, "The Norm of Reciprocity," *American Sociological Review*, vol. 25, 1960, pp. 161–178.
21. *Ibid.*
22. *Ibid.*
23. Burns, *op. cit.*

THE THIRD FOUNDATION

*The Functional Context of
Educational Administration*

II

Problems of Supervision

The moral maxim never to use a man as a mere
means is actually the basis of modern organization.[1]

ADMINISTRATION has typically been defined in terms of three processes—supervision, leadership, and personnel management—which
center on problems of evaluation and morale. Although these are
closely related and not completely distinct functions, they are certainly
not identical. Supervision, the subject of this chapter, concerns the tactics
of efficient and proper management of personnel. The leadership function
involves broad policy formulation and strategies to achieve the organization's long-range goals. Although both processes necessarily have a bearing on personnel evaluation, advancement and morale, and personnel policies, these latter functions are so essential for implementing broader
policy that they merit particular attention.

Preceding chapters were concerned with the internal inconsistencies
within organizations, dilemmas between ends and means, and strains produced by discrepancies between the ideal model and organizational practice. Certainly the nature of supervision cannot be unaffected by such
problems. On the contrary, many of the serious problems of supervision
must be attributed exclusively to the complicating features of organization itself because they are so widespread that they cannot reasonably be
attributed to either the personal quirks or the incompetence of particular
supervisors.

Supervision, as the term is used in this chapter, is concerned with those
aspects of administration which are aimed at maintaining the efforts of
personnel in line with the goals of the administration. There will be no
attempt at this point to differentiate between those aspects of supervision
which are "line" in nature and those which are "staff." Indeed, the au-

thors would argue that much of both staff and line administration *is* supervision. Because supervisors are in close contact with nearly all members of the organization, they, more than any administrator, are responsible for the resolution of incompatible demands that personnel are supposed to comply with. By his informal policy and his demeanor, the supervisor chooses between certain official standards and cultural values when there is conflict. He is daily confronted with pressures to favor the socially privileged, to ignore violations of official norms, to "pass the buck," to assume responsibility, to delegate or to retain control. He finds that he cannot treat all persons of the same official rank alike; the old, the young, the female, the college "brain," the confidante, the ambitious all receive their due. In a word, the nature of supervision is conditioned by the nature of organization itself and must be viewed in that context. Some of the major problems arising from the supervisory function are those related to subordination on the one hand and the proximity (distant or close) of the supervision on the other.

Subordination

The fact that individuals in organizations are subordinate to one another is a source of both serious resentment and personal satisfaction; it often culminates in a pervasive ambivalence that characterizes the supervisory relationship.

PERSONAL SATISFACTION

Imputing superior status to those in command makes subordination bearable; stressing the superior's unique qualifications justifies one's subordination without implying inferiority.[2] Subordination can be a source of satisfaction, for subordinates are guaranteed a minimum number of *rights* as well as obligations. The subordinate's rights clearly define his place within the system, providing him with a sense of identity. The slave, for example, is guaranteed food and shelter; the Marine private knows that his salute must be returned from officers; and the janitor has the right to expect gratitude for his personal services to teachers.

But as low-ranking persons are guaranteed only a *minimum* number of these rights, they are often among the most ardent defenders of the *status quo;* for, when there is only a minimum of security, any change can be a threat. These observations may help to explain a finding in Manwaller's study that most teachers accept the demanding prescriptions that the public places on their personal life.[3]

It is, however, difficult for subordinates to completely respect supervisors who were promoted over them from the ranks they now command. On the one hand, the supervisor cannot claim superiority to persons who were a short time ago his equals; his promotion is a constant reminder to the subordinates of their own misfortune rather than their former competitor's uniqueness. On the other hand, the personal friendships and commitments he developed within the group while their peer imposes restrictions on his authority.

INDIVIDUALISM

Supervisors and administrators in American society face a prevalent problem arising from the inconsistencies which subordination poses in a democratic society. As Simmel puts it, "The moral maxim never to use a man as a mere means is actually the basis of modern organization." [4] As a consequence, subordinates often develop profound feelings of inequality, which arouse resistance to supervisors. One writer maintains that the worker's ". . . self-esteem is based on a sense of justice which on principle challenges the presupposition of the employer's authority." [5] For reasons which are familiar enough, many employees regard it as unjust and immoral that they should be so completely dependent on an employer's will.

The tensions resulting from the egalitarian ideology are experienced by supervisors as well as subordinates. The comments of an industrial superintendent are illustrative: "Sometimes I wonder who the hell I am, to tell these guys what to do." [6] Similar ambivalence toward the supervisory roles is reflected in this confused statement of a high school superintendent:

I don't think though—in my honest opinion—that an administrator should bring himself down to the level in all cases; of course I do think we're all teachers. But, at the same time, if you become one of them maybe you don't always accomplish. Yes, but maybe you do. I don't know. In fact, I have several [teachers with whom] my wife and I are very good friends.

Another superintendent was even more defensive:

We shouldn't fear our superiors, and yet I do think that there should be respect. We shouldn't have contempt for a person just because he's a superior. [7]

AMBIVALENCE

The severest problems of subordination are often encountered by the intermediate rather than lower echelons in organization. Located between the highest and lowest ranks, intermediate personnel are not only less resigned to subordination than the lowest group, but their identification with the upper group prevents coalitions with lower ranks. [8] Assistant superintendents, supervisors, and principals occupy a middle status position in school systems. Very seldom do these personnel identify with coalitions of teachers. There are also likely to be few coalitions among teachers of relatively low status disciplines, such as shop and homemaking, and higher status positions, such as English, history, science, and foreign languages. The very highest and the lowest ranks, in fact, sometimes identify more closely with each other than with adjacent intermediate ranks. Teachers may express more animosity to their own principal than to the superintendent; superintendents may get along better with janitors than teachers do; similarly, the janitorial and secretarial staff are probably more loyal to the administration than to the teaching staff.

There is always the possibility that the superior's official authority will be construed as personal and social superiority. Partially to separate official authority from social status, organizations utilize two principles to prevent this development: representative administration and "supervision at a distance."

Representative Administration

The right and responsibility of employees to participate in administrative decisions is one of the tense issues of modern organization. A more detailed consideration of the question will be reserved for a subsequent chapter, but the advantages and disadvantages of decentralization as an exclusively supervisory property deserves consideration here.

DIRECT PARTICIPATION

The ambivalence of management toward the participation of subordinates in the decision process is obvious. On the one hand, the participation of subordinates can be threatening in the sense that a suggested improvement is easily interpreted as a criticism of the superior's personal competence. This is the reason for using such devices as the suggestion box which assures a measure of anonymity. Administrators are reluctant to take seriously suggestions which, in effect, require admission that they have "been wrong all these years." Also, some suggestions jeopardize the authority of the higher office itself, as when a teacher suggests that the principal's authority over the English program be completely relinquished to English teachers.

On the other hand, administration may gain in several respects by encouraging subordinates to participate in several types of decisions. Because they work within the task environment itself, specialists are in a good position to see possible improvements. Teachers, for example, often have a better idea about the proper size budget for new books than the administrator who is less likely to see either daily waste or common deficiencies. Teachers may also be in a better position than the superintendent to contribute to certain phases of curriculum development. For example, the junior high school teacher is in a better position to know what elementary school children have and have not learned when they come to the junior high school than is the curriculum coordinator in a central office.

Subordinates can at times be menacing precisely because they are so close to the task, because they tend to perceive the total organization only from the standpoint of their own specialty and their special problems. They can be unaware of and fail to understand the total organization and the outside pressures on it. Consequently, their interests and perspectives may conflict with those of management. A change proposed by specialists may upset the internal power balance and alienate the chief executive's supporters; or it may be ultimately intended only to change undesirable aspects of their personal position, which may be irrelevant to the formal goals. To gain personal insight into these questions, administrators would be well advised to classify each suggestion on the basis of the amount of threat to his own position, the enhancement of subordinates' interests, its potential for technical improvement, and its consistency with long-range goals.

Perhaps a more common reason for utilizing employee participation is that it increases identification with administrative policies and with the regulations that are adopted. If personnel have contributed to the formation of a program, they will be more willing to support it. Representative administration is, in other words, an effective *strategy* for soliciting support for policies, independent of its contributions to efficiency. The effectiveness of this strategy will be considered in the subsequent chapter on morale.

SPHERES OF AUTHORITY

There is an alternate form of representative administration. In contrast to conventional representative administration where many subordinates have small roles in many decisions, the final decision-making authority may be *distributed* among subordinates. The personal sensitivity to subordination may be partially offset if each subordinate has at least one sphere of supremacy. This principle is in fact built into the "pecking order" of hierarchy; most persons who are subordinates also have subordinates of their own. Sometimes one only has subordinates outside of the organization, as in the case of the janitor who is at least the head of his household.

Superiority and subordination may alternate between the same persons as they engage in different tasks. In fact, the supervisor must usually defer to the authority of his subordinates on some issues. The high school principal may overrule the superintendent's idea on a class schedule, and the drama coach may be able to overrule the principal's judgment in matters of selecting and costuming of performers for the senior play. This somewhat parallels the military situation where the sentry is authorized to arrest his own commanding officer for improper conduct. These are extremely complex relationships to manage. In one study of teachers in the military, the fact that classroom teachers were often officially subordinate to the officers in their class was a source of embarrassment and confusion.[9] Nevertheless, the alteration of subordinate and superior positions between individuals helps to offset the derogatory aspects of the former when each subordinate has other clearly established spheres of authority.

But even where it is accepted in principle, the sphere of authority plan is difficult to put into practice. For one thing, it can create serious coordination problems when many persons are responsible for their own areas of competence. The existence of separate spheres also creates delegation problems. The person who learns of a problem and comprehends it may not be the one who is officially supposed to solve it. If there is a time pressure, it may take too much time to delegate it. But if a person acts out of his own sphere, he threatens the authority of the legitimate official. In the process of attempting to maintain or clarify spheres of authority, the entire authority structure can be undermined. Some of these problems are exemplified in the following case study: [10]

Triangles Can Exist in School Administration

Al Bennett knew why he was being summoned to the superintendent's office for a conference. His most recent dispute with the Art Supervisor was the culmination of a series of rather heated disagreements between the two. Mr. Bennett had been principal of the Greenly High School for eight years and no one could doubt that they were successful years. He was accepted and respected by the students, the faculty and the community. His professional colleagues in the state had the highest regard for his administrative abilities and scholarly activities. Greenly High was a senior high school and enrolled 500 students. In addition the city of 12,000 had a junior high with 560 pupils and five elementary schools with a total of 1300 children.

Each building had its own principal. The supervisors were attached to the superintendent's central office staff and consisted of (1) an elementary supervisor who devoted her time primarily to the content fields in elementary education; (2) a physical education supervisor whose activities were confined to the first six grades; (3) an instrumental music supervisor for the elementary grades; (4) a vocal music supervisor for the elementary grades; (5) an art supervisor whose jurisdiction included all schools—elementary, junior high and senior high; (6) a psychologist who was available to students at all grade levels; and (7) a speech correctionist who worked at all grade levels.

Al Bennett knew Miss Smith, the high school art teacher, was involved in the argument. He regarded Miss Smith as a top-notcher. Her ability and hard work was responsible for the present fine reputation enjoyed by the high school Art Department. Before Miss Smith took over, the Art Department was in a most deplorable condition. It was under her energetic leadership, however, that the art classes developed new life. In the place of the formal atmosphere in which students all worked on the same lessons she developed an art laboratory where students in the same classes were working in many different areas. The demand for art by high school students exceeded the facilities and the program received wide attention in the community and in the state. In addition to being an outstanding artist in her own right, Miss Smith was a profound student of art education and loved to teach.

Bennett knew there was little love between Miss Smith and the Art Supervisor, Miss Crosby. It irritated Miss Smith no end to have the Art Supervisor behave as if Miss Smith was just a struggling young teacher experiencing difficulty. But then Miss Smith just didn't like supervisors, period. Miss Crosby, the art supervisor, would come to Miss Smith's classroom and observe for a half of a day at a time. Never had the supervisor taken over the class for demonstration or offered suggestions of a constructive nature, according to Miss Smith. Occasionally she would ask, "Why are you doing this?" or pick up the project of a very poor student and eye it critically as though much improvement was needed. Miss Smith had her feelings hurt because Miss Crosby failed to remark that Miss Smith was doing a good job. Miss Smith concluded that the Art Supervisor was jealous over her success and popularity. It appeared that the supervision was disconcerting to the teacher.

On one occasion Bennett spoke to Miss Crosby about reporting to the office when she came into the building. Other supervisors did this. Often, he suggested, there were matters he would like to call to her attention or discuss with her and it would be easier to do this if she would stop by the office on her way to visit the Art Department.

But Miss Crosby continued to come and go as she pleased. Bennett recalled one of the early flare-ups between Miss Smith and Miss Crosby. Miss Smith reported to Bennett that she had entered some projects, not recommended by Miss Crosby, in the Scholastic Art Exhibit Contest. It so happened that each of Miss Smith's entries had won an award or honorable mention while only one entry from the selection the supervisor had made received attention. While this may have been a credit to Miss Smith's ability to select the right material for an art contest, it didn't help relations with the supervisor.

Miss Crosby came to Greenly as art supervisor the same year Al Bennett was made principal of the senior high school. Miss Crosby had a fine teaching record. She had been an elementary art teacher in the school in which Superintendent Baumgartner had formerly served. The superintendent liked her work and brought her to Greenly when a new art supervisor was needed. She had experience at the secondary level but liked elementary art the best. Teachers in the elementary school were loyal to Miss Crosby. They liked her very much and enjoyed working with her. Miss Crosby was a craftsman in her own right, and well informed in methods of teaching art.

Miss Crosby issued statements of policy and other directives directly to teachers. In some schools the program of art tied in closely with the instruction of other subject areas, while in other areas art was taught for the sake of art alone.

Superintendent Baumgartner was a great believer in full and complete delegation of responsibilities to his supervisors. He had delegated to the Art Supervisor full authority to organize the art program and to establish working policies as a guide to all of the teachers of art. Miss Crosby sometimes confused the role of an administrator with that of supervisor in the normal concept of line-staff hierarchy. Her intent to improve the teaching of art and to establish policy was sincere but inflexible. Little allowance was made for varying personalities and abilities of teachers and even students in some situations.

Miss Crosby gained great favor with Superintendent Baumgartner and kept him well informed of her plans. Such items as central purchasing, establishing lists of approved materials, procedures relating to art contests and order of units of instruction received a favorable reception with Superintendent Baumgartner. He was impressed with her work and was convinced she was doing an outstanding job. Whenever criticisms were lodged against Miss Crosby he dismissed them as expected reactions to any new policies that worked well.

Bennett had no difficulty remembering the problem which resulted in the conference with Superintendent Baumgartner. On Friday Miss Smith came to Mr. Bennett for advice. She had been approached by a group of parents who were enthused over the interest of their children in puppet work in the art class. They wondered if it would be possible for their children to show the puppets during the coming workshop for the university. They had planned to take their children to the workshop anyway but it would be so much nicer, they thought, if the children would really enter their accomplished works of art.

The time was late and any reservations for booths at the workshop would have to be made immediately. Miss Smith was not able to obtain Miss Crosby's permission as the supervisor was out of town. Would she dare go ahead and make arrangements? Mr. Bennett said that he was still principal and such decisions would be within his province. He thought the idea was fine, would make for good public relations and encouraged Miss Smith to make the arrangements.

Arrangements were made by Miss Smith for the demonstration booth. Upon the return of Miss Crosby she advised the Art Supervisor of the developments. In a very unkind way Miss Smith was told she had no authority to take such action. All the requests concerning out-of-school art activities must be approved or disapproved by her supervisor and no exceptions were permitted. With this she picked up the phone, called the university long distance and cancelled the previously made reservation by Miss Smith.

The art teacher was on the verge of tears when she explained the action to the principal. Mr. Bennett felt that this was a direct slap in his face as well and immediately called Miss Crosby and demanded that she regain the facilities cancelled at the university. He was told instead by Miss Crosby in no uncertain terms that he had acted completely out of his jurisdiction and that she had no intention of rescinding her action, in fact, she felt the superintendent should know about the matter immediately. Her irritation with Bennett's call was not only evidenced by the firmness in her voice but also by the resounding bang as the receiver hit the hook.

This was the situation Al Bennett knew he had to work out with the superintendent as he proceeded to the administrative office. He felt he ran a good school and could provide instructional leadership without supervisors. Supervisors were all right for elementary schools but were unnecessary in a second-ary school where the principal knew his business. Superintendent Baumgartner, he was sure, had heard the Art Supervisor's full report and Bennett's pedigree as well, à la Miss Crosby's version. As a defense attorney she was unsurpassed.

After the usual amenities following his entrance to the superintendent's office, Al Bennett asked for clarification of the principal and the supervisor's role in the high school program. Superintendent Baumgartner listened intently and couldn't help but be impressed with the sincerity of Bennett's action in the matter and his desire to run a good school. At the same time Baumgart-ner felt that Miss Crosby's outstanding art supervision in the system as a whole could not be disregarded. He felt that the school system should operate as a unit rather than as separate groups encased within the walls of each school. Miss Crosby derived her authority from the superintendent but then so did Principal Bennett. Baumgartner had great respect for both persons involved in this dispute as well as for the high school art teacher, Miss Smith. How to extricate himself out of a difficult position which could well result in losing an outstanding high school principal, outstanding supervisor of art, or a fine teacher of art would require all the administrative ingenuity he could muster, thought Superintendent Baumgartner.[11]

DISADVANTAGES OF REPRESENTATIVE ADMINISTRATION

Representative administration would logically seem to be an effective way of bolstering subordinates' pride, yet one of its greatest inadequacies is in this very respect, for it is by no means certain how much decision-making responsibility employees wish to assume. Direct participation not only places the subordinate in a threatening position, but the participation itself may be perceived as "unauthentic" by the subordinate when he is asked to assume the responsibilities of leadership without having power to either protect himself or to effectively implement his proposals. The situation merely increases the likelihood of his failure and is a potential source of embarrassment to him. Students are often placed in the same position by teachers who wish to have a "democratic" classroom, but who actually manipulate the decisions and are reluctant to accept the actual wishes of the majority of the students. Representative administra-tion has a propensity to turn into a sham at precisely the most crucial moments of decision. For these reasons, supervision at a distance is often a more effective tactic.

Supervision at a Distance

CLOSE SUPERVISION IN EDUCATION

Some years ago a writer in educational administration proclaimed, "When a teacher's weekly report shows that addition of fractions will soon be finished, the supervisor should make sure that this skill is properly

mastered before the teacher goes on to the subtraction of fractions . . .
It is for the supervisor to say whether or not the class should go on." [12]
This is an extreme example of close supervision in education. More re-
cently, the following situation was reported:

> In a Chicago suburb a social studies teacher of eight years' service paused
> in the hall to talk to another teacher after the bell had rung and his pupils
> were in the classroom. The assistant principal came by on his regular checkup
> and reprovingly pointed at him and then at the door of his room. "I was to
> go into the room like a sheepish child," said the teacher. "When I complained
> to him, he said, 'You don't believe in discipline.' " [13]

This may not be atypical; 46 of 105 Massachusetts school superintendents
say that they keep a watchful eye on the personal behavior of their subordinates. [14] At times administrators have sponsored espionage among
subordinates in order to maintain this "watchful eye." In six of sixteen
cases involving questionable administrative practices in the schools a few
years ago, it was alleged that administrators encouraged spying among
teachers. In New York there were attempts to compel teachers to inform
when requested. [15]

STRUCTURAL CAUSES OF CLOSE SUPERVISION

Certain characteristics of the superior-subordinate relationship itself
promote close supervision. First, the nearer the authoritative one stands
to subordinates in respect to origin, experience, knowledge, education,
rank of office, and level of earnings, the more insistently he may have to
rely on the authority of his office rather than personal respect, and the
more arbitrary his supervision will seem. [16] Similarly, where differences
in the authority of superordinates and subordinates are slight, small deviations by the subordinates may be interpreted as a threat to the superiors'
authority. Second, a supervisor's perception of his subordinates' motives
helps to determine how much supervision is in order. [17] If, for example, a
supervisor perceives that a subordinate is unwilling to do a job, he will
tend to direct the worker more closely. The way he perceives a subordinate in turn depends on the pressures that are operating on the supervisor.
If he is anxious to be promoted, or if he has had little opportunity to test
his subordinates' loyalty, he is more apt to perceive his subordinates as
unmotivated.

Third, the methods used by the central office administrators and supervisors also affect the type of supervision exercised at lower echelons. In
general, a supervisor probably tends to duplicate the kind of treatment he
receives from his own superiors. If he himself is closely supervised, he
will be inclined to reciprocate with his own subordinates. For the more
closely his own work is controlled, the more closely he must control the
work of his subordinates in order to meet the demands from above. How-

ever, while pressures from above occur sporadically—that is, superintendents may examine the work of their principals only periodically—there seems to be a tendency for close supervision to persist for longer periods of time down each level of the hierarchy.

Span of Control. A "short span of control" (a small ratio between the number of subordinates and supervisors) is the major structural means for promoting close supervision, while the "flat" pattern (a large number of subordinates per supervisor) fosters autonomy for the subordinate. As several writers have pointed out, a short span of control is efficient in terms of logical organizational goals. However, a flat pattern permits more initiative and personal responsibility and is more personally satisfying to the individual. They also observe that while the short span of control gives the immediate supervisor more control over his own subordinate, it requires more authority levels, which removes subordinates (and their supervisor) from the chief administrators. It would seem, however, that a flat pattern will be more personally satisfying to the extent that the subordinate is not inaccessible to the flow of information within the system.

Finally, the method of supervision is intimately linked with the physical space which the superior and subordinate occupy. Space conditions the access to and the privacy from people as well as information, and insulates entire parts of the organization. There are usually organizational rules about what can be legitimately hidden and observed in particular work situations.

Observability. The extent to which subordinates and supervisors are mutually observable, for example, induces different types of conformity. *Behavioral* (or "outward") conformity is all that is technically required for an organization to operate. Although they may prefer more than the minimum, supervisors are generally satisfied when "everyone does his job." They seldom bother to question how personally "involved" personnel are with every aspect of their work. Considering the range of activities that educators commit themselves to during the course of a week—committee work, public lectures, personal consultations, reading, school board meetings, preparation of reports, and other miscellaneous requirements of the job, in addition to family and other social obligations—it is unreasonable to expect them to be personally involved with every duty they must perform.

However, emotional involvement (or belief) is demanded at times. The fact that employers are extensively concerned with the "morale" and "loyalty" of their employees suggests that personal involvement with the job is considered to be important, even though it is not always entirely necessary. Personal involvement seems to be most demanded of workers whenever performance is inaccessible to the supervisor or to the public. Their personal involvement with their jobs provides assurance that workers will perform properly and above the minimum when they are not being directly observed by others. Coser proposes a similar argument concerning "attitudinal conformity," or consensus on the belief that certain values are legitimate. Some hypothesized relationships between observability and attitudinal conformity which seem to be suggested by Coser's analysis are summarized below.[18]

First, as observability of performance decreases, demands that workers be highly involved (that they "conform attitudinally") increase. Coser reports that rigid attitudinal conformity is demanded by the senior medical staff of resident psychoanalysts, since the privacy which prevails between the doctor and his patient prevents the senior staff from observing much of the doctor's work. A similar situation prevails in educational organizations where the performance of principals is usually not directly observable by superintendents who are physically distant, and where the behavior of teachers who work within the sanctity of classrooms, behind closed doors, is unobservable to principals or even to other teachers. This helps to account for some of the conservative community expectations of teachers, such as the rigid personality and moral qualifications often imposed. This unobservability of classroom teaching is also a reason why administrators try to assess the teacher's philosophy, attitude, and general outlook on life during interviews.

Second, as the work of persons becomes observable, attitudinal conformity (similarity of belief) becomes less essential and less subject to scrutiny. Politicians who are in the public eye are perhaps judged more on the way they conform to outward expectations than on their personal beliefs.[19] It is interesting to speculate that teachers in fields which are easily observed by the public, such as the athletic or drama coach, may undergo less moral and attitudinal scrutiny and may be judged more directly on the basis of their performance than are classroom teachers.

Gouldner has distinguished between conformity behaviors in the organization, which are voluntary, with others, which are the result of rules.[20] What we are referring to here, however, is the kind of conformity which is exerted upon organizational members externally—pressure from the culture and value-laden expectations from the larger community.

When people are completely observable, all that may be required of them is what Coser describes as "doctrinal" conformity, that is, verbal or symbolic conformity to the hallowed traditions displayed externally through ceremonial gestures. Examples of "doctrinal conformity" are attendance at commencement addresses, saluting the flag, and standing at national anthems. Because they are always verbal or behavioral, these acts are entirely observable and so need not be accompanied by any personal involvement with the act. School ceremonies such as the principal's annual address to the PTA, an annual ceremony with the school board, and attendance at graduation ceremonies do not usually require any evidence that those who are there personally believe in the meaning of the occasion. Flag saluting, for example, is a visible act, and because it is so visible it seems to require little additional evidence of attitudinal conformity or personal involvement other than the act itself.

Third, in situations where there is lack of consensus among workers regarding appropriate conforming attitudes while at the same time, their personal involvement in such situations is high, there is greater propensity for conflict.

The above propositions can be extended in several ways in application to the superior-subordinate relationship: (1) When there is *direct* observability by the superior, the normal concern is with assuring appropriate *behavior* rather than assuring attitudes or involvement; conversely, when personnel are assumed to lack initial involvement, close supervision is invoked. (2) Subordinates often make themselves inaccessible to persons in higher authority, which protects both parties. It protects subordinates to the extent that observability restricts their behavior; persistent observability by a superior may lead to extreme conservatism on the part of the subordinate, a tendency which increases as the rank of the superior increases. Insulation also protects superiors to the extent that it prevents development of either friendly or hostile feelings toward subordinates, which could affect their impartiality and otherwise confound the rationality of their decisions.

When a superior is directly observable by his subordinates, he will also tend to increase his behavioral conformity just as his observation of subordinates increases theirs. When he is observable, his subordinates have access to his personal affairs. The boss' private secretary is a convenient example. She often participates in "guilty" knowledge concerning the informal behavior of the organization, such as conflict among the administrative staff or illicit uses of school property, which may increase her involvement with her job and her loyalty to her boss; but it also makes her a threat to him. Perhaps superiors must sacrifice a certain amount of social distance and respect in exchange for the personal loyalty of their subordinates.

One disadvantage to superiors who remain unobservable to their subordinates is that such remoteness fosters gossip about the boss. Since access to secret knowledge is a source of informal power, teachers can enhance their status by relating gossip about their administrators. Superiors try to protect themselves from gossip even in public by isolating themselves through ceremonial gestures with respect to subordinates. "Officiousness" is a defense against personal approaches from others. A ceremonial announcement of the superintendent's forthcoming personal visit to the school will provide both parties with an opportunity to prepare a formal setting in which their informal lives can be disguised in official activities.

In conclusion, avoidance of direct observability has advantages for both superiors and subordinates. When the superior directly observes the subordinate, the superior also leaves himself open to scrutiny. Yet, if he is entirely unobservable, he leaves himself open to gossip.

ALTERNATIVES TO CLOSE SUPERVISION

In a society which stresses equality, close supervision is a constant reminder to the worker of his inferior position. It implies that the subordinate is incompetent and suggests an outright distrust of him by superiors; it often borders on invasion of professional competence. Personnel may view close supervision as a form of strict punishment which arouses their resistance and apathy.[21] Of course, the intensity of these effects will depend on the complexity of the task (subordinates will look for help as it becomes more difficult), the level of training of both subordinates and supervisor (the greater the differential, the more tolerable is supervision), and the degree of freedom which subordinates have in accepting and rejecting instructions.[22]

Close supervision has been advocated largely as a means of implementing efficiency. Yet, paradoxically, close supervision may have *adverse* effects on productivity. For example, in one study of twenty-four clerical sections of an insurance agency, closely supervised sections whose heads gave detailed instructions and frequently checked up on them had lower productivity than sections where workers were given more freedom to do their work.[23] Moreover, the supervisors who were primarily concerned with maintaining a high production level were less successful than superiors who were more interested in the welfare of subordinates than in sheer production.

There are at least three alternatives to close supervision: rules, strategic leniency, and diffuse ratings.

Rules. Close supervision clarifies power. Visible power tends to become a threat to the individual. He may become defensive, nervous, or he may withdraw much of his initiative. He may even quit the organization. The real question facing administrators and supervisors is how to maintain control without letting it become a threat to individual productivity and initiative. Control would thus be defined as orderly and effective pursuit of organizational goals.

One alternative is to evolve procedures of control which are impersonal —that is, "fair" to all—and which can be applied generally to all personnel in many situations. This is what Gouldner refers to as "general and impersonal rule."[24] Rules help to protect the individual against excessive demands from superiors by establishing the limits of authority so that persons hired for a job know in advance the extent of their burden. However, rules normally do not prescribe the kinds of informal demands that are made on a person, such as the number of hours that will be required each week for extracurricular activities or the percentage of salary expected to be given to charity.

Rules also relieve the tensions of close supervision for the supervisor by permitting him to demonstrate that he is not exercising arbitrary or personal power; [25] for they stand as impersonal principles above the caprice of the immediate supervisor, who is also bound by them. Much of the derogatory aspects of a job are removed simply by the knowledge that the superior is commanded from above just as the workers are. In falling back on rules imposed from above, the superior is at the same time distributing blame throughout the hierarchy, and with it the antagonism of workers. Failure to do so tends to arouse hostility to particular supervisors, which in turn threatens their authority.

However, as a consequence, bureaucracy often appears to be the rule of "no one," a rule by rules; the same impersonal quality of rules which makes supervision bearable may also promote an even more oppressing element—the sense of powerlessness. Under rule by law, a person may feel he can in no way influence justice which renders him insignificant.[26]

The use of faculty meetings to announce a new regulation is less personal and less threatening to an individual than calling him into the office and telling him about it personally. The use of teacher handbooks to inform the staff about rules, regulations, and policies for operating the organization are less threatening, and have lower power visibility than calling each person into the office individually and going over the rules with him personally; the threat is less for both the administrator and the teacher. In a personal situation the teacher may object and put the administrator on the defensive. At this point, the level of interpersonal relations rises, and the administrator is in danger of losing control of the situation, or losing the respect of his subordinate. A simplified diagram of Gouldner's thesis (Figure 13) schematically shows this relationship.[27]

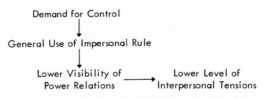

FIGURE 13. Schemata illustrating relationship of impersonal rules to the facilitation of organizational control. (From Alvin Gouldner; see J. G. March and H. A. Simon, *Organizations*, New York: Wiley, 1959. p. 45.)

The conditions outlined in Figure 13 facilitate the maintenance of control.

Unanticipated Consequences of Impersonal Rules. Rules, regulations, handbooks, and impersonal announcements regarding behavior and procedure have the effect of describing only the *minimal* behavior tolerated by the organization. But if all personnel acted only minimally, it is doubtful that the organization could achieve its goals. In fact, the school system would probably not function if everyone followed the "letter of the law." As the "buck private" knows, the way to ruin the army would be to follow every rule to the letter and not do one thing more. When the handbook states that teachers are due in their rooms by 8:30 A.M., the administration of course hopes that many, if not most, of the teachers will come earlier and that they will have enough to do and are interested enough in their work to begin it once they are there.

Since rules and regulations effect only minimal behavior, it is difficult for organizations to officially require extraordinary effort. Rules tend to increase the distance between the goals of the organization and the achievement of the goals. As the distance between the achievement of the goals and the goals themselves become great, personal supervision must be increased. When this happens power becomes visible, interpersonal relations are intensified, general and impersonal rule diminishes, and control is jeopardized. This is illustrated by Gouldner as in Figure 14.[28]

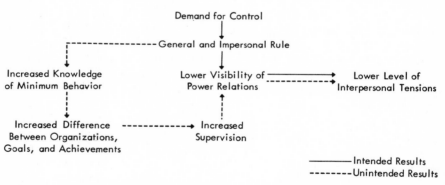

FIGURE 14. The unintended consequence of the tendency for rules to promote minimal behavior is an increase in the distance between the goals and their achievement. (From Alvin Gouldner; see, J. G. March and H. A. Simon, *Organizations*, New York: Wiley, 1959. p. 46.)

Strategic Leniency. While leniency has "democratic" connotations, it does not mean rule by majority; rather it is a means of increasing the effectiveness of control from above.[29] A supervisor's leniency toward his subordinates in such matters as tardiness, "no smoking" rules, or the use of first names may be used by him as a weapon by threatening to withhold such privileges when workers fail to perform properly. In this sense, Gouldner describes rules as "chips" to which the organization stakes its supervisors to play the game; when a number of small tensions accumulate between personnel and their supervisor, the privileges are withdrawn and the official standards are reinvoked.[30] It is because of strategic noncompliance with rules that superiors join their subordinates in resisting efforts of chief executives to enforce rigid compliance to such rules as no smoking, punctuality, prescribed lunch hours, and so on. The chief administrator may overlook the fact that in requiring his supervisors to enforce the letter of the law, he is reducing their own effectiveness.

Diffuse Rating Procedures. "Diffuse" rating refers to procedures for rating subordinates on their ability to meet performance standards. It involves periodic ratings spaced at long intervals. The procedure avoids the constant reminder of status differences that otherwise occur when ratings are used repeatedly to enforce *particular* commands. Determination of a teacher's right to tenure after several years of performance is an example of a diffuse rating procedure. (The difficulty with the tenure system is that in the course of the probationary period, teachers may become so personally involved in their school and the school so committed to them by the mere fact that they have been retained, that it is difficult to release them without arousing antagonism from their personal supporters.)

It is difficult to utilize periodic rating policies wherever the ultimate goals are as abstract or intangible as they often are in education. In education it may take years to evaluate the success of a school's graduates, and then only on intangible and sometimes controversial criteria. It may be noted in passing that this factor is perhaps one reason for the emphasis on methods (rather than achievement of aims) in teacher training and evaluation criteria.

Supervision as Consultation. Apart from the *process* of supervision which is inherent to some degree in any superordinate-subordinate relationship there is a unique supervisory function in education. We refer to the traditional "supervision of instruction."

In this regard there is a particularly relevant alternative to "close" supervision. It is, in effect, to redefine the role from one of supervision to one of consultation. When the instructional specialist is seen as consultant by the teacher, the resulting relationship is more likely to be viewed as a "helping" one rather than an "evaluative" one. Where supervision is the principle emphasis, the teacher tends to be more guarded and defensive, identifying the supervisor with the central hierarchy. On the other hand, when the specialist is performing a consultative role, the teacher is more likely to respond to the technical expertise that is exhibited and to identify the specialist with the instructional rather than the administrative goals of the school. Of course, the consultant must also internalize the new role expectations. Merely changing the name doesn't make the rose smell any differently.

Some school districts have realized optimal results with consultants by making their services available only when teachers request them. This tends to solidify the teacher-consultant relationship as one of a technical nature rather than of a superordinate-subordinate nature.

SUMMARY

The problems of supervision arise from the complexity of the organization itself. Subordination is the condition in which a person is used as a means to an end. It is a particularly acute problem in a democratic society. Subordination is in some ways more satisfying to those at the extremes of the relationship than to those in intermediate positions, since the status extremes of the hierarchy are clearly defined and are guaranteed at least a minimum of rights.

Representative administration is a technique which may help to offset the sense of inferiority which is a natural product of subordination. However, direct participation of subordinates in the major decisions can be threatening to subordinates and superiors alike; moreover, the logical advantages of participation by subordinates are offset by their limited perspectives of the overall organization, its history, and the pressures on it from both internal and external sources. Rotating the authority in such a way that everyone has his own sphere of authority in which to make decisions provides some compensation for some of the derogatory aspects of subordination; however, this practice may create an extremely complex set of contradictory relationships which persons find difficult to manage.

Supervision at a distance is another way of offsetting the derogatory effects of subordination. However, there are features within the work setting itself which promote its opposite—close supervision. These include some special aspects of the interpersonal relations between subordinates and superiors, methods used by top administration, and the extent to which subordinates are observable. Observability, in particular, influences close supervision. Overt conduct, rather than attitudes, is stressed to the extent that the work of subordinates is observable, while inaccessibility to the subordinate encourages superiors to stress attitudinal conformity.

Close supervision can be avoided by at least four interpersonal techniques. First, rules protect against arbitrary uses of authority by stressing the rights as well as the obligations of subordinates. The impersonal quality of rules relieves suspicions of caprice on the part of supervisors; however, to the extent that rules treat people categorically, they are insignificant and powerless to influence a situation. Second, strategic leniency is a way of relaxing the oppressive elements of supervision without losing control; it is, in fact, a way of enhancing control without restricting permissiveness. Third, periodic rating procedures stressing achievement of goals more than the means used to achieve them minimize some of the reminders of status differences that are otherwise inherent in the evaluation situation.

Finally, another alternative to close supervision may be available in certain specialized areas by changing the role of the supervisor to that of the consultant. This tends to suppress the sensitivity of the teacher to superordinate-subordinate considerations by supplanting a sensitivity to technical expertise. The choice among such alternatives and their probable consequences are properties of leadership. It is to this concept that we now turn our attention.

BIBLIOGRAPHY AND NOTES

1. G. Simmel, *The Sociology of Georg Simmel,* trans. by K. Wolff. Glencoe, Ill.: Free Press, 1950, p. 182.
2. Simmel, *op. cit.,* pp. 190–303.
3. L. V. Manwiller, "Expectations Regarding Teachers," *Journal of Experimental Education,* vol. 26, 1958, pp. 315–354.
4. Simmel Wolff, *op. cit.,* p. 182.
5. H. De Mann, "Reaction to Subordination," in *Joy in Work,* London, 1929, cited in *Human Relations in Administration,* R. Dubin, ed., p. 279. Englewood Cliffs: Prentice-Hall, 1951.
6. A. W. Gouldner, *Patterns of Industrial Bureaucracy.* Glencoe, Ill.: Free Press, 1954, p. 162.
7. Quoted by M. Seeman, "Role Conflict and Ambivalence in Leadership," *American Sociological Review,* vol. 18, 1953, pp. 373–380.
8. Simmel, *op. cit.,* p. 220.
9. J. W. Getzels and E. G. Guba, "Role Conflict and Effectiveness: An Empirical Study," *American Sociological Review,* vol. 19, 1954, pp. 164–175.
10. Iowa Case Studies in School Administration #3, State University of Iowa, College of Education.
11. Points of departure for a discussion: If you were in Superintendent Baumgartner's position, what would you do?
12. F. B. Knight, "Possibilities of Objective Techniques in Supervision," *Journal of Educational Research,* vol. 16, 1927, p. 9; *cf.* also W. C. Bagley, *Classroom Mannent,* New York: MacMillan, 1907, pp. 262–265.
13. R. Meryman, "How We Drive Teachers to Quit," *Life,* Nov., 1962, p. 106.
14. N. Gross, *Explorations in Role Analysis.* New York: Wiley, 1958, p. 331.
15. Summarized by H. O. Dalke, *Values on Culture and Classroom.* New York: Harper, 1958, p. 451.
16. De Mann, *op. cit.,* p. 279.
17. Gouldner, *op. cit.,* Ch. 8.
18. R. L. Coser, "Insulation From Observability and Types of Social Conformity," *American Sociological Review,* vol. 26, 1961, pp. 28–38.
19. *Ibid.*
20. *Cf.* Gouldner, *Patterns of Industrial Bureaucracy, op. cit.,* p. 160.
21. *Ibid.*
22. *Cf.* J. G. March and H. A. Simon, *Organizations.* New York: Wiley, 1959, p. 55.
23. P. Blau, *The Dynamics of Bureaucracy.* Chicago: Univ. Chicago Press, 1955.
24. Gouldner, *Patterns of Industrial Bureaucracy, op. cit.,* p. 165.
25. *Ibid.,* pp. 164–166.
26. *Cf.* Simmel, *op. cit.,* p. 250.
27. *Cf.* Gouldner, *Patterns of Industrial Bureaucracy, op. cit.,* pp. 174–180, as depicted by March and Simon, *op. cit.,* p. 45.
28. *Ibid.,* p. 46.

29. P. Blau, *Bureaucracy in Modern Society*. New York: Random House, 1956, Ch. 6; *cf*. pp. 114–115.
30. Gouldner, *Patterns of Industrial Bureaucracy, op. cit.*, p. 173. *Cf*. Gouldner, "Organizational Analysis," *op. cit.*, pp. 423–426.

CHAPTER

12

Scope and Character of Administrative Leadership

But what determines the structure of a society is not the majority but the leaders.[1]

No institution can possibly survive if it needs geniuses or supermen to manage it. It must be organized in such a way as to be able to get along under a leadership composed of average human beings.[2]

THE IMPORTANCE of leadership is generally conceded. The execution of policies developed in the school superintendent's office has repercussions throughout the community; examples of how educational leadership with respect to consolidation or school building programs infect the life blood of the broader society have been mentioned in previous chapters. In this chapter the significance of mature leadership will be more systematically explored.

The Leadership Setting

It is fashionable to discuss leadership as a separate topic, apart from the nature of organization itself. But this is a misleading, if not warped, perspective of the process. It is an inescapable fact that the nature of leadership is conditioned by the nature of organization and of the society. Educational leadership cannot be understood apart from its complex, bureaucratic context and the "power" environment. For although leaders deal directly with individuals, ultimately it is organizations—that is, group traditions, established relationships, and vested interest groups—which are their main concern. Clearly, the problems, dilemmas, and inconsistencies of the organization and of the society are the problems of the leader. They constitute the leadership setting. For this reason, the following analyses of leadership rely heavily on projected implications of the preceding chapters.

AMBIGUITY FROM STRUCTURAL INCONSISTENCIES

Ambiguity is an important and common element of the leadership setting. The school executive in particular lives in a world that is frequently inconsistent. He must set school policy in the face of conflicting public demands and internal factions. As stated earlier, just as effective supervision constitutes the ability to compromise organizational inconsistencies in the course of day-to-day relationships with personnel, so effective leadership involves the ability to live with the ambiguities created by such compromises and to incorporate them at the level of policy formulation and implementation.

The ambiguous setting is created largely by the problems so far discussed. It is instructive to enumerate them again. First, there are problems dealing with the competing demands of the public and various pressure groups. Indeed, the contemporary importance of administrators is largely due to their strategic relationship with the *public*, rather than to the inherent worth of internal coordination. Second, there are a series of tensions generated by myths that organizations either are, or ideally should be, rational, impersonally commanded, rule-directed, and harmonious, with consensus on ends and means, and, above all, on overall policy. Though these standards are never completely fulfilled, the belief that they should be fulfilled creates official pangs of conscience when performance falls below the ideal. Third, innumerable problems are created from processes of delegation. The leader is expected to maintain control and at the same time delegate his authority. Questions concerning the amount of authority that should be granted to subordinates and the amount of autonomy that is expected from them are perennial. Fourth, a series of problems arise because of inconsistencies between official and societal demands. Of extreme importance is the dilemma of exercising authority in an egalitarian society. The leader must strategically regard men as means, which is ideologically taboo in a democratic society. Differences between official and social evaluations concerning sex, age, ethnic and social origins, level of education, religion, and income must also be considered. Fifth, there is a recurring tendency for means to displace goals. The leader encounters special problems of maintaining his own position against poachers and the intrigues of other departments, while at the same time contributing to the welfare of both his own organization and to the social institutions for which he is responsible. Maintenance of office often entails greater attention to techniques and details and to internal politics than can be logically justified—that is, securing internal and external support, pleasing superiors, public relations, and so on. Finally, the leader must initiate change while at the same time maintain organizational continuity and stability. Line-staff conflicts and cleavages between local- and cosmopolitan-oriented personnel are natural adjuncts of this struggle.

The normal strains created by environmental pressures, inconsistencies of internal principles, conflicts between office and status, ends-means dilemmas, and change-stability questions can easily become inadvertently exaggerated by certain leadership policies. At the same time, however, initiative and creativity are sometimes stimulated by the tensions that arise from these conflicts.

MORAL COMPLEXITY

It is also apparent that the leader lives in a morally complex environment where he must not only choose between right and wrong, but between two or more "rights." Consequently, to be effective, leaders must be morally complex themselves. This does not mean that effective leaders lack a conscience, but rather that they need a flexible and temperate one, as well as a sense of justice that is not rigid and takes into consideration the rights of all parties concerned. Indeed, all that many subordinates expect of their leader is that he will, over the long run, give them a "fair shake," and earnestly *try* to do what is "right" in situations where there is little consensus.

From one study of school executives comes evidence that "strong" leaders have a more realistic conception of the difficulties of administrative choices than "weak" leaders. Neither the school men who naïvely denied the extent of difficulties, nor those who greatly exaggerated the difficulties involved, received high leadership ratings from their subordinates.[3] Effective leadership requires a realistic perception of dilemmas and some ability to clarify issues. Another writer suggests that weak leaders are feaful of conflict situations and seek merely to avoid trouble. They hesitate to act without consulting their superiors and fall back on official rules when they encounter problems, whether the rules are adequate or not.[4] In relying on rules rather than ingenuity, the weak hold leadership positions tenuously (with seniority and experience as their only justifications for their position). They are easily displaced as rules go out of date. On the other hand, effective leaders tolerate dilemmas and seek to turn them to their own advantage or to the advantage of their organization. They are least morally threatened by a compromise because they are aware of moral complexities. Indeed, it is these complexities which provide the leader with an enormous opportunity to be creative and to "lead."

FORMAL AND INFORMAL BASES OF LEADERSHIP

The simultaneous existence of formal and informal modes of organization provides the leader with at least two bases of authority, popularity
and respect. Respect may be derived from either technical competence to
lead the group to its goals, or from customary respect for the office itself
independent of the person who occupies it.[5] At times the leader is forced
to decide whether to be popular with subordinates (by subverting official
principles in their favor), or to uphold his official duties at the expense of
his popularity. Sometimes he can do no more than cater to the will of his
subordinates in order to maintain their goodwill; but the leader is also in
many ways a group "deviate," who exercises a latitude in obeying and
carrying out group norms which other members do not have. In extreme
cases, a strong leader will be willing to contradict the sentiment of his
subordinates and take a morally courageous stand at the risk of losing
popularity. While the leader may be justly concerned about his popularity, it must be remembered that there is another basis of authority; he
may be able to win the respect of subordinates with whom he is not especially popular if they agree with the ideals that he is trying to uphold.
Although the leader needs strong support, he does not need unanimous
support. Courageous leaders risk criticism without necessarily sacrificing
their effectiveness.

It is unfortunate that many people somehow assume that the human relations approach to management requires that the leader be "liked" by his
subordinates. Research in the field of group dynamics disputes this; it has
been shown repeatedly that persons who exert important influence are
frequently disliked. Bennis points out that the position of psychoanalysis
would tend to concur. He states that this position ". . . follows along
these same lines, that productive work is partially a function of hostility
to the leader." [6]

Whether or not a leader has the "courage" to risk unpopularity for the
sake of upholding official or moral principles depends partially on how
secure the leader feels and how much investment he has in his office. It is
difficult for a leader who is primarily concerned about maintaining his position to jeopardize it for the sake of his ideas. Conversely, the courageous
leader is probably among those whose involvement with principles at
some point exceeds his personal commitment to his office. Commitment to
office probably increases with age, marital status, property ownership,
parenthood, and aspiration to succeed, and it probably declines with the
existence of alternative career lines, outside income, and outside support.

COMPROMISE

The leader is, in effect, a middle-man between conflicting interests and
values. He is a representative of third parties mediating a bargaining

process. In this compromising setting no party will be completely satisfied with any action. Therefore, the leader often finds himself in the position where *any* choice will detract from some of the organization's major goals and will meet with some disapproval; his problem is to make concessions which *least* deflect the organization from its overall goals. Consequently, the administrator must have more than technical skills, or even "human relations skills" designed to enhance his popularity. It requires the ability to anticipate the effects of alternative decisions on the organization's future course of action and the courage to deal with cultural and organizational dilemmas in the face of criticism.

Views of Leadership

The conceptualization of leadership, the skills that it requires, and its explanation apparently depends on an understanding of the forces within the leadership setting. Four views of leadership will be reviewed with respect to their relevance to the organizational context as outlined thus far: leadership as personality traits, as a set of functions, as social relations, and as a social process.

LEADERSHIP AS PERSONALITY TRAITS

People are inclined to explain leadership in terms of the leaders themselves, that is, their personal traits independent of their cultural, social, and situational context. One writer suggests that explanations of leadership in terms of personalities is so tempting to administrators because they conveniently seem to imply that administrators are personally superior.[7] Certainly the picture of workers as irrational beings, moved by sentiment and tradition and utilized as means to official ends, provides a convenient contrast to the image of administrators as rational, creative, free-willed decision makers. The overemphasis on the conformity of subordinates is excelled only by the distorted stress placed on the personal, individualistic qualities of leaders.

The Case Against Personality. There are several reasons for discounting the role of personality in leadership. First, it is not the leader's personality which makes him important. The administrator is important because of his job—his coordinating, public relations, policy formulation, and representative functions. Second, there is not one but a range of leadership personalities. Probably most people with sufficient motivation and of average intelligence and experience could learn to be adequate administrators. The number of qualified persons tends to outnumber the jobs available at every level of employment. There is little reason to assume that the personal traits and abilities of administrators are more significant factors in their achievement than are their loyalties, aspirations, connections, and the chances of vacancies occurring at a crucial time in their career. In fact, leadership is so important that its fulfillment could scarcely be left to the chance that particular individuals with unique personalities will appear at the proper times. Also, except for gross estimations gleaned from interviews or brief contacts between subordinates and superiors, the leadership traits of promotables may not even be systematically or directly assessed before they assume important positions. Moreover, whatever minimum personality traits that are demanded for a particular job may very well develop after the leadership position has been assumed; the often noticeably altered attitudes of the worker who becomes boss, the student who becomes a teacher, or in fact the pedestrian who becomes a driver, are notable examples of the effects of status change on personality. Finally, whatever leadership traits which leaders may be observed to have in common may reflect the traits that are required to *achieve* positions of leadership rather than the traits necessary for actual leadership.

The above statements are not intended to completely deny the relevance of personality to leadership, but to place personality in its proper perspective. Generally, extreme personality traits may set the minimum limits for effective leadership. Extreme personality types are disqualified. Completely insane persons sometimes cannot lead effectively, although some psychopathic types, such as Hitler, have been effective leaders; and persons who are filled with hatred for their subordinates or extreme self doubt and withdrawal probably do not make good leaders. But it is generally easier to identify the persons who do *not* make good leaders in these terms than those who do.

Empirical Findings.   Empirically speaking, the search for the ideal personality of "born leaders" has proved fruitless. Bird's review of the literature revealed that only five per cent of the purported traits were common to four or more empirical investigations of leadership. Stogdill's review of the trait studies seems to justify a pessimistic appraisal.[8] For example, six studies on the importance of age find that better leaders are younger, but ten studies also report that they are older, and seventeen report that it "differs with the situation." Similarly inconsistent results are typical of studies on height, weight, energy, health, emotional stability, appearance, I.Q., and self-confidence; although it is commonly purported that leaders have "insight," it is by no means apparent what that is.

On the other hand, personal attributes that involve social skills, ambition, and social direction seem to be important. Stogdill reports that effective leadership was found to be consistently related to "social skills," such as language fluency, humor, sociability, diplomacy, tact, and popularity.[9] Leaders also seem to be highly motivated. Henry has found that American business leaders express strong mobility drives—achievement desire, respect for superiors, decisiveness, and somewhat severed obligations from parents.[10] These may be the very traits which help a leader to deal with the frequently ambiguous social situations that he will encounter in a morally complex environment. Language skills, ambition, and decisiveness, the ability to maintain poise in potentially embarrassing situations, to act diplomatically and with tact under pressure, are all useful skills in complex situations. However, even such qualities are not necessarily generalized, inherent qualities of personality. Persons who can tolerate ambiguity in some situations may be completely overwhelmed in others, and even "ambitious" persons are not necessarily ambitious in every undertaking. In fact, whenever such traits as self-confidence and ambition do carry over between situations, it may be because of similarity between the situations.

LEADERSHIP AS A SET OF FUNCTIONS

Leadership can be understood better in terms of what the leader does rather than who the leader is. Several functions common to leaders will be outlined below.

Policy Formulation. In formulating policy, the leader must squarely face decisions about means, aims, and values; in this respect leadership is ultimately a moral concern. However, while all leaders are responsible for policy, the influence which a particular leader has over the policy of his organization varies. The leader is charged with the responsibility for both establishing the abstract goals of the organization and specifying the more specific working policies that guide the organization in its daily operations. While these two elements of policy are supposed to be logically related, there is a tendency for operating policy to become distinct from the abstract goals. Because many of these problems are fundamental concerns to persons who do not agree among themselves, the leader must endure much criticism.

Implementation. Once the policies have been formulated, they need to be put into effect by means of specific *plans* of operation. This involves making everyday, routine decisions which will help to achieve the goals. Needless to say, while the chief administrator is responsible for seeing that decisions are made, he normally does not make them himself. If he were the only person deciding these matters, his job would be much simpler than it is. His role is to see that *someone* assumes the responsibility to make decisions. In the course of daily pressures and disagreements among the staff who have these decision-making powers, the leader is often not in a position to follow the course of action that he would personally prefer.

Often the leader's only function is to prevent certain decisions which deviate too far from overall policy. For example, the superintendent may give his new secondary school principal complete responsibility for developing a sound in-service program in the high school, but when the superintendent hears that the principal plans to dismiss children early twice a month for faculty meetings, the superintendent may be inclined to intercede in order to clarify the school's policy by specifying the conditions under which the children may be dismissed; dismissal time is usually closely tied to policies, rules, and regulations regarding transportation and bus drivers—even to statutes. Weekly meetings of principal and central administrators are partly aimed at preventing decisions which deviate too far from overall policy.

Maintenance of Functional Autonomy. In policy formulation and decision-making, the leader has a dual responsibility—responsibility to the public and responsibility for the welfare of the internal operations. This somewhat jaundiced aspect of leadership is a source of considerable strain. For maintenance of the internal organization frequently requires some sacrifice to outside pressure groups, while external demands ordinarily deflect much of the leader's attention from the organization's long-range course of action. The leader must decide on the amount of internal control over policy and procedures which will be sacrificed for external and internal support.

The fact that leaders represent the interests of the organization to the external environment is often ignored. However, one writer divided twenty-three principals into two major groups: one group was high on both "consideration" and "initiation," and the other was low on both dimensions. Each major group was further divided into two subcategories: those who were high in both "procurement" functions (acquisition of support for the school) and "disposal" functions (marketing of the product), and those who were low on both dimensions. These dimensions concerned the leader's ability to obtain for the school what it needs from outside sources and to protect the staff from outside interference. For each of the major groups, those who ranked high on procurement and disposal received higher effectiveness ratings from the staff; teachers' job satisfaction was higher and they expressed more confidence in the principal's leadership.[11]

Besides guarding the organization's welfare, a leader is also responsible for coordinating the ends of the organization with the *institutional* values of the broader society. This is normally difficult, particularly in cases where upholding institutional values means jeopardizing the organization's prestige, as in cases when some schools must be discontinued in order to consolidate for the sake of improving education.

LEADERSHIP AS SOCIAL RELATIONS

While leadership is not merely a personality characteristic, neither can it be understood exclusively in terms of the leadership *tasks* just alluded to. Drucker says of an institution that it is "like a tune; it is not constituted by individual sounds but by the relations between them." The same can be said of leadership; it is a function of the social relations expected of certain social positions. These expectations both support leadership actions and restrain them.

The content of the leader's orders is normally as important as he who gives them. For no matter who the leader is, his orders cannot be arbitrary, that is, outside the realm of normal expectation. For example, it has been found that small group leaders cannot maintain their leadership positions unless their orders are in agreement with the traditions of the group.[12]

The view of leadership as a social relation directs attention away from the personal qualities of the leader and toward the fundamental nature of leadership: the *demands* made by one party on another. Leadership occurs when subordinates comply with an order. A leader's acts cannot be understood out of context of his relationship with his subordinates. The nature of that relationship is reviewed below.

Shared Dependence. The leader has a unique role with respect to his subordinates. It is a role which is indispensable to their jobs and to the organization. It is characteristically a role on which others depend. This characteristic is a matter of degree and is present in many roles. Thus, a member of a group is a leader to the extent that others in the group must depend on him to fulfill his tasks.[13] Leadership, in other words, is not an all-or-none category, but is a variable. People are not simply either leaders or followers. There are as many leaders of an organization as there are shared dependency roles; the same person may lead and be led as he changes roles.

The criterion of a leader, then, is the fact that all other members must depend on the leader more than he depends on any *one* of them. Thus, while every member of the assembly line performs a minor task, the foreman is less dependent on a particular assembly worker than each is on him—for parts, for wages, vacations, and so on. As specialization increases, there is opportunity for more individuals to become indispensable at various times during their careers; but conversely, it becomes increasingly difficult for a single individual to be completely indispensable and dominate the leadership structure.

This element of shared dependency differentiates "small group" leaders from large organization leaders. In the former case, group functions are limited and so there are only one or two leaders because all members can be served by a single person. But in complex organizations with diverse functions, it is difficult for any one or two persons to serve the entire membership. They have neither the skill nor the social capacity to do so. This difference makes it hazardous to generalize in both small and large group leadership studies.

Initiation and Consideration. Two components of the leader's relationships to his subordinates are of special importance. On the one hand, the leader is expected by superiors to initiate ideas, maintain group norms, and act as final arbitrator of decisions. At the same time his relationships to subordinates concern "taking care of others," maintaining a humanitarian or, at least, an objective attitude, and in general not acting "like a big shot." When emphasis is placed on the consideration role, the leadership is sometimes loosely characterized as "democratic," while emphasis on initiating activities is often attributed to authoritarianism. Several studies have shown that skills in fulfilling these "initiation" and "consideration" roles are associated with good leadership ratings. One investigator concluded from a study of chairmen of liberal arts college departments that chairmen with good reputations as administrators are those who rate high on both the consideration and initiation dimensions.[14] A similar conclusion was reached from a study of eighty-nine aircraft commanders. Good ratings of the commander by his superiors were associated with high initiation structure scores (originating new ideas or practices, maintaining standard operating procedures with his crew, giving regular and clear assignments to subordinates). Good ratings by his subordinates, however, were associated with high consideration scores (doing personal favors for crew members, being friendly, treating the subordinates as a social equal, looking out for the crew welfare).[15]

There are times when these two relationships require the leader to behave inconsistently. Telling others what to do and maintaining official standards may create resentment among subordinates, while establishing equal relationships with subordinates may prevent the leader's taking official action against them, and may jeopardize his relationship with his own superiors. A division of leadership labor is one solution to the dilemma. Some leaders seem to depend more on their initiation role, letting other members of the group take care of the needs and feelings of subordinates. This division creates at least two distinct types of leaders: those responsible for pursuing the group tasks and supporting its official structure, and those who are responsible for maintaining group sentiments, or its cohesiveness.

There is also reason to believe that the relative emphasis which an official leader gives to each of the elements is conditioned by his rank and his advancement opportunities. In one study of military leaders, it is reported that army officers, more than noncommissioned officers, competed openly with their peers and with their superiors, while they competed less with their own subordinates.[16] On the other hand, although noncommissioned officers were more aggressive with their subordinates, they maintained less "social distance" from them than officers did. The lower ranking officials seemed to rely on the consideration leadership behavior more than higher ranking officers did. The consideration function is perhaps left to *informal* mechanisms to a greater extent at high levels of command than lower ones. Similarly, initiation seems to be more informal at lower echelons.

Like so many other characteristics of organization, the initiation and consideration behaviors often necessitate compromise in practice. Styles of leadership are undoubtedly associated with the nature of these compromises. Halpin has developed a typology of leadership styles in terms of four combinations of initiation and consideration structure.[17] School superintendents who were high on both dimensions were assumed to be the most effective; only eleven of fifty superintendents were placed in that category by both their staffs and the school board.

Social Distance. The initiation and consideration roles are so different that subordinates and superiors, leaders and followers, are characteristically separated by formal and informal barriers. Of this, one school superintendent has said, "You can become too—maybe too—putting yourself on too much of an equal—to be too friendly. Now there has been some little thought that has come to my mind that maybe I have been a little too friendly." [18] Some of the superintendents in a Massachusetts study followed a policy of having no intimate friends in the community in which they worked, and they were reluctant to develop friendships with their staff members.[19] The social distance that characterizes leader and subordinate relationships is most apparent in the military where there are official restrictions against fraternization, and separate social, eating, and sleeping places (they even wear their status on sleeves and shoulders).

In maintaining social distance from subordinates, the leader is handicapped in understanding them and their wishes, which generally prevents the most effective fulfillment of the consideration role. This is a structural source of ignorance which may leave the needs of subordinates unanswered. This social distance is one reason that informal leaders arise within the subordinate ranks—to take care of the consideration roles neglected by distant superiors.

If it handicaps the consideration role, then why is social distance so characteristic of leadership positions? From an examination of this question, one investigator concludes that it is not because subordinates' feelings of familiarity with their leader hinder their own effectiveness; nor is it because the knowledge which subordinates have of their leader's defects reduces their confidence in him. Rather, social distance is designed to protect the leaders' performance of initiating behaviors. Barriers protect the leader from any involvement with subordinates which might influence his ability to reach decisions that contribute to the goals.[20] As one school superintendent put it, "I mean they would feel, 'He's an old buddy of mine.' If you had to crack the whip a little bit, or set down some rules, then they'd be offended quicker." [21] Social distance seems to produce an atmosphere favorable to rationality by preventing unnecessary personal commitments from interfering with the leadership role.

This is not to say that social distance is without benefit to subordinates, for it does benefit them. At the same time that he is aloof to his subordinates, the leader is associating with other, perhaps more influential people —that is, school and community leaders. This puts him in a position to make contacts with those who can achieve salary increases and otherwise protect the interests of his subordinates, advantages which they could not have achieved themselves.[22]

One researcher suggests that social distance is partly explained by virtue of the fact that the satisfactions realized through peer relationships might be jeopardized by too close relationships with superiors.[23]

It is relatively more difficult for leaders in some positions than those in others to maintain social distance. Lower ranking officials are often in closer physical proximity to the subordinates than higher officials are to theirs. This may help to account for relatively greater emphasis (noted earlier) that lower officers give to consideration. Teachers, for example, having no office of their own, cannot completely withdraw from students as principals can withdraw from teachers. They are under pressures to be popular and a "good Joe," with no intermediary to bear the brunt of resentments; and not having particularly high social status, as well as being subject to the ridicule of their students and parents, teachers are especially likely to rely on their consideration role, which makes them vulnerable to the charge of "favoritism." There is always a threat that the teacher will succumb to humanistic conceptions of students rather than to official ones, that they will like some of their pupils and dislike others, because of their close special relationship.

The Nature of "Subordinates."   The concept of leadership is meaningless except as it implies a set of relationships. It cannot be understood without understanding the other positions with which leaders must deal. Of particular importance is the nature of the subordinate position. The practice of speaking about subordinates categorically obscures their characteristic diversity. Subordinates do not represent a unified front, but rather a mixture of subgroups which support or resist different leaders in various degrees. In a study of sociometric choices in a training school for girls, for example, it was reported that there was very little overlap among individuals who supported different group leaders.[24] Large organizations, particularly, are characterized by heterogeneity and dissent among subgroups who are divided among themselves on the basis of their allegiance to different leaders.

This heterogeneous character of subordinates influences the structure of leadership. An array of leaders develop who are supported by various *factions* of subordinates. A portion of the power of the leader is dependent on the relative power of his supporting faction compared with the elements that oppose him.

LEADERSHIP AS A SOCIAL PROCESS

Although there is, of course, a leadership environment, and a set of functions, requirements to compromise, and networks of interpersonal relationships, and although all of these and more impinge upon the leader and those led, leadership is perhaps best understood in the final analysis as a social (interaction) process. Bennis has characterized leadership in operational terms as comprising the following fundamental elements: (a) an agent; (b) a process of inducement; (c) subordinates; (d) the *induced* behavior; and (e) a particular objective or goal. He explains that the process of inducement may be defined as *power*—that is, the ability to control rewards and punishments and thereby control the means for the satisfaction of subordinates' needs. The behavior that is induced is defined by Bennis as *influence*. Putting these elements together, leadership may then be defined as ". . . the process by which an agent induces a subordinate to behave in a desired manner." [25]

Interaction and Informal Leadership.   Like the ancient alchemists who sought a man-made substitute for gold, administrators understandably seek a set of rules, or "principles of administration," which apply unconditionally to most situations. There are at present no such rules. However, also like alchemists, the belief in them causes some persons to glibly accept the prescriptions of "more experienced" persons on faith. One writer cautions that it would be dangerous if there were such rules because, although they might work for a time, they would become inappropriate under new conditions.[26] This in fact is the epitome of "trained incapacity," that is, the substitution of rules for aims. Yet this is precisely what the administrator who wishes to learn only from experience seems to be seeking.

Rather than look for a set of administrative rules, the administrator is better advised to look for underlying principles of human interaction in large scale organizations which will provide a method for understanding *situations* in which the aims must be achieved. Although the search for rules of administration assumes that situations are consistent, the quest for principles of interaction starts with the variability of situations.

Homans chooses to investigate small group processes in terms of four concepts: *activity, interaction, norms,* and *sentiment.*[27] *Activity* refers to the tasks of the work group. *Interaction* occurs whenever one person's activitity is stimulated by the activity of another; it includes verbal and nonverbal communication. A *norm* is a standard held by work group members that prescribes what ought to be done; orders are norms which anticipate changes in established ways of doing things. *Sentiment* refers to the subjective qualities of members, their likes and dislikes, drives, emotions, motives, and attitudes. The underlying assumption of the conceptual system is that a change in one element modifies the others. Thus, for example, by increasing the group's activities, interaction will increase among the members, and in increasing interaction they are more likely to "get to know one another on a personal basis, either as friends or personal enemies." Thus, Homans proposes that "persons who interact frequently with one another will tend to like one another." [28] Sentiments are also conditioned by status relationships: "The more frequently persons inter-act with one another, when no one of them originates interaction with much greater frequency than the other, the greater is their liking for one another and their feeling of ease in one another's presence." [29] On the other hand, ". . . the more frequently one of the two originates interaction for the other, the stronger will be the latter's sentiment of respect (or personal hostility) toward him . . ." [30] That is to say, hostility or respect, rather than friendship, is a more likely outcome when superiors interact with subordinates.

The concept *originating interaction* provides a clue to the detection of informal status relationships. Action is originated for another when he obeys requests, volunteers to satisfy the wishes of others, seeks information, and so on. Often persons who are not in official leadership positions originate interaction for others. The assignment of persons to high-ranking offices does not guarantee that they will necessarily exercise leadership initiative, for there are many factors in the official structure that may prohibit the exercise of initiative. Key subordinates may be in a better position to exercise unofficial leadership because of their close affiliation with the public, with pressure groups, or with influential community leaders. Leadership depends partially on access to crucial information about what is going on in the group and within the community; this may involve access to files. For example, the school psychologist is in a position of leadership because he controls secret information about students.

Since intelligent leadership requires that outside influence be considered and used in making decisions, the leadership position will be one that provides a wide variety of outside contacts. That is, the higher the formal or informal social rank, the more interaction there is between that position and the outside groups. For similar reasons, informal leaders will have contact with more of the organization's personnel than those who are not leaders, and consequently they are in a position to develop intimate knowledge of the group norms.[31] That is to say, the leader's knowledge of group norms is no accident. It is gained through a complex network of communication with all members of the group. In other words, "the higher the person's social rank, the wider will be his range of initiation" within the group as well as outside it.[32] This suggests that informed leaders arise from those group positions which afford a range of internal and external contacts and that provide ready-made channels of communication. Because communication generally flows toward and away from the leader in greater volume than to other members, it seems reasonable that informal leadership develops at communication centers. Thus, the higher an individual's informal rank, the larger the number of persons for whom he will initiate interaction.

Just as formal status differences reduce interaction among unequals, higher rates of interaction occur among persons who are nearly equal in *official* rank. This high rate of interaction of informal peer group leaders with other group members facilitates the development of mutual sentiments; informal leaders, therefore, can be expected to rely more on consideration and friendship and less on deference, respect, and initiation than official leaders.

The view that leadership is a social relations process calls for special consideration of sociological explanations. Some of these approaches will be considered subsequently.

Leadership Tactics

Viewed as interaction, effective leadership is partly dependent upon the leader's skill at (1) maintaining his position (position maintenance), (2) initiating ideas and commands (initiation), and (3) supporting the interests of his subordinates (consideration). Below are some general tactical approaches to the first and last of these problems. Initiation is related to the decision-making process already discussed, and to professionalization which is the subject of Chapter 15.

INTERNAL POLITICS AND POSITION MAINTENANCE

Holding a position of leadership does not insure the power to lead. For example, nothing can be so corrupting to a new leader's authority as his attempt to radically alter established ways before he first guarantees his own position. Consequently, much of the strong leader's time is devoted to the tactics of position maintenance—concerns which are often labeled "political." The fact that leaders must "play politics" probably discourages some otherwise promising persons who dislike using personal power and contacts and other political tactics to achieve leadership positions. It is also conceivable that persons who do achieve and maintain their positions of responsibility sometimes do so almost exclusively because of political skills, which is no assurance of their wisdom in policy formulation. Undoubtedly, some people who hold responsible positions in education go to great lengths to secure their positions—ranging from bribery and forged academic degrees to a career of hand-shaking at national conventions and impression management before important audiences. The relationships between *achieving* leadership positions, ability to lead, and devotion to institutional values poses a crucial problem for understanding the nature of leadership.

With Respect to Superiors. When a leader senses that his position is threatened by other departments or by his own subordinates, there are several devices that he can adopt. With respect to his official superiors he can either (1) attempt to enhance his personal relations with them, or (2) attempt to please them by increasing the objective standards of his work.

The first tactic seems to be more effective when there is one powerful superior (for example, a strong superintendent or a strong school board member) who can protect and support the leader. However, if there are cleavages among the top leadership, pleasing one of them may simply incur for the leader the displeasure of his superior's own enemies. Also, since it is usually easiest to please persons who are weakest among the top leadership group, the support that he receives is likely to be from the least influential superior, or from one who will be reluctant to publicly risk his own insecure position in defense of a subordinate. Where many people hold power, the subordinate may attempt to please several of the top leaders, but if this requires him to adopt inconsistent "faces," that may also be dangerous.

On the other hand, the leader may enhance his position by stressing his competence; he may seek election to a state or national professional office, publish in trade journals, or increase his efficiency by cutting costs or by winning an important bond issue. Since "competence" can be easily advertised to other organizations, this approach has an added advantage; for nothing is so enhancing to the leader's current position as public knowledge that another organization wants him.

With Respect to Subordinates. The principal or superintendent who spends all of his time worrying about what his superiors think of him is inclined to ignore the influence that his teachers and students can have on his fate. "Neutral" subordinates are especially crucial, because their reaction is least predictable. Neutrals may sometimes be "won over" by raising their salaries, offering them personal considerations (such as a little time off, a new desk), or by paying them personal attention (such as going to their office rather than requesting them to come to his). Opponents are also obviously important. Their power can be weakened by transferring them to other departments, by offering them promotion or otherwise breaking down their solidarity. In general, the strong leader will support the position of some of his subordinates and simultaneously attempt to weaken the position of his adversaries.

The skilled leader uses a variety of tactics to maintain his position against the opposition of subordinates. Tactics that prevent their becoming united are crucial. Henry suggests that by using a common classroom technique, teachers are able to dissipate any unified resistance from students. He maintains that teachers encourage children to destructively criticize another child who differs in opinion from the teacher; this renders them "docile," that is, more concerned about finding the answer which the teacher wants, and giving it to her, than about expressing ideas and interpretations that oppose hers. Students who are critical of their classmates and who come to the teacher's defense receive recognition from her. Thus pitted at odds among themselves, students are reluctant to voice a discrepant opinion, and the peer group is effectively disintegrated. Unsure of support from their peers, students anxiously seek the approval of their teachers.[33] Apparently teachers then do ordinarily use the kind of leadership tactics designed to counteract resistance from their subordinates which are being described in this chapter.

MAINTAINING SUBORDINATES' POSITIONS

Communication. Subordinates tend to support superiors who confide in them. A principal is likely to support a superintendent who at least informs him of the decisions as soon as they are made. Nothing undermines a principal's authority so much as when his superintendent or some member of his school board fails to consult him before issuing a statement to his teachers. In addition to consulting his direct subordinates, the superintendent must give them information for them to function effectively. If a principal must consult his own superiors about policy every time someone on the faculty or in the public has a question, he jeopardizes his own authority and embarrasses the organization.

Likert compared groups of workers in industry which expressed favorable and unfavorable attitudes towards their official leaders.[34] Nearly half of those who were favorable said that their superiors informed the men what was happening in the company and how well they were doing; less than thirteen per cent who were unfavorable to their supervisors gave that description. Nearly two-thirds of those who were favorable said that their supervisor hears complaints and grievances compared to less than one-third of those who were unfavorable to their supervisors. The favorable group reported virtually unanimously that they felt free to discuss important things about the job with their supervisor and that it does some good to discuss them, while only six in ten or less of the unfavorable group reported the same. Two-way communication, it appears, is crucial for effective leadership because it helps to maintain the subordinate's position (even when it is not logically essential for him to accomplish his task).

However, the fact that top executives need some freedom to be flexible and to compromise as situations arise imposes limits on the amount of policy-making, which superintendents can pass on to principals, for it is often strategically unwise to make any more policy statements than immediately necessary.

Praise and Blame. Another way the leader can influence the security of his subordinates is through his use of praise and blame. Homans asserts that the leader will neither blame nor praise a member of his group before other members.[35] Blaming individuals in public creates a threatening situation for the other members as well, who have engaged in the practice and who fear similar reprisals.

Generally, leaders will not place their positions in jeopardy more often than necessary, and then only when something is to be gained by doing so. Oddly enough, this principle applies to the use of praise too. For in publicizing praise, the leader unnecessarily runs the risk that his opinions will not be shared by his subordinates or by the public; the subordinates often have more information than he does. This is one of the daily hazards that confront teachers whose evaluation of pupils often does not correspond with peer group and parental evaluations.

KNOWLEDGE OF SUBORDINATES' POSITIONS

Leaders can show personal consideration only to the extent that they are legitimately aware of their subordinate's interests and problems. However, a leader has two handicaps. First, because his position is threatening to his subordinates, a leader's efforts to learn about their activities are resisted. This tempts him to use unofficial, informal, even unethical procedures to obtain information, such as spy systems. But if the spies are discovered by subordinates, it clearly signifies a state of open "warfare" between the leader and his followers. Second, the leader can officially acknowledge that he has only that information which he should "legitimately" know. This condition restricts the amount of interest he can officially display in a personal problem of a subordinate which he learned about informally.

Unofficial channels provide one means of learning about subordinates. Personal interests are frequently revealed in the gossip of informal gatherings. In fact, the "office party" offers one of the few occasions where people can step out of their official roles and proprieties and speak their minds. Both social status and personality differences are obscured in the party for the sake of maintaining the situation itself. A person can speak his mind at a party precisely because it is intended to be a depersonalized and egalitarian situation.[36] The leader who remains inconspicuously present may sense a great deal, provided that his presence does not dampen the party with an air of officiousness. However, there is always a danger that when an administrator abandons his official rank in order to be taken into the confidence of his subordinates in such gatherings, he will jeopardize his official leadership role later in the formal setting. This dilemma between "officiousness" (or initiation) and informal interaction with subordinates (or consideration) may be partially resolved if informal interaction with subordinates is confined to private places and small groups.[37] The ways which particular leaders compromise their official and informal interaction habits underly a variety of personal leadership patterns.

A leader's moral tone also promotes or restricts permissiveness in both the official and informal settings. Subordinates will not speak openly if they fear reprisal or an officious moral stance from the leader. A "strong" leader sees moral complexities and does not seek to impose a single standard on everyone. Information gained through personal confidence places a special obligation on the leader not to act as a judge or reveal personal information. Paradoxically, the same principle of moral neutrality also severely restricts the available alternatives for dealing with problems learned in this way.

Uses of Informal Organization. The informal organization of subordinates can be strategically utilized by leaders to support their own position. Many times, for example, the informal organization may be entrusted to handle discipline problems. There are usually compelling reasons why subordinates disobey, often inherent in the organizational structure itself, and subordinates may have a better sense of these reasons and causes for undisciplined behavior than the superior.[38]

The leader can gain the support of subordinates by supporting their leaders. For example, there is evidence that leaders of inmates in prisons have more favorable attitudes than nonleaders toward authority in their prison camp, are less likely to escape, and are less likely to request transfer or to be transferred for "maladjustment."[39] These cooperative and sympathetic attitudes of the leaders of prisoners toward the administration were due largely to the support which the administration gave to the informal leaders. The latter were generally more concerned about the inmates who were after their positions than about the shortcomings of the administration or prison guards. The administration gave the informal leaders of inmates more desirable jobs on labor gangs, and they were more likely to receive high status bottom bunks despite official "random" assignment procedures. In return, inmate leaders promoted administrative goals.

This kind of cooperative arrangement which can develop between officials and the informal leaders of subordinates suggests that informal teacher and student groups can be enticed to support the administration by recognizing and promoting their leaders.

Carlson reports that new superintendents were able to counteract long-standing informal resistance by (1) stopping their social contacts with the adversary (that is, increasing social distance), (2) bringing in an outside agency to conduct a survey and confirm the need for change, and (3) promoting the leadership of the adversary group (that is, a teachers' union) to a position of administrative responsibility where it can be co-opted. The first principle was used by an inside successor who had a history of personal relations with the adversary, and the third principle was used by a successor from the outside who was unencumbered by personal relations.[40] Teachers often utilize this third principle of co-optation, when student leaders are invited to "sit in" on faculty meetings and to have representatives at important committee meetings which affect the lives of the students. The fact that student leaders are recognized by the system develops in them a sense of commitment to that system. Gordon reports that teachers with insight into the student's informal system were able to secure their support.

It is partly because teachers must support the informal status system for practical reasons that social class discrimination occurs in public schools. Since informal leaders often come from the middle class, the tendency of teachers to favor the middle class is as much a part of their strategy for dealing with student leaders as it is their own personal bias. Making the school more "democratic" not only threatens to undermine the teacher's own personal prejudices, but it also jeopardizes their ability to support the student leader from the middle class.

OUTSIDE SUPPORT

A leader's position is enhanced to the extent he can maintain a wide range of external as well as internal "contacts" which provide him with information and potential support. He may establish a personal following among the students or parents which makes it difficult for the school board to fire him, or he may attempt to establish cooperative relationships with community influentials. For example, a school milk contract may be awarded to the company which will return the greatest support for the school's forthcoming bond issue, rather than to the low bidder. While "fixing" of school contracts is in itself unethical, it often occurs within the context of an exchange of favors which is essential to the existence and effectiveness of the organization.

Some Sociological Foundations of Leadership

The influence of the situation on leadership is unmistakable. Roosevelt and Hitler were products of their time who would not have risen to fame and infamy apart from the situation. The nature of the situation greatly influences the type of leader that will be selected. The shy boy may become an aggressive leader when an issue close to his heart arises or when his special skills are demanded; as one writer points out, the lowly army private may assume command under severe battle conditions when his lieutenant's skills are no longer sufficient, and the most flagrant criminal who has knowledge to survive under times of stress may be intrusted with leadership during a community disaster.[41] It must be concluded that leadership is a combination of a situation, demand for special skills, and a sense of common destiny, as well as personal ambition.

SMALL GROUP STUDIES

The situational influence on leadership raises questions about the applicability of studies of leadership in small, *ad hoc* groups to the leadership process in general. There are several reasons why the useful ideas which have been advanced in small group research may be essentially irrelevant to other types of leadership *situations*. In the first place, although traditions are often a determining influence on the leader's behavior, *ad hoc* laboratory groups have no traditions. Second, the rewards of leadership in laboratory situations are usually so small that they will motivate few persons to any significant degree. Third, the laboratory situation operates independently of outside pressures which are normally major determining influences on leadership. Finally, and perhaps most important, the size of the group is itself a determining influence on leader behavior. For these reasons, if there is any connection between *ad hoc* laboratory groups and the broader context of leadership, it is probably because of the conditioning influence of the broader culture that is held in common among the participants.

MOBILITY PATTERNS

The fact that the situation is important does not make personal background irrelevant, however. Personal career patterns (as opposed to personality traits), for example, constitute one aspect of the "situation." Most administrators of the largest and most influential school systems achieve their positions after a long succession of upward moves. The exact degree of mobility among chief school administrators is variable. Carlisle reports an eight per cent average turnover of local administrators. Turnover is inversely related to size of units; administrators tended to move because of desire for higher salary.[42] In New Jersey, districts look for a new superintendent at least once every six years,[43] while turnover in twelve midwestern states was found to be nearly twenty per cent annually; the highest turnover there was reported in the smallest districts, and the greatest stability was reported in medium-sized disricts of 40 to 200 teachers.[44]

Local and Cosmopolitan Leadership Patterns. Carlson notes several principal ways in which the patterns of leadership differ among local (*place-bound*) and cosmopolitan (*career-bound*) public school superintendents.[45] Place-bound superintendents are "insiders" promoted from within the system; they constituted thirty-five per cent of a nationwide sample of 859 superintendents, while sixty-five per cent were "outsiders." Three types of outsiders were identified: hoppers, specialists and statesmen. *Hoppers* move frequently without benefiting their status and without leaving a lasting impression on the schools they serve. Specialists are hired to do a special job—financing or building—and do leave a lasting impression, but go away when their job is finished. The statesman leaves only when he feels he can do no more for the system. Largely because of what the statesman has been able to do for the system, the school board is usually satisfied with the system as he leaves it, and hires an insider as his successor. Insiders are often represented in larger systems. There are nearly twice as many insiders as outsiders in systems over 100,000 inhabitants, and sixty-one per cent of the superintendencies in cities over 500,000 in population are held by insiders (who constitute one-third of the superintendents).

Outsiders are more likely to be hired where the school board is unsatisfied with the present system. Outsiders are looked to for creativity, while insiders are hired to maintain stability. No insider reported that his board was dissatisfied with his predecessor. It would be difficult for the insider to effect change even if he wanted to. He would not be as likely to have the school board's support and he risks being identified, on the basis of his past and by virtue of his promotion, by the teachers as the "school board's man." If there is any creativity in such a system, it must come from the teaching profession rather than from the administration. Carlson concludes: "The insider adapts or modifies himself to fit the office; his performance adds nothing new to the role. It is not creative. . . . The place-bound superintendent seems to derive satisfaction from the office; he does not bring status to it. Coming from the outside, cosmopolitans are in a better position to bargain than are insiders, and accordingly they receive between $1,000 and $5,000 more a year than beginning insiders, and the insider never catches up. This demonstrates the crucial relationship that connections with the outside market have on the salary level. Persons not willing to enter the market or leave their present employment cannot command the present market salaries.

Both types of superintendents studied by Carlson engaged in rule-making upon taking office.[46] Rule-making creates the impression that the successor is engaged in important activities, that he is going to "do" something, forcefully bringing to everyone's attention the fact that he is on the scene; in the process of making rules, the successor also learns who will support him on larger issues and who will resist. Insiders and outsiders, however, were concerned with different types of rules. Insiders made rules which essentially sustained the *status quo*, while eighty-five per cent of the outsiders' rules altered internal commitments or external ties of the system. Insiders' rules typically pertained to the technical-managerial facets of the school; for example, "All individuals are responsible for making classroom observations and follow-up conferences." [47] But outsiders' rules affected the institutional level of the organization and changed its character; for example, the outsider might establish a kindergarten or employ social workers to serve the school.

When the successor was an outsider, the informal organization also showed signs of change and realignment of conflict relations. One noticeable effect of the outsider was a temporary solidification of informal relationships *within* each level of the hierarchy; that is, interaction increased among elementary principals and among secondary principals, but decreased between them. Such solidification was less likely where the successor was an insider, and when it occurred it took place across hierarchical levels. This means that, unlike the insider, the outsider inherits strong, neutral units which can be mobilized against him, or for him.

Insiders and outsiders also made different uses of "strategic replacement." [48] The outsider is more concerned than the insider with developing personal loyalties. The insider knows who his friends are and who his enemies are, and he has had years in which to build up a personal following. Consequently, outsiders more frequently increased their staffs than did insiders. Even new outside superintendents added more positions than old outside superintendents, while the reverse was true for new and old insider superintendents, which indicates that additions by the outsiders are viewed as strategic replacements necessary in the early years. Thus, school systems changed more quickly when outsiders were brought in.

Insiders "lasted" in office longer than outsiders. The mean time in office for insiders was ten years, while outsiders lasted a mean average of eight years. There was some evidence that insiders were able to persist longer because of more thorough political adaptation to outside interests. One insider who served twenty-seven years in one system never permitted himself to take a position in conflict with his school board, but he was willing to sacrifice principle for expediency; he also spent his time in community projects making personal contacts.

Although there are periods when insiders are needed, Carlson concludes that "two insiders in a row may be one too many." Two consecutive insiders would mean that the system has endured an average of twenty years of leadership without any major adaptations to the environment. Less than ten per cent of the instances of succession were concurrent insiders. However, about half of the cases were consecutive outsiders, fifty-three per cent of 209 instances were outside to inside, and thirty-nine were inside to outside successions. Carlson conjectures that by comparison with business organizations, which exist in a "wild" environment where adaptation is necessary, public schools are "domesticated" in the sense that they are assured of clients and income. They can exist longer without adapting.[49]

Thus, it is apparent that turnover is a crucial aspect of the school's character, and that the type of person a board hires—outsider or insider—may be a more significant determinant of his leadership than personality traits.

Mobility Aspirations.   This process of promotion, mobility, and aspiration to positions of greater authority affects the leadership style. In a study by Seeman of fifty school administrators, results of a leader behavior description questionnaire developed by Halpin disclosed that while measures of career mobility showed little relationship to administrative behavior, it was significantly related to a mobility aspiration scale designed to test the administrator's ambition to succeed. By combining mobility history with mobility aspiration, a four-way typology of administrators was developed: mobile nonstrivers, mobile status-seekers, stable nonstrivers, and unsuccessful status-seekers. Both the mobile strivers and the stable nonstrivers had low receptivity to organizational change, while the mobile nonstrivers and unsuccessful strivers were receptive; the mobile nonstrivers displayed relatively uniform controls over the organization and low responsiveness to needs of the group. The findings demonstrate that the career pattern and aspirations influence the style of leadership.[50]

Mobility Goals. Another facet of the mobility pattern which conceivably influences leadership style concerns what leaders strive *for.* Some ambitious persons seem to be seeking to "*become* something," and are awed by the style of life or the prestige of the leadership position itself. On the other hand, some ambitious persons seem to aspire to leadership in order to "*do* something"—they want to effect a program, or change one currently in effect. Conceivably, these two types of leaders display different leadership styles upon taking office. For example, the "strong" leaders, who resist pressures that deflect from their goals, are perhaps more likely to be found among the latter type. "Weak" leaders, who succumb to power of outside interests or who allow subordinates to ultimately assume command, are conceivably of the former type; for having no program, they seek out clues from others about how the role is to be played. In this case, it is the interplay between ambition and social pressures that constitutes the "situation."

Often, the personal goals that lead individuals into an occupation are not the ones that hold them there. One investigator classified nurses on the basis of shifts in their goals during their career: the "dedicated" had initially strong allegiance to nursing, which was retained throughout the career; the "convert" entered nursing with a low estimation of it, but radically altered her opinion of her career; the "disillusioned" entered the occupation with a high estimation of it, which later deteriorated; the "uncommitted" had neither entered the occupation with a high estimation of it nor developed one during the career.[51] In short, it is conceivable that the leadership styles change with fluctuations in degrees of emotional involvement and formal commitment during the career.

The mobility pattern and expectations regarding it have far-reaching significance for the style of leadership. The question can be analyzed further by directly examining aspects of the succession process separately.

THE VACANCY

A person's style of leadership can be affected by his anticipation of promotion to another office. This anticipation, in turn, can modify the behavior of the promotable's own subordinates who are "next-in-line" and develop new expectations because of it. The leader's behavior seems to change with a cycle of promotion which includes the opportunity to be promoted, the promotion itself, and re-entrenchment afterward. Levenson has observed, for example, that while striving to gain favorable recognition, the leader who is under consideration tends to enforce the rules more strictly than before he was being considered.[52] However, once he knows that he will be promoted, he again relaxes control, having less time or incentive to police subordinates as he learns his new job. At this same time, the leader also scrutinizes his subordinates for a replacement which, in turn, undoubtedly constrains some of them. Moreover, in training someone to fill his position, the leader exposes much information about the work that was formerly secret. Then, for a time following his promotion, the promotable is obliged to "prove" himself to his superiors. He may retighten control at this time, but once he has demonstrated himself, the leader may adopt still another style of leadership, until there are prospects for another immediate promotion.[53] Thus, cycles of authoritarian and democratic control, and other leadership characteristics, which are often attributed to personality traits, are actually variables produced by the pressures of the situation itself.

The *un*promotable supervisor probably has as significant an effect on his subordinates' behavior as the promotable.[54] For when the supervisor is unpromotable, his subordinates' opportunities are restricted as well. Levenson outlines four possible reactions to unpromotability. First, the unpromotable one may *withdraw*, that is, leave either the organization or the profession. However, whether this alternative is feasible depends on still other situational factors, such as age, commitments to the community, and financial and social commitments. Or, he may *resign himself* completely to the situation by abandoning ambition and accept other rewards, such as esteem and seniority. He may also adopt *innovative tactics* designed to make supervisors notice him; he may "overcompete," or try to please indirect superiors, or become assertive at meetings. Finally, the unpromotable may *rebel*, and seek to displace his immediate superior; he may stage a show-down, seek to embarrass his supervisors, display himself more cleverly, and so on.[55]

The presence or absence of opportunity, then, clearly demonstrates the influence that the situation has on behavior. Aggressiveness, withdrawal, and ritualism can be accounted for by the dead-end character of some jobs rather than personality traits. To the extent that the "dead-end" career is characteristic of the teaching profession, the above thesis is a promising point of departure which may have far-reaching significance for an understanding of the behavior of teachers and their supervisors.

THE CRISIS

In periods of organizational crisis, leaders tend to assume more authority, to centralize power, and to demand greater conformity from subordinates. Conceivably, as organizational stress relaxes, decentralization may increase (though not necessarily as quickly as centralization develops from crisis).

In crises, the maintenance of authority is so crucial that leaders sometimes compound them. Arbitrary deadlines, unannounced visits, memoranda, and delays at promotion and contract time are well designed to imbue the organization with an element of minor crisis.

A great deal can be learned about patterns of leadership by observing organizational *tempos*, the rise and decline of pressures generated by deadlines and by close supervision. For example, the school principal will sense that he has more authority, greater responsibility for the school, and more obedience from subordinates when the school is being "inspected" by the superintendent or visited by State Department of Education representatives or by a parent group. Similarly, teachers seem to be more "official" with students on the first day of school, and more informal on the last day; they also probably assert more officiousness at test time. When an important bond issue or consolidation vote is deciding the fate of the school, the administrator tends to become more directive. In general, during crises the consideration role declines in favor of the initiating functions, and subordinates' wishes become less relevant to the concerns of the leadership. Halpin's typology of leaders based on their relative stress on initiation and structure (mentioned in the previous chapter) needs modification to include the cyclical changes in these styles over a period of time as pressures ebb and flow. Theories of action provide the best means for confronting those organizational variables which are complicated by changes through time. We refer to natural system models such as that of Talcott Parsons. More will be said about this toward the end of this chapter.

Precisely because he is granted more authority in times of crises, the leader's position is most vulnerable then. To fail at a time of major crisis usually means the loss of the leadership position, for ineffective leadership is at no time more apparent nor more fateful. Consequently, the defeat of an important bond issue may result in a change of administration.

However, even the administrator who has won his cause—a bond issue, or a fight with the city council or the school board—may have jeopardized his position if he had to wield too much power or alienate too many persons in the process. The successful leader usually makes enemies in the process of a fight, or he may have become so committed to his supporters that the alternatives which remain open to him are so severely restricted by his obligations to them that his power is virtually destroyed. Often his best recourse after an all-out fight is to resign, whether he won or not.

"Busy-ness." An element of crisis, at least the appearance of it, is also used by some subordinates to strengthen their authority. "Busy-ness" is the art of appearing busy. It must be admitted as one of the effective ploys of "impression management." It conveys to observers the subordinate's assumed importance. Indeed, "busy-ness" is so effective that the casual observer cannot distinguish the busy from the productive members of the work group. However, in announcing his presumed importance, the busy person is announcing his ambition to be important, which is sig-

nificant in itself. It is this common element of "ambition" which links the unimportant and the important busy persons.

"Busy-ness" assumes characteristic levels of activity among various occupational groups. Most nurses, for example, complain that they are "too busy." Yet upon observing them at work in hospitals, it seems that the complaint is voiced more consistently than the actual work load would warrant. That is, even when she is not personally busy, a nurse will complain of it.[56] Occupation-wide ideologies create exaggerated illusions of overwork: the statement that "most people in the occupation are busy" comes to mean that "I am busy." Characteristically, occupations striving for greater social status, including those in the process of professionalization, complain most about being busy. It is symbolic of dissatisfaction and ambition. Applied to teaching, the question is, to what extent do teachers' complaints about being overworked reflect dissatisfaction with their *status*. Without implying that most teachers do not work hard, it may be that complaints about hard work are indicative of a more fundamental condition of the occupation—the drive for the status that comes with busy-ness.

STATUS SECURITY

The way a leader performs the leadership function depends to some extent on the risks he is both able and willing to endure. The leader's feelings about the security of this position vary independently of such personality traits as "confidence." His security is dependent on the permanency of his position and the guarantees that he will continue to occupy it. His personal commitment to the position is also important, of course. His position is important to him to the extent that there are few other acceptable jobs available to him. In short, his security is a function of the permanency of the position, his power to hold it, and the available alternatives. During periods of proposed change his position is particularly vulnerable. A principal may resist efforts of the school board to bring in an "outsider" to fill the position for which he aspires. He may also resist the establishment of a position which has authority over his, thus decreasing the authority of his position. But he will not resist such a position if he expects to be promoted to it.

Similarly, for example, whether one reacts conservatively to proposed school district reorganization plans depends not only on whether the plans threaten to displace him, but on his commitment to the job. It is precisely because volunteer groups such as the PTA are *not* fully committed to their position that they are in a position to take a liberal stand on proposed educational changes.[57]

As suggested, the amount of commitment to a position depends upon the relative availability and importance of other positions. For example, as a homeowner and parent, the principal may dislike a new industrial plant locating in his town, but as a taxpayer and professional educator he may see advantages for this school. Whether he reacts conservatively to the plan will depend partly upon the relative commitment to his parental and professional roles.

In addition to personal commitment to his position, it was also suggested that the leader's behavior depends on the security of the position itself. A person needs a certain amount of security to take a risk. So, it can be expected that the leaders who support educational changes hold positions in the largest school systems in the country which have the backing of the nation's most powerful economic and political leaders. This is somewhat contrary to the stereotyped notion that persons most entrenched in power are the most conservative defenders of the *status quo*. This may have some basis in fact; the upper class is both powerful and conservative—but historically the striving middle class has probably been more anxious and insecure about its status than the upper class.

Considering the organization, the question of who is the most conservative leader depends on the relative balance between commitment to office and the security of the office. Where commitment is lowest and the office is most secure, leaders can afford to be less conservative. Conversely, conservatism is highest among leaders who are most committed to relatively insecure, unpowerful positions.

SIZE OF ORGANIZATION

The size of an organization is another facet of the leadership situation. From one study of 500 students who described the groups of which they had been a member, it was found that as a group becomes larger, demands upon the leader's role become greater and more numerous, tolerance for leader-centered direction of group activities increases, and the group generally becomes more bureaucratic—that is, rules are enforced impartially, concern with administrative problems increases, and firmness toward subordinates increases.[58]

These findings have several implications. First, they stress the fact that the problems of leadership become accentuated with bureaucratization. The challenge of leadership in the future will increasingly be the problems generated by bureaucracy, and as these problems become more complex there is little prospect that they will be solved by "experience" or with mediocre training. Second, with his organization increasing in size, it is difficult for the leader to give attention to the special problems of subordinates. It becomes more difficult to display the special leadership qualities of consideration; but perhaps consideration is also less demanded of the official leader as informal leaders assume this function through specialistic divisions of leadership functions. Finally, the evidence points to the dangers of projecting *small* group laboratory studies of leadership to complex organizational settings.

IMPLICATIONS

The skills of leadership, like other skills, are developed through training and experience. However, because of the variety of situational contexts, it is by no means apparent what type of training and experience are most beneficial. However, there is reason to believe that, in face of the overwhelming variety of situations, the most effective training is at the level of principles of interaction and social analysis.

The highly specialized courses in administration, which grew like Topsy, do not seem to reflect these theoretical principles. Separate administrative courses usually offered for elementary, secondary, and other special types of school organization did not emerge as a result of evidence that there are different leadership principles for each level of school organization; they emerged instead from "experience"-oriented assumptions that what is important to know are the specifics of the system. But contrary to this, research evidence indicates there is more similarity between large organizations of different purposes than there is between small organizations of different purposes.[59] Such characteristics as system size, school size, situational influences, complexity, and degree of bureaucratic administration perhaps provide a more meaningful basis of differentiating course work in administrative training programs than grade levels when it comes to examining leadership problems in education.

The situational context also challenges the fetish of experience. Not only may experience in one situation be unrepresentative of another, but it may close alternatives and become so technique-oriented that the broader *principles* of administration are never fully realized.

From the situational viewpoint, the training program is another "situation," and from that perspective it also influences leadership patterns. When, for example, the training program is closely geared, either officially or unofficially, to a *particular* school system, or when the training amounts to on-the-job training, the practical benefits are often more than offset by the lack of perspective and critical imagination which could be derived from systematic consideration of theoretical principles.

The recent trend toward theory development, utilization of social science models, and the application of these to case situations appears to be a move in the right direction. Training programs which include intensive study in discovering the world of reality through social science techniques, and the application of their knowledge to analysis of the administrative world through case studies, field studies, and simulated situational materials are recent and promising additions to preparation programs for administrators in many universities.

Societal Influences

Although the situational approach calls attention to the influence which the immediate setting has on leader behavior, it still underestimates the extent to which social factors condition the leadership role. For beyond the official organizational setting is a cultural one, the outside society, which seriously influences the leader's internal functions.

SOCIAL STATUS

Seeman broached the question of how the leader's social status influences his leadership roles in a sample of seventy-five public school superintendents in Ohio.[60] It was found that their leadership style was affected by their conception of the place they hold in the community and in the general culture. Measures of status were designed to assess (1) the leader's community status, (2) discrepancies between economic and social status, and (3) distortions between the leader's perception of his social status and his followers' perception of it. The measures were compared to the subjects' ideologies of leadership and to subordinates' evaluations of their leadership effectiveness. Regarding status differences, when the leader gave himself high self-ratings on community status, he also claimed high responsibility and authority and a tendency to delegate authority to his subordinates. Also self-rated, high-status leaders who perceived a significant difference between themselves and their followers were judged by subordinates to be receptive to change, communicated frequently with subordinates, and did not express "separateness" (social distance) attitudes toward subordinates. Moreover, those high-status leaders who perceived a relatively great status difference between themselves and their subordinates received favorable evaluations from subordinates.

Because this last finding seems to be contrary to the egalitarian concept of leadership, it bears further consideration. Given a democratic bias among subordinates and a demand for personal consideration, one might expect that subordinates would prefer school executives who are similar to themselves in community status. But the reason they do not is suggested in the same data: there is a positive correlation between "separatism" of superintendents as described by teachers, and percentage increase in teachers' salaries.[61] That is, higher-status leaders were in a better position to enhance their subordinates' positions by virtue of their social distance, that is, the fact that they associated with community influentials rather than with teachers.

Leaders who exaggerated their status in relation to teachers' placement of them, and who "underestimated" teachers' status (relative to teachers' self-placement), exhibited high separatism attitudes toward teachers and were unresponsive to change; these leaders received low ratings from their subordinates.[62] In general, the findings suggest that a basic requisite of good leadership is the ability to accurately judge the attitudes of the total membership on relevant issues (though not necessarily on nonrelevant issues).

The importance of social status appears to lie in the relative security it provides. When the leader is clearly of higher status than his subordinates, he is not threatened by them, and his response is both one of high communication and delegation of authority. Also, his community status places him in a more opportune position to support his subordinates. However, when his community status is not clear, either because of disparities between economic and prestige ratings, or because his own status aspirations create distortion, the leader is threatened by his subordinates. Under these conditions, his leadership style displays personal status enhancing and conserving tactics, which probably reduces his overall leadership effectiveness.

Besides the limited sample and its obviously exploratory nature, one major shortcoming of the study, recognized by Seeman, is that no attempt was made to differentiate the school leaders' status in the local community from his status in the general *society*. The findings may apply only to "locally-oriented" executives, whose reputation and status in the local community is important to them. To the extent that school executives are mobile, often marginal community members, operating in a nationwide or statewide framework, their overriding status identification may typically be to professional and national sources outside the community rather than to the local community. This reservation does not detract from the study's significance, however. It is evident that training in "human relations" and "social skills" do not encompass the leadership task. Leadership training stops no shorter than consideration of the cultural context.

ORGANIZATIONAL VERSUS INSTITUTIONAL LEADERSHIP

The cultural context in which the organization operates determines its ends. The values of the broader society, and the fact that education is a culture-wide institution, have an undeniable influence on policy formulation. However, the institutional values which regulate and guide education are not always compatible with the goals of a particular organization or school. The administrator is sometimes forced to choose between the welfare of his school and the improvement of education. Such a choice constitutes a fundamental aspect of educational leadership. The interplay between organizational and social leadership deserves some brief comment.

Technique and Policy. Much modern administrative thought stubbornly encourages a mythical separation of value and fact, of "policy formulation," and "administration." This analytical separation is difficult to maintain in practice. Which is a matter of policy and which is application of the policy: "learning social studies," "learning history," or a course in American history in the eleventh grade? Each of these statements has been treated by school boards as a policy function within their province. Moreover, the distinction conveniently justifies a passive administrative posture toward policy formulation, and produces in administrators a characteristic retreat from concern with long-range planning and purpose. It also encourages its counterpart, an excessively technical orientation. Accordingly, one writer states of educators: ". . . Those concerned with administration too seldom look beyond the machinery of administration to see what purpose it serves . . ." [63] Newlon's study of eighteen textbooks of administration between 1882 and 1932 reported that fiscal administration, business administration, buildings and equipment were, at that time, the prominent emphasis in courses for preparation of administration. None of the texts were concerned with purposes or factors that influence policy.[64]

Harlow has held that the most neglected and yet among most important aspects of administrative preparation is concerned with the processes of purpose definition. He states, ". . . public, wide-scale education is not a given in any social order; it is a creation. It comes into being as the servant of social purpose. Its content and processes are altered to accommodate changes in these purposes. And education itself bears most intimately upon the formation and revision of the purposes which it in turn is required to serve.[65]

Later writings in educational administration have included statements of purpose, and objectives for education. Moehlman's book, *School Administration*, which was popular during the 1940's and early 1950's, devoted a substantial amount of space to the background of educational science, and purposes of education.[66] Yet, even then, and to some extent today, the statement that the purpose of administration is to "facilitate instruction" was accepted as a *raison de être* for administration. This has become a well-worn cliché among school administrators. It really says nothing except that administration is dedicated to providing machinery, tools, and techniques to develop that which is already set up. The emphasis has been on means, techniques, and operational recipes for "baking a good cake." Ends and means have been considered inappropriate concerns for school administrators. Consequently, to this day the organizational objectives of school organization, as they apply to the internal organization, have not been clearly defined, and very little study or thought has been given to the extent of conflict between the internal organizational objectives of school and the broader societal objectives of education. Developing from this orientation is an ideal image of an administrator who is a skilled technician but essentially neutral, and therefore adaptable to any goal that he is hired to serve.

This "cult of efficiency," the stress of technique-orientation, as it has been called, not only reverses the relative theoretical importance between ends and means, but it obscures the impact that purely technical decisions may have on organizational purposes. The seemingly technical decision to organize schools in terms of the so-called "comprehensive classroom," by including nonintellectual and intellectual students in the same classroom, has made it very difficult to emphasize scholarship in the contemporary classroom. It is misleading to visualize organizational purposes as given, in view of the fact that they are continually being modified by the "technical" decisions that are being made every day. Even so mundane a decision as the purchase of new desks, which on the surface appears to be a purely technical problem best determined by the logic of efficiency, places limits on policy formulation; the use of funds in this way commits the organization to use out-dated textbooks for another year, for example. Once a technical decision has been made, it may be simpler to change policy than reverse the initial decision. Because of the interdependence of means and ends, the administrator is forced into a position of institutional leadership, whether it is recognized as such or not.

Institutionalizing. Although they are created as a technical expedient to achieve certain institutional goals, organizations readily become embodied with value and transformed into temples of tradition. Thus, the five- or six-period day, the summer vacation, and educational television are defended, or resisted, because they disturb traditions and for sentimental reasons other than their demonstrated educational value. This fusion of organizational technique with institutional value is the process whereby means become transformed into ends.

The institutionalizing process has a significant influence on both the nature of internal relationships and on the leadership role. Established ways of doing things provide a source of personal satisfaction, a sense of continuity, a fixed plan of action, and a fixed personal image, all of which commit personnel to a particular way of organizing. But all of this may be costly, for it binds the organization to specific aims and procedures, limits the freedom of leaders, and reduces the organization's ability to adapt to changing conditions.

While reducing the organization's adaptability, institutionalization increases its autonomy: [67] because institutionalization does fix the operation and the responsibilities for it more precisely, external social forces will have less effect upon the organization. One writer suggests that the opportunity and need for strong institutional leadership diminishes as institutionalization proceeds; the need to standardize declines as the homogeneity of personnel increases. Conversely, schools with numerous and ambiguous goals require strong internal leadership; leadership is dispensable only in fully institutionalized stable organizations, and then at the expense of their flexibility.

Institutional Responsibilities. Institutionalization is a two-way process. Besides the fact that the internal operations become infused with value, the organization is forced to live up to the broad institutional values that define the purpose of the school. That is, the institutional setting forces upon the administrator a responsibility for improving education which involves more than the concern with his own school. As Selznick points out, the leader is in a position, to act as an "agent of institutionalization" exerting influence over the haphazard direction of institutions.[68] Because of his official position, and the implications that the decisions which pertain to his school may have throughout the institutional fabric, the executive of the local school does in fact help to shape and direct the development of education in this country.

A leader who is aware of his institutional leadership responsibility will probably proceed differently from one who is not. In fact, Selznick believes that the most serious default of leadership is failure to face up to the problems of *institutional* success while seeking *organizational* success. Of this Selznick says, ". . . he [the leader] fails if he permits sheer organizational achievement, in resources, stability, or reputation to become the criterion of his success. A university led by administrators without a clear sense of values to be achieved may fail dismally while steadily growing larger and more secure." [69] The administrator who resists consolidation, who ignores the problems of his colleagues in other school systems, who fails to support his colleagues before the state legislature or their own school boards, and who seeks to advance his school at the disadvantage of other schools, is failing as an institutional leader even while improving the welfare of his own school. His failure to recognize the implications of his actions for institutional development may permit the organization to drift along a course of short-run adaptations to unintended institutional changes which ultimately sacrifice student and social welfare. But for those leaders who recognize them, institutional considerations provide another aspect of the environment which must be taken into account. The institutional leader will not sacrifice the welfare of education in the name of his school's success. It is this fundamentally moral character of the institutional leadership which makes the administrative task so difficult and challenging.

Internal decisions may be viewed either in terms of the environmental forces which shape them, or in terms of their potential effects on the environment. The decisions which most directly involve the broader society, such as personnel policies and proposed cooperation with other organizations, are usually more crucial ones. At such times, the organization must reappraise its general aims and adapt them without seriously corrupting the institutional values. It is precisely these decisions which have been ignored by the stress on routine problems of management.

Leadership Autonomy. Because of the strategic limitations which the environment places on policy formulation, Selznick proposes that the leader's ability to maintain institutional values depends on his autonomy, that is, independence from outside pressures.[70] As schools are exposed to the demands of outside groups, the special identity and the standards and ethics of professional educators are endangered by countless compromises with public pressure groups.

Selznick proposes that administrative decisions should take into account the different capacity of subordinate units to defend their values from outside pressures. One defense is to attach weaker divisions to stronger units which are capable of defending themselves.[71] However, the risk remains that the stronger unit will encroach on the goals of the subordinate unit. For example, a school administrator may have to justify a large expenditure of funds for data-processing equipment for purpose of research and self-study in education. Because research divisions are not usually recognized as justifiable operations by the public, the data-processing equipment is often incorporated into a stronger, more acceptable department, such as business and finance. But as a result, the research and study tends to be dominated by the finance department, with an emphasis on finance and business rather than learning or instruction.

From this analysis, it is apparent that the decision capacity of administrators can be improved by more effective methods of analyzing power structures. This is not equivalent, Selznick points out, to more "human engineering." "Human engineering" stresses skill in getting others to *accept* decisions, but ignores the basic problems of decision-making itself. Nor will improved decision capacity be achieved by more concern with "public relations;" the role of the leader is not defined by his ability to create *harmony*, which can be achieved regardless of what the end may be.[72] Analysis of decisions must focus on the forces that deter the organization and the pressures which bear on it to sacrifice its distinctive competence, its social purposes.

THE PARSONIAN MODEL

Such an intensive analysis requires, first of all, a more "systematic" view of organizations; that is, executives must be cognitively capable of conceiving the organization as a total entity. Such a cognitive view necessitates a rather abstract reconstruction of the organization's significant components; a *model* meets such requirements and one that is useful and appropriate is that of Talcott Parsons.[73]

According to Parsons, there are four basic levels of organization in a social system which may be said to constitute a structural hierarchy. These levels extend from the most highly unified at the top to the most highly differentiated at the bottom. "At the bottom of the structure, the social system is rooted in the concrete human individual as a physical organism acting in a physical environment."[74] This individual participates in processes of social interaction through various roles. At the top is the so-

ciety as a total system such as a single political collectivity which institu-
tionalizes an integrated system of values. Thus, at the bottom where there
are many millions of individuals, the system is highly segmented and
differentiated; while at the top of the system, unity is attained through
the medium of a common culture and a generally homogeneous value system. The various levels may therefore be interpreted as constituting intermediate structures which are necessary to the functioning of the general system.

The lowest level Parsons designates as the *technical* or *primary* level of
the system, and as such it produces outputs of significance to other levels
and receives inputs from other primary subsystems. The next level may
be designated as the *managerial*. Two further levels are the *institutional*
and the *societal*.

Parsons asserts that all social systems are organized about two major
axes and when these axes "are dichotomized, they define four major
'functional problems,' with respect to which they differentiate." [75] These
four functional categories apply at any of the four fundamental levels of
organization referred to above.

The first of the two major axes represents the relationships that exist
between the organization itself and its external environment:

First Axis

External

Internal

The second axis of differentiation is ". . . central to what Durkheim
called the 'division of labor' through which parts are differentiated and
concomitantly integrated through 'organic solidarity.' It is analogous to
the differentiation between means and ends in terms of action as such." [76]
When these two axes are dichotomized, they produce the following
schema:

	Instrumental (Means)	Consummatory (Ends)
External	The problem of adaptation	The problem of goal-attainment
Internal	The problem of tension-management	The problem of integration

THE FOUR FUNCTIONAL PROBLEMS

In the above schema, the dichotomization of the two organizational
axes generates what Parsons has termed variously as "imperatives,"

and "functional problems." He has used the latter term in his more recent writing.

Although the four functional-problem dimensions may shade into each other, they must be considered as qualitatively differentiated categories. The four categories that are derived are (1) adaptation—the external-instrumental reference; (2) goal-attainment—the external-consummatory reference; (3) latency (or in some of Parsons' writings, pattern-maintenance and tension-management)—the internal-instrumental reference; and (4) integration—the internal-instrumental reference. *The processes which involve these functional categories, or organizational problems, generate what is known as an "action cycle."*

Chandler Morse provides a lucid interpretation of these categories.[77] He points out that goal-attainment represents the termination of an action cycle. By the same token, an action cycle of a subsystem terminates when it has completed its contribution (at any given moment in time) to the functioning of the larger system. Thus, a school system completes an action cycle when it contributes high school graduates to society. This represents the ultimate goal of the school even though there may be a number of highly important intermediate goals—for example, changes in behavior of pupils as they progress through school. More acceptable behavior therefore acts as an output of the school and an input for the societal system because it is required by the societal system in its various functioning.

Adaptation, according to Morse, involves the process of mobilization of the means for goal-attainment and tension-management. The adaptive problem is that of properly perceiving and rationally manipulating the external world for the attainment of ends. The two best simple examples of the adaptive function as interrelated task-conditions are public relations on the one hand, and the securing of facilities, personnel, supplies, and so on, on the other hand, which allows the system to continue to operate as a system pursuing culturally prescribed goals.

Integration is the process of achieving and maintaining appropriate emotional and social relations (1) among those directly cooperating with the goal attainment process, and (2) in the system of action viewed as a continuing entity. The integrative problem generates those management tasks associated with holding cooperating units "in line" and of creating and maintaining "solidarity" despite emotional strains which normally accompany goal-attainment; important to this also is the development of whatever devices are necessary to the sharing of rewards in the cooperation process. In other words, integration concerns the mutual adjustment of units or subsystems from the point of view of their contributions to the effective functioning of the system as a whole.

Latency, or tension-management, is an interlude between successive goal-attainment phases. It is not a period of inactivity, but rather the activities consist of restoring the energies, motives, and values of cooperating units and do not explicitly advance the larger system toward its goals. Generally, this function refers to the maintenance of the structural pattern of the system. Such functions in the public school system could be those of pupil accounting, building maintenance, preparation of lesson plans, in-service training, and general housekeeping responsibility.

The most important thing to remember about this theory of action is that for each level of the hierarchical structure of organization, the next operational level is the most significant. If it is remembered that Parsons specifies four levels in the hierarchy—the technical, or primary; the managerial; the institutional; and the societal—then for a school system we have:

Political entity . . . . Societal level

Fiduciary boards . . . . Institutional level

Administrators . . . . Management levels

Teachers and pupils . . . . Technical, or primary levels

Using the paradigm developed by Parsons, Curtis surveyed as many studies as he could find (going back to 1890) which dealt with the functions of the school superintendent in an attempt to determine which of the four functional problems were dominant. Among other things, he concluded that the superintendent "has primarily been responsible, for performing the 'instrumental' functions of the organization." And Curtis further concludes that more recently ". . . the superintendency not only has become more 'instrumental' but more 'adaptive' " [78]—in other words, more concerned with external-instrumental activity than with internal-instrumental, but in any case not much concerned with what Parsons has called "consummatory" (ends) functions. This reinforces the writers' view that decision analysis must focus on those sociocultural forces that deter from the school's purpose; needless to say, purpose analysis is itself essential.

SUMMARY

Leadership is not best understood by asking the question, *who* can best lead? In the first place this question does not distinguish between the skills necessary to become a leader and those necessary to lead once the position has been acquired. However, besides this theoretical inadequacy, the approach deflects attention from the underlying sociological conditions which influence leadership. The problem posed here is, under what *conditions* can the leader best lead? These conditions which influence leader behavior involve such structural and cultural limitations as mobility patterns, vacancies, crises, organizational size, security of position, and the leader's cognizance of his social position and the institutional purpose that his organization was designed to fulfill. Although it is often more difficult to alter the organizational and cultural setting than to sift out personalities, the approach will clearly have implications for organizational alterations.

It is clear that when decisions are based exclusively on *organizational* welfare, they may violate ideologies of "individual interest" on the one hand, and broader institutional values on the other. Here is where the institutional leader clearly stands apart from the organizational leader in terms of his courage to face the problems of leadership. But if the conditions for staying in power are corrupting, as in the case of some labor union leadership and urban political positions, the demands of the job can erode the good intentions of the most idealistic of leaders. The sociological approach to leadership may eventually call for a major reorganization of school administration itself.

Implicit in any conceptualization of leadership is an assumption of superordinate-subordinate relations even though (as with small, informal groups) it may not be clearly visible. With formal organizations, however, leaders are usually charged with the responsibility of appraising the efforts of subordinates and this inevitably affects morale. In the following chapter, aspects of evaluation and morale are considered.

BIBLIOGRAPHY AND NOTES

1. P. Drucker, *Concept of the Corporation.* Boston: Beacon Press, 1960, p. 6.
2. *Ibid.,* p. 26.
3. M. Seeman, "Role Conflict and Ambivalence in Leadership," *American Sociological Review,* vol. 18, 1953, pp. 371–378.
4. M. Dalton, *Men Who Manage.* New York: Wiley, 1959, p. 247.
5. *Cf.* G. Simmel, *The Sociology of Georg Simmel,* trans. by K. Wolff. Glencoe, Ill.: Free Press, 1950, pp. 183–184.
6. W. G. Bennis, "Leadership Theory and Administrative Behavior," in *The Planning of Change,* W. Bennis, K. D. Benne, and R. Chin. New York: Holt, Rinehart, Winston, 1961, p. 438.
7. W. Moore, *Industrial Relations and the Social Order.* New York: Macmillan, 1951, p. 125.
8. R. M. Stogdill, "Personal Factors Associated With Leadership: A Survey of the Literature," *Journal of Psychology,* vol. 25, 1948, pp. 35–37.
9. *Ibid.*
10. W. E. Henry, "The Business Executive: A Study in the Psychodynamics of a Social Role," *American Journal of Sociology,* vol. 54, 1949, pp. 286–291.
11. R. J. Hills, "The Representative Function: Neglected Dimensions of Leadership Behavior," *Administrative Science Quarterly,* vol. 8, 1963, pp. 83–101.
12. F. Merci, "Group Leadership and Institutionalization," *Human Relations,* vol. 2, 1949, pp. 23–39.

13. T. Newcomb, *Social Psychology*, New York: Dryden Press, 1950, pp. 650–660.
14. J. K. Hemphill, "Leadership Behavior Associated with the Administrative Reputation of College Departments," *Journal of Educational Psychology*, vol. 46, 1955, pp. 385–401.
15. A. W. Halpin, "The Leader Behavior and Effectiveness of Aircraft Commanders," in *Leader Behavior: Its Description and Measurement*, R. Stogdill and A. Coons, eds. Columbus: Ohio State Univ. Bureau of Business Research, #88.
16. S. A. Hetzler, "Variations in Role-Playing Patterns Among Different Echelons of Bureaucratic Leaders," *American Sociological Review*, vol. 20, 1955, pp. 700–706.
17. A. W. Halpin, *The Leadership Behavior of School Superintendents*, Columbus: Ohio State Univ. 1956. However, it is significant that superintendents and staff both believe that the superintendent should initiate far less structure than the boards prefer; the staffs prefer even less structure than superintendents. It is possible that if a leader is high on *either* dimension he is effective in one sense or the other.
18. Quoted by Seeman, *op. cit.*
19. N. Gross, *Who Runs Our Schools?* New York: Wiley, 1958, p. 58.
20. F. E. Fiedler, "A Note on Leadership Theory: The Effect of Social Barriers Between Leaders and Followers," *Sociometry*, vol. 20, 1951, pp. 89–94.
21. Quoted by Seeman, *op. cit.*
22. Cf. *Ibid.*
23. E. Jaques, "Social Systems as a Defense Against Persecutory and Depressive Anxiety," in *New Directions in Psychoanalysis*, XX, M. Klien *et al.*, eds. London: Travistock, 1955.
24. H. H. Jennings, "Leadership and Sociometric Choice," in *Readings in Social Psychology*, G. Swanson, T. N. Newcomb, and E. L. Hartley, eds. New York: Holt, 1952, pp. 312–318.
25. Bennis, *op. cit.*, p. 440.
26. F. J. Roethlesberger, *Management and Moral.* Cambridge, Mass.: Harvard Univ. Press, 1941, pp. 156–159.
27. G. Homans, *The Human Group.* New York: Harcourt, Brace, 1950, pp. 34–40. This discussion has been recently updated by Theodore Caplow, *Principles of Organization*, New York: Harcourt, Brace & World, 1964. For example, "the status order is unequivocal, transitive, and inclusive" (p. 68); "there is a tendency for followers to initiate interaction and for leaders to initiate activity" (p. 99); "the power of a superior over an inferior cannot vary above the power of his own superiors" (p. 107).
28. *Ibid.*, p. 111. This, however, is true only if members do not have inherent value conflicts or other conflicts of interests. A more acceptable statement of the hypothesis is simply that interaction influences the intensity of sentiment; increasing interaction between enemies may merely increase their hostility.
29. *Ibid.*, p. 243.
30. *Ibid.*, p. 247.
31. *Ibid.*, p. 141. Homans conjectures that the higher the rank within the group, the more nearly activities conform to the norms of the group. However, this may be an overstatement, for certainly the leader is also in the best position to violate group norms. For example, he may be late for official meetings without repercussions, and he may be granted certain illegal privileges, such as the use of the custodial staff to take care of his own home. In fact, because he is responsible for making decisions about new situations, his orders and actions often require that he violate at least some established norms. But it is probably true that in no case can the leader violate the fundamental traditions of the group. A more exact statement of the principle, then, is that the leader is one who *knows* the norms of the

group and knows which ones may be violated under certain conditions.

32. Homans, *Ibid.*, p. 145.

33. J. Henry, "Docility, or Giving Teacher What She Wants," *The Journal of Social Issues*, vol. 2, 1955, pp. 33–41.

34. R. Likert, "A Motivational Approach to a Modified Theory of Organization and Management," in *Modern Organization Theory*, M. Haire, ed. New York: Wiley, 1959, pp. 188–189.

35. Homans, *op. cit.*, p. 433.

36. *Cf.* Simmel, *op. cit.*, p. 346.

37. Homans, *op. cit.*, p. 433.

38. *Ibid.*, pp. 434–435.

39. O. Grusky, "Organizational Goals and the Behavior of Informal Leaders," *American Journal of Sociology*, vol. 65, 1959, pp. 59–67.

40. R. O. Carlson, *Executive Succession and Organizational Change: Place-Bound and Career-Bound Superintendents of Schools*. Chicago: Midwest Administration Center: Univ. Chicago, 1962.

41. A. J. Murphy, "A Study of the Leadership Process," *American Sociological Review*, vol. 6, 1941, pp. 674–687.

42. W. T. Carlisle, *Turnover and Demand by Public School Administration*. New York: CPEA Digest Series, Teachers College, Columbia University, 1953.

43. "The Superintendency in New Jersey as Viewed by the Presidents of Boards of Education." Trenton: State Federation of District Boards of Education of New Jersey, 1954.

44. E. E. Mosier and J. E. Baker, "Midwest Superintendents on the Move Typify the Hazards of School Administration; Medium-Size Districts Offer Greatest Security," *The Nation's Schools*, January, 1952.

45. Carlson, *op. cit.*

46. *Ibid.*

47. *Ibid.*, p. 29.

48. *Ibid.*

49. *Ibid.*

50. M. Seeman, "Social Mobility and Administrative Behavior," *American Sociological Review*, vol. 23, 1958, pp. 633–642.

51. L. Reissman and J. H. Rohrer, eds., *Change and Dilemma in the Nursing Profession, Studies of Nursing Services in a Large General Hospital*. New York: Putnam, 1957, pp. 50–80.

52. B. Levenson, "Bureaucratic Succession," in *Complex Organizations: A Sociological Reader*, A. Etzioni, ed. New York: Holt, Rinehart, & Winston, 1961, pp. 262–275.

53. *Ibid.*

54. *Ibid.*

55. *Ibid.*

56. Reissman, *op. cit.*, pp. 262–264.

57. *Cf.* M. Bressler and C. F. Westoff, "Leadership and Social Change: The Reactions of a Selected Group to Industrialization and Population Influx," *Social Forces*, vol. 32, 1954, pp. 235–243.

58. J. K. Hemphill, "Relations Between the Size of the Group and the Behavior of 'Superior Leaders,'" *Journal of Social Psychology*, vol. 32, 1950, pp. 11–22.

59. T. Caplow, "Organizational Size," *Administrative Science Quarterly*, vol. 1, 1957, pp. 485–505.

60. M. Seeman, *Social Status and Leadership: The Case of the School Executive*. Columbus: Bureau of Educational Research, Ohio State Univ., 1960.

61. *Ibid.*

62. *Ibid.*

63. E. V. Sayers and W. Madden, *Education and the Democratic Faith*. New York: Appleton-Century-Crofts, 1959, pp. 418–419.

64. J. Newlon, *Educational Administration as Social Policy*. New York: Scribner, 1934, p. 92.

65. J. G. Harlow, "Purpose-Defining: The Central Function of the School Administrator," in *Preparing Administrators: New Perspectives*, J. A. Culbertson and S. P. Hencley. Columbus, Ohio: University Council for Educational Administration, 1962, p. 62.

66. A. Moehlman, *School Administration: Its Development, Principles and Future in the United States*. Boston: Houghton, Mifflin, 1940.

67. P. Selznick, *Leadership in Administration*. Evanston, Ill.: Row, Peterson, 1957.

68. *Ibid.*

69. *Ibid.*

70. *Ibid.*

71. *Ibid.*

72. *Ibid.*

73. *Cf.* T. Parsons, "General Theory in Sociology," in *Sociology Today*, R. Merton *et al.* New York: Basic Books, 1959, pp. 3–16.

74. *Ibid.*, p. 7.

75. *Ibid.*, p. 5.

76. *Ibid.*, p. 6.

77. C. Morse, "The Functional Imperatives," in *The Social Theories of Talcott Parsons*, M. Black, ed. Englewood Cliffs, N.J.: Prentice-Hall, 1961, pp. 100–120.

78. V. K. Curtis, Jr., "The Evolution of the Public School Superintendency as Indicated by the Application of a Paradigm for the Analysis of Social Systems," unpublished Ed.D. thesis, College of Education, University of Oklahoma, 1965, p. 67.

CHAPTER

13

Evaluation and Morale

A careful study of the matter would seem to
suggest that in many instances supervisory ratings
are basically not efficiency ratings, but compatibility ratings.[1]

THE STRUCTURE of "personnel relations" has many features—
from publicity to morale and from sorting, selecting, and manipulating workers to helping them solve their daily problems. In this
chapter *two* conceptually distinct but interdependent control issues pertaining to the management of personnel will be considered—evaluation
and morale.

It is clear that personnel are evaluated frequently in the decision process; at the time of recruitment, during periods of allocation and realloca-
tion of resources, at promotion time, and in planning sessions. They are
judged daily on the basis of the success or failure of their decisions. The
procedures, criteria, and influences on which evaluation is based are less
than clear. Throughout previous chapters, it was asserted that the structure of the organization has a determining influence on the leadership
process. This chapter will attempt to illustrate how organizational dilemmas can complicate evaluation.

Like the basis of organization itself, there is not one, but a variety of
foundations, or basic criteria, that contribute to the assessment process.
The presence of these criteria, and the dissent regarding them, provide, at
the least, a somewhat insecure occupational foundation for the American
worker.

Underlying the evaluation problem is the question of how stated and
actual operating goals, and workers' relations to them, affect criteria used
to judge and advance personnel.

There are two sets of criteria for evaluating personnel. One is official,
the other informal, and there are certain contradictory factors within and

343

beween each of these. The official bases of evaluation are (a) competence and (b) seniority (sometimes guaranteed by tenure provisions). But unofficially, such criteria as (c) consensus with superiors and (d) personal compatibility with them and with peers are perhaps of equal importance. Accordingly, evaluation is a mechanism for steering the various features of official and informal expectations into a compromise. That is to say, to evaluate personnel is to assess unofficial as well as official demands. The ways in which each of these considerations impinge upon the evaluation process will be considered in the following discussion.

Competence

In practice, the *use* of teacher rating and merit rating plans has been declining during the last half century, even though there is still an occasionally loud public demand for merit ratings. In 1922, nearly sixty per cent of schools surveyed reported use of teacher rating procedures, and in 1940, forty percent reported use of teacher rating; but by 1961, only eight per cent of 539 schools studied by the NEA reported the use of merit rating plans.[2] The reason given by over a third of the schools for discontinuing the plans is that there was no procedure developed for selecting excellent teachers; a third of the schools reported simply that use of the plans created dissension among the staff; another thirteen per cent reported that a sense of injustice was created by attempts to assess teacher competence. Some of the problems involved in using "competence-to-teach" as the criteria of evaluation are reflected in one study of over 3,200 teachers.[3] While eighty-nine per cent of the men and seventy-six per cent of the women said that they were willing to be evaluated on the basis of their competence, only half of those who were willing thought that such evaluation should affect their salaries; and resistance to evaluation increased among those with more than nine years of service. In view of the continued decline in usage of such plans, these inconsistent attitudes toward the use of teacher ratings in the ideal and in practice is indicative of some of the practical problems of evaluation.

Two questions will guide the following discussion of issues which underlie the problem of competence: (1) What is evaluated? and (2) Who evaluates? Although these questions raise analytically distinct issues, in practice they turn out to be aspects of the same problem; reaction to the criteria used frequently depends on who makes the evaluation.

The answer to what is evaluated is initially determined, within broad limits, by several special institutional characteristics of education itself. Each characteristic interferes with complete objectivity toward evaluating teaching competence. Among these limiting characteristics are vague institutional goals, limited observability of teaching performance, and limited advancement opportunity within teaching.

VAGUE GOALS

The goals of most school systems are so vague, and so comprehensive, that it is difficult to measure the extent to which a teacher is contributing to them. "Character development" and "development of intellectual curiosity" are goals which are too vague to provide practical evaluation criteria, and, more important, the simultaneous existence of such independent goals provides little indication of their *relative* importance. For example, is the ability to supervise the extracurricular recreation of students evidence of teaching "competence"? Is such a teacher more competent than an English teacher who "knows her subject" and communicates it well? This is precisely the choice that often must be made at the time of promotion or evaluation for merit pay. The following are among the variety of goals by which teachers may be judged.

1. *Knowledge of subject matter.* In one study, Edson and Davies found that academic achievement was second in a list of five criteria used to select and retain students in nineteen teachers' training institutions, and that academic achievement is emphasized more than it was previously.[4] Also, Shannon found that teaching skill and knowledge of subject matter were among four elements associated with the supervisor's evaluation of 782 elementary and secondary school teachers.[5] Nevertheless, it will become evident as this chapter progresses that such technical competencies are by no means the only important ones in evaluating teachers. According to a study of 419 presidents of liberal arts colleges, for example, it is not intellectual distinction and attainment which college presidents stress in evaluating their faculty, but rather social skills and organizational competency.[6] An earlier study by Kelley also concluded that knowledge and mastery of subject matter were only secondarily related to human and social qualities of personality by college students.[7] Similar evidence pertaining to public school officials will be reported subsequently.

2. *Personality and popularity.* An early attempt to predict the quality of teaching among 560 elementary teachers showed a high correlation between their personality and the "efficiency rank" received from principals ($r = .88$); but, significantly, the relationship with their college marks was less impressive ($r = .29$).[8] To a considerable extent, compatible personalities are essential to the effectiveness of both the informal and formal organization. Since the informal organization relies heavily on consent, work groups are as interested in hiring and rewarding persons who are agreeable and interested in maintaining good relations as are the higher officials. Moreover, teachers with adaptable and pleasant personalities are not as likely to aggravate public relations and discipline difficulties. Personality is visible and understandable to parents, but technical competence is more obscure.

Consequently, in the public schools there is considerable concern about teachers' "personalities," including such traits as kindliness, affection, pleasantness, and so on. Lieberman suggests that the reliance which teachers and the public place on personality in teaching success obscures the basic factor of technical competence, which is a basis of judging other professionals, and that it holds the teacher to a standard of judgment requiring little more skill than that possessed by the average layman.[9]

3. *Public relations and the ability to work with children.* The stress on public relations in education is reflected in a New York law (cited by Lieberman) which provided for merit rating of teachers based on such considerations as their service in youth organizations (such as the Boy Scouts, Girl Scouts, 4-H Clubs, Future Farmers of America, and Future Homemakers of America).[10] In general, teachers are viewed as representatives of the school who are responsible for public diplomacy. Emphasis on "getting along" in the community is reflected in the stress put on the "teacher morality"—manners, proper modes of dress, and other social or sociability qualities that enable the teacher to get along with influential citizens.

Stress on teacher-pupil relationships is similarly partly a function of the need to maintain good public relations with students who report to their parents.[11] Even in schools where attendance is required, the popular teacher can have a function, for large enrollments and satisfied students justify expansion of programs and requirements for more funds. The popular teacher may also be potentially useful for smoothing relationships between students and parents and for acting as a buffer between the administration and other teachers.

4. *Efficiency.* The use of efficiency as a basis of evaluation is so prevalent that it is sometimes equated to teacher-rating in the literature. Efficiency itself appears in a variety of forms. Discipline in the classroom, for example, is stressed in the name of efficiency—a disciplined classroom is efficient. Conversely, the so-called progressive classroom is objectionable to many administrators and parents partly because the noise seems, in a bureaucratic setting, to be a characteristic of distasteful inefficiency. In fact, Shannon reports that poor discipline in the classroom is the major problem contributing to the failure of public high school teachers,[12] which corroborates a negative correlation ($r = -.53$) between discipline in the classroom and teacher success reported by Sommer.[13]

Fearful of the students' insubordination, each new teacher faces every class period dimly aware of an impending clash with some student and the subsequent challenge to his authority. In dealing with insubordination, the teacher is necessarily dependent on his own resources, for, as Gordon notes, if too many children are sent to the principal's office, the principal hears only the child's side of things and the teacher's reputation is endangered by the public assumption that he cannot handle his own problems. Sensing this, children soon learn when and how much they can misbehave in class before the teacher will risk bringing in a higher authority. The anxiety in such an atmosphere breeds rumor. In one study, for example, it was rumored that the principal kept a mythical "black book," in which he recorded the number of students which teachers sent to the office, and to which he referred at contract time.[14] In general, it seems that the less support given to a teacher by the principal, the more frequent informal compromises will develop in the classroom which, in effect, increases the relative authority of students.

Ability to "handle large classes" is another mark of efficiency. This, however, is sometimes a dubious ability in that it may force a disturbing wedge between the teacher, the administrator, and the department head. Department heads and the teaching staff tend to favor the small-class philosophy of teaching, which, of course, justifies departmental expansion in direct proportion to enrollment increases. However, administrators, aware that they are judged partially for their ability to keep costs down as enrollment increases, are forced to look for alternatives to staff expansion, which easily predisposes them to at least seriously consider larger classes. A teacher who is ready to handle large classes, and can rationalize the practice, may be approved by the administration; but partly for the same reason he may suffer some disapproval of his peers or department head.

Disputes over teaching pedagogy may also be viewed as part of the larger problem of teaching efficiency. Within any profession, certain technical procedures are considered to be more effective than others. Their use is considered in evaluation. At the same time, however, the stress on technique provides a convenient substitute for the more difficult concern of evaluating the ultimate end which that technique is supposed to achieve. In some cases, the mere use of a technique may be taken as sufficient evidence of competence, although its use obviously does not guarantee the hoped-for outcome. By judging technique, administrators and supervisors may be deluded into assuming that somehow the teaching outcome is being evaluated.

LIMITED OBSERVABILITY OF OUTCOME AND OF PERFORMANCE

Another characteristic of teaching which makes it difficult to evaluate is that, at best, there is only limited *observability* of the teaching outcome and of the teaching performance itself. In other words, even if there were consensus on goals it would be difficult to assess the extent to which teachers are fulfilling them because of a number of factors. *Bureaucratization* of education is a major one. Because of the extreme interdependence of different teaching functions, no one teacher can be held responsible, for example, for the mathematical performance of a particular person, or even for a particular class. Spelling, to take an exteme case, in considered to be the responsibility of almost every teacher throughout the various levels of the school system. It is difficult, then, to determine the degree of influence which an eighth-grade English teacher has had on the career of a successful group of businessmen, or delinquents (who in both cases may be bad spellers). Even if it were possible to do so, the fact is that most decisions that the teacher and administrator make are seldom re-evaluated after a lapse of time. In fact, in some schools with high personnel turn-over rates, persons are not around long enough to be evaluated.

In the face of these problems, administrators and teachers have searched for an objective way of assessing merit independent of direct observation of teachers at work. The substantial number of investigations, tests, and measurements relevant to efficiency and effectiveness reported in the literature attest to the sincerity of the educators' concern. National testing programs for students, student test scores on various subjects mat-ter areas, and teaching tests provide a limited, but empirical, means of judging specific areas of merit. Despite such research, however, the fact remains that there is little consistency in the rating criteria actually used by students, teachers, and administrators, and inconsistency characteristic within each group as well. Over twenty-five years ago, for example, Brookover reported that correlations between students' and administra-tors' ratings of teachers were not significant. Ratings by two adminis-trators of the same teachers were as low as $r = .25$, and ratings among twelve students, although higher, were still relatively low ($r = .63$).[15] Similarly, Lins reported little relation between either pupil or supervisory ratings of teacher success and other measures of competence and achieve-ment.[16]

Students and administrators not only use different criteria of teaching competence, but, as already suggested, they have differential opportunities in which to directly observe the teaching performance itself. While im-mediate superiors have the authority to visit classes in most schools, the practice is not utilized systematically, especially in larger urban systems. Visitation poses supervisory problems; it is also time-consuming. While most administrators advocate class visits as an effective way to evaluate teachers, they themselves do not place primary reliance on it because of insufficient time to visit.

It seems likely that different bases of evaluation will be used when the performance of the person being evaluated is immediately observable and when it is not.[17] In the latter case, more stress is placed on attitudinal conformity than where performance is directly observable. Thus, what is objectively irrelevant to technical competence—personal attitudes and values—may assume major importance when the performance itself is not public.

On the basis of a large-scale study conducted by NEA's Research Division, a little more than twenty per cent of elementary teachers indi-cated they had not been observed teaching; 33.9 per cent of secondary teachers indicated they had not been observed.[18]

Another interesting result of the NEA study was the finding that superintendents were more confident in their school system's evaluation program than were principals, and they in turn had more confidence than the teachers. Negative expressions toward evaluation were voiced by 38.3 per cent of elementary teachers and by 54.7 per cent of secondary teachers.[19] Major criticisms were that evaluation was inaccurate, and that administrative staffs were too busy to evaluate effectively.[20]

LIMITED OPPORTUNITY FOR ADVANCEMENT AND STANDARDIZATION OF WORK

The problems of adequately rewarding and evaluating public school teachers are compounded by supply and demand fluctuations characteristic of employed professionals. Among professional workers especially, where the initial screening procedures are relatively rigorous, a number of people are likely to be competent enough to qualify for a limited number of high positions. Beyond a point, the relative competence of a person is difficult to measure; considering licensure, most people can agree that they are "competent," without having any clear measure of its degree. Teaching jobs have been deliberately designed and standardized so that many teachers of average ability and experience can qualify for most other teaching positions in their field. It is this quality about large-scale organizations that make interchangeability and replacement, and therefore continuity, possible. But this quality also accounts for the restlessness of competent teachers who are unlikely to be recognized for exceptional ability through no fault of their own. The result is that, without refined standards of measurement to distinguish among the group of highest competence, and confronted with relatively uniform teaching positions and conditions, officials can never adequately *reward all* competent teachers; and favorable evaluation that brings no official reward is rather tasteless for those who must try to comprehend the dubious honor.

Standardization does not encourage the chief executive to reward officially some of the very behaviors which some school administrators would say characterize a meritorious teacher. Creativity, novel innovations, imaginative planning, unique methods, and so on are all limited by standardization of jobs. Not only are teaching jobs standardized, but the means of promotion are also; and the concept of equal work for equal pay permeates the organization. Standardized promotion is limited to single salary schedules composed of even steps based on experience and preparation.

When teaching jobs are highly standardized, the individual teacher (no matter how meritorious) has little or no control over the situation. Thus "competence" is of dubious value if it is constrained by standard work procedures. Even if the objectives were clear and if measures could be developed to assess the effects of teacher performance on goal attainment, the underlying question—whether it was the teaching or the standardization of the teacher's job that generates results (either negatively or positively)—would remain unanswered. Teaching positions, as they are generally organized today, allow the teacher complete freedom so long as he confines each class session to forty-five to fifty minutes, meets five sessions a day, and tends to other duties carefully prescribed as to length of time, time of day, and student personnel involved; he must also agree to follow a system-wide course of study and the preferred teaching methods. Until teaching positions become less standardized, and the teacher has real control over what he does and the way he does it, it would seem that evaluation of the teacher and his effects on the goals of the organization may be perfunctory.

IMPLICATIONS

Because our measures of competence are not refined enough to select those few who can qualify for limited rewards on that basis alone, for all but those of the most exceptionally obvious merit selection will naturally be based on other than technical performance. This helps to explain why, in many cases, otherwise "fair" administrators use officially irrelevant criteria to make decisions about promotion—there are simply too many candidates qualified on a purely objective basis. It also injects a note of arbitrariness into even the most objective of existing reward systems, and it is the actual basis for prevalent feelings among subordinates that those promoted over them are no more qualified than themselves. However, while the use of criteria other than competence may seem logically arbitrary from the standpoint of teaching excellence and Johnny's education, these other criteria are not necessarily irrelevant to the needs of the *organization* and to the prejudices and values of the broader society.

Seniority and Tenure

Partly because the task of judging competence is so difficult and because of the persistent intrusions of personal and community values and certain arbitrary judgments, seniority has developed as another official basis of evaluation. Particularly where longevity rights are guaranteed by tenure provisions, seniority has the advantage of providing a clearly assessable and a culturally sanctioned basis of recognition. The seniority principle is so well accepted that it occasionally takes precedence over the principle of ranked authority, as in cases where experienced secretaries unofficially "run" the office for the inexperienced principal.

ADVANTAGES

Although seniority implies no direct assessment of competence, it has a sense of social justice about it. As an evaluation standard, it is less subject than competence to ambiguous, unknown, irrelevant, and arbitrary factors. It might simply be said that seniority is easier to measure. Seniority provides official recognition for loyalty to the system, which will probably be taken into consideration anyway, and it is not normally subject to the personal whims of the person evaluating.

Seniority also inhibits any impulse toward extreme competition among workers. In this respect, it establishes an age-graded, ascribed status system which helps to counteract some of the visible pressures typical of a highly achievement-oriented society. For although competitive achievement is usually identified as democratic, it has some very "undemocratic" consequences. For example, older persons who have not achieved as well as their younger successful counterparts are left without recognition at the end of their careers. At the other extreme, persons who have achieved while young may suffer a "destination sickness" in which they are left relatively early without further goals to pursue. Seniority provides a remedy for those who suffer in the first case, and a life-long goal without the pain of anxiety and persistent revisions of goals that an achievement-orientation system requires.

Although it is obvious that seniority provides some advantage to workers, the principle also saves administrators from some of the difficult problems already discussed which are inherent in attempts to evaluate the technical competence of subordinates. It permits administrators to escape some of the frustrations of evaluation and the consequent friction and guilt over arbitrary and misinformed judgments; yet it systematically provides recognition for loyalty to the organization in the face of professional orientations and other cosmopolitan influences that undermine commitment to it.

DISADVANTAGES

While experience may provide the necessary practice that enhances competence, the mere fact of being on the job for a specified time is obviously not a sufficient measure of competence. Seniority does not guarantee competence. The absence of a necessary relation between these two official alternatives is a frequent structural source of conflict. Each factor, seniority and competence, justifies a different conception of justice and represents alternative philosophies of recognition, status achievement, and status ascription.

Seniority obviously does not encourage the conflict between persons of various levels of training and skill within the organization that occurs when achievement is stressed; but the use of seniority in an achievement-oriented society encourages another form of conflict—conflict between the generations. It may be expected that younger, well-trained individuals will support the criterion of competence, while older and less well-trained persons prefer to rely on seniority guarantees; that seniority frequently prevails is reflected in the reluctance of organizations to demote their incompetents.

The pervasiveness of conflicts between the generations is perhaps best symbolized by the disc jockey, Dick Clark, whose popular newspaper columns are devoted to explaining children to their parents, and explaining parents to their children. His publication of teen-age vocabularies to enlighten parents on the meaning of their children's language is a commentary on the gulf that exists between adults and adolescents today. In an era when an entirely novel vocabulary, dress, speech, taste, and motive accompanies each new generation, it seems reasonable that younger teachers are best suited to communicate with youth and to understand their perspective. Seniority, however, accelerates the average age of the most esteemed teachers and administrators, which in turn contributes to conservatism of the public schools and constricts their flexibility. On the other hand, however, by the very nature of their age, older teachers may receive more respect from the older, often influential adults in established communities. Comparisons of school systems with age extremes of teachers and administrators would be enlightening. In any event, the *prospect* that the seniority principle may defeat the essential characteristic of teaching—communication with youth—underscores the neglected fact that it is not the amount, but the type of experience, which is most relevant to teaching competence.

As a reward for sheer loyalty to the organization rather than for professional achievement, seniority simply encourages incipient discrepancies between a person's professional reputation and his official rank. Since seniority is, at best, incompletely transferable between organizations, the prospects of official advancement may inhibit mobility within the profession to jobs of equivalent rank but of greater prestige; conversely, professional advancement sometimes requires a sacrifice of seniority which the newcomer must normally expect to encounter. As a result of these disparities, senior employees, whose major achievement may be no more than having endured in the local system, can capture influence far in excess of their demonstrated professional competence or acknowledged perspectives on education.[21] There is a strong possibility that because of the dilemmas incorporated into professional and employee roles in rewarding seniority, professionalism is undermined.

To place the discussion in its proper perspective, it must be noted that strains from simultaneous use of seniority and competence are part of the broader problems produced by the competing representative and authoritarian styles of bureaucracy. Representative bureaucracy, where authority is based on skill and knowledge, logically requires that competence be rewarded; but in authoritarian, or punishment-centered, bureaucracy authority rests on sheer incumbency in office, which would logically seem to require recognition for seniority in the office. Since most organizations represent compromises between these bases of authority, it is hardly surprising that most organizations are also confronted with the dilemmas that accompany these inconsistent dual systems. Significantly, in choosing between these evaluation methods, the administrator is implicitly moving the organization toward one or the other bureaucratic type.

TENURE

Struggles to guarantee seniority rights seem to have paralleled the history of seniority systems. In 1931, only twenty-eight per cent of school districts sampled in a study reported the use of tenure or protective contracts, but only twenty years later, fifty-six per cent of the school districts in an NEA study used tenure or protective continuing contracts to protect their teachers; twenty-eight per cent used spring notification types of continuing contracts, and only fifteen per cent used annual or periodic election. The use of tenure appears to be associated with urbanization and with the bureaucratization of public education.[22] Only forty-six per cent of the smallest cities reported tenure arrangements, compared to ninety-four per cent of the largest cities. Six per cent of cities over 500,000 reported annual election, compared to one-fifth of the cities between 2,500 and 5,000.[23] Continued efforts of teachers to secure and maintain protective rights are evident in the fact that seventeen of fifty-four legal cases involving teachers reported in 1960 concerned questions of tenure.[24] It is doubtful that this situation has changed much since that time, although the effect of more militant teacher organizations remains to be rigorously examined.

One reason for the popularity of tenure is perhaps implicit from an earlier study which reported that forty-four per cent of the teachers interviewed expressed concern that they might lose their jobs regardless of their competence. Between one-third and one-half, feared other types of arbitrary treatment, such as transfer to a less desirable job, withholding of promotion, false charges by authorities that would hurt their reputation, and withholding annual contracts until after other teachers had received theirs.[25] The struggle of teachers to implement tenure provisions appears to be motivated by these anxieties.

The actual guarantees that tenure does in fact provide should not be overexaggerated. One NEA study of dismissals of experienced teachers reports that thirty-five per cent of the dismissals occurred in cities with annual elections and thirty-seven per cent in cities with continuing contracts, but twenty-two per cent, or one out of every five dismissals, occurred in cities with permanent tenure.[26]

Conformity

The conformity of the American people has recently attracted unprecedented attention among scholars and social critics. It is one type of *informal* evaluation criterion. Although the fact is sometimes ignored, contemporary statements of the problem do not differ greatly from those of y Gasset and de Tocqueville a century ago. That is, it is not the fact of *conformity* itself which is unique to the modern setting; men, in fact, have always conformed. It is *what* is conformed to that constitutes whatever is unique in the modern situation.

HISTORICAL ANTECEDENTS

Historically, a shift has occurred between conformity in what one writer terms the "private" and the "public" realms.[27] Pressures to conform in work habits appear to have increased as work places have been transferred from the privacy of home to public offices. Since the industrial revolution, work has become a public activity of course. Workers and clients are on public display in large shops, offices, and even classrooms under scrutiny of co-workers and the public. Partly as a result, a person's success in his career has become more dependent on what other people think of him (implicit in the notion of evaluation) and less dependent on his own achievements. The necessity of group work has further made interpersonal compatibility a precondition of success. All of this has promoted emphasis on conformity to others—the boss, the public, co-workers. Accordingly, the individual tends to be evaluated in terms of how his behavior reflects on the propriety of the organization and how well he fits into it. He is an approximation of the model of the "organization man" whose loyalties, identity, and values are determined by pressures to get along with others.

CONFORMITY IN EDUCATION

The emphasis on conformity and compatibility also inescapably finds its way into the standards by which public school teachers are evaluated.[28] The student-teaching recommendation forms used by a bureau of recommendations in a large state university preparing teachers contain more than a hint of this influence. The supervisors check the student's ability or disability, at some point on a scale, for several criteria, among them the following: (1) How does his personal appearance impress you? (2) How does his personality affect other people? (3) Is he emotionally well poised? (4) How does he react to suggestions? (5) How do pupils react toward him? (6) Does he express himself clearly? (7) What is his attitude toward pupils in school activities? (8) What is the atmosphere of his classroom? (9) How does he control unexpected situations?

TABLE 3
Teacher Evaluation

Teacher: Socrates

	RATING (HIGH TO LOW)	COMMENTS
A. *Personal Qualifications*		
1. Personal appearance	1 2 3 4 (5)	Dresses in an old sheet draped about his body
2. Self-confidence	1 2 3 4 (5)	Not sure of himself—always asking questions
3. Use of English	1 2 3 (4) 5	Speaks with a heavy Greek accent
4. Adaptability	1 2 3 4 (5)	Prone to suicide by poison when under duress
B. *Class Management*		
1. Organization	1 2 3 4 (5)	Does not keep a seating chart
2. Room appearance	1 2 3 (4) 5	Does not have eye-catching bulletin boards
3. Utilization of supplies	(1) 2 3 4 5	Does not use supplies
C. *Teacher-Pupil Relationships*		
1. Tact and consideration	1 2 3 4 (5)	Places student in embarrassing situation by asking questions
2. Attitude of class	1 (2) 3 4 5	Class is friendly
D. *Techniques of Teaching*		
1. Daily preparation	1 2 3 4 (5)	Does not keep daily lesson plan
2. Attention to course of study	1 2 (3) 4 5	Quite flexible—allows students to wander to different topics
3. Knowledge of subject matter	1 2 3 4 (5)	Does not know material—has to question pupils to gain knowledge
E. *Professional Attitude*		
1. Professional ethics	1 2 3 4 (5)	Does not belong to professional association, PTA
2. In-service training	1 2 3 4 (5)	Complete failure here—has not even bothered to attend college
3. Parent relationships	1 2 3 4 (5)	Needs to improve in this area—parents are trying to get rid of him

Recommendation: Does not have a place in Education. Should not be rehired.

From J. Gauss, *Phi Delta Kappan*, Jan. 1962 (Used with permission.)

(10) Are the lessons well planned and executed? (11) What use does he make of materials of instruction? (12) Does he show initiative and ambition? (13) How does he provide for equipment? (14) Will he be likely to grow in effectiveness? The first five of these criteria concern interpersonal relations, ability to impress others and willingness to conform to suggestions. The effect of such considerations on the quality of public school teachers is dramatized in a satirical evaluation of Socrates by John Gauss, on a standard teacher evaluation from (Table 3). Significantly, by the official criteria, the grim conclusion is that Socrates would not qualify as a teacher in the public schools.[29]

There is little empirical evidence of the importance that schools place on conformity relative to technical competence. However, in one study Stout found that eighty-five per cent of 385 institutions preparing teachers said that their program required academic admission standards at least equal to undergraduate preprofessional programs, but nearly half of these institutions said that they consider personal, social, ethical fitness *more frequently* than any other single factor in the admission of teaching candidates to their program.[30] This stress on general personal acceptability bears a remarkable resemblance to the concept of the "organization man." [31]

IMPLICIT MEANINGS OF CONFORMITY

Actually, the concept of "the organization man" turns out to have a confusing array of meanings. The concept of conformity itself is multidimensional, each dimension having several referents. There are, however, two major meanings of conformity which are particularly relevant to the evaluation problem. Each is reflected in well-known ideologies of success. On the one hand, there is a popular belief that "it isn't what you do, but whom you know, that counts in getting ahead." This criterion is based on compatibility or "sentiment," characteristic of congeniality and primary groups. On the other hand, there is a widespread belief that being a "yes-man" is a definite advantage in the promotion system. Whereas the first ideology suggests the importance of compatibility— personal friendship, connections, or simply popularity—as the basis of advancement, the second ideology stresses agreement with the *ideas* of others (rather than personal feelings toward them) as the basic ingredient of advancement.

Each quality stresses a different aspect of the informal organization, sentiment and ideas. Together, consensus and compatibility constitute a separate and dual system of informal evaluation criteria. Not only may each conflict with the official standards as discussed, but they may create inconsistent informal expectations.

Consensus

SIGNIFICANCE

Today approximately ninety per cent of the population earns its living in large-scale organizations. The success of these people is as much a function of other people's evaluation of them as it is of their own performance. They must cooperate and meet the approval of others in order to succeed. Accordingly, the modern hero is portrayed in literature and in mass media as a person who can subordinate his personal interests to those of the organization.[32] This context of work has had some very important consequences on the nature of organization as Durkheim, Weber, and more recently Whyte, have observed.[33] Apparently, the facility to agree with the opinions of superiors is an effective way to get ahead in public school teaching, at least if the findings of one study are any indication. Guba and Bidwell found that the ratings of effectiveness which principals give to their teachers are functions of the degree to which the principal perceives that the teacher conforms to his expectations of the teacher's role.[34] There is, in other words, a direct correlation between the agreement of principals with teachers on work roles and the teacher's rated effectiveness.

ASSUMPTIONS

There are at least three assumptions which underlie a variety of designs to increase consensus. The first assumption is that it is possible to adjust persons to organizations. Personality-testing programs can be utilized to screen out or reallocate students, teachers, and administrators who are potentially or actually troublesome. The widespread reliance on personality tests is undoubtedly having unnoticed effects on the perceptions of students and of teachers. In fact, these tests probably fix the place of personnel on a prejudged basis in the same way that family background has traditionally done. It is as difficult for a student or teacher to "live down" his test results as his family's station in life. This is all the more remarkable in view of the low predictability of most of the tests.

Some vigorous designs on consensus seek to "re-educate" personnel to a common value system; seminars on *how* to listen, *how* to handle discipline, and the *art* of compromise are among examples of such programs, as well as thousands of in-service education programs devoted to similar themes.

The second assumption is that deviation arises from either personality problems or lack of understanding. To deal with the personality problems, a battery of personality tests, such as the Minnesota Multi-Phasic Inventory (MMPI), may be given to staff and students to discover their personal inadequacies; nonconformity may thus be first perceived as a form of emotional instability. For example, in at least one state university women students who repeatedly violated curfew were customarily given MMPI's; in one case, it was (purportedly) given to a college man who wore odd-colored clothing and to a married graduate student who sponsored raucous parties. When the personality is found to be sound, explanation next turns to some "misunderstanding" which the efficiency expert is called upon to correct. Neither approach recognizes the possibility that nonconformists may have reasonable disagreement with the official values, and that value conflicts are the basic cause of low morale, low productivity, and other forms of nonconformity.

Finally, those who design procedures to improve consensus assume that consensus is necessary for organizational effectiveness. As a matter of fact, there is little empirical evidence concerning what consensus does to or for organizational effectiveness. One study shows the expected relation over the short run.[35] On the other hand, Rose found that industrial workers who were critical of their labor union were also among those most loyal to its principles.[36] It is possible that over the long run, consensus merely perpetuates ineffective practices. In a Michigan study relating to a variety of communication issues concerning schools, it was concluded that patrons who indicated high satisfaction with schools were least well-informed about them, while those who were most critical were well-informed.[37] The custom of appointing and tolerating only agreeable subordinates effectively insulates officials from critics whose insights might have otherwise benefited their administration. In fact, it is precisely this effect of consensus that stagnates governments in power too long and, conversely, adds vigor to new administrations. The dilemma is that, although there is an immediate need for subordinates who are loyal to administrative aims, the practice of strategically replacing disloyal with loyal personnel limits the official's perspective and stagnates his decisions.

CONSENSUS IN THE CLASSROOM

Jules Henry describes the process by which American school children learn to conform to the teacher in the modern classroom.[38] Henry suggests that the child learns to be docile, or to conform without the use of external force; relatively few of the child's acts are a function of personal choice, Henry maintains, but rather the child reacts in anticipation of the will of others. For example, in one situation second-grade pupils are shown a film about birds, and asked by the teacher, "Did the last bird ever look like he would be blue?" The children don't understand the slant of the question, so the teacher rephrases the question: "I think he looked more like a robin, didn't he?" The children then respond "yes" in chorus. The children, in other words, seek to answer the way the teacher desires, as indicated by the fact that they cannot reply until her slant is made known. Henry concludes that the teacher reinforces a tendency for children to destructively criticize one another, which heightens their anxiety. They seek to alleviate this anxiety by gaining the teacher's approval through giving her the correct answers. This, he concludes, is a peculiarly middle class kind of docility based on fear of loss of love rather than fear of corporal punishment.

One unanticipated consequence of the emergence of representative forms of bureaucracy in the classroom is a modified basis of the teacher's authority. In its extreme form, consensus is a threat to the traditional basis of knowledge which is scholarship. There is always the danger that the principle, "everyone has the right to his own opinion," will be translated to mean that everyone's opinion is equally right; in such an environment, there is a temptation to settle matters of empirical controversy by vote rather than by scholarship.[39]

Students' opinions determine the subject matter, its treatment and resolution. In the name of achieving agreement among students through class discussion, the teacher may have to compromise the very nature of evidence itself—evidence derived from scholarship. The teacher who stresses scholarship—the intellectual "authority" with ideas of his own—seems out of place in a "democratic" classroom, while the teacher who gets "a lot of discussion going" is considered good, sometimes because he is engaged in the process of developing consensus. In the long run, the reputation of a teacher may depend more upon his ability to involve students in discussions about a subject, than upon his knowledge of that subject.

Compatibility

Unlike consensus, which is a congruence of view and opinion, compatibility is based on like feeling or sentiments. It may be said that consensus is characteristic of the informal *structure* of the organization, while compatibility concerns friendship *sentiments* of the people there. Excessive stress on sentiment (for example, friendship and personal approval) is sometimes deplored as "togetherness." In quest of approval, men develop what has been called an "other-directed" personality which is malleable to the personal values and ideals of others and to group pressures.[40]

ITS FUNCTION

While togetherness produces a "groupy" society ruled by the "sales personality," and while it may be criticized for its lack of inner-directness, togetherness nevertheless represents a solution to a fundamental problem of modern man—the tendency for a specialized society to lose its solidarity and humane perspective. It provides men with a form of group security which replaces extended kinship and the security of the feudal system of the preindustrial era. Approval, belongingness, and friendship help to ease the tensions of an anxious and competitive world.[41] Where one's friends and competitors are at the same time in the work group, the need to regulate competition and reinforce friendship is particularly acute.

COMPATIBILITY IN EDUCATION

"Togetherness" has made a number of inroads in education. Among its obvious forms are the proliferation of conferences, workshops, project teams, buzz sessions, discussion groups, and committees. These group efforts partly reflect an explosion of knowledge, and of population, and emergent problems that no specialist, isolated in scattered segments of the organization and throughout the country, can face alone. As a consequence, however, people of diverse backgrounds, representing distinct personal and group interests, are brought into close, short-term contacts, which for these very reasons are partially disruptive. Under these conditions, it is perhaps natural that attention turns to compatibility as a means of integrating work groups. There are general norms which emerge to encourage teachers to get along with one another, with the public and with the administration—the nobility of compromise, the ability to "accept" suggestions, intolerance of disturbance, stress on flexibility of ideas, the impropriety of maintaining a rigid principle, and the propriety of disguising true feelings to prevent fundamental underlying hostility and resentment from becoming apparent; all of these and more are "togetherness" norms. Amiability is as admired in teachers as it is in salesmen, and those who do not "fit in," who are too sensitive, dogmatic, or competitive are looked upon as malcontents, insubordinates, and generally unsatisfactory workers. Although such judgments have always affected personal and community reputations, it is significant that today such judgments are very important for career advancement.

Precisely how these considerations affect the evaluation of teachers is still a subject of speculation. In one report, Singer found that the social competence of teachers benefits their success.[42] Several measures of success—teacher self-rating; ratings by local administrators, state department of education, and students; and observation—were intercorrelated with a variety of measures of social competence, including sociometric scores, judges' opinions of teachers' social competence and teachers' self-ratings. Twenty-five of fifty-five correlations were significant. In further analyses, the three most successful teachers received twice as many friendship choices from students as the three least successful teachers.[43] From their review of such literature, Stiles and others conclude, "A careful study of the matter would seem to suggest that in many instances supervisory ratings are basically not efficiency ratings, but compatibility ratings." [44]

Under the rule of compatibility, the teacher who is isolated, who is "unadjusted," who refuses to belong to the proper community associations or to attend the proper social functions, appears "incompetent." Indeed, "belongingness" appears to be emerging as a new secular morality which is replacing the Puritanical standards by which communities controlled teachers in the past. The proportion of parents who expect teachers to attend or to participate in activities in the community is probably double the proportion who expect them to attend church.[45] Teachers are expected to join local civic and social organizations, attend PTA meetings, consult with parents, visit students an their homes, chaperone extracurricular activities, sponsor Boy Scouts, Campfire Girls and other adolescent activities, and in general to be in "the swim of things"; organized interpersonal activities are precisely where togetherness, or compatibility, pays off. Kuvlesky and Buck report that eighty per cent of the teachers in a Pennsylvania sample had higher community participation scores than the average white-collar workers, and one-third of them participated at a higher rate than top business and professional people.[46] But although they participate *in* community activities, teachers are not *of* them; they seldom hold influential positions. Cook and Greenhoe found that with the exception of religious organizations (where one-fourth of the teachers were officers) only a small minority of teachers hold offices in the community organizations in which they participate, and very few of them are officers in the most influential community organizations.[47]

Leadership skills also reflect these developments. In effect, the modern teacher must have at his command a set of techniques for guiding, persuading, and perhaps manipulating others in order to secure cooperation without jeopardizing his own popularity. "Expressive" leadership, or the ability to control the sentiments of the group and maintain its morale, is at least as important as instrumental leadership, which concerns the achievement of basic group tasks. Teaching skill is probably strongly dependent on personal relations with students and their opinions of the teacher as a person. Brookover, for example, reports a correlation of $r = .86$ between the interaction of teachers with their students and their students' ratings.[48]

Implications

CONSENSUS VERSUS COMPATIBILITY

One preliminary attempt to explore the relative importance of consensus and friendship raised some problems of general importance for administrative and organizational theory.[49] Although the study concerned hospital staff nurses, the implications are relevant to teaching. Supervisors were asked to use several criteria to evaluate the competence of forty-eight nurses working under them. These ratings were compared with (1) the consensus between nurses and their superiors on an inventory of items pertaining to their specific job definitions, and (2) the friendship superiors showed toward each nurse (based on her desirability as a person to work with, as a friend, and as a lunch partner). It was found that consensus with superiors was not significantly related to success ratings, but friendship choices were. Superiors tended to like high-success nurses better than low-success nurses. This modest finding calls attention to a significant aspect of the evaluation process, for it suggests that sentiment may play a more important role in the way supervisors evaluate their subordinates than job definitions.

Friendships formed at work are normally determined by the basic values of the society. Several studies suggest that friendships based on ethnic, religious, and class similarities are preconditions for the success of industrial employees. For example, in a few factories it was found that being a Mason, associating with the right crowd, being Republican, being a member of the yacht club, and "proper connections" were all factors associated with promotion through the supervisory ranks.[50] In one case, workers went on strike when a member of a minority ethnic group was promoted from among them to foreman. Collins also reports that sponsorship and rejection for promotions at the factory he studied were based on ethnic background. Certain jobs were held by the ethnically acceptable, and large areas of the hierarchy were almost completely occupied by members of one ethnic group. The principle was so well incorporated that a work stoppage materialized when management went over the foreman's head and chose a subforeman for him who was not a member of the dominant group. Similar opposition, however, did not arise when eligible minority persons were not promoted.[51]

This is not peculiar to industry. Hall describes in vivid detail the similar "institutional compatibilities" that physicians must demonstrate in order to be accepted among their professional society.[52] In addition to his competence, which colleagues often simply assume, a physician's access to the desirable hospitals depends on such criteria as popularity, "connections," and seniority. In this regard, Caplow and McGee also report that ability to get along with other members of the academic department in universities plays a significant role in the selection and promotion of professors.[53]

It is proposed that the use of friendship as a basis of evaluation contributes to dominant organizational values. Friendship frequently is based on similarity of basic values. By endorsing friends over other subordinates, superiors are able to insure that official control of the organization will remain in the hands of employees who are sympathetic with the basic values. Dissent over work roles—that is, disagreement over the particular means, techniques, and work procedures—can be tolerated as long as personnel are compatible, for their compatibility expresses a shared definition of the basic ends of the organization.[54] When subordinates disagree with the superior's basic understanding of the organization, it is reasonable to suspect that their industry and ambition, no matter how great, will not be rewarded with a favorable evaluation that could put the organization in the hands of "enemies."

Hughes observes that industry encourages ambition and complains about the lack of it, but at the same time it praises some people for not having it and complains of others who do.[55] He concludes that this seeming inconsistency occurs because personnel are not merely technical help, but are also (a) potential participants in a struggle for power within industry and (b) potentially close colleagues. Personnel who are friendly with management constitute the least threat to the organization.

The relationship between competence and popularity as a basis of promotion is undoubtedly complex. It would be useful to investigate whether the organizations which emphasize friendship with superiors over job consensus are significantly different from those that emphasize the latter. It can be hypothesized that the more visible and demonstrable is a person's competence, the less important is his popularity as a basis for advancement. Organizations differ on the measurability of the performance of employees; and, of course, in any organization there is some variability in the competence of individuals to do the work. Since most persons are not so singularly qualified that their competence alone justifies their incumbency, popularity is usually taken into account.

CONFORMITY AND BUREAUCRATIC TYPES

There is at least enough evidence that consensus and friendship are determinants of organizational behavior to warrant further analysis of their place and effect in complex organization. Gouldner's descriptions of bureaucratic types was considered earlier.[56] Competence gives rise to a representative form of bureaucracy, while the sheer power of office gives rise to authoritarian bases of bureaucracy. However, competence and power seem to apply primarily to the official bureaucracy and to an instrumental basis of leadership; the unofficial bases of bureaucracy and expressive leadership are explicitly unaccounted for in Gouldner's typology. The typology in Table 4 incorporates consensus and compatibility as separate bases of authority within the representative and authoritarian (or punishment-centered) bureaucratic types.

Table 4 indicates that consensus is more relevant to representative bureaucracy than to authoritarian bureaucracy. In the former, opinions of subordinates are supposed to be taken into account, but it is less necessary in authoritarian settings where employees are simply expected to obey the regulations; here also informal role conception is normally less relevant than in representative forms, since subordinates have comparatively little opportunity to influence the way in which roles are fulfilled.

Compatibility is probably stressed in both representative and authoritarian bureaucracies, but for somewhat different reasons. But it is especially important between superiors and subordinates in authoritarian bureaucracy because employees are expected to be officially adaptable and compatible to superiors and because of the need to cooperate formally even if they do not agree with official directives. In representa-

TABLE 4

Bases of Authority in Bureaucracies

Bases of Authority	Representative Bureaucracy		Authoritarian Bureaucracy	
	INFORMAL (EXPRESSIVE)	OFFICIAL (INSTRUMENTAL)	INFORMAL (EXPRESSIVE)	OFFICIAL (INSTRUMENTAL)
Knowledge		X		
Power of office				X
Consensus	X			
Compatibility	(X)		X	

tive bureaucracy, compatibility may be simply an adjunct of the need to cooperate informally and arrive at some kind of consensus on work roles and basic policy.

Morale

Morale is composed of a complex of factors, which range from satisfaction with the material and the nonmaterial aspects of the job and with interpersonal relations, to specific work behaviors, such as efficiency, productivity, and dependability of workers. However, underlying all of these are "vitality" and "enthusiasm" for the task, which are fundamental to morale. The level of this vitality and enthusiasm is strongly dependent upon the degree of meaning that a man finds in his work, the extent to which he contributes to, and identifies with, the goals of his job.

There is nothing inherently stagnant or boring about teaching itself; the great teachers of the world—from Socrates and Christ to the lonely few really inspired teachers who stand out in some of the present-day classrooms—are a testament to this assertion. Yet, most of the trends and problems introduced in the foregoing chapters impinge upon initial enthusiasm and threaten to stifle it. The logic of efficiency and the need to coordinate classroom activities from year to year and from state to state under the watchful eye of state agencies, generates a routine which suffers under the welter of problems created by curriculum guides, close supervision, rules and hierarchy, red tape, educational television, transfer policies, seniority, propriety and manners. Overshadowing the entire teaching process are foreboding community pressure groups which must be mollified and an elusive power structure of restraints and demands.

The future holds in store longer school days and a year-'round operation for teachers who already work more hours than most other workers each week, and who at least feel underpaid. The teacher's work year has increased from 159 days in 1910 to 180 to 185 days in 1962, excluding summer workshops, conventions, and summer schools.[57] Teachers work five to fifteen hours longer each week than industrial workers, because of increased student load and because of increasing extracurricular functions which are assumed by teachers; a teacher spends an average of four hours a week on extracurricular activities alone, and teachers participate in more community activities than most professional groups. After impressive salary increases the salaries in teaching are still not as high as those of many other vocations.

Frustrated by a system of inarticulate goals, amidst ambiguous avenues of success, the teacher looks for some stability in his work role in the daily routine of classes, repetitious courses, papers, committees, and extracurricular activities. Stability in the career easily becomes anchored in the routine of the job rather than in firmly fixed role conceptions of it, which further depresses the vitality of the job itself.

This statement does not deliberately ignore the more optimistic elements of teaching such as the challenge of solving its problems and stimulation from students; in world, and in historical perspective, to say nothing of alternatives available for millions of teachers in this country, teachers are not among the underprivileged of mankind. Yet, these negative developments do provide a general setting to be reckoned with, for they suggest *relative* deprivation—that is, a discrepancy between expectations and reality—which makes morale one of the significant aspects of the teaching-administrative relationship.

It is in any event safe to assert that the state of the morale of teachers affects the climate of the entire school; an uninspired faculty can hardly inspire an indifferent student body, who themselves are shuffled through the same heartless routine of classes, papers, attendance checks, assignments, and planned activities day after day.[58]

SYMPTOMS

To underline the vague suspicion that many teachers are really not doing their best, and either restrict their energy or feel overworked and complain extensively, one need only examine the statistics on turnover and vocational commitment to find a basis for the suspicion. In a 1954 study, three out of five persons trained to teach were not in the vocation at any one time; teachers annually vacate their jobs at the rate of seventeen per cent (twelve per cent of whom leave teaching), and administrative turnover approaches twenty per cent in the midwestern states and ten per cent in the west.[59] A recent Iowa study indicates little change in this picture.[60] Only sixteen per cent of the women and twenty-nine per cent of the men in a sample of first-year school teachers in 1956–1957 expected to stay in classroom teaching until retirement.[61] Of course, morale is not the only cause of these negative data (some actually represent increased morale as people move to administrative jobs within teaching and as discontents leave the field). Yet in one study, only twenty-seven per cent of the male elementary teachers stated that they would choose elementary teaching if they had to start all over again, and less than thirty-five per cent said they actually liked teaching.[62] It is safe to assume that morale plays an important role in such attitudes.

In an NEA report made more than two decades ago, it was found that only thirty-eight per cent of the teachers surveyed were classified as "high morale" teachers on each of three questions: whether they wanted to start over in teaching; whether they get a fair deal if they have a complaint; and whether they enjoy teaching. Only eight per cent of urban teachers were certain that they would start over again in teaching, and nearly two-thirds of them said that they probably would not or certainly would not start over in teaching again.[63] In an NEA report ten years later, educators had lower morale than business-industrial comparison groups. The majority expressed confidence in their school administrators, but one-half of the teachers in that study lacked confidence in their school boards and two-thirds complained that facilities for personal comfort could be improved.[64]

Significant as morale is, the problem has often been treated in the literature, and perhaps in the minds of some administrators, with an air of superficiality that has merely aggravated the sense of insignificance which already depresses many teachers. It should be apparent that these problems arise from the situation rather than from the personalities of those involved—and they will not be solved with the addition of a new teachers' lounge.

PERSONAL ASPECTS

Although it is natural enough to envision the problem of morale solely in personal terms, extended concern for the way individuals feel is not a substitute for a theory of morale. Whyte admonishes:

In much of the work done on organizations today, and particularly in studies using the questionnaire as the major research instrument, the focus of attention has been on attitudes (or sentiments) . . . There have been important technical advances in methods of measuring sentiment with a questionnaire . . . However, if we can demonstrate that sentiments are changed by changes in interactions and activities and that all three are subject to influence from forces in the environment, then it follows that any methodology or any theory which focuses exclusive or primary attention upon sentiments (personal attitudes) is seriously deficient.[65]

It is the *situation* in which the personality is operating that must be given primary consideration.

SITUATIONAL APPROACHES

The premise that human relations are exclusively problems of personal character, or personality, is plainly short of the mark. Human relations, group solidarity, and cohesiveness are produced by the institutional order. Murray suggests, for example, that the morale of an organization is influenced by its turnover rates, which in turn are determined partially by the way workers are treated.[66] Transfer policies were found to affect the absentee rates among hospital aids; workers were treated as interchangeable. Similarly, the fact that there is an annual turnover of nearly twenty-five per cent among school teachers and students may have a devastating effect on the relations between the remaining teachers and pupils.

PERSONAL AND SITUATIONAL FACTORS AMONG ADMINISTRATORS

Eighty-three of the 105 Massachusetts school superintendents studied by Gross said that they like the superintendency very much, and only twenty-six found quite a few features about the job that they disliked. The major dissatisfaction (cited by seventy-five of them) concerned inadequate leisure time.[67] Seventy-two of them said that the school superintendency is at least one of the most satisfying careers they could follow, and an additional thirty-two said that it is as satisfying as most careers.

Barry studied morale of school administrators and found the following factors to be related to their high morale: (1) recognition for ideas in the community, (2) cooperative relationship with school boards, (3) cooperative relationship among administrators within the district, (4) responsibility and power in the community (on important committees with professionals and laymen), (5) participation in projects to improve education, (6) satisfaction with material factors (salary and facilities), and (7) attendance at professional meetings.[68]

TEACHERS

Classroom teachers apparently do not fare so well. The sources of their dissatisfaction appear to be related to (a) their social backgrounds and (b) their situation. Place of work, facilities provided, recognition, responsibility, administrative practices, and the structure of the work setting all seem to be related to the job satisfactions of teachers.

There is some evidence which seems to point to the importance of control over one's work and to a promising future as factors in morale. Chase, for example, reports five factors that are important to the job satisfaction of a nationwide sample of over 2,000 teachers in forty-three states: freedom of the teacher to plan his own work, quality of professional leadership and supervision, opportunity for the teacher to participate in educational planning, salary, and adequate physical facilities.[69] All but the last two of these are definitely related to the teacher's autonomy over his work. There was also a close correspondence between teachers' ratings of their administrators and their job satisfaction. Schultz found that ninety-eight per cent of the most satisfied teachers in his study agreed that they had sufficient voice in school plans and policies, and only twenty-three per cent of the least satisfied teachers agreed on this point.[70] The least satisfied teachers also said that there was a lack of helpful supervision. Table 5 reports similar implications from another study.

TABLE 5

Major Sources of Dissatisfaction and Frustration in Teaching

Percentages of teachers, administrators and college faculty checking each of eleven sources of dissatisfaction *

SOURCE OF DISSATISFACTION	CLASSROOM TEACHERS (%)	ADMINIS- TRATORS (%)	COLLEGE TEACHERS (%)
a. Too many duties other than actual teaching.	34.9	26.6	23.8
b. Don't really care for teaching.	0.4	0.0	1.3
c. School board or community interference.	10.1	5.7	2.6
d. Principal or supervisor difficult to work with.	7.9	3.9	5.1
e. Pay too low.	44.6	40.2	38.8
f. Large classes and over-crowded rooms.	33.6	22.2	22.8
g. Pupils not interested in learning; disciplinary problems	25.7	11.6	11.7
h. Lack of materials and equipment for teaching.	14.6	14.0	11.5
i. No chance for promotion.	11.8	9.4	10.3
j. No intellectual stimulation.	5.0	2.8	3.8
k. Can never get completely away from kids.	2.1	9.3	1.3

* This table is based on a follow-up study of 250 school teachers, 82 college teachers, and 126 school administrators who were tested while in the military service during World War II, and again in 1955. (From R. L. Thorndike and E. Hagen, *Characteristics of Men Who Remained in and Left Teaching.* New York: Columbia University, Teachers College, undated.) Used with permission.

As the foregoing suggests, administrative practices are undoubtedly a crucial part of the situation, especially since they play a large part in determining the amount of control an employee exercises over his work and the quality of advice he receives. Schultz reports that the most significant differences between satisfied and unsatisfied teachers in his study were in the area of administrative practices and staff relations. The least satisfied teachers felt handicapped by unpleasant staff relations, and they felt that they received insufficient consideration from their administrator.[71] Eighteen of the twenty-eight most satisfied teachers mentioned administrators favorably as reasons for liking their present position, and fifteen of the least satisfied teachers mentioned administrators as the reason for their dissatisfaction.

Chase likewise found that the most frequently mentioned factor contributing to the job satisfaction of teachers was stimulating leadership of the principal.[72] In particular, the principal is expected to allow the teacher considerable latitude in choosing teaching materials and methods, and he is expected to respect her rights and dignity when offering his advice.[73] The significance of this administrative relationship will be considered further in connection with the problem of alienation.

THE MEANINGFULNESS OF WORK

Some programs have attempted to recharge work with meaning merely by assigning personnel men with the responsibility of paying personal attention to employees, by attempting to break down impersonal barriers with a monthly party or an annual picnic, or by redecorating the work place. Other programs have sought to increase harmony by encouraging consensus and excluding the outspoken, the nonconformists, and those with atypical political and social backgrounds. Still other programs have more recently sought to ignite a sense of purposefulness by creating an *esprit de corps* at the level of basic goals by using group incentive plans and group competition.

Yet, none of these methods is in itself sufficient to provide a complete sense of purposefulness and significance, so long as the worker is denied respect for his opinions and the dignity of control over his work. Attempts to create consensus on the basic organizational goals will be of little avail if the worker has no avenue to personally shape these goals and effect their accomplishment. It is control over work which makes work a "joy" and which gives work its meaning. Accordingly, for meaning to be restored to work, the worker must be allowed to maintain control over the work that he performs.

SUMMARY

The relationship between evaluation of teaching personnel and morale is a curious mixture of cause and effect. Teachers know and expect that they will be assessed in some fashion, because accountability for one's work performance is a definite part of American organizational procedures.

By and large, teachers have not only expected to be evaluated, but they have recognized that good evaluation programs are beneficial.[74] To be truly effective, however, evaluations ". . . must be given high priority on the list of administrators' duties [and] time must be allowed to plan a good program and set up realistic criteria." [75]

The maintenance of a sense of personal worth, relative satisfaction within the task environment, and meaningful interpretation of the relationship between personal goals and organizational purposes constitute the significant dimensions of morale. When teacher evaluation programs take these dimensions into consideration and also recognize the importance of encouraging (and therefore allowing) the teacher to maintain considerable control over the technical aspects of the job, evaluation contributes to morale; it is more clearly viewed not only as a means for appraising performance, but also as a nonthreatening technique for improving it.

It is obvious that evaluation and morale clearly influence the career patterns of educational workers; it is therefore appropriate that the following chapter examines some of the "avenues of success" available to educators.

BIBLIOGRAPHY AND NOTES

1. L. J. Stiles *et al.*, *Teacher Education in the United States.* New York: Ronald Press, 1960, p. 150.
2. NEA Research Division, "Why Few School Systems Use Merit Ratings," Bulletin 39, 1961, pp. 861 ff.
3. *Teacher Competence and Its Relation to Salary.* New England School Development Educational Council, July, 1956.
4. W. H. Edson and D. Davies, "Selectivity in Teacher Education," *Journal of Teacher Education,* vol. 11, 1960, pp. 329 ff.
5. J. Shannon, "Elements of Excellence in Teaching," *Educational Administration and Supervision,* vol. 27, 1941, pp. 168–176.
6. M. R. Trabue, "Characteristics of College Instructors Desired by Liberal Arts College Presidents," *Bulletin of Association of American Colleges,* 1950, pp. 374–379.
7. R. L. Kelley, "Great Teachers," *Bulletin of Association of American Colleges,* 1929, pp. 49–68.
8. A. L. Odenwiller, *Predicting the Quality of Teaching.* New York: Columbia University Teachers College, 1936.
9. M. Lieberman, *Education as a Profession.* Englewood Cliffs, N.J.: Prentice-Hall, 1956.
10. Cited by Lieberman, *Ibid.,* p. 398.
11. *Cf.* Shannon, *op. cit.*
12. *Ibid.*
13. G. T. Sommer, *Pedagogical Prognosis Predicting the Success of Prospective*

Teachers, T. C. Contributions to Education, no. 140. New York: Columbia University Teachers College, 1923.

14. W. Gordon, *The Social System of the High School*. Glencoe, Ill.: Free Press, 1957, p. 44.

15. W. B. Brookover, "Person-Person Interaction Between Teachers and Pupils and Teaching Effectiveness," *Journal of Education Research*, vol. 34, 1940–1941, p. 287.

16. L. J. Lins, "The Prediction of Teaching Efficiency," *Journal of Experimental Education*, vol. 15, 1946, pp. 2–60.

17. R. Coser, "Insulation from Observability and Types of Social Conformity," *American Sociological Review*, vol. 26, 1961, pp. 28–39.

18. NEA Research Bulletin, "Methods of Evaluating Teachers." NEA Research Division, vol. 43, 1965, p. 14.

19. NEA Research Bulletin, "What Teachers and Administrators Think About Evaluation," NEA Research Division, vol. 42, 1964, p. 111.

20. *Ibid.*, p. 111.

21. *Cf.* A. W. Gouldner, "Cosmopolitans and Locals: Toward an Analysis of Latent Social Roles, I and II," *Administrative Science Quarterly*, vol. 2, 1957, pp. 281–306; and vol. 2, 1958, pp. 444–480.

22. NEA Research Bulletin, "Teacher Personnel Procedures: Selection and Appointment," March, 1942, p. 73; and NEA Research Bulletin, "Teacher Personnel Practices, 1950–51," Feb., 1952, p. 22.

23. *Ibid.*

24. NEA Research Report, "The Teacher's Day in Court: Review of 1960." NEA Research Division, 1961, R7, p. 5.

25. *Certain Personnel Practices in the Chicago Public Schools*. National Commission for the Defense of Democracy Through Education, NEA, May, 1945.

26. NEA Research Bulletin, *Teacher Personnel Procedures: Employment Conditions in Service*, May, 1942, p. 106.

27. H. Arendt, *The Human Condition: A Study of the Central Dilemmas Facing Modern Man*. New York: Doubleday, 1958.

28. R. G. Corwin, *A Sociology of Education*. New York: Appleton-Century-Crofts, 1965.

29. J. Gauss, *Saturday Review*, July 21, 1962, p. 54.

30. R. Stout, "Selective Admissions and Retention Practices in Teacher Education," *Journal of Teacher Education*, vol. 8, 1957.

31. W. Whyte, *The Organization Man*. New York: Simon & Schuster, 1956.

32. *Cf.* H. J. Friedsam, "Bureaucrats as Heroes," *Social Forces*, vol. 32, 1954, pp. 269–274.

33. *Cf.* E. Durkheim, *The Division of Labor*, trans. by G. Simpson. Glencoe, Ill.: Free Press, 1947 (Copyright Macmillan, 1933); ct., W. H. Whyte, *The Organization Man, Ibid.*

34. E. Guba and C. Bidwell, *Administrative Relationships*. Chicago: Midwest Administrative Center, Univ. Chicago, 1957.

35. *Cf.* A. H. Stanton and M. S. Schwartz, "Observations on Disassociation as Social Participation," *Psychiatry*, vol. 12, 1949, pp. 339–354. On the other hand, other researchers in a similar setting report contrary findings: *Cf.* A. Wallace and H. Rashkis, "Staff Consensus and Patient Disturbance," *American Sociological Review*, Dec. 1959, pp. 829–835.

36. A. M. Rose, *Union Solidarity*. Minneapolis: Univ. Minnesota Press, 1952, p. 70.

37. W. Roe, L. Haak, and E. McIntyre, "Creating an Informed Citizenry," *Michigan Educational Journal*, vol. 32, 1954.

38. J. Henry, "Docility, or Giving Teacher What She Wants," *The Journal of Social Issues*, vol. 2, 1955, pp. 33–41.

39. Cf. D. Riesman and N. Glazer, *The Lonely Crowd*. Garden City, N.Y.: Doubleday, 1956, Ch. 2.
40. *Ibid.*, Ch. 1.
41. Cf. K. Polonyi, *The Great Transformation*, Boston: Beacon Hill Press, 1957.
42. A. Singer, "Social Competence and Success in Teaching," *Journal of Experimental Education*, vol. 23, 1954, pp. 99 ff.
43. *Ibid.*
44. Stiles, *op. cit.*, p. 50.
45. L. V. Manwiller, "Experimentations Regarding Teachers," *Journal of Experimental Education*, vol. 26, 1958, pp. 315–354.
46. W. P. Kuvlespy and R. C. Buck, *The Teacher-Student Relationship*. Philadelphia: Univ. Pennsylvania, 1960.
47. Cf. L. A. Cook and E. F. Cook, *A Sociological Approach to Education*, 2nd ed. New York: McGraw-Hill, 1950, p. 444.
48. W. Brookover, *op. cit.*, pp. 272–287.
49. R. G. Corwin, M. Taves and J. E. Haas, "Social Requirements for Occupational Success: Internalized Norms and Friendship," *Social Forces*, vol. 39, 1960, pp. 135–140. See also by same authors, *Role Conception and Success and Satisfaction*, Bureau of Business Research, Ohio State University, 1963.
50. M. Dalton, *Men Who Manage*. New York: Wiley, 1959, pp. 178–191.
51. O. Collins, "Ethnic Behavior in Industry: Sponsorship and Rejection in a New England Factory," *American Journal of Sociology*, vol. 51, 1946, pp. 293–298.
52. O. Hall, "The Informal Organization of the Medical Profession," *Canadian Journal of Economics and Political Science*, vol. 12, 1946, pp. 30–44.
53. T. Caplow and R. McGee, *The Academic Market Place*. Glencoe, Ill.: Free Press, 1958.
54. E. C. Hughes, "Queries Concerning Industry and Society Growing Out of Study of Ethnic Relations in Industry," *American Sociological Review*, vol. 14, 1949, pp. 218 ff.
55. *Ibid.*
56. A. W. Gouldner, *Patterns of Industrial Bureaucracy*. Glencoe, Ill.: Free Press, 1954.
57. NEA Research Division, "Time Devoted to School Duties," Research Bulletin, vol. 40, no. 3, 1962, p. 83.
58. Anderson reports that pupil achievement is related to teacher morale. L. W. Anderson, "Teacher Morale and Student Achievement," *Journal of Education Research*, vol. 46, 1953, pp. 693–698.
59. D. Wolfle, *American's Resources of Specialized Talent*, New York: Harper, 1954, pp. 52–53; W. S. Mason and R. K. Bain, *Teacher Turnover in the Public Schools*, 1957–58, USDHEW, Circular No. 608, Washington, D.C.: U.S. Govt. Printing Office, 1959.
60. P. Brunsvold, "The Relationship Between Selected School District Variables and Teacher Assignment Based on Preparation." Unpublished Ph.D. thesis, Univ. of Iowa, 1966.
61. W. S. Mason, R. L. Dressel, and R. K. Bain, "Sex Role and Career Orientations of Beginning Teachers," *Harvard Educational Review*, vol. 29, 1959, pp. 370–383.
62. Cf. L. Kaplan, "Causes of the Man Teacher Shortage," *American School Board Journal*, vol. 115, 1957; also "More Men for Elementary Schools," *Phi Delta Kappan*, vol. 19, 1948, pp. 299–302. However, eighty-eight per cent of the beginning teachers in 1956–57 said they would enter again; the figures ranged from eighty per cent of the male secondary teachers to ninety-three per cent of the women elementary teachers, cf. *Ibid.*
63. NEA, "The Teachers Look at Personnel Administration," Research Bulletin,

vol. 23, no. 4. Washington, D.C.: U.S. Govt. Printing Office, December, 1945.

64. NEA, *Trends in Public School Relations.* NEA School Relations Association, 1953.

65. W. F. Whyte, "An Interaction Approach to the Theory of Organization," *Modern Organization Theory,* M. Haire, ed. New York: Wiley, 1959, p. 180.

66. M. Murray, "Absenteeism Among Psychiatric Aides," *American Sociological Review,* vol. 26, 1961, pp. 14–22.

67. N. Gross, W. S. Mason, and A. W. McEachern, *Explorations in Role Analysis: Studies of the School Superintendency Role.* New York: Wiley, 1958, p. 355.

68. F. Barry, "Factors Affecting Administrative Morale," unpublished Ed.D. project, Syracuse University, 1956, cited by D. Griffiths, *Human Relations in School Administration.* New York: Appleton-Century-Crofts, 1956, p. 157.

69. F. S. Chase, "Factors for Satisfaction in Teaching," *Phi Delta Kappan,* vol. 33, 1951, pp. 127 ff.

70. R. Schultz, "Keeping Up Teacher Morale," *Nation's Schools,* vol. 50, 1952, pp. 53–56.

71. *Ibid.*

72. Chase, *op. cit.*

73. Yoroborough, "Morale is a Number of Things," *Illinois Education,* 38, p. 162.

74. NEA Research Division, "What Teachers and Administrators Think About Evaluation," *op. cit.*

75. *Ibid.,* p. 111.

14

Avenues of Success

We may suppose, in advance of further analyses, that competence will be most heavily weighted by one's fellows, that personal relations will assume great importance in a hierarchy, and that in those occupations which are subject to evaluation by the public the rating of individual merit will be least predictable.[1]

FROM THE preceding chapter it is apparent that "competence" encompasses a complex system which offers many avenues for advancement to many types of employees. With this development of multiple bases of achievement, "teacher" no longer evokes an image of a single stereotype in the popular imagination. The successful teacher is not necessarily an intellectual, just as he (or she) is not necessarily popular with children and parents; nor is he necessarily a "progressive" teacher, nor a political conservative. All of this, as emphasized in the previous chapter, compounds the problems of evaluating competence.

The difficulties that surround attempts to evaluate competence, however, do not prevent attempts from assessing it. Teachers *will* be judged for their ability to teach; and often those who judge it are least able to evaluate it. But since such judges, and their judgments, are often influential in the teachers' career, they will be taken into account. The variety of people who feel obliged to evaluate the work of teachers, the differences in perspectives used, the scope of career alternatives, and dead ends that typify much of teaching all complicate the problem of advancement and anticipate the complex picture of the avenues of success that will be considered in this chapter.

Perhaps the term "avenue" of success is inappropriate, for it may appear more like a haphazard maze of footpaths as this chapter unfolds. If the dissent among various parties who appear at the scene of evaluation and direct traffic up the promotion ladder appears overstated, it is because evaluation is so crucial to the organization's basic direction that even minor inconsistencies can be fateful. In this chapter, evaluation will be viewed as a relationship between parties, and success will be defined in terms of the variety of advancement opportunities and inopportunities.

Evaluation as a Relationship

Insofar as it is a judgment of one party over another, evaluation constitutes a relationship; the party evaluating is as important a factor as the party being evaluated. The following discussion attempts to estimate the particular criteria which various parties tend to choose from the array of available criteria discussed in the preceding chapter.

REMOTE SUPERIORS

The initial interviewing and screening of teaching candidates may be done by the superintendent, principal, a committee of faculty, or by a board of education. Which official or group has primary responsibility depends to a considerable extent on the size of the system. For example, in 1952, faculty committees interviewed teacher candidates in one-third of the cities over 500,000, while school board members interviewed the applicant in approximately one-quarter of the communities between 2,500 and 4,999; that proportion declined with city size.[2] Superintendents assumed the chore in ninety-two per cent of all 1,484 school systems studied, while principals also interviewed candidates in sixty-two per cent of the systems. An earlier study also indicated that the proportion of principals who assumed responsibility for interviewing candidates increased from eighteen per cent in schools of 500 to 999 to sixty-four per cent in schools with a pupil population of 2,500 and up.[3]

The majority of teachers probably prefer to be evaluated by less remote superiors, especially by their principal. Two-thirds of over 3,000 teachers in one study said they preferred their supervisors' evaluations, and forty-six per cent listed superintendents as a preference; but significantly, only fifteen per cent listed a preference for faculty committees.[4]

EVALUATION CRITERIA

Discrimination. The kind of criteria which remote superiors, such as superintendents, use to evaluate teachers probably reflects the pressures of their situation. The more remote the superior, the less probable are personal feelings (sentiments of like and dislike) to be used as the basis of his evaluation, and the greater reliance that will be placed on observable measures of performance and on the opinions of his subordinates.

However, the fact that evaluations by remote superiors tend to be impersonal does not imply that they are impartial; on the contrary, their responsibility for the overall public image of the organization predisposes chief administrators toward partiality to certain types of people. Green-hoe concluded that the type of teacher preferred by school board members is a Protestant, native-born, white, conservative, without foreign name, and born and raised in the local community (see Table 6).[5] School board emphasis on local residence varies by city size. According to an NEA survey of 1,615 school systems in 1951, twelve per cent of the cities

TABLE 6

Employability Quotients of Potential Applicants for Teaching Positions in the Public Schools

Percentage of Group Preference

POTENTIAL APPLICATION FOR TEACHING POSITION	SCHOOL BOARD MEMBERS (356)	LAY PERSONS (2,095)	PUBLIC SCHOOL TEACHERS (9,122)	EDUCATION STUDENTS (3,054)
1. A known Protestant	76.5	84.9	93.5	93.5
2. Native-born, foreign name	56.3	73.2	88.5	89.9
3. Nonlocal resident	48.3	46.0	78.4	89.1
4. City-reared person	45.8	66.6	85.4	90.8
5. Out-of-state applicant	15.4	27.5	69.4	64.9
6. A known Catholic	−21.3	9.5	53.1	68.0
7. A known pacifist	−22.8	5.3	29.7	40.4
8. A married woman	−32.1	−12.0	36.5	12.4
9. A known Jew	−41.3	2.3	44.8	41.5
10. A known militarist	−62.0	−50.1	−42.1	−25.1
11. A light Negro	−82.1	−54.2	−54.7	−33.6
12. A dark Negro	−85.7	−66.0	−63.4	−49.4
13. A known radical	−88.0	−72.5	−63.6	−48.2
14. A person in bad health	−93.3	−87.9	−54.7	−89.6
15. A known Communist	−94.1	−83.2	−77.5	−57.9

From F. Greenhoe, *Community Contacts and Participation of Teachers,* American Council on Public Affairs, 1941, p. 32.

with a population of 500,000 or over favored local applicants, while forty-eight per cent of the cities of 100,000 to 499,000 favored local applicants.[6] It is significant that favoring of local applicants is especially characteristic of larger cities. NEA trouble cases (six of sixteen) show that school boards show favoritism on the basis of kinship and friendship. Some boards of education hired relatives or close friends for administrative and clerical positions, and one attempted to reinstate a demoted school principal to his former position because of a common religious affiliation.[7]

The study of Massachusetts superintendents is representative of evidence that superintendents and school boards are partial to the local values and feelings regarding race, religion, national origin, and other cultural values in filling vacant superintendency positions. Forty per cent of the school board members said that such considerations must be, or should be, considered in filling vacant positions, and only fourteen percent said that such considerations absolutely must not be used.[8] Similarly, well over half of the superintendents report that they actually do consider such criteria in filling vacant positions.

The predispositions of school superintendents to favor the culturally acceptable are also reflected in the kind of persons that superintendents say they would recommend for replacement for their own job. Ninety-three of the 105 superintendents say that they either must or should give preference to married persons; seventy-two of them would give preference to church members, and ninety-six of them say they either should not or must not consider persons over sixty years of age. Similar preferences were shown toward white male Protestants. Aversions were shown toward socialists and Negroes; eighty-seven of the 105 school superintendents said they either should not or must not consider Negroes in recommending a replacement for their own vacancy. The same superintendents overwhelmingly considered divorced females entirely unacceptable.[9] Marital status, however, is not discriminated against to the extent that it was in 1941. Ninety per cent of the cities studied in 1951 report that the status of employed married teachers was not affected by the marriage; [10] however, the majority of schools do still show a preference to single women at the time of employment.

It is actually not surprising that schools recruit teachers on the basis of their values and background. For despite the bureaucratic and democratic ideologies that prohibit the practice, the necessity of appeasing outside groups and of maintaining control over internal values requires screening on that basis in order to prevent unintentional commitments and problems by the accident of membership. What remains surprising, however, is that these illicit screening practices are so infrequently used to support the long-range organizational and institutional goals; in fact these practices often actually undermine them. Although recruitment can be used strategically to enchance the administrative's internal support, it is often no more than a reflection of local prejudices. In this sense, the problem is not that there is discrimination, but that it is being used dysfunctionally.

Perhaps because of this discrimination, there is little evidence of a close association between superintendents' ratings of teachers and other measures of teachers' technical competence. For example, while 102 of the 105 superintendents in the Gross studies say that they evaluate on the basis of merit alone,[11] thirty years ago Anderson reported low correlations between superintendents' ratings of over 500 teachers and their college scholarship.[12] Similarly, in 1937 Stuit reported a low correlation between scholarship and superintendents' ratings, which explained less than ten per cent of the variance.[13] In a more recent study, Becker reports low correlations between the superintendent's evaluation of good teachers and such considerations as pupil interest ($r = -.30$), physical condition of the classroom ($r = .24$), attitudes of pupils ($r = .18$), pupil activity ($= .17$), and teacher aims ($r = .15$).[14]

Incompetence to Evaluate. The criteria by which remote superiors evaluate are influenced by several other considerations besides their natural prejudices and outside pressures on them to use technically irrelevant criteria. In the first place, the remote superior is often not trained in the special fields of competence of the subordinates whom he evaluates; this is a source of tension within many types of organizations. It is not much of an overstatement to say that top school executives are normally incompetent to evaluate the specialized skills of their subordinates. Principals and superintendents must evaluate physical science and English teachers, vocational guidance counselors, and a battery of other specialists, the content of whose work they know little about.

Even more remote is the evaluation that comes from State Departments of Education which issue *restrictive* teaching certificates that prevent teachers from teaching in any but specified areas. As Lieberman points out, in few other professions does the certifying board presume to judge the professional competence of professionals to practice in a specific field; this is normally a judgment reserved for professional colleagues in the field of specialization concerned.[15] That state departments make this decision is indicative of the extent to which the practice of evaluating specialists by remote superiors has proceeded in education. The practice encourages further separation between those responsible for making judgments and those who are competent to make them.

Bureaucratic Considerations. Another problem stems from the normal drive of organizations to render workers interchangeable by standardizing their work. In opposition to this is the equally normal drive of subordinates to prove their uniqueness and irreplaceability. This propensity of subordinates to display some unique ability in the face of standardization has an economic incentive; as Caplow points out, the chances for advancement are greatest where interchangeability is lowest.[16] However, because interchangeability permits flexibility and continuity of administration, there is a reluctance at some levels of administration to encourage exceptional performances from subordinates. The very exceptional employee has disproportionate bargaining power and his departure will tend to upset the organization once it becomes accustomed to rely on a person who always performs "beyond the call of duty." Simmel cites the story of a German military officer who, when it was suggested that an outstanding German official transfer to another branch of government, asked his minister: "Is the man indispensable to us?" "Entirely so, your high-ness." "Then we shall let him go. I cannot use indispensable servants." [17]

This quest for interchangeability sometimes discourages school systems from vigorously attempting to retain superior teachers when they are bid away by other schools. The salary and working conditions necessary to retain them can totally upset the existing order of rank. The tendency to assign equal units of work also restrains the amount of work a teacher can do; a person probably could not volunteer to teach a double teaching load for long because it would threaten the work loads of colleagues. The net effect is to restrain any tendency to emphasize competence to the exclusion of bureaucratic considerations.

Power of Subordinates. Whether or not excellence will be recognized by remote superiors depends upon the power of their subordinates and upon the holding power of the organization. Strangely enough, teachers and administrators must sometimes threaten to resign in order to force a favorable evaluation. That is, those who have the power to quit are in a better position to force a conclusion about their merit, which, if favorable, gives them an advantage over their peers, their relative technical competencies notwithstanding. Conversely, an older teacher who is in debt, or who is otherwise attached to the community by close family and friendship ties, is less likely than his peers to receive tangible evidence that his work is appreciated. The influence that resignation threats have on evaluation is due partially to the fact that without the threat of departure evaluation might not otherwise have occurred; but the threat to quit also forces merit to be judged in "the open market" where it is less easily exploited by specific holding powers of the organization. Consequently, those who receive recognition are not necessarily the only most able subordinates; they include those who are able to quit or to otherwise jeopardize the organization.

The prevalence of the resignation threat as a leverage to gain favorable recognition and advantage is a common practice in most industries and universities,[18] but its use in education provides a special impetus to an otherwise remarkable turnover rate. Each school system is, in effect, a local monopoly which teachers must leave in order to enhance their careers.

IMMEDIATE SUPERVISORS

Although there is little tangible evidence of it, when subordinates are evaluated by their immediate (or direct) superiors, there is probably a tendency for personal considerations to be used—that is, beyond the impersonal social status symbols that remote superiors take into account. The welfare, or convenience, of the immediate superior becomes particularly relevant. By virtue of his position, the subordinate's personal life can be closely observed by his immediate supervisors. His personal loyalty to them, of course, critically influences their own careers. Because he is under constant temptation to stress personal loyalty and anticipate disloyalty, the immediate supervisor's judgment is easily distracted by officially irrelevant attitudes, personal feelings and tastes, and ostensible signs of loyalty to him. (This is indicative in some of the evidence pertaining to the influence of consensus and friendship between subordinates and immediate superiors presented in the preceding chapter.)

However, if subordinates are at times judged by criteria that are not officially relevant or publicly endorsed, in all fairness it is probably due to reasons beyond the sheer subjective preferences of supervisors. Frequently administrators with the best intentions of evaluating technical competence are prevented from doing so by situations beyond their normal control, such as time limitations, incompetence to judge, lack of observability, and other problems previously mentioned. At times there seems to be little other basis for judgment left except personal impressions and demonstrated personal loyalties and consensus.

PEERS

Despite the anxieties that evaluation by superiors often create for subordinates, there is probably more reason for subordinates to prefer that the evaluation come from their superiors rather than from their own peers. As previously indicated, less than fifteen per cent of teachers in one New England study indicated a preference to be evaluated by faculty committees.[19] There must be a variety of reasons, but undoubtedly among them is the common belief that peers impose harsher penalties than would superiors. For example, army enlisted men reputedly choose military officers disproportionately to enlisted men to sit on their own court martials, because the latter are assumed to be less tolerant. This popular belief is likely to be true whenever a peer's acts cast negative reflections on the other members of his group, who will find him guilty in order to absolve themselves.

Caplow suggests that peers stress technical competence more than do their superiors.[20] Since peers are more technically qualified and are more in touch with one another's work performance, there may be some truth to this. The fact that superiors do take into account social background, as already suggested, further supports the contention. In support of the proposition is a 1954 report by Guthrie who surveyed student and faculty ratings of the effectiveness of college teachers. Although there was substantial disagreement in the ratings, the faculty rated scholarly attainments (that is, their technical competence) as more important compared to students, who tended to accent specific personality and teaching qualities.[21] Which aspects of competence are stressed varies. When teachers were asked by Domas to describe effective and ineffective teaching "incidents," effectiveness appeared to be more closely associated with "teaching technique" (that is, literally, another aspect of technical competence) and with philosophy of teaching than with content taught or knowledge of subject. Heading the list for the effective teacher was encouraging every child to "participate" and "encouraging the child to learn by doing." Teachers also rated high who solved their own problems and prepared lesson plans. The ineffective teachers were described as those who ordered children to obey them, became angry when criticized or corrected, became vindictive toward pupils, and failed to recognize individual differences.[22]

There is, on the other hand, little evidence that the particular aspect of technique which teachers stress is very much different from the criteria that a random sample of laymen might emphasize. One study reports relatively little difference in the importance which teachers and laymen attach to such roles as student-centered behavior, maintaining social distance, teacher-centered methods, and other social skills used in the classroom.[23] For example, while fifty-four per cent of the community members stressed such student-centered qualities as kindness and personal consideration of students, only slightly more of the teachers stressed this (sixty-five per cent), and most of the other differences were smaller. This study, it should be noted, did not involve the actual evaluation of *particular* teachers, but it invoked general ideology. The compatibility between teachers and laymen was suggested in a study fifteen years ago which reported that three-fourths of the teachers either favored social and moral restrictions on teachers or were unconcerned; only sixteen per cent said they would rebel or protest.[24] Also, the views of laymen are endorsed by teachers in an official statement of the National Educational Association which declares that teachers are obligated to maintain higher standards of personal conduct than members of other occupational groups. A study by Richey and Fox which compared student teachers and nonteaching students, provides further indication of the similarity of expectations between teachers and the outside communities.[25]

One implication is that if there is a difference in the standards by which peers and the outside community and superiors judge teachers, the difference probably cannot be attributed to greater reliance of teachers on criteria of technical competence. They appear to show the same concern as laymen and superiors with nontechnical, social, and personal propriety in their evaluations, and at times stress these factors even more than would laymen.

The element of personal jealousy must be considered when analyzing the dynamics of evaluation by peers. Personal competition is, of course, potentially present among peers in a way that it is not present among unequals. The subordinate who has sought advancement may have done so, directly or indirectly, at the expense of his co-workers, if only because he carries out the orders of remote superiors with greater zeal or because he has capitalized on limited opportunities. Also, unencumbered by the restraining proprieties of social distance, peers sometimes develop intense personal animosities which in turn can influence their evaluations of their colleagues. Thus, while peers are in an objectively better position to assess their co-workers' competence, the facts of personal competition can easily color their evaluations with latent personal sentiments. There is a strong possibility that these sentiments, in turn, will provoke competitors to stringently stress technical competence in such a way as to legitimate and validate their own negative attitudes. Complaints about the technical incompetence of a more successful peer, for example, may be no more than a front for the real source of complaint.

It should be noted in passing that school superintendents do not seem to stress intellectual competence in evaluating their peers. Gross asked Massachusetts school superintendents how important intellectual brilliance is for a superintendent whom they might recommend to replace them. None of the 105 superintendents said that a superintendent "absolutely must" be brilliant, and sixty of them said he "must not" be brilliant. Nearly twice as many thought he "probably should" be a stern disciplinarian as thought he "probably should" have intellectual brilliance.[26] It is evident from such a response pattern that most superintendents do not base their authority and competence on specialized knowledge which would increase with intellectual competence. Rather, they seem to base their authority on their legal status which can be maintained by disciplinary control over subordinates. This evidence alone does not warrant a conclusion that superintendents fail to respect intellectual competence, but neither does it provide much evidence that they do. Somehow educational leadership does not, in their minds, require intellectual competence. Does this also mean that they do not respect intellectually brilliant teachers?

In conclusion, teachers and administrators may emphasize technical considerations in evaluating other teachers, but their conception of technical criteria is hardly more sophisticated than that of the general public, and teachers are perhaps just as concerned with nontechnical, social considerations and with personal competitiveness as they are with classroom performance. However, regardless of their bases, the judgments of co-workers about their peers must be taken into consideration by administrators as a way of anticipating the consequences of advancing certain personnel over others. In some cases, promoting a person over co-workers who do not approve of him, no matter how competent he is, may increase the resistance of subordinates to the administrative program and reduce the total level of morale.

SUBORDINATES

Despite professional canons against being evaluated by the public and by clients, the reputations that teachers have with their students are commonly taken into consideration at evaluation time. Of course, the extent of the influence of student opinion depends on *which* students are heard by the administration, and this in turn depends on the existing pattern of informal channels of communication.

There is reason to believe that, in contrast to peers and superiors, subordinates stress technical competence. From early studies comes evidence that capability and knowledge of subject matter lead the list of criteria on which pupils judge their teachers. Schaffle found that impartiality and knowledge were stressed by public school ninth and twelfth graders in evaluating their teachers.[27] Recent studies of what college students expect of their professors show that they stress presentation of the material, its organization, the professor's command of the subject, and his willingness to give personal help.[28] Stress on personality and ability to motivate students ranked relatively low in that study, as it has in a number of others.

T. McDaniel studied teachers in North Carolina who were rated by superintendents, patrons, teachers, and pupils as "excellent" teachers.[29] (Each person rated "the" most excellent teacher in their opinion.) Of the 192 sample statements concerning why the teacher was excellent, a sizeable portion of the superintendents, patrons, other teachers, and pupils rated *personality* above preparation and knowledge of subject matter. The majority of these were statements from patrons and teachers. Superintendents seemed to especially favor the positive attitudes of teachers toward the administration and community. By contrast, among the first reasons that *pupils* gave were statements like, "She would explain things so you could understand them," and "She knew what she was talking about."

In general, the most salient characteristics by which students described their most excellent teacher were in the category of "knowledge of professional methodology." No matter what the teacher's personality and background, the pupils were more appreciative of his methods of educating. Fifty-six and four-tenths per cent of those named by these pupils as excellent held a bachelor's degree, while fifty per cent of superintendents' excellent teachers held B.A.'s. Twenty-eight per cent of those named by other teachers held B.A.'s and thirty-three per cent of those named by patrons did. It took teachers who were not college graduates twelve years longer than the graduates to be thought of as excellent teachers.

However, while technical competence is probably more important than personality or background, personal sentiment probably is taken into account. Thirty years ago, Hart found that eighty per cent of 3,700 high school seniors evaluated the teachers they *liked* best as their best teacher.[30] Brookover (1940) found in a similar study that high school teachers who stimulate a great deal of discussion are better liked by their students than those who do not, and there was a strong correlation ($r = .64$) between their rated ability and their rated friendliness as a teacher.[31] By contrast, however, the more authoritarian types of teachers, who were not so well liked, nor so inclined toward discussion, seemed to teach more history.

Despite some inconsistencies among these findings, the weight of available evidence seems to indicate that students place more stress on the technical competence of their teachers to teach than on their personalities, social background, and public relations skills. Their emphasis on technical competence in the classroom may be due to the fact that they are the "subjects" who are being operated on and who must bear the marks of the teacher's technical competence or incompetence to teach. This stress on competence may also account for the prevalent lack of consensus between administration's and students' judgments of teacher competence. In this regard, Symonds reports that the *highest* correlation which he found between principals and pupil evaluations of teachers was only in the magnitude of r— .6, which accounts for less than forty per cent of the variance.[32]

OUTSIDERS

Laymen. As public employees, teachers are obviously dependent on persons *outside* of their organization to validate their positions within it. This is particularly true where community power intrudes into the internal system as it does when school boards govern. "Connections" with persons on the outside who wield influence over school officials is an important source of personal power. Teachers who get along splendidly at the local chapter of the PTA and those who are popular speakers at the local businessman's club luncheon may be retained on their own terms.

To the extent that schools depend on outsiders—parents, businessmen, and self-appointed correspondents to the editor—the expectations of outsiders will penetrate the organization. Because of the unfamiliarity that outsiders have with the work and because the intrinsic information is not usually available to them, they are prone to use evaluation criteria which are extrinsic to the job itself. Clues to the standards that the public uses have been illustrated and are provided in a number of nationwide surveys of public expectations of teachers. One Roper survey, for example, indicated that when asked what would be the most important consideration in hiring a school teacher, thirty-eight per cent of the public said how well the teacher "handles children"; twenty-nine per cent said their "education"; sixteen per cent mentioned "experience"; eleven per cent "morals"; and two per cent "religion." [33] It is likely that teachers would in general agree, although they might reverse the relative order, particularly of the first and second statements.

However, even if there is agreement on the basic criteria, workers generally try to escape evaluation by lay audiences whom they feel do not really *understand* their work. For example, to evade his lay audience the jazz musician retreats to his after-hours "jam sessions," which provides him with an opportunity to play the music which the audience does not fully appreciate.[34] Despite similarities between the views of many teachers and their various publics (students, parents, and administrators), differences between them on the evaluation of competence also seems inevitable. In defense, at least some teachers regularly retreat to private areas where they congregate to reinstate their own views and undermine judgments imposed by the uninformed persons outside the profession. The school cafeteria, furnace room, classrooms after hours, private offices, and homes all function as sanctuaries, removed from outsiders' purview, where the fraternity gossips about their good and poor students, the troublesome and decent parents, the querulous and compliant administrators. In such retreats their own value systems are recharged.

Outside Professionals. Local and cosmopolitan types of teachers logically diverge in their preference for evalution by outsiders; they may also have different preference for certain outsiders. Because the reputations of "locally" oriented teachers rest on the opinion of community influentials, these teachers may be counted on to sustain local community opinions and to defend local criteria. The cosmopolitan teacher, however, oriented to a regional, nationwide, and international scene, and identified with the outsiders—colleagues around the country, their "discipline," university professors, and professional leaders—finds greater incentive to ignore the opinions of the uninformed locals. Both teachers and school administrators must face *two* ways at once, walking a tightrope between evaluations emanating from inside and from outside the organization. The local and cosmopolitan teacher each walks that tightrope in somewhat different postures.

As surely as professional expertise is a basis of authority in modern organization, there is a definite threat that personnel will be more committed to their discipline, profession, and colleagues outside of the organization than to their interests within it. From the viewpoint of the organization, this externally directed attitude produces high turnover rates, introduces dissenting views, and increases resistance to some administrative practices and, ultimately, reduces administrative control over subordinates (and so enhances professionalism). Gouldner suggests that much of industry's recent efforts to induce loyalty to administrative goals in employees, reflected in the well-known image of the "organization man" and manifested as a quest for consensus and morale, is an attempt to counterbalance this shattering influence that attention to the opinions of persons outside the organization has on the organization's solidarity.[35]

CONCLUSION

Although it is hazardous to form generalizations on the basis of the sketchy, unsystematic, and often methodologically questionable studies that are available, it may be strategically useful to advance some working hypothesis at this time. It might turn out that emphasis on personal compatibility and technical competence increases down the hierarchy. More specifically, it is hypothesized (a) that stress on conformity to cultural values increases directly with the rank of the official evaluating; (b) that immediate supervisors primarily stress personal loyalty, consensus, and friendship with their subordinates in evaluating them, and that they stress these criteria more than any other single group considered; (c) that peers stress technical competence less than they stress personal compatibility with their colleagues, but perhaps more than remote superiors stress it; and (d) that, in teaching at least, subordinates place greater stress than other groups on technical competence.

Advancement

FORMAL ADVANCEMENT

The advancement of subordinates is so closely connected with the general problems of evaluating them that it is unjustifiable to discuss one process without considering the other. The choice of evalution criteria is, for example, an obviously crucial determinant of the career of any particular employee.[36]

Career Aspirations. Most teachers are willing to be evaluated, and all teachers must be. However, the majority of teachers probably do not aspire to great heights in their careers. There is, for example, little reason to suppose that the majority of teachers long for promotions which will require of them more responsibility, time, and energy. In fact, most teachers do not have strong commitments to their careers at all. This statement is supported by national statistics: three out of five public school teachers are not teaching ten years after graduation, and a substantial proportion of them are not teaching after two years.[37] If most teachers do not plan to remain in teaching, they are unlikely to work hard for promotion.

Promotion seems to be especially unattractive to the women of this society, and women, of course, constitute the majority of public school teachers. According to a study of mature, single women in various careers, which was conducted by the Women's Bureau of the U.S. Department of Labor in 1950, only forty per cent of those interviewed wanted to continue working; they were more interested in steady and comfortable working conditions and companions.[38] Among the school teachers in that study, twelve per cent of the men wanted to keep their present jobs, while the rest wanted promotions; on the other hand, both single and married women wanted to quit teaching to be housewives. In a more recent study, seventy per cent of women teachers said that they expected to leave teaching sometime to become housewives, and over forty per cent of them never expected to return; only sixteen per cent of the women and twenty-nine per cent of the men planned to stay in the profession until retirement.[39]

Some of the lack of commitment to teaching that is written into the foregoing figures undoubtedly reflects a realistic assessment of the limited opportunities for promotion available to classroom teachers. In view of the relatively few official grades of classroom teachers, it is a "dead-end" career for the majority. The relatively restricted opportunity for promotion undoubtedly has an overwhelming influence on teachers' career patterns, morale, and aspirations.

Professional and Administrative Success. The major promotions which are available are to administrative or semi-administrative jobs. Advancement through this restricted administrative route has the effect of removing specialists from their fields of competence and, many times, from their major interests. The present promotion system removes able teachers from the classroom where they can be most effective. The decision to forego teaching for administration is probably a difficult one for many of the most committed teachers whose emotional involvement remains, nostalgically, at the early stages of their career. At the same time, and for these very reasons, those teachers who were originally less committed to classroom teaching are likely to.be among the most ambitious who work for and accept promotion; the circuit of promotion in education naturally directs aspiring administrators through the classroom where many have little desire to be.

Besides affecting the quality of *teaching*, this dead-end barrier between professional and administrative careers can erode the quality of administration. The curious fact is that in the past, advancement to administrative positions has often been a reward for either seniority in the classroom or for competence in a speciality other than administration—for example, classroom skills. As a result, the important posts are often filled by persons who are untrained, if not emotionally unprepared, for administrative work.

In a study of nursing, Corwin reports that staff nurses who aspired to administrative hospital posts were among those with the greatest bureaucratic loyalty, but they were also among the nurses who expressed the lowest professional loyalty. The aspirants also expressed extremely low certainty as to their role conceptions.[40] This could mean that administrative posts provide definite social identities to persons who are the least certain of their roles within the organization.

SALARY

Uniform Salary Schedules. Salary schedules usually correspond to the promotion system, but they also provide an independent and alternate ladder of official advancement. Richey and Fox found that the pay advancement system is one of teaching's five major advantages, according to the student teachers in their sample.[41] Yet, the use of scheduled salary raises which guarantee regular salary increases, now in effect in ninety-six per cent of all communities over 2,500, has several distinct disadvantages. While the systematic and uniform pay raises guaranteed by such schedules may help to reduce competitive anxieties over salaries and a sense of arbitrariness about salary increases, and while they may partially compensate for the lack of promotion opportunities, uniform across-the-board guarantees create other, often more basic problems. One problem is that by regularizing such increases, the administrator loses control over the reward system. He is less able to reward either merit in a designated skill or personal loyalty.

The major difficulty, however, is that in solving the immediate internal problems that arise in a system where salary is competitive, uniform schedules blatantly ignore the supply-and-demand ratios of the teaching market. The existing long-range problems of recruiting teachers in areas for which there is great demand are aggravated by insistence on uniform salaries. Lieberman contends that a single salary schedule makes it infinitely more difficult to retain good physics teachers, for example, because, receiving no more salary than the Latin teacher or driver's education teacher, they are bid away by industry.[42] There is some truth in this; in 1960 only seventy per cent of the needed math and English teachers were graduated—they can get much higher salaries elsewhere.[43] At the same time, the salaries of driver education teachers and men's physical education teachers become artificially inflated above their market value because of excessive supply. The same argument would apply to the custom of paying uniform salaries to both elementary and high school teachers in a system, for they usually have different supply-and-demand ratios on the labor market. Competitive salaries, of course, do not solve all problems. Under a competitive salary schedule, for example, some scarce teachers in extrinsic programs, such as successful athletic coaches, generally receive inflated salaries that detract from the salaries which can be paid to teachers in the intrinsic program.

Salary Levels. Always lurking behind salary problems are the persistent reminders from a number of public-spirited groups, to say nothing of the NEA, that, relative to the amount of training required, the standard of living which the schedules provide is low. The average salary of classroom teachers in 1965–1966 was $6,792 or $6,293 for elementary teachers and $6,792 for secondary teachers.[44] The differences between elementary and secondary teachers have diminished since 1950, but the overall variability in teaching salaries, particularly by region, is relatively great. For example, the average salary in California was $7,000 in 1961, in New York State it was $6,700, and in Alaska it was $5,527. On the other hand, Mississippi was at the bottom with an average salary of $3,560. Despite the fact that over the past ten years Mississippi salaries have risen over 125 per cent, the absolute differences are increasing rather than diminishing. Nearly five per cent of all teachers were paid less than $3,500 in 1963, nineteen per cent were paid between $3,500 and $4,999, twenty-seven per cent were paid between $4,500 and $5,499, twenty-four per cent were paid between $5,500 and $6,499, while twenty-five per cent were paid $6,500 or more. In comparison, the median salary for accountants in 1961 to 1963 ranged from nearly $6,000 to over $10,000, and for attorneys the median salary ranged from $6,500 to over $20,000. The median teacher's salary was equaled by accounting clerks and exceeded by a category of tabulating machine operators.[45] A beginning accountant with a B.A. could expect to earn $1,200 more the first year than a beginning teacher.

However, salary inadequacies can be overestimated. These salaries are above the median for all *women* college graduates,[46] and for men the *starting* salaries are not much different than they would be in many other professions. Moreover, it must be recognized that the salaries of public employees in all fields are normally below those paid in private industry. The purchasing power of teachers has increased ten per cent in the last decade.

Indeed, some writers have maintained that comparisons of salaries between teaching and industry may be misleading. Parsons contends that the meaning of wages within an institution depends on the institutional goals, which are quite different for different types of organizations.[47] Because the success of a business firm is normally measured in terms of its profits, the executive's salary is also an appropriate measure of his success. By the same token, however, salary may be a less appropriate success symbol in non-profit organizations, such as schools, where the money available is a greater tribute to skills at begging contributions than to teaching competence. Operating on public benevolence, the teacher's success is perhaps more appropriately measured by service, loyalty, technical skill, popularity, leadership, responsibility, and internal power. Teachers, in fact, apparently do not regard making a high salary of first importance in considering a vocation. It is reported that only five per cent of student teachers agree that salary is of first importance (compared to thirteen per cent of a non-student teaching group studied); at the same time, fifty-three per cent of the student teachers agree that being of service to mankind is of first importance in considering a vocation (compared to thirty-eight per cent of non-student teachers).[48]

Salary Range. The major problem of salary schedules in teaching is not their inadequacy compared with industry and other professions, but rather the limited *range* of advancement opportunities that they provide *within* the teaching profession. To a considerable extent, above its gross purchasing power a worker's salary reflects his relative utility to the institution. Thus, in teaching invidious comparisons between positions *are* made on the basis of salary. In fact, a study of the prestige ratings of school superintendencies reports that the prestige of superintendent positions was most highly correlated ($r = .9$) with superintendents' and teachers' salaries.[49]

The amount of official recognition which an administrator can give to his personnel is directly limited to the distinction he can accord them through salary differentials, and this is independent of the absolute salary level as compared to other types of institutions. An administrator working with a $15,000 salary differential between top and bottom, for example, can give considerably more recognition to deserving teachers (and thus increase the holding power over his teaching staff) than one working with a salary differential of $5,000. With these considerations in mind, it is beneficial to look at the median salary ranges existing in teaching in 1960–1961, according to NEA reports (Table 7).[50]

It is significant to note that the average public school teacher with a B.A. will start at $4,500 in the largest city system and can move in that system up to a maximum of $7,400, a salary differential of less than $3,000 over a period of perhaps ten years. According to one estimate, a teacher with a B.A. can expect a sixty-seven per cent salary increase in fourteen years, compared to a typical male college graduate working in a corporation who could expect a ninety-nine per cent increase in his salary within five years. An ambitious teacher can return to graduate school and earn a doctorate and then expect to typically earn about $9,000 in the largest school systems—a $2,000 increase over the B.A. maximum for four years of graduate study.[51] It should be pointed out also that according to a 1965 NEA report, fewer than five per cent of all teachers were receiving top maximum scheduled salary.[52]

Table 8 summarizes the salary levels of school administrators, indicating why it is necessary for teachers to accept administrative positions in order to achieve an appreciable increase in their salary differential that will give them a real sense of official recognition.

There is at present no teaching salary comparable to the $25,000 customarily paid to metropolitan superintendents. However, it is worth noting that one consequence of "team teaching," now in effect in some major cities throughout the country, will be to create a teacher hierarchy and a new avenue of opportunity in what is now a dead-end career for most teachers. Recent estimates are that a master teacher may expect to earn up to $15,000 annually.

TABLE 7

Median Salaries for Urban Classroom Teachers, 1950–51 and 1960–61

PREPARATION LEVEL	Population of Districts					
	500,000 AND OVER	100,000– 499,999	30,000– 99,999	10,000– 29,999	5,000– 9,999	2,500– 4,999
Bachelor's degree (or 4 years):						
Minimum, 1950–1951	$2,660	$2,471	$2,466	$2,437	$2,412	$2,417
Minimum, 1960–1961	4,500	4,300	4,270	4,200	4,150	4,100
Percentage increase	96.2%	74.0%	72.3%	72.3%	72.1%	69.6%
Maximum, 1950–1951	$4,700	$4,158	$3,938	$3,725	$3,499	$3,377
Maximum, 1960–1961	7,100	6,750	6,500	6,100	5,725	5,655
Percentage increase	51.1%	62.3%	65.1%	63.8%	63.6%	67.5%
Master's degree (or 5 years):						
Minimum, 1950–1951	$2,863	$2,656	$2,652	$2,608	$2,567	$2,556
Minimum, 1960–1961	4,650	4,600	4,600	4,418	4,400	4,400
Percentage increase	62.4%	73.2%	73.5%	69.4%	71.4%	72.1%
Maximum, 1950–1951	$4,980	$4,439	$4,259	$4,049	$3,990	$3,848
Maximum, 1960–1961	7,380	7,305	7,100	6,600	6,200	6,105
Percentage increase	48.2%	64.6%	66.7%	63.0%	55.4%	58.7%

From National Education Association, Research Division. *Salaries and Salary Schedules of Urban School Employees*, 1960–1961. Research Report 1961-R17. Washington, D.C., Oct., 1961, p. 82.

TABLE 8

Average Salaries Paid Selected Central-Office Administrators, 1964–65,
Reporting Systems with Enrollments of 12,000 or More
(These are NOT national averages)

*Reporting systems
with enroll. of 12,000 or more* [a]

POSITION	NUMBER OF PERSONS	AVERAGE SALARY PAID	RATIO TO AVERAGE SALARY PAID CLASSROOM TEACHERS
Classroom Teachers	567,491	$6,669	100.0
Superintendents	391	20,372	305.5
Assistant and/or deputy superintendents	1,041	15,849	237.7
Administrative officers for finance, business, and school plant administration			
General finance and business	282	12,122	181.8
Purchasing	258	9,775	146.6
Accounting and Auditing	277	9,417	141.2
Building operations and maintenance	431	9,728	145.9
Building planning and construction	216	11,306	169.5
Administrative officers for			
Employed personnel	350	12,005	180.0
Research	183	12,207	183.0
Food Services	338	8,981	134.7
Health Services	330	11,754	176.2
Administrators for instructional services			
General instruction and curriculum	320	11,830	177.4
Elementary education	988	10,997	164.9
Secondary education	472	12,044	180.6
Special education	413	10,922	163.8
Instructional materials and audiovisual ed.	351	10,699	160.4
Administrators for special subject areas			
Art	339	10,318	154.7
Home Economics	149	10,823	162.3
Industrial arts	146	11,351	170.2
Physical and health education	480	10,833	162.4
Vocational education	230	10,995	164.9
Administrators for pupil personnel services			
General	230	11,306	169.5
Attendance	429	9,154	137.3
Guidance	284	10,849	162.7
Psychological and psychiatric	439	10,223	153.3
Tests and measurements	150	9,530	142.9

[a] Information was received from 392 of the 443 systems in this enrollment stratification.
From NEA Research Bulletin, vol. 43, No. 3, 1965. p. 83.

TABLE 9

Distribution of Administrative Schedules in Relation to Schedules for Classroom Teachers, 1962–1963

SYSTEMS BY ENROLLMENT	NUMBER OF SCHEDULES	RATIO DIFFERENTIAL	INDEPENDENT	DOLLAR DIFFERENTIAL	RATIO AND DOLLAR DIFFERENTIAL
25,000 or more	106	44.3%	38.7%	17.0%	—
12,000 to 24,999	119	47.9	31.9	17.7	2.5%
6,000 to 11,999	115	52.2	34.8	10.4	2.6
Selected suburban systems, enrollment 1,000 or more	64	57.8	36.0	3.1	3.1

From NEA Research Bulletin, Vol. 41, No. 1, Feb., 1963.

UNPROMOTABILITY

A major difficulty that is often unnoticed in connection with a teaching career concerns the negative effects that promotion may have on the morale of the unpromotables. This problem, of course, is by no means limited to public education. Co-workers may resent their superiors' choice of persons who are promoted over them. The problem may be partially avoided by consulting with subordinates prior to the promotion. But once an objectionable subordinate has been promoted over his peers, he will probably have difficulty in re-establishing his authority over those who were formerly his co-workers. Transfer to another area at the time of promotion is one solution to this problem; in this sense, the successful man is necessarily one who has moved away from those who "knew him when." Another strategy is to bring in experienced, often more prestigious, outsiders to fill the position; but this practice may still alienate subordinates, since they stand to benefit by a policy of inside promotions, and since they can have no guarantee that the outsider will understand and observe the organization's informal codes. In buying the objectivity and prestige of an outsider, the organization may also be buying trouble.

INFORMAL ADVANCEMENT

Those who do not stand to benefit immediately from the formal system can turn to the informal system. In the future, informal recognition for principals will probably frequently compensate for decreasing economic and official differentials between the principal and his staff as teachers successfully raise their salaries.

Salary may play a significant role even in this informal sphere, for reasons beyond purchasing power. For example, annual and monthly salaries carry more prestige than the equivalent income earned at hourly rates. Similarly, Gardner suggests that workers are sometimes more concerned about the fact that their co-workers earn five cents more an hour than about the total size of their paycheck.[53] These are the kinds of symbolic differentials that comprise informal systems of advancement.

In many respects, school administrators can exert as much influence over the informal status symbols as they do over formal advancement by working with and supporting the informal system. For example, a transfer to a more desirable classroom location, or to a more desirable school within the system, is sometimes as effective as an official promotion. Change of title, special parking privileges, name plates, allocation of a secretary's time are all informal kinds of recognition which a perceptive administrator can manipulate.

By the same token, administrative decisions which ignore the unofficial hierarchy may meet a cool reception from employees. One writer tells of a competent industrial executive who suddenly became sullen, anxious, and unmotivated. After some investigation, someone happened to learn that his desk had been changed from a two-pedestal to a one-pedestal model, which he had interpreted as a demotion since his peers' desks had not been changed.[54] Decisions made in this way from exclusively "rational" considerations may inadvertently, but no less effectively, damage the status of the very workers whom the administrator wishes to support.

The following analysis, based on observations of Homans about specialization, will illustrate the unanticipated effects that rational decisions may have on informal status systems.[55] On the basis of rational need work is often divided into more specialized jobs. Upon specialization a chain of events may follow that seriously undermines the status of subordinates. For as specialization increases, specialists begin to confine their interaction to one another while their interaction with other personnel and with outsiders declines. Accordingly, their opportunity to direct the work of a subordinate group diminishes, as does their frequency of contact with the chief executive. The resulting insulation—from subordinates, outsiders, and the chief executive—in effect lowers the specialist's social rank. For similar reasons, the status of principals in a system may be threatened when a new administrative assistant is appointed over them because his presence increases the social distance between them and the top administration, as well as increasing the likelihood of close administrative supervision.

Inadequate Performance

School boards have the implied power to dismiss any teacher for good and sufficient cause. The definition of a "sufficient cause" is sometimes specified by state law, but generally the grounds for dismissal of teachers are less clearly specified than they are for some other professions. Only ten states specify ambiguous grounds such as "good," "reasonable," or "sufficient cause" as adequate legal grounds for dismissal of doctors, and only one state so specifies for lawyers, but in most states these are legal grounds for dismissing teachers. Fifteen states do not provide teachers with the right to notice, hearing, or appeal, and only eleven states provide the right to appeal a case to a higher school official or court; only one has provision for possible reinstatement after dismissal.[56] The most frequently reported causes for trials for revocation of teaching licenses have been immorality, intemperance, and unprofessional conduct.[57]

In practice most incompetents are probably not dismissed from the profession. Caplow suggests that the reluctance of a profession to dismiss its incompetents increases with the level of training required to enter it.[58] Among the reasons for tolerating incompetents is the sense of responsibility that a profession itself accepts for having admitted an incompetent at the initial screening period, which, of course, reflects on its own competence and standards. This sense of responsibility for mistakes is also tempered by humanitarian considerations within some professions, that is, the psychic and social damage it can cause to an individual who has committed his life to a career. Haas and Collins found that the treatment of a university professor who is a known incompetent depends to a great extent on the degree of humanitarianism of his department as compared to its professionalism.[59] The data show that humanitarianism is more commonly found among disciplines based on the social sciences, while direct and abrupt procedures for dealing with incompetents are more likely to be found among professions based on the physical and biological sciences. The paradox is that short-sighted views of humanitarianism, which focus on the personal damage which a colleague might suffer from dismissal, obscure the social damage that an incompetent professional can do to his clients.

Besides the ethical and humanitarian considerations, however, the fact is that open declaration of the inadequate performance of personnel can prove to be a source of embarrassment to an organization. To publicly discharge a teacher for incompetence is to publicize the fact that incompetents have been harbored within the school's offices. Moreover, exposure of one incompetent threatens the security of others who are perhaps more competent but less secure, who fear that they may be next. An additional personal factor may be involved as well; the exposure of an incompetent can embarrass the party who was responsible for initially screening and engaging him, particularly if the exponent found it necessary to plead his cause originally.

For these and other reasons, known incompetents are often handled secretly, behind fronts. They are sometimes promoted upward, to more responsible jobs where the work is less visible and where they can be more closely regulated by the chief executive. A similar technique is to divide their work and create new positions from which the crucial tasks have been removed. In this way, incidentally, competents inadvertently foster bureaucratic growth; recognition of this fact may provide a tongue-in-cheek argument in support of the caustic charge that bureaucracy is a way of compensating for lack of competence. In short, there are commitments and restraints concerning the disposition of incompetents that are not entirely spelled out in either the contract or in the professional codes of ethics. These solutions for handling incompetents are not "rational" in the narrow sense of the term, since such roles are not filled with the logic of the job in mind, but they may rationally avoid even greater problems.

Summary

It is perhaps fitting to conclude a speculative chapter such as this with a question: What evaluation standards, professed and practiced, are *actually* used in the sponsorship and rejection of teachers? Some of the questions that might be raised are these: What is the relationship between formal policy statements and actual evaluation practices used in school systems? How does the evaluation and recognition system reward or undermine the logical objectives? What conditions and pressures, internal and external to the school system, influence the evaluation standards?

As a general proposition, it can be safely assumed that the dominant values of the American culture generally determine the evaluation practices used in the schools. But the precise relationship between cultural values, the internal organization, and evaluation standards, and the route by which they get there, can be understood only by comparing these variables in a concrete setting—that is, a sample of public schools. Such a study would provide some insight into the specific relationships between education and the rest of the culture; on the other hand, it would provide knowledge about the particular values that dominate in practice instead of theory.

Several writers—among them for example, William Whyte and David Riesman—have proposed that evaluation standards are becoming more "people" oriented or, in other words, that there is more emphasis on conformity, compatibility, and consensus. There is reason to believe that this orientation is associated with the bureaucratization of American society in which people must work together and in which the ability to please supervisors has become crucial for advancement in the system. Thus, it is expected that the degree of bureaucratization of *particular* public schools will be associated with evaluation practices found there. In particular, it is proposed that the degree of bureaucratization of a school—as measured by degree of centralization, standardization, and specialization—is directly associated with the emphasis placed on the teachers' (1) personal popularity with other teachers, administrators, and students, and (2) loyalty to the local culture of the school. Conversely, it is proposed that the extent to which teachers are professionalized—as measured by activity in professional organizations and personal attitudes—is directly associated with emphasis on technical competence, including knowledge of subject matter, level of education, and ability to communicate. The relationship among these variables and the emphasis on personal background characteristics such as ethnic, religious, and political background and age and sex also deserves investigation. Within a particular system different standards of evaluation are probably used by various levels of administration, the school board, teachers in general and teachers in various positions, and students at various grade levels.

BIBLIOGRAPHY AND NOTES

1. T. Caplow, *The Sociology of Work.* Minneapolis: Univ. Minnesota Press, 1954, p. 113.
2. NEA Research Bulletin, "Teacher Personnel Practices, 1950–51: Appointment and Termination of Service," vol. 30, 1952, p. 18; see also NEA Research

Bulletin, *Teacher Personnel Procedures: Selection and Appointment*, March, 1942, pp. 66–68.

3. S. A. Hamin, *Organization and Administrative Control in High Schools*. Northwestern University Contributions to Education, No. 6, 1932.

4. *Teacher Competence and Its Relation to Salary*, New England School Development Educational Council, July, 1956.

5. F. Greenhoe, *Community Contracts and Participation of Teachers*. American Council on Public Affairs, 1941, p. 32.

6. NEA Research Bulletin, 1952, *Ibid*.

7. Cited by H. O. Dalke, *Values in Culture and Classroom*. New York: Harper, 1958, p. 447.

8. N. Gross, W. S. Mason and A. W. McEachern, *Explorations in Role Analyses: Studies of the School Superintendency Role*. New York: Wiley, 1958.

9. *Ibid.*, pp. 335–338.

10. NEA Research Report, 1952, *op. cit.*

11. Gross, *op. cit.*, pp. 535–539.

12. H. J. Anderson, "Correlations Between Academic Achievement and Teaching Success," *Elementary School Journal*, vol. 32, 1932, pp. 22–29; for bibliographies on the relatively unfruitful but extensive efforts to relate teacher competence to personality and training, see S. J. Domas and D. V. Tideman, "Teacher Competence: An Annotated Bibliography," *Journal of Experimental Education*, vol. 19, 1950, pp. 101–128; and A. S. Barr, "The Measurement and Prediction of Teaching Efficiency: A Summary of Investigations," *Journal of Experimental Education*, vol. 16, 1947, pp. 203–283.

13. D. B. Stuit, "Scholarship as a Factor in Teaching Success," *School and Society*, vol. 46, 1937, pp. 382–384.

14. D. Becker, *The Evaluation of Teachers*. Syracuse, N.Y.: Syracuse Univ. Press, 1949.

15. M. Lieberman, *Education as a Profession*. Englewood Cliffs, N.J.: Prentice-Hall, 1956.

16. T. Caplow, *op. cit.*, pp. 145 and 113.

17. G. Simmel, *The Sociology of Georg Simmel*, trans. by W. Wolff. Glencoe, Ill.: Free Press, 1950, p. 199.

18. T. Caplow and R. McGee, *The Academic Marketplace*. Glencoe, Ill.: Free Press, 1958.

19. *Teacher Competence and Its Relation to Salary, op. cit.*

20. Caplow, *op. cit.*, p. 43.

21. E. R. Guthrie, *The Evaluation of Teaching: A Progress Report*. Seattle: Univ. Washington Press, 1954.

22. S. Domas, *Report on an Exploratory Study of Teacher Competence*, New England School Development Council, 1950.

23. W. Kuvleshy and R. C. Buck, *The Teacher-Student Relationship*. Philadelphia: Univ. Pennsylvania, 1960.

24. M. Lichliter, "Social Obligations and Restrictions on Teachers," *School Review*, Jan. 1946, pp. 17 ff.; see also L. V. Monwiller, "Expectations Regarding Teachers," *Journal of Experimental Education*, vol. 26, 1958, pp. 315–354.

25. R. W. Richey, W. H. Fox and C. E. Fauset, "Prestige Ranks of Teaching," *Occupations*, vol. 30, 1951, pp. 33–35.

26. Gross, *op. cit.*, pp. 335–338.

27. A. E. Schaffle, "Pupil Checks the Teacher," *School Executive*, vol. 51, 1931, pp. 151–153.

28. J. W. Riley, B. F. Ryan and M. Lifshitz, *The Student Looks at His Teacher*. New Brunswick: Rutgers Univ. Press, 1950.

29. J. M. Daniel, *Excellent Teachers*. Columbia: Univ. South Carolina, 1944.

30. F. W. Hart, *Teachers and Teaching, by Ten Thousand High School Seniors*. New York: Macmillan, 1934.

31. W. B. Brookover, "Person-Person Interaction Between Teachers and Pupils and Teacher's Effectiveness," *Journal of Educational Research*, vol. 34, 1940, pp. 272–287.

32. P. M. Symonds, "Characteristics of the Effective Teacher Based on Pupil Evaluation," *Journal of Experimental Education*, vol. 23, 1954, pp. 289–310.

33. E. Roper, "Higher Education: The Fortune Survey," Supplement to *Fortune* magazine, Sept. 1949, pp. 6–7.

34. H. Becker, "The Professional Dance Musician and His Audience," *American Journal of Sociology*, vol. 57, 1951, pp. 136–144.

35. A. W. Gouldner, "Organizational Analysis," in *Sociology Today*, R. K. Merton et al., eds. New York: Basic Books, 1959, pp. 400–428.

36. R. G. Corwin, *A Sociology of Education*. New York: Appleton-Century-Crofts, 1965.

37. D. Wolfle, *America's Resources of Specialized Talent*. New York: Harper, 1954.

38. *E.g.*, see U.S. Women's Bureau, "Women in Higher Level Positions," Bill No. 236, 1950.

39. W. S. Mason, R. J. Dressel, and R. K. Bain, "Sex Role and Career Orientations of Beginning Teachers," *Harvard Educational Review*, vol. 29, 1959, pp. 370–383.

40. R. G. Corwin and M. J. Taves, "The Criteria of Occupational Success: Internalized Norms and Friendship," *Social Forces*, Dec., 1960.

41. Fox and Richey, *op. cit.*

42. Lieberman, *op. cit.*

43. *Cf.* R. N. McKeon and J. Kershaw, "A Solution for Teacher Shortages," *The Saturday Review*, Nov. 17, 1962, pp. 62 ff. The extent to which uniform salary schedules have adversely effected the salaries of teachers in scarce fields is illustrated by chemical engineers who in 1939 received, on the average, an annual salary of $2,640—sixteen per cent less than the average salary of high school teachers in large cities. Twenty years later the average salary in chemical engineering was $11,000—sixty-five per cent *more* than that of high school teachers.

44. NEA Research Division, "Facts on American Education," Research Bulletin, vol. 44, 1966.

45. *National Survey of Professional, Administrative, Technical and Clerical Pay*, Winter 1961–62. U.S. Dept. of Labor, Bureau of Labor Statistics, Bulletin No. 1346, p. 11.

46. "First Jobs of College Women," and "Status of Women in the U.S.," U.S. Dept. of Labor, Women's Bureau, Bulletins No. 268 and 249, 1953 and 1959.

47. T. Parsons, "Suggestions for a Sociological Approach to the Theory Of Organizations," *Administrative Science Quarterly*, vol. 1, 1956, pp. 225–239.

48. Fox and Richey, *op. cit.*

49. W. S. Mason and N. Gross, "Intra-Occupational Prestige Differentiation: The School Superintendency," *American Sociological Review*, June, 1955.

50. NEA Research Division, "Median Salary Ranges," Research Bulletin, vol. 40, 1962.

51. *Teachers for Tomorrow*, Fund for the Advancement of Education, New York, 1954, p. 37.

52. NEA Research Division, "Few Teachers Get Top Salaries," Research Bulletin, Vol. 43, 1965, p. 9.

53. B. Gardner and W. Morse, *Human Relations in Industry*, rev. ed. Chicago: Irwin, 1950, pp. 106 ff.
54. *Ibid.*, p. 113.
55. G. Homans, *The Human Group*. New York: Harcourt, Brace, 1950, p. 406.
56. Cited by Dalke, *op. cit.*, p. 77.
57. *Ibid.*
58. Caplow, *op. cit.*, Ch. 5.
59. E. Haas and L. Collen, "Administrative Practices in University Departments," *Administrative Science Quarterly*, vol. 8, 1963, pp. 44–60.

15

Professional Persons in Public Organizations *

We had three younger teachers in the math department who were very enthusiastic about the
newer approach in mathematics, but the administration and Board of Education no doubt went
along with the superintendent who did not want
the new approach brought in suddenly. They preferred to stick with the old established program,
and this brought on conflict . . . Our best math
people left—they were all very brilliant teachers.

From a high school teacher

Conceptualizing Organizational Conflict [1]

THE INDIVIDUAL VERSUS THE ORGANIZATION

A perennial question which philosophers and social scientists alike
have asked in one way or another concerns the individual's conflict with society. Hobbs stated the question bluntly in terms of
individuals versus other individuals: "How is society possible in a state of
war of all against all?" Since such frightful issues were first raised, social
scientists have become sophisticated enough to realize that man is basically
a group-centered creature and hardly in a constant state of warfare with
his fellows. On the contrary, critics complain of the opposite, an "organization man" with little independent will of his own.[2] With this prospect of

* This chapter previously appeared as an article by Ronald G. Corwin in *Educational Administration Quarterly*, vol. 1, 1965, pp. 1–22. It is used here with permission.

conformity in view, contemporary scholars have posed the issue in a slightly different form—the individual versus the organization.

Contemporary literary and social critics have been aware of the apparent problems that organizations have posed for individuals. The influence of this issue is quite apparent in American literature. Plots of many current novels analyzed by Friedsam center around the fact the hero is a bureaucrat.[3] The dilemma posed in such novels as Wouk's *The Caine Mutiny* is that, while the employee ought to be able to afford the luxury of his own integrity, bureaucracy increasingly erodes his intellectual responsibility and compromises his moral integrity. Social scientists also have formulated the issue in a similar way. Argyris' work, for example, is based on a presumed conflict between the needs of "mature" individuals for independence, variety, and challenge and the demands of organizations for dependent and submissive employees.[4]

TOWARD AN ORGANIZATIONAL CONCEPTION OF ORGANIZATIONAL PROBLEMS

Such statements of the problem pit *the* individual against *the* organization. There are, however, serious disadvantages in this way of formulating the problem. One disadvantage stems from the component of "the individual" in the equation; it prompts analysts to explain what are essentially *organizational* problems in individualistic terms. This approach deflects the focus of attention from the central problem of organization to philosophical speculation on the nature of individuals, which is a residual problem from the standpoint of organization theory. Given this formulation, the person in trouble is defined either as a hero or a maladjusted personality, depending on one's point of view. But personality seems to be significant precisely *because* a given way of organizing is taken for granted; if a specific organization is assumed to be legitimate, then nonconformity will, by definition, appear as a personal "maladjustment."

Still other problems are associated with conceptions of organization that seem implicit in this way of formulating the issue (individual versus organization). The organization is portrayed as an overbearing entity, a unified set of values and goals which are in opposition to personal values and needs. This unitary conception of organization is fostered by two common implicit preconceptions of organization held by those who study organizations: (1) institutional favoritism and (2) organizational bias.[5] Institutional favoritism refers to the exaggerated attention that customarily is given to legitimate institutional ideals embodied in an organization. For example, theorists tend to focus almost exclusively on educational values in schools, religious values in churches, or efficiency in businesses. Correspondingly, with a few exceptions, value conflicts within each of these settings have been neglected.[6]

This institutional perspective tends to emphasize the static image implicit in the very concept of organization. Not only does the study of structure tend to be preferred over process, but structure itself is conceived statically; earlier formulations of structure as a set of "positions" (of teachers, administrators, etc.) obscured the role conflicts or tensions built into each position. Subsequent developments in role theory have helped to correct the impression that structure is necessarily consistent, but the almost exclusive attention to the normative quality implicit in the concept of role (or expectations) has continued to distract attention from the perplexing discrepancies that exist between role conceptions and actual behavior. Finally, little attention has been given to longitudinal studies of the outcomes of role conflicts; consequently little is yet known about the forces within organizational structure itself that produce systematic changes in roles.

The term organizational bias refers to the related prominence given to a presumed set of overriding organizational goals. If it is assumed that it is "normal" for all personnel to work toward a set of organizational goals, then conformity to a rational decision-making model is also "normal"; and, conversely, nonrational behavior can only be attributed to "abnormal" sources. Hence, given these assumptions, any behavior which does not conform to the organizational logic—i.e. the logical means for fulfilling the organization's official objectives—is difficult to explain except in terms of "problems" and personal deviations. Consequently, all forms of behavior which do not "fit" the assumed logical structure are usually grouped into a *residual* category—that is, a category consisting of elements which have little in common except the fact that they don't correspond to the logic. Whenever behavior cannot be explained in organizational terms, it is explained in such residual categories as accident, circumstance, personality, or that amorphous creature bred for the purpose, "informal organization."

To summarize, when the logic of organization is taken for granted, behavior unsuitable to the organization in question tends to be explained in individualistic rather than organizational terms. The problem is that organizational tension, despite its prevalence, cannot be incorporated into existing models of organization in other than a residual way.[7]

PROFESSIONAL VERSUS EMPLOYEE PRINCIPLES OF ORGANIZATION

There is another alternative. Using a different line of reasoning, behavior that is deviant in one form of organization may be seen as conformity in another. It is well known, of course, that the bureaucratization of American society is one of the fundamental developments of this century and that bureaucracy presently represents a dominant form of organization. Drucker, in fact, has termed this an "employee" society;

that is, one in which the rights and obligations between employers and employees (i.e. those who work for another for wages) determine the character of the society.[8] As individual employers have disappeared, these relationships increasingly have been defined by impersonal administrative principles.

However, it is equally true that the social forces which have produced this bureaucratic society have also created alternative forms of organization. Professional principles constitute a prominent but competing way of organizing an employee society.[9] In a professional-employee society, the fundamental tension is not between the individual and the system, but between parts of the system—between the professional and the bureaucratic principles of organization.[10]

Dual professional and bureaucratic principles have been evolving in teaching for some time. The employee status of teachers has been reinforced, first by a strong tradition of local, lay control over educators, and then by the subsequent growth of complex school systems, which have required more administrative control to maintain coordination.

At the same time, the growth of systematic knowledge in teaching and a firm sense of responsibility for students' welfare supports teachers' claims to an exclusive monopoly over certain aspects of teaching, which is the basis of a *professional image* that points teaching in quite another direction. Behind professionalization is a "drive for status," or the efforts of members of a vocation to gain more control over their work—not only more responsibility, but more authority.[11] For decades teachers have subscribed to the idea that they have professional obligations (such as staying late to work with students); now they are demanding professional rights as well (such as the right to select their own teaching materials and methods).

Professional associations were, of course, originally formed in order to free vocations from lay control; and the efforts of teachers to professionalize are no exception. The process of professionalizing publicly-supported vocations, then, is likely to be militant. It represents a challenge to the traditional ideologies of control by laymen and their administrative representatives. The professionalization of any vocation (including school administration) will involve boundary disputes among laymen, the professionals, and public administrators. These boundary disputes, it should be noted, also infect the vocation itself, breaking it into segments or coalitions which compete among themselves: one, a small but active militant leadership group, spearheads the movement, while other coalitions constitute small groups of supporters and the opposition. Each segment then attempts to control the conditions of work in terms of its own definitions.

In teaching, the immediate issues concern the amount of autonomy which teachers should have over the selection of textbooks, over methods, and over curriculum development. But the underlying issues are not peculiar to teaching. One issue concerns the appropriate role of professional-employees in complex organizations. A second involves the place of experts in a democracy. In a sense, this conflict between expertise and democratic principles has already been waged by administrators of public organizations. In these struggles, on the one hand, the growth of knowledge has almost forced laymen to forego their right to make many technical decisions; but on the other hand, many people feel that ultimately only public control will safeguard public interests. Militant professionalism, then, is intended to compromise both the control that administrators have gained over public education and the control traditionally exercised by the lay public.

Despite the efforts of many occupations to professionalize, the characteristics of complex organizations do not uniformly support professional behavior. In fact, there is evidence from a variety of settings that inconsistencies between professional and employee principles are responsible for tensions. As one example, the professional roles of physicians in the military have been found incompatible with the bureaucracy in which they operate.[12] The professional person's self-conception as an individual capable of critical ability and capacity for original thought could be only superficially followed in the structure of the military organization, according to McEwan, who believes that the bureaucratic principles on which the military is organized—such as standardization of positions and superordination-subordination by rank—are, in practice, incongruent with the need for creative thinking and peer relations that prevail among professionals.[13] The principle of delegating authority seems inconsistent especially with the idea that professional authority is independent of the sanctions applied by a particular organization.[14]

PROFESSIONAL-EMPLOYEE ROLE CONFLICTS

Bureaucratic principles can serve as a point of departure for conceptualizing organizational role conflicts.[15] These principles include: (1) specialization of jobs, (2) standardization of work, and (3) centralization of authority. Each may be visualized as a separate continuum, ranging from more to less bureaucratic (see Table 10). The configuration of these variables influences the opportunity that members of an organization have to act professionally in their relations with clients, colleagues, the administration, and the public, and the amount of pressure that is exerted on them to behave as bureaucratic employees in these relationships.[16] For example, group practice of medicine is characterized by a highly specialized but uncentralized form of bureaucracy. On the other hand, school systems probably do not differ from factories in degree of centralization, or even of standardization, but they differ fundamentally in level of specialization of their personnel. Therefore, because of these different configura-

TABLE 10

Contrasts in the Bureaucratic- and Professional-Employee Principles of Organization

ORGANIZATIONAL CHARACTERSTICS	BUREAUCRATIC-EMPLOYEE EXPECTATIONS	PROFESSIONAL-EMPLOYEE EXPECTATIONS
Standardization		
Routine of Work	Stress on uniformity of clients' problems	Stress on uniqueness of clients' problems
Continuity of Procedure	Stress on records and files	Stress on research and change
Specificity of Rules	Rules stated as universals; and specific	Rules stated as alternatives; and diffuse
Specialization		
Basis of Division of Labor	Stress on efficiency of techniques; task orientation	Stress on achievement of goals; client orientation
Basis of Skill	Skill based primarily on practice	Skill based primarily on monopoly of knowledge
Authority		
Responsibility for Decision-Making	Decisions concerning application of rules to routine problems	Decisions concerning policy in professional matters and unique problems
Basis of Authority	Rules sanctioned by the public	Rules sanctioned by legally sanctioned professions
	Loyalty to the organization and to superiors	Loyalty to professional associations and clients
	Authority from office (position)	Authority from personal competence

tions of bureaucratic principles, different types of tensions would be expected in schools, medical centers, and factories.

As professionals, teachers are expected to defend the welfare of students, even against *organizational* practices that are likely to be detrimental; so professional teachers will be disposed toward supporting school consolidation and toward defending the right of students to read significant American authors such as Steinbeck or Faulkner, and they will adjust their teaching to the unique capacities of their students. As bureaucratic employees, however, they will be expected to subscribe to the expectations of the administration and the community. Hence, it is possible for a teacher to be successful as an employee while failing to fulfill professional obligations, or vice versa.

Some of the tensions arising from these bureaucratic principles are illustrated in the case of *specialization*. As Gouldner observes, much organizational tension can be attributed to the fact that administrators frequently supervise and evaluate professional subordinates who are more competent in their work than they.[17] This situation, in turn, raises such questions as whether the criteria for promotion should be seniority and loyalty to the organization or professional skill and competence, which is difficult for non-specialized administrators to evaluate. The problem of evaluation is compounded by the fact that the reputations of professionals are based on the opinions of their colleagues outside the organization. Blau and Scott report that of the social welfare workers they studied, those who were most closely oriented to their profession were also less attached to the welfare agency, more critical of its operation, and less confined by its administrative procedures.[18] On the one hand, the expert is expected to be loyal to the organization, and on the other hand, his primary identification often is with groups on the outside. (However, there also exist locally oriented professionals who are primarily concerned with the opinions of their peers in the organization.)

Similar tension exists between the professional and his client, for while professionals are obliged to serve the best interests of their clients and to provide them with needed services regardless of other considerations, they are not obliged to accept their advice; professionals develop ways of rationalizing their clients' evaluations of them. This indifference to clients' opinions poses a problem in public organizations like public schools where neither the professional nor the client has much choice in entering the relationship.[19]

Second, *standardization* presents another problem, not because it is incompatible with individualism, but because it probably discourages creative and original thought, which is so necessary if organizations are to adapt to changing environments. Watson concludes, for example, that team work is a substitute for creativity, and is responsible for much mediocrity in academic institutions.[20] From the short-run perspective in which administrators and workers see their daily problems, predictability and consistency often appear more convenient than change and the risk of applying new ideas. (It is interesting, for example, that usually it is not sufficient to demonstrate that a proposed change will be no *worse* than the existing situation; change is avoided when possible.)

However, despite the complaints of professionals, standardized procedures do have advantages for them. From his examination of school systems of varying degrees of bureaucratization, Moeller concludes that, contrary to his expectations, standardized systems can provide teachers with a sense of power that does not exist in systems where there is a lack of policy; for policy reduces particularism and increases predictability. Hence teachers demand rules, especially in dealing with other groups such as students.[21] What the professional employee resists is the imposition by outsiders of rules which do not support him; even then, rules are preferred to their absence unless the group has such power that it can maintain its interests without them. The major difference between professional- and bureaucratic-employees in this respect is the established ideology which grants professionals the right to make the rules, and which sanctions the diffuseness of the rules that are made.

In considering the procedures by which rules are established, the third bureaucratic dimension, *centralized authority*, has been introduced. The problems of centralized authority, however, are more extensive than the mere question of the organizational level at which rules are made. For the very basis of authority in complex organizations is involved: bureaucratic and professional principles provide different ways of legitimizing authority.[22] In bureaucratic organization, one derives his authority primarily from the position that he holds. He may be competent in the profession, but the amount of deference that is due him is based directly on his rank rather than on, or at least in addition to, his personal or technical competence. In bureaucracies, a superior has the right to the last word because he *is* the superior.

The notion of hierarchical authority, on the other hand, is not central to professional organizations; the last word presumably goes to the person with greater knowledge or the more convincing logic. In other words, the professional employee, in comparison with the bureaucratic employee, distinguishes between his obligations to accomplish his work and his obligations to obey; the bureaucratic employee is hired to "do what he is told," while the professional already knows what he is to do and how to do it. Thus, the professional's loyalties are split between the organization and the profession according to these competing bases of authority.

In this connection, when Peabody compared school employees, police officers, and welfare workers on the degree to which each group stressed each basis of authority, he found that the most striking contrast among the three groups was in the relative importance that the elementary school teachers attached to the professional basis of their authority.[23] Yet, their typical reaction to conflict was acquiescence to the authority of position, particularly among the less experienced members of the sample.

However, this presumed tension between professional and bureaucratic principles of organization will vary systematically with different types of organizations. Two variables are especially important: the *complexity* of the organization, and the degree of *technical* specialization that employees have achieved. Specialization gives employees power; the more specialized they are, the less competent are administrators and laymen to supervise and evaluate them. On the other hand, the more complex the organization, the greater the need for internal coordination, which enhances the power of administrators whose primary internal function is coordination. Lay control is challenged simultaneously by the development of both conditions: and at the same time the concurrent development of specialization and complexity has fertilized the soil for conflict between administrators and professional employees.

The implication is that if a particular organization is structured around several, often divergent but legitimate principles, then the personnel in it can legitimately disagree on the appropriateness of each principle.

Some Preliminary Research Findings

In view of some of these considerations, a research project was outlined to explore some of the implications of possible tensions among professional-employees in the public schools.[24] The general working hypothesis was that professionalism in bureaucratic organizations is a militant process.

METHODOLOGY

In the conceptual model, the teaching position was visualized as a product of the teacher's role expectations concerning students, the public, administrators, and colleagues. Professional and bureaucratic (or employee) role conception scales containing items pertaining to each of these role expectations were constructed and administered to 284 teachers who represented seven secondary schools of varying sizes (from 9 to 120 teachers) located in Ohio and Michigan. Each scale consisted of Likert-type pretested items derived from the focal concepts: centralization, standardization, and specialization. The professional orientation scale contained sixteen items and the employee orientation scale consisted of twenty-nine items, selected from among those judged by a panel of sociologists to be relevant to the several dimensions of each concept. These dimensions were referred to as "subscales." [25] Possible responses weighted on a five point scale ranged from "strongly agree" to "strongly disagree." Using critical ratio tests and scale value difference ratios, the final set of items proved to be internally consistent, in the sense that they discriminated between groups of respondents whose total scale scores were in the extreme quartiles.[26]

Each major scale also discriminated between respondents who exemplified logical extremes (high versus low) of professional and of employee conduct. Criteria found to be associated with the extreme professional groups included a combination of levels of education, time devoted to reading journals and number of journals subscribed to, number of articles published, and professional activities; extremes of the employee groups were identified from a combination of loyalty to the administration as rated by principals, expression of agreement and disagreement with criticisms toward the organization and administration, and absenteeism. Also, a group of university high school teachers, who technically are members of the university faculty, and whose professional orientation is reputedly high, scored at the expected extremes of each scale. The employee scale differentiated among the means of the set of seven schools in the sample, and the professional scale differentiated between the means of the two extreme schools.

Total professional scale scores of the sample were not significantly correlated with total employee scale scores, which bears out the conceptual model hypothesizing professional and employee expectations as part of independent systems. The absence of correlation between the two major scales suggests that analysis of the way respondents organize their professional and employee conceptions is of promising importance for studying role conflicts. A significant difference was found in the proportion of the faculties at each school who were simultaneously highly committed to both conceptions, simultaneously low on both, or simultaneously high on one and low on the other.

In addition to the scale analysis, 143 teachers were randomly selected for open-ended interviews and were asked to describe friction incidents involving themselves or other staff members. Respondents identified 326 separate incidents, which were then classified by methods of content analysis as to the openness of the conflicts, the type of issue, and the parties involved.[27]

There was general consensus within schools on the frequency with which different types of problems have created incidents, although not all incidents described were specifically corroborated by a second respondent. Many of the incidents which were not directly corroborated were mentioned by "reliable" respondents, i.e., those who did report at least one corroborated incident; nearly half of the incidents are either corroborated or reported by reliable respondents. The frequency with which corroborated, reliable, and non-corroborated types of incidents were mentioned is not significantly different, as tested by chi square.

It was found that the number of conflicts reported in a school increased directly with the number of the staff interviewed, but this was not related to either the size of the school staff or to the proportion of the staff interviewed. Therefore, in order to avoid a measure of conflict rates which is a simple function of the number of interviews, the number of incidents reported per interview is the index of organization conflict rates that was used.

This method of computing the rate of conflict was compared to a "global tension" measure in the questionnaire which asked "how much tension" exists between each of thirteen types of role partners in each school (e.g., teacher-administrative role, teacher-teacher role, etc.). The alternatives ranged from severe to none. There was a direct Spearman rank order correlation of .82 between the total number of incidents reported per interview and this global measure of tension. The rank order correlation between this global measure and the rate of "open or heated discussions or major incidents" reported per interview was even higher: .93. Also respondents were asked to indicate "how much tension exists" between them and each other member of the faculty. When schools were ranked only on the basis of the proportion of faculty mentioning "severe" tension, the rank order correlation with the number of "open or heated discussions or major incidents" per interview was .86, and with rate of "open or heated discussions or major incidents per interview" that specifically involved teachers and administrators it was .89.

The rates of conflict computed from interviews also correlated with other independent measures of conflict, such as the frequency with which respondents reported that their contacts with the principal have involved disputes, the proportion of teachers checking at least one negative statement about their principal, and the proportion of teachers who mentioned that compliance impresses their principal.

TYPES OF CONFLICT

Approximately forty-five per cent of all the incidents involved teachers in opposition to members of the administration; about one-fifth of these disputes were "open" discussions involving direct confrontations of parties in an argument or "heated" discussions (as judged by content analysis), or "major incidents" including a third party in addition to those teachers and administrators initially involved; this is a larger number of open conflicts than reported among teachers themselves. About one-half of all incidents involved *groups* of teachers (teacher's organizations in seven per cent of the cases).

Twenty-four per cent of all conflict incidents fell in the categories of classroom control, curriculum management, and authority in the school; these incidents embraced such issues as the use of proper teaching techniques and procedures, changing the curriculum and selection of text-

TABLE 11

Frequency of Occurrence of Incidents Involving Authority,
the Distribution of Scarce Rewards, and Values,
by Level of Intensity

TYPE OF ISSUE INVOLVED	NUMBER OF OPEN OR HEATED DISCUSSIONS OR MAJOR INCIDENTS	PROPORTION OF ALL INCIDENTS *
I. Authority, Total	81	48.7
A. Over the classroom		
1. with respect to superiors (curriculum management and authority over classroom)	35	17.4
2. with respect to subordinates (student discipline and problems)	23	15.6
B. Within the school		
1. with respect to superiors (authority over school)	7	6.8
2. with respect to public (school-community relations)	2	1.8
3. with respect to peers (disputes among teachers' organizations)	14	7.1
II. Distribution of Scarce Rewards, Total	48	25.2
A. Teachers economic and job status (salary problems, distribution of physical facilities and job status)	23	13.1
B. Scheduling problems	21	10.4
C. Economic status of the educational program (school finances)	4	1.5
III. Value Conflicts, Total	26	22.1
A. Moral, ideological and interpersonal issues	9	8.6
B. Educational philosophy	3	4.9
C. School policy	14	8.6
VI. Unclassifiable (Insufficient Information)	4	3.9
TOTAL NUMBER	159	—

* Based on total number of incidents of all types, including complaints and impersonal competition. N = 326.

TABLE 12

Rates of Conflict in Schools Whose Faculty Have High, Middle and Low Professional Orientations

LEVEL OF PROFESSIONAL ORIENTATION	RATE OF INCIDENTS PER INTERVIEW			RATE OF OPEN, HEATED DISCUSSIONS OR MAJOR INCIDENTS PER INTERVIEW			RATE OF OPEN, HEATED DISCUSSIONS OR MAJOR INCIDENTS PER INTERVIEW INVOLVING TEACHERS AND ADMINISTRATORS		
	NUMBER			NUMBER			NUMBER		
	CONFLICTS	INTERVIEWED	RATE	CONFLICTS	INTERVIEWED	RATE	CONFLICTS	INTERVIEWED	RATE
High Schools 3 and 7 $\overline{X} = 58.69$	93	27	3.44	50	27	1.85	24	27	0.88
Middle Schools 1, 5, and 6 $\overline{X} = 57.17$	131	83	1.58	94	83	1.13	38	83	0.46
Low Schools 2 and 4 $\overline{X} = 56.76$	102	36	2.83	15	36	0.42	4	36	0.11
Total	326	146	2.23	159	146	1.08	66	146	0.45

books. About half of these involved administrators (Table 11). Of the 159 incidents that were in the open, about one-fourth were with the administration over these issues of authority.

PROFESSIONAL MILITANCY

There was a significant rank order correlation ($r_s = .91$) between the mean professional orientation of the seven schools and their rates of conflict per interview. The seven schools also were grouped into three categories on the basis of their rank on mean professional orientation (2-high, 3-middle, and 2-low schools) (Table 12). The two high ranked schools (combined) reported a rate of open or heated discussions or major incidents per interview several times as great as that of the low-ranked schools (.4 compared to 1.9 per interview). There was a parallel ranking on such incidents that specifically involved the administration. The reverse also tended to be true; schools with higher rates of conflict had higher mean professional scores than schools with lower professional orientations.

Finally, persons who held simultaneously high-professional and low-employee orientations had higher rates of conflict than persons who held low-professional and high-employee orientations, or any of the other possible role combinations (Table 13). Nearly half of the group with combined

TABLE 13

Organization of Status Conceptions and Rates of Conflict

STATUS ORGANIZATION	N	NO. OF CONFLICTS PER PERSON	PER CENT INVOLVED 1 OR MORE	2 OR MORE
High Professional— High Employee	67	0.61	.34	.16
High Professional— Low Employee	60	1.27	.47	.28
Low Professional— High Employee	59	0.56	.29	.14
Low Professional— Low Employee	71	0.89	.31	.17

high-professional and low-employee orientations were involved in one or more incidents, and about one-fourth of them were involved in two or more incidents. This finding illustrates that it is as important to ascertain what a group is *against* (low-employee orientation) as to determine what it is for (high-professional orientation).

The weight of evidence from this very limited sample suggests that there is a consistent pattern of conflict between teachers and administrators over the control of work, and that professionalization is a militant process. In future phases of the study, larger samples will be collected. Also, more intensive analysis of concomitant variations between professionalism and organizational variables eventually will help to assess the relative significance of each type of variable in relation to conflict.

Implications

COMPLEX AUTHORITY SYSTEMS

It seems likely that if the sources of organizational tension are structural, then potential solutions to organizational problems also will be found at that level. Hence, use by administrators of more benevolent methods in working with teachers will not necessarily solve the problems unless these administrative practices are supplemented with structural changes. Many school boards and administrators today are talking about "allowing" teachers to participate more in the decision process. However, teachers appear to want the authority to make certain types of decisions, not merely the opportunity to become involved with some stages of decision-making at the discretion of the administration. The problem with so-called "democratic" administration is that the participation of subordinates usually continues to be at the discretion of the administration. As an uncertain privilege, the opportunity to participate may be withdrawn or withheld in practice. Lefton, Dinitz, and their associates, for example, found that when wards in a hospital were operated according to so-called "democratic" principles of administration, the actual result was far from democratic;[28] moreover, professionals working in this situation, where only an illusion of democracy was perpetuated, were more frustrated and negative than those working on wards that were admittedly less democratic. Hence, those who regard the problem simply as one of creating "good administration," ignore the very condition that professionalization is designed to remedy—that, under benevolent authoritarian administration, the status of the teacher's authority still depends on the discretion of the administration.

When the problem is viewed as one of organization, it becomes apparent that the teacher's professional authority will be in jeopardy until it is supported by the structure of the organization itself. For example, in one study dual lines of authority which developed between physicians and administrators in a hospital helped to minimize professional-employee conflicts.[29] On the one hand, the hospital administration maintained the right to make certain administrative decisions, such as scheduling and chart review, and the right to give advice. However, physicians reserved the right to accept or reject administrative suggestions about patient care. It was up to the physician actually attending tht patient to make the final decision. Physicians interpreted the official right of the administrator to supervise as the right to "advise" rather than to make the decisions. This consulting relationship was even more acceptable because respected physicians held the administrative positions. Whether or not physicians accepted advice with which they disagreed depended on whether they considered the sphere of authority in question to be administrative or professional in nature. Although following administrative regulations was not very important to physicians when these regulations conflicted with their professional tasks of taking care of patients, they did otherwise comply with them; for, by complying in strictly administrative spheres, physicians gained freedom from administrative responsibility, which they considered to be onerous.

Goss, the author of the study, concludes that although the hierarchical organization of the hospital in which professionals work might appear to conflict with the essence of professional autonomy, in fact the hospital avoided this conflict by using this kind of separation of spheres of authority.

In thinking of organizations, administrators often seem to have had in mind a stereotype implicitly based on the military bureaucracy, which they have attempted to apply wholesale to virtually every type of organization, under the myth that a central office must have authority over every decision throughout the organization. This myth can bridle professionals, who have first hand acquaintance of their client's problems and who have specialized *training* for dealing with them, but who have insufficient *authority* over the way clients are treated. Conversely, those who are most removed from the operating level are put in the impossible position of being held *responsible* for the decisions that must be made there. Moreover, these discrepancies among authority, competence, and responsibility have more significance for professional-employee organizations than, for example, for factories or prisons.

Perhaps more than any other factor, the myth that a central office must stand responsible for every decision throughout an organization is now deterring administrators from considering alternative designs by which organizations could be adapted to accommodate the fact of professionalization.

ADMINISTRATIVE TRAINING PROGRAMS AND CONFLICT

The prospect of growing conflict among professionals within school systems also is likely to transform traditional leadership functions of the school administrator. Increasingly, his functions will involve mediation between groups; his job will be less that of "directing" the organization, as legal theory stipulates, and more one of just holding it together sufficiently to enable the professionals to improve their own effectiveness. His influence will be felt, but less directly than formerly, by the support that he gives to, or withholds from, the innovations that his subordinates suggest.

If conflict is a routine and normal occurrence within the administrative process, then administrative training programs should address themselves systematically to the proper role of conflict—its positive as well as its negative functions. Yet, to the extent that conflict has been fully recognized, it probably has not been considered with the intent of redefining administrative roles in terms of these conflict functions. Training programs seem to have focused on ways of limiting and managing conflict by screening people on the basis of their backgrounds or personality tests or teaching-group dynamics in hope of establishing cooperative and harmonious relationships among people on the job. However, in the first place, the disadvantages of such harmony have not been thoroughly explored; nor have the boundaries within which conflict can fruitfully occur been established. And secondly, it is possible that even the most peaceable, reticent person will become militant when he is operating under certain pressures. Perhaps it is these pressures that school administrators, especially, need to understand.

EVALUATING PROFESSIONAL EMPLOYEES

Finally, many administrators lack a coherent philosophy for evaluating their professional employees and for guiding their own conduct with respect to professional employee conflicts. The principal fact is that the teachers who are the most loyal employees, and the ones who make the administrator's job easier, are not always the most professional teachers. Conversely, those professionally oriented teachers who also want to be good employees are likely to receive little recognition, but endure much blame, for the moral responsibility that they do demonstrate when they are forced by an administrative regulation or by public fiat to compromise one set of principles in the interests of their school's or their students' welfare. What is to be the fate of a teacher who is guilty of "insubordination" while attempting to protect his students from a textbook or a curriculum guide which he believes would be ineffective, or detrimental, to students? How will an otherwise competent teacher who leaves the building early be treated? The same issues, of course, apply to administrators. Will a superintendent who has been requested by a school board to violate a professioinal ethic (e.g., fire a competent teacher for prejudicial reasons) dare to be insubordinate?

The answers to these questions depend upon the relative merits of professional and employee norms. The question of merit is in part a value judgment, but it is also partly an empirical question. Are professionally oriented teachers more effective? The answer, of course, depends on the criteria used to assess effectiveness. Are professionally oriented teachers better liked by students and parents? Do they have a better grasp of subject matter, and do they communicate more effectively? Perhaps professionally oriented teachers are not superior in all these respects. But, one hypothesis does merit further consideration. That is, professionally ori-

ented teachers, in comparison with less professional ones, can be expected
to protect the interests of clients against both bureaucratization and the
special interests of laymen. For example, because classroom teachers interact daily with slum-school children, they are probably under greater
direct pressures than the central city administration to adapt the organization to the problems of this unique clientele and environment; increased
professional autonomy for these teachers might tend to alleviate those dis-
criminatory practices otherwise fostered by standardization.

Professional norms also can counteract community pressures to maintain an outmoded curriculum or to censor the literary works of major
American authors. More generally, because many professionals have less
reason than administrators to be committed to a particular form of institutional structure, with the support of a strong organization they would
be in a more opportune position than the administration to exercise leadership in changing the structure. Also in this regard, if more autonomy
were granted to professionals (especially the younger ones trained recently), who may be partially insulated by the administration and their
own professional organizations from outside pressures, the diffusion of
those educational innovations most in harmony with professional values
might be accelerated; and, conversely, teachers would be in a better position than administrators to resist adverse outside pressures.[30] If so, then
the preference of administrators for loyal, compliant employees may be
in conflict with their responsibilities as professional educators.

SUMMARY

In conclusion, while individual personalities do become involved in
conflicts, the individual-versus-the-organization hypothesis has obscured
some potential contributions that studies of conflict can make to organization theory. A more fruitful approach to the problem focuses on the
contrasting organizational principles which individuals uphold. From this
perspective, one function of conflict is to defend conflicting but valued
principles and to effect creative compromises between them. Group conflicts, in other words, function as "checks and balances."

Yet, although traditional theory has been concerned with divisions of
labor, and more recently some attention has been given to distinctions between formal and informal organization, the conflicts among other
largely ignored structural divisions, such as professional and employee
modes of organization, have been relatively neglected. Moreover, to the
extent that organizational structure has been recognized as a potential
source of conflict, it often has been with the intent of showing only that
the known principles of organization have not been applied, as in the case
where illogical work flows have been discovered.

Behind the current interest in professional-employee organization is the
idea of process, the simultaneous professionalization and bureaucratization

of American society. It is not possible to consider the problem of organization without considering the possibilities and probabilities of organizational change. In considering potential reorganization of large scale systems, administrators will have to take into account one of the most powerful phenomena of our times—the professional organization of employees.

BIBLIOGRAPHY AND NOTES

1. This is a revision of a paper written for a conference on "Developments in Professional Staff Relationships: Research and Practices," sponsored by the U.S. Office of Education, Washington, D.C., May 27–28, 1964. I wish to thank Russell Dynes, Willard Lane, and Robert Howsam for their thoughtful comments on an earlier version of this paper.

2. William H. Whyte, *The Organization Man* (New York: Simon and Schuster, 1956).

3. Hiram J. Friedsam, "Bureaucrats as Heroes," *Social Forces*, XXXII (March, 1954), 269–74.

4. Chris Argyris, *Personality and Organization* (New York: Harper and Brothers, 1957), pp. 50–51.

5. Cf., Willard R. Lane, Ronald G. Corwin, and William G. Monahan, *Foundations of Educational Administration* (New York: The Macmillan Company, 1967). Ch. 10.

6. Callahan's study, which analyzes the effects of business principles on education, is a notable exception. See Raymond E. Callahan, *Education and the Cult of Efficiency* (Chicago: University of Chicago Press, 1962).

7. For criticisms of social scientists' neglect of a conflict models, see: Ralf Daerendorf, "Out of Utopia: Toward a Reorientation of Sociological Analysis," *American Journal of Sociology*, LXIV (September, 1958), 115–27; Jessie Barnard, "Where is the Modern Sociology of Conflict?," *American Journal of Sociology*, LVI (July, 1950), 11–16; also, Dennis H. Wrong, "The Oversocialized Conception of Man," *American Sociological Review*, XXVI (April, 1961), 183–93.

8. Peter F. Drucker, "The Employee Society," *American Journal of Sociology*, LVIII (January, 1952), 352–63.

9. Cf., Ronald G. Corwin, "The Professional Employee: A Study of Conflict of Nursing Roles," *American Journal of Sociology*, LXVI (May, 1961), 604–15.

10. Parsons has warned of the dangers in analyzing occupational behavior on the basis of individual motives. See Talcott Parsons, "The Professions and the Social Structure," *Social Forces*, XVII (May, 1939), 457–67.

11. The term profession is conventionally applied to a set of structural characteristics (i.e., an organized occupational group with a legal monopoly over recruitment and knowledge); but most of what might be called professional behavior is in fact the striving of a group to achieve the right to claim the title of a profession. In other words, to study professions is to study process. See also Howard S. Becker, "The Nature of a Profession," *Education for the Professions*, Sixty-first Yearbook of the National Society for the Study of Education, Part II (Chicago: University of Chicago Press, 1962).

12. William J. McEwan, "Position Conflict and Professional Orientation in a Research Organization," *Administrative Science Quarterly*, I (September, 1956), 208–24.

13. There is also a hierarchy among professionals, but it has a different basis of

authority; and communications between ranks of professionals are more nearly reciprocal.

14. Walter I. Wordwell, "Social Integration, Bureaucratization and Professions," *Social Forces*, XXXIII (May, 1955), 356–59.

15. Of course, there are many similarities between professional and bureaucratic expectations, but the differences will be the focus of this discussion.

16. For an empirical study showing low inter-correlation among these variables, see Richard H. Hall, "The Concept of Bureaucracy: An Empirical Assessment," *American Journal of Sociology*, LXIX (July, 1963), 32–40.

17. Alvin W. Gouldner, "Organizational Tensions," *Sociology Today*, ed. Robert Merton *et al.* (New York: Basic Books, 1959), pp. 400–28.

18. Peter Blau and W. Richard Scott, *Formal Organization* (San Francisco: Chandler Publishing Company, 1962), p. 244.

19. The factor of choice is an important control mechanism for both clients (who can boycott professionals from whom they receive little benefit) and for professionals (who can do a more effective job with clients who have faith in them). Private practice, however, overcompensates for the first problem, because of the professional's dependence on private fees; and bureaucratic employment accentuates the second problem. The fact that teachers are arbitrarily assigned students who are compelled to accept the service is a serious strain in the teacher-student relationship.

20. Goodwin Watson, "The Problem of Bureaucracy, a Summary," *Journal of Social Issues* (December, 1945), 69–72.

21. Gerald H. Moeller, "Relationship Between Bureaucracy in School Systems and Teachers' Sense of Power" (Unpublished Ph.D dissertation, Washington University, 1962). Centralized authority systems support professional autonomy by resisting outsiders (as when principals defend teachers against interfering parents) and by refusing the use of essential facilities to competing groups.

22. Gouldner, *op. cit.*

23. Robert L. Peabody, "Perceptions of Organizational Authority," *Administrative Science Quarterly*, VI (March, 1962), 463–82.

24. Ronald G. Corwin, *The Development of An Instrument for Examining Staff Conflicts in The Public Schools*, U.S. Office of Education Cooperative Research Project No. 1934, Department of Sociology and Anthropology, The Ohio State University, 1964. The research reported here was supported through the Cooperative Research Program of the Office of Education, U. S. Department of Health, Education, and Welfare in cooperation with The Ohio State University.

25. *Employee Orientation "Subscales":* Administrative orientation, loyalty to the organization, competence based on experience, interchangeability of personnel and standardization of work, stress on rules and procedures, and public orientation. *Professional Orientation "Subscales":* Client orientation, orientation to the profession and professional colleagues, competence based on monopoly of knowledge, decision-making authority, and control over work.

26. The corrected split-half reliability of the employee and professional scales is .85 and .70, respectively.

27. An "incident" is defined as a description of a discrete episode in which a verbal complaint or attack was made against a person or group. A single episode was considered to be one incident regardless of the number of teachers involved or the number of times it was reported.

28. Mark Lefton, Simon Dinitz, and Benjamin Pasamonick, "Decision-Making in a Mental Hospital: Real, Perceived, and Ideal," *American Sociological Review*, XXIV (December, 1959), 822–29.

29. Mary E. W. Goss, "Influence and Authority Among Physicians," *American Sociological Review*, XXVI (February, 1961), 39–50.

30. At the same time, of course, while professional autonomy can protect clients, professions in a status struggle also can jeopardize the interests of clients because of their own self interests, special viewpoints, and status hierarchies. For example, most professions seem to give preferential treatment to clients with more power. Similarly, in our study of conflicts between teachers it was clear that teachers were competing with each other for students for their extra curricular activities in order to enhance their own positions, and apparently at the expense of the students' welfare in some cases.

Index

A

B

C

D

E

F

G

H

I

M

N